WORK IN PROGRESS

A Guide to Writing and Revising

THIRD EDITION

WORK IN PROGRESS

A Guide to Writing and Revising

THIRD EDITION

Lisa Ede
OREGON STATE UNIVERSITY

St. Martin's Press New York

Senior editor: Karen J. Allanson
Development editor: Edward Hutchinson
Managing editor: Patricia Mansfield-Phelan
Project editor: Nicholas Webb
Production supervisor: Joe Ford
Art director: Sheree Goodman
Cover design: Laura Ierardi
Cover photo: Jim Finlayson

Library of Congress Catalog Card Number: 94-65174

Manufactured in the United States of America.
9 8 7 6 5
f e d c b a

For information, write:
St. Martin's Press, Inc.
175 Fifth Avenue
New York, NY 10010

ISBN: 0-312-10107-4

Acknowledgments and copyrights can be found at the back of the book on pages 291–92, which constitute an extension of the copyright page.

To my students
and
(of course)
to Gregory

To Instructors

With the first edition of *Work in Progress*, I wanted to write a theoretically sophisticated but commonsensical and relatively brief textbook, one that would enrich but not dominate the life of the classroom, one that would support but not impose a collaborative approach to the teaching of writing. Traditional textbooks have too often placed students and teachers in opposition: the teacher acts as the provider of knowledge, the students as passive absorbers of this wisdom. *Work in Progress* would, I hoped, foster the development of a genuine collaborative community, grounded in mutual respect and a shared commitment to inquiry. Learning and teaching are, after all, both works in progress.

Work in Progress has, fortunately, been successful enough to warrant subsequent editions; thus it continues as a work in progress for me. In working on this third edition, I have attempted to build on the strengths of earlier editions and to respond to the needs and suggestions of instructors and students who have used the text. The central goals of *Work in Progress* remain unchanged; these goals are reflected in a number of features that characterized earlier editions:

- full discussion of the concept of the rhetorical situation
- explicit support for and reinforcement of collaborative learning and writing activities
- extensive attention to the process of reading and to reading and writing as dynamic, interdependent activities
- full discussion of the demands of academic writing
- a strong emphasis on the importance of social context and of textual conventions of writing
- a variety of student and professional examples, including numerous comments by students about their writing practices
- activities interspersed throughout the text, as well as at the end of each chapter, that encourage students to apply the concepts and strategies discussed in the text
- "Guidelines" sections throughout the text that distill the discussions into concise, accessible forms

Several new features distinguish this third edition of *Work in Progress*:

- New "Guidelines for Collaborative Writing" sections, integrated into the writing chapters, expand the text's treatment of group invention activities and peer review to encompass the writing of actual collaborative projects—a kind of writing that is increasingly being assigned in college-level courses across the curriculum. These sections draw on Andrea Lunsford's and my ten years of research on this subject.
- A new prologue, " Entering the Conversation," and a new epilogue, "Going On," present statements from current and former students about their own writing experiences and how the concepts discussed in *Work in Progress* have affected them as students and as professionals. These statements (many more of which are interspersed throughout the text) demonstrate in the most concrete ways how much students can learn from each other; they also indicate how much we as instructors oversimplify and reify when we talk about "the" student writer.
- A new mini-anthology of reading selections, on the theme of education, appears in Chapter 9, "Understanding the Reading Process." This section provides flexible opportunities for teaching the reading strategies under discussion and for source-based writing assignments.
- An expanded discussion of research strategies in Chapter 5, "Strategies for Successful Invention," now includes discussions of questionnaires and field research.

This edition incorporates further additions and changes. There are a number of new professional and student essays as well as other texts for analysis. Throughout, I have added references to the roles that electronic technologies play in writing. Finally, with this edition I continue to refine my effort to convey complex theoretical ideas in a way that is accessible and engaging to students.

Work in Progress is divided into three major parts. Part One, "Writing: An Introduction," comprises four chapters:

- Chapter 1 Writers Writing
- Chapter 2 Understanding the Writing Process
- Chapter 3 Understanding the Rhetorical Situation
- Chapter 4 Writers Reading

These four chapters establish the conceptual and pedagogical framework for the text. Together, they enable students to develop a sophisticated yet commonsensical understanding of writing as a means of communication, the writing process, and the rhetorical situation. The discussion and activities in these chapters also encourage students to begin to think of themselves as writers participating in a community of writers.

Part Two, "Practical Strategies for Writing," contains the following four chapters:

- Chapter 5 Strategies for Successful Invention
- Chapter 6 Strategies for Successful Planning and Drafting
- Chapter 7 Strategies for Successful Revision: Managing the Revision Process
- Chapter 8 Strategies for Successful Revision: Revising for Structure and Style

As the title of Part Two suggests, these four chapters introduce students to a variety of practical strategies they can use as they plan, draft, and revise. Rather than emphasizing a single, prescribed series of steps or strategies that students must follow, *Work in Progress* encourages students to develop a repertoire of strategies they can use (working alone and with others), depending on their purpose and situation.

Part Three, "Connections: Writing, Reading, and Reasoning," consists of three chapters:

- Chapter 9 Understanding the Reading Process
- Chapter 10 Understanding Academic Audiences and Assignments
- Chapter 11 Understanding Academic Analysis and Argument

This final part of *Work in Progress* initiates students into the reading and writing they will do as members of the academic community. Students learn approaches to analyzing texts that will help them read more critically and write more effectively. The text offers suggestions for analyzing disciplinary conventions and for understanding what is expected for assignments. In these and other ways, *Work in Progress* shows students ways to approach the writing of academic analysis and argument.

Work in Progress is an innovative textbook, but it is also a practical textbook. It provides a conceptual framework and activities that stimulate effective classroom instruction, yet it also offers teachers considerable autonomy and flexibility. Some teachers will particularly appreciate the book's emphasis on reading and on academic writing, for instance, while others may draw more heavily on its numerous collaborative, workshop-oriented activities. The *Instructor's*

Manual to Accompany Work in Progress provides further elaboration of ways in which the text can be used.

Before I wrote *Work in Progress*, acknowledgments sometimes struck me as formulaic or conventional. Now I recognize that they are neither; rather, acknowledgments are simply inadequate to the task at hand. Coming at the end of the preface—and hence twice marginalized—acknowledgments can never adequately convey the complex web of interrelationships that make a book like this possible. I hope that the people whose support and assistance I acknowledge here not only note my debt of gratitude but also recognize the sustaining role that they have played, and continue to play, in my life.

I would like to begin by thanking my colleagues at the Center for Writing and Learning at Oregon State University. I could accomplish little in my teaching, research, and administration without the support and friendship of Barbara Hogg, Jon Olson, and Saundra Mills. They, along with our writing assistants, have taught me what it means to collaborate in a sustaining, productive fashion. Others in the English department, my second academic home, supported me while I wrote and revised this text. I am indebted to my colleagues Chris Anderson, Vicki Collins, Cheryl Glenn, Anita Helle, and Simon Johnson for their friendship and their commitment to writing over the years.

I have dedicated this book to my students, and I hope that it in some way reflects what *they* have taught me over the years. I also owe a great debt of gratitude to another friend and teacher, Suzanne Clark, who allowed me to persuade her to interrupt her own important works in progress to collaborate with me on the *Instructor's Manual*. Colleagues and students play an important role in nurturing any project, but so do those who form the intangible but indispensable community of scholars that is one's most intimate disciplinary home. Here, it is harder to determine who to acknowledge; my debt to the composition theorists who have led the way or "grown up" with me is so great that I hesitate to list the names of specific individuals here for fear of omitting someone deserving of credit. I must, however, acknowledge my friend and frequent coauthor Andrea Lunsford, who writes with me even when I write alone. And I would also like to thank the many dedicated teachers of composition I have worked and talked with over the years. By their example, comments, suggestions, and questions, they have taught me a great deal about the teaching of writing.

A number of writing instructors took time from their teaching to read and comment on drafts of this edition. Their observations and suggestions have enriched and improved this book. These reviewers include Wendy Bishop, Florida State University; Deborah S. Bosley, University of North Carolina at Charlotte; Rebecca E. Burnett, Iowa State University; Patsy Callaghan, Central Washington University; Suellynn Duffey, Ohio State University; Cheryl Glenn, Oregon State University; Jan Probst Goggans, University of California at Davis; Glenn Harris, Troy State University; Mara Holt, Ohio University; Lawrence Musgrove, University of Southern Indiana; Carol Nowotny-Young, University of Arizona; John Trimbur, Worcester Polytechnic Institute; and Dennis Young, James Madison University.

I wish to thank the dedicated staff at St. Martin's Press, particularly Edward Hutchinson, whose supportive but tough questions have challenged me to clarify and extend my ideas, and Nick Webb, whose patient attention to detail proved especially valuable.

Finally, I want to (but cannot adequately) acknowledge the support of my husband, Gregory Pfarr, who by his example has shown me what it means to be both dedicated to one's work and in love with life. I'm trying, Gregory.

LISA EDE

CONTENTS

PART ONE

WRITING: AN INTRODUCTION

Prologue

ENTERING THE CONVERSATION

It's late on a Thursday afternoon, and a group of students have gathered to talk with me about writing. It doesn't take long for us to realize how diverse we are. Robin Cross, for instance, is an agricultural economics major returning to school after running a sheepshearing and lambing business. Monica Molina, a sociology major who just finished an internship in Oregon State University's Affirmative Action office, is a disk jockey on the student radio station and an active member of OSU's Hispanic Students' Organization. Tina Fowlks is majoring in psychology, while Michael Lundin and Audrey Meier are English majors: all are students in their early twenties who are involved in a variety of campus activities. Chris Jones has a double major in science and technical writing; we can't guess his age (and, he laughingly says, he won't tell). James Fowell is a sociology major, computer whiz, and veteran of the Internet. Jim Hogan, Kelly Rayle, Terrell Ratchford, Karen Zielinski, and Donna Anderson are all education majors; older-than-average students, each has returned to college after working at various "real-world" jobs.

I asked these students to meet with me because I wanted to understand writing from *their* perspective—and I wanted to share their thoughts with you. My twenty years of experience teaching writing have taught me many things, and one of the most important is that students can learn an enormous amount about writing by talking, working, reading, and writing with other students. In this prologue to *Work in Progress,* then, you will have an opportunity to discover what students like yourself have learned about how writing works.

I begin our conversation by asking about the kinds of writing these students currently do. At first they laugh: "What kind of writing do you think we do?" Terrell Ratchford responds. Essays, summaries, tests, lab reports, letters of application: the familiar forms are named and discussed. But as we talk, the list grows.

"I have quite a few friends who I write to save on phone bills—and also because I enjoy getting mail," Michael Lundin observes. "I dabble in creative writing and poems mainly to see if I can do it and also just to have fun with words. Keeping a journal helps me think about what I'm doing and also encourages me to pay attention to life."

Others comment on similar writing efforts—the poem written to express strong feelings, the pro-and-con lists sketched out to help make a difficult decision. Some of those present publish their writing: Robin Cross still writes occasional columns for his industry journal, and Chris Jones writes ads for the student newspaper. James Fowell and Kelly Rayle describe themselves as "addicted to E-mail."

Kelly keeps in touch with her parents through E-mail letters: "They usually take the form of stream-of-consciousness writing, unpunctuated, uncorrected. Often we try to make puns and coin new words. It keeps us in touch—and it makes us laugh."

James also corresponds with family and friends through E-mail, and he contributes to several bulletin boards: "I regularly post to several newsgroups on the Internet," James tells us, "including alt.discordia, orst.soc.418, orst.soc.324, and alt.my.head.hurts."

Like most in college, these students must juggle many pressures and demands, and writing sometimes add to them. As we talk, they acknowledge the pressures that writing can bring. "Writing can make me really uptight," Donna Anderson observes—and the conversation evolves into an alternately humorous and heated discussion of the best way to respond to the pressure of imminent deadlines. That pressure is quite real, all the students agree. "Even when my writing's going well," Robin Cross notes, "there's always some element of worry and stress."

Given that inevitable worry and stress, what keeps you going, I ask them. What does writing do for *you*? The first to respond is Audrey Meier: "Writing gets me organized." She laughs. "I'd be nowhere without my 'to do' list, my short-term and long-term goals. Writing keeps me in line with life!"

"And it keeps me in line with my studies," Tina Fowlks adds. "When I need to work through my ideas, really need to understand them, I write. I may just scribble ideas or freewrite about questions I have—I do whatever feels right at the time. The more difficult the reading is for me, the more I need writing to help me figure it out."

"Writing's important to my schoolwork too," Kelly Rayle agrees; "it allows me to process information, to let it sink in. Sometimes before a test I write just to find out what I know, where the gaps are. But I don't want to be a slave to my studies. I try to keep some fun in my writing—that's why I like my E-mail letters—they're pure enjoyment. You should see some of the words we've come up with!"

"E-mail is a real tension breaker for me too," James Fowell agrees. "When I'm feeling uptight, I like to just sit at the computer and vent."

"I'll tell you what keeps me going as a writer," Jim Hogan says, capturing the group's attention. "What I like about writing is having written!" We turn to him for clarification, so Jim continues: "I get a lot of satisfaction from the products I produce when I write, from winning the mental struggle to get my ideas on paper. But the struggle itself can be the pits! There are times when I hate writing. But when I read a paper that I'm really proud of, when someone tells me they can really see what I mean, then I love having written."

Jim's comment seems somehow definitive, so our talk shifts to other matters. Audrey wonders, for instance, whether others are as much an "organization freak" as she is. "I plan and plan and outline and then plan some more," she says. Some students agree—but others protest in mock horror. Tina Fowlks doesn't ever do outlines, she says, but rather freewrites and clusters—and this only after several days of thinking through her ideas. Jim Hogan describes his process differently: "I can't describe it very well, but everything seems to happen all at once while I draft, including revising. I hate freewriting—can't seem to let it flow. And though I spend some time jotting down ideas, I don't really spend much time planning. I just start writing and then I kind of revise my writing as I go."

"Boy, it's a wonder anyone ever gets anything written, isn't it!" Chris Jones exclaims. We laugh and start to discuss whether despite their differences, the students do share some common experiences as writers. "One thing I've learned," Michael Lundin observes, "is that the more I write, the easier it gets. Not that I can count on that every time," he quickly adds. "But overall I can see that it gets easier."

"It's kind of like an inchworm, isn't it?" Monica Molina asks. "You inch along and inch along. First a two-page paper seems impossible to write; a year later that's not so hard but a five-page paper is a challenge."

"I'll tell you one thing that I've learned always works for me," Karen Zielinski comments. "I've learned that my writing's always better if I get other people to read it. Sometimes it's a friend, sometimes a writing assistant at the writing center, sometimes my mom and sister—in fact, given deadlines, it's often my mom and sister!"

Others chime in. "I need feedback too," Donna Anderson observes. "But I also need people I can talk about my ideas with separate from my paper."

"Talking about my ideas is important for me too," Tina Fowlks adds. "If I can see that my topic interests somebody else, that gives me the push I need to keep going."

Anything else, I ask? "Well, I've learned to trust to the process," Donna Anderson responds. "I've learned not to expect a perfect product immediately. When I'm feeling tense, I just keep repeating my mantra: 'I can always revise; I can always revise; I can always revise. . . .' "

"That's my mantra too!" Robin Cross exclaims, as group members laugh and agree. "Poor spelling used to discourage me from getting started. But now I know that I don't have to worry about that, that I can accept imperfections, be patient, and let the process develop."

"Absolutely," Donna responds. "Knowing I can revise is a pressure valve for my ego. So much of my own self-image can be tied up in what I write that I can get all balled up and expect too much too fast. It's been a relief to learn that if I ease up a bit and let my writing develop naturally, it'll be better in the long run."

The hour is growing late, and the cookies and coffee that I've provided are almost gone. There's just one final question I want to raise: What advice, I ask these students, would you give to other students, especially those who are just beginning a college writing class?

"You mean that we get to be the experts for once?" Monica Molina jokes.

"Absolutely," I reply. "So what do you think?"

"Write about topics that you really care about," Terrell Ratchford quickly replies. "If you don't care, you can't write well—it'll just be a game to see if you can get a good grade."

"I agree," Michael Lundin adds. "Life's too short to just get by."

"Get to know your teacher and other students in your class," Tina Fowlks observes. "They'll be reading your writing, and the better you know them, the more comfortable you'll be."

"But get other readers too," Donna suggests. "I meet regularly with a writing assistant, and I wouldn't give that up for anything. I like it that she's not in my class; it takes the pressure off and gives me a new perspective on my writing. And then there's my roommate—boy do I owe her!"

"How's this for some simple but important advice?" Jim Hogan interjects. "Get started as early as you can. The more you put off writing, the harder it is. As that Nike commercial says: 'Just do it!' And do it often—the more practice you get the easier it'll come, and the better you'll get."

"Yes, and speaking of 'doing it,'" Tina interjects, "I've got a four-pager due for my psych class tomorrow."

Others begin to talk about chapters to read, tests to study for, reports and essays to write. It is time, we recognize, to end our conversation. We stand, stretch, and begin to pack up our belongings, all the while commenting on how quickly our time together has passed. I thank the students, urging them to take the last few cookies home.

As I listen to these thoughtful students chat about what they need to do that night, about how quickly deadlines and the end of the term are approaching, I think back to my own student experiences, wishing that I'd known then what they know now. When I was an undergraduate, I was simply told *to write*; no one, not even my English teachers, talked to me about *how* to write—and that made writing a scary, lonely business. And my teachers certainly didn't encourage me to learn from other students; that, they warned me, would be cheating. Fortunately, the teaching of writing has changed considerably since my undergraduate years. I have tried in *Work in Progress* to incorporate the best of these changes. And I've also included many additional comments by students and examples of student writing. All, I hope, will help you grow in confidence and skill as a writer and thus help you find your own place in the conversation of the academy.

CHAPTER 1

WRITERS WRITING

WHY WRITE?

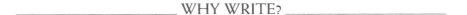

Why do people write? Let's take a look at some representative writing situations.

> A psychiatric social worker *takes notes, jottings that make sense only to him, as he meets for the first time with a client. Later, after reviewing the client's history with colleagues at a staff meeting, he will use these notes to dictate a summary recommending appropriate therapy for the client.*
>
> A retired librarian who is chairing his local school board *learns that a group of parents plans to petition the board to have several young adult books removed from the middle school library. Aware that petitions such as this can develop into major controversies if not handled properly, the librarian decides to ask others how they have responded on similar occasions, so he logs into School Board, an electronic bulletin board for members of school boards and others interested in local educational issues, and types in his query. Checking in several hours later, he finds that his question has generated a lively exchange. After reading the responses, he prints a number of suggestions, then types in his thanks and adds his own comments to the ongoing conversation.*

A consulting engineer *meets with colleagues to begin work on a proposal for a major construction project. Knowing they have just a month to meet the deadline, she assigns duties to group members. Some will begin research on technical issues, others will consult with resource people within the firm, and still others will begin writing nontechnical sections of the draft. Her role will be to organize and monitor the group effort and edit the final proposal. After the meeting, she works out a schedule for preliminary reports, E-mails it to her colleagues, and reminds them that their company's new network can now both send and receive faxes. Even when they're in the field, she observes, they should now be able to get reports to her on time.*

A college student in mathematics education *decides to keep a journal during his student teaching practicum. He uses the journal to reflect on his students' problems, to record observations about the school where he is teaching, to analyze the effectiveness of his lesson plans, and to cope with the inevitable highs and lows of his first experience in the classroom. At the end of the term, for an advanced seminar in his major, he draws upon the journal to write an essay on the relationship between theory and practice in mathematics education. "It's a good thing I kept that journal," he tells a friend. "It helped me get beyond clichés about teaching to what I really know works in the classroom."*

A newly hired department-store manager *meets with her supervisors to discuss her store's goals for the next three months. Wondering how she is actually going to meet these goals, she goes back to her office, asks her secretary to hold all calls, and brainstorms at the computer for two hours. When she is done, she has the outline of a plan to present to her staff for discussion. Afterwards, she will incorporate the group's ideas in a memorandum to her supervisors.*

A team of government safety inspectors *visits a meat-processing plant for its annual inspection. After three days of interviews and observations, they compile an annotated list of problems that have appeared since their last visit and fax it to their main office.*

Two students in an introduction to literature class *learn that they must write an analysis of Mrs. Ramsey, a character in Virginia Woolf's* To the Lighthouse. *They decide to meet to discuss possible essay topics. At first their conversation moves slowly; they both liked the novel and found Mrs. Ramsey interesting, but they're not sure how to move from a general response to a specific topic. Finally one of them suggests that they write down all the*

> *questions they have about Mrs. Ramsey. They do so and are reassured by their list. But what to do next? Why not try to imagine how different characters in Woolf's novel might respond to their questions, one of them suggests. Perhaps the characters' responses will help them see something that they might otherwise overlook. They quickly make a list of characters, divide them up, and agree to meet the next day to discuss their experiment. As they say goodbye, they comment with relief on how good it feels to have gotten started.*
>
> A retired teacher, *after visiting her grandchildren, realizes that they know very little about what her own parents and grandparents were like. So she spends several days writing about them on her home computer. As she prints her first draft, she decides that this is the time to learn how to use her new desktop publishing program. It will be worth the effort, she muses, if she can produce a first-rate family history.*

People write for a variety of reasons. Many people write because they are required to. Term papers, business letters, reports, proposals, articles in magazines—most are written by a person, or a group of persons, who has been asked to take on the responsibility for the project. Sometimes this writing simply reports the results of analysis or observations, as in the safety inspectors' list. But often the writing functions in more complex ways, providing the means by which individuals solve problems, make difficult decisions, and come to understand complex situations.

People also write to fulfill important personal needs. The grandmother describing her parents and grandparents, bringing them to life for her grandchildren, writes because she wants to record her family's history. The student teacher uses his journal to help make sense of—and survive—his difficult but rewarding first experience in the classroom. People write to solve problems or interact with others in the world, but they write to look inward as well.

Exploration

What do you typically write, and why? Make a list of the kinds of writing you regularly do. (Be sure to include *all* kinds of writing, even shopping lists and class notes.) What kinds of writing do you do most often and what kinds least often? What are your usual reasons for writing? Which of your writing experiences are generally productive and satisfying? Unproductive and unsatisfying? Write one or two paragraphs exploring why some writing experiences are productive and satisfying while others are not.

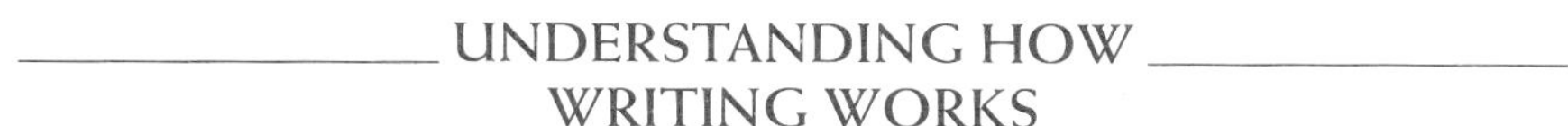

UNDERSTANDING HOW WRITING WORKS

At first glance, the writers described previously might seem to have little in common. But if you look more closely, you can see a number of similarities—similarities that can tell you something about how writing works.

1. All these people are writing under some sort of pressure, either external (from a job or school) or internal. They *need* to write.
2. The writing that they do *matters* to these people; it helps determine how successful they are in school or on the job or how they feel about themselves.
3. These writers are not working in isolation. Although all of these writers spend some of their time thinking and writing alone, they also *interact* regularly with others. Sometimes they do so to generate ideas or to get responses to their own projects; electronic media have extended the possibilities for these and other collaborative activities. On other occasions, they not only learn from and work with but also write with others.
4. Whether writing alone or collaboratively, these individuals are writing in a *specific context or situation.* As writers, they are influenced by such factors as these:
   - their reason for writing and the nature of their writing project
   - the issues they want to explore or points they want to make
   - the readers for whom they are writing
   - textual conventions, like report or business letter formats, that help define the form their writing takes
   - their feelings about the writing they need or want to do
   - the amount of practice they have had with a particular kind of writing
   - external factors, such as deadlines and access to electronic media

5. No matter what they write, from the moment they begin to think about their writing, these individuals are faced with a complex series of *choices*. Some of these choices will involve the writing process. To make practical decisions about their writing, these writers ask themselves questions such as the following:
   - Do I know enough about my subject? Do I need to do additional reading and research?
   - When should I begin writing? What deadlines should I establish for this project? How much time should I spend planning, drafting, and revising?
   - At what points in my writing might I benefit from interactions with others?

   Other questions involve the writing itself:
   - What do I hope to accomplish? Are my goals for the writing realistic, and do they respond to the needs, interests, and expectations of my readers?
   - How can I organize and develop my ideas most effectively?
   - How much supporting detail, and of what types, do I need to provide?
   - What tone or style should I adopt, given my subject, purpose, and audience?

   These writers may not ask these questions in the same way and at the same time in their writing process, but they all understand the importance of considering these and other issues.
6. These individuals recognize the significant role that writing plays in their personal and professional lives. Writing doesn't necessarily come easily to them, but they are willing to spend the time and energy necessary to write well. Writing, they know, is important *work in progress*.

Exploration

The previous exploration asked you to consider the role that writing plays in your life and the kinds of writing experiences that you find productive and unproductive. Now recall a successful writing experience. (Don't limit yourself to academic writing, by the way.) What factors enabled you to complete this writing successfully? Write a paragraph or more describing this experience and analyzing the reasons you were successful.

MAKING CHOICES: DEVELOPING RHETORICAL SENSITIVITY

How do writers make choices as they compose? Experienced writers, like those described at the beginning of this chapter, draw on *all* their resources when they write. They use their knowledge of writing gained through reading, and they also analyze their own situation as writers. They think about their purpose—the meaning they wish to communicate, their reasons for writing—and their readers. They explore their own ideas, challenging themselves to express their ideas as clearly and carefully as possible. They play with words and phrases, sentences and paragraphs, to make their writing stylistically effective. In all of these activities, successful writers are demonstrating their *rhetorical sensitivity*—even though they might not use this phrase to describe their thinking and writing.

You may not be familiar with this phrase, either. It derives from the word *rhetoric,* which means the art or discipline of effective communication. Rhetoric is one of the oldest fields of intellectual study in Western culture; it was first formulated by such Greek and Roman rhetoricians as Isocrates (436–338 B.C.), Aristotle (384–322 B.C.), Cicero (106–43 B.C.), and Quintilian (A.D. 35–96). Originally developed to meet the needs of speakers, rhetoric quickly was applied to written texts as well.

In your daily life, you have already developed considerable rhetorical sensitivity. As you make decisions about how you wish to present yourself to and interact with others, you naturally (if often unconsciously) draw on your commonsense understanding of effective communication. Imagine, for instance, that you are preparing to interview for a job. In deciding what to wear to and how to act during the interview, you will make a number of decisions that reflect your rhetorical sensitivity. Much of your attention will focus on how you can present yourself best, but you also recognize the importance of being well prepared and of interacting effectively with your interviewers. And if you are smart, you will consider the specific situation for which you are applying. Someone applying for a position in a bank might well dress and act differently than someone applying for a job as a fund-raiser for a small nonprofit arts group. Successful applicants know that in all that they do—in the way they dress, present themselves, respond to questions, and interact with interviewers—they are attempting to communicate their strengths and persuade their audience to employ them.

As this example indicates, when you think rhetorically, you consider how you can communicate most effectively with others, given what you know of the specific situation. And many of the decisions you make are informed by the common sense that you've acquired simply by participating in the life of your culture. You don't have to think about it too consciously to recognize that you would dress and act one way at a job interview and another way at a sports event. When writers think rhetorically, they apply their understanding of human communication in general, and of written texts in particular, to the decisions that will enable effective communication within a specific writer-reader situation.

Seeing the key elements of rhetoric in context

Rhetoric, as applied to written texts, involves the following key elements:

1. One or more *writers* who have (or must discover) something to convey
2. One or more *readers* with whom the writer (or writers) would like to communicate
3. A written *discourse* or *text*—an essay, poem, chart, set of directions, letter, report, or other writing—that makes this communication possible

The relationship among these elements is dynamic. As Chapter 9, "Understanding the Reading Process," emphasizes, communication between writer and reader is not a one-way operation, like a radio tower transmitting messages to be passively decoded. Writers select and arrange language to express their meanings, but readers are equally active. Readers don't simply decipher or decode the words on the page; they draw on their own experiences and expectations as they read. As a student, for instance, you naturally read your economics textbook differently than you read a popular novel. You also know that the more experience you have reading certain kinds of writing—science fiction novels or the sports or financial pages of the newspaper, for example—the more you get out of them.

Writing and reading do not occur in a vacuum. Like all people, writers exist in a particular time and place; they are influenced by the environment in which they live and by the institutions within which they work. Just as a person interviewing for a job dresses and acts in a manner appropriate to the situation, so too do writers respond to their situation. Neither students nor businesspersons, to cite two examples, are free to write whatever they wish. Their participation in larger institutions limits their freedom, just as it also provides opportunities for communication with others. A student writing an essay about a controversial issue and a middle-level manager writing an annual sales report are both taking advantage of institutionally sanctioned opportunities to communicate their own ideas. But if the student and the manager wish to have their ideas taken seriously, if they wish to be effective with their intended audience, they know that they must write in a form acceptable to their readers.

How do forms or genres become acceptable to readers? Like languages, such forms as the business letter and the scientific report develop over time. And like languages—which evolve in response to the needs of particular people in particular times and places—forms also respond to the needs of readers and writers. The scientific report and the business letter, for instance, evolved along with and in response to the rise of modern science and of Western capitalism. Different forms of writing thus have histories, just as languages and countries do.

What difference does it make to you as a writer that reading and writing occur in a context and that readers and writers both draw on and adhere to certain forms and conventions? It means that as a writer you are both limited and free. You cannot ignore the situation within which you are writing or the forms and conventions your readers expect you to follow. But unless you are writing a legal contract or filling out a renter's agreement, you also have considerable flexibility and opportunities for self-expression.

An example from my experience in writing *Work in Progress* may help clarify this point. When I started, I knew that I needed to follow certain conventions. Some of these conventions—such as the requirement that a textbook have headings, subheadings, and activities at the end of each chapter—are very general; others are more specific to composition textbooks. I didn't feel burdened or limited by these conventions; in fact, they reassured me, for they provided a framework I could use to develop my ideas. When you write, you must work within conventions appropriate to your situation, purpose, and subject, but these conventions generally are enabling, not limiting.

Demonstrating rhetorical sensitivity

Writers who demonstrate rhetorical sensitivity consider all the elements of rhetoric when they compose. They think about their own purposes and intentions—the meanings they want to convey to readers. They reflect on the image of themselves, the writer's *persona,* that they want to create in their writing. They consider the needs, interests, and expectations of their readers. And they draw on the knowledge they have gained about language through speaking, listening, reading, and writing.

All writers, including you, have some degree of rhetorical sensitivity. Because you learned language as a child and have used it in your daily life ever since, you have already developed sensitivity to oral language. When you converse with others, you automatically adjust your language to the situation. You naturally speak differently when you chat with friends than when you talk with your minister, employer, or teacher, for instance.

If you are like many students, you may be more confident of your ability to communicate effectively through oral language than through written discourse. How can you increase your rhetorical sensitivity as a writer? You can do so by reading broadly, writing often, and discussing your writing with others. Helping you achieve this rhetorical sensitivity is also, of course, a major goal of this textbook and of your composition course.

Exploration

Take a few moments to reflect on your understanding of the terms *rhetoric* and *rhetorical sensitivity.* You may find it helpful to recall an incident in your daily life when you demonstrated what you now recognize to be rhetorical sensitivity. If so, describe this situation. Then write a paragraph or more stating your current understanding of these terms. Finally, write one or two questions that you still have about *rhetoric* and *rhetorical sensitivity.*

USING COMMONSENSE ANALYSIS TO UNDERSTAND WRITING "RULES"

Writing is hard but rewarding work. Sometimes people think that they can make that hard work just a little easier by establishing rigid rules. You may have been warned, for instance, never to use the pronoun *I* in your writing. This rule may have confused you; you may not have understood what's so terrible about having a few *I*'s sprinkled throughout your essay.

If you think commonsensically about how language works, drawing on the rhetorical sensitivity you have developed as a reader and a writer, you can begin to understand how rules like this got established. More importantly, you can decide when this and other rules make sense and when they are overly rigid or unnecessarily limiting.

Let's look at the rule I've just mentioned: *Never use* I *in your writing.* Teachers sometimes discourage students from using *I* because they are aware that most academic writing is intended to focus on the subject being discussed, on arguments and evidence, rather than on the writer's individual experiences and opinions. A history professor who assigns an essay exam on the causes of the civil rights movement of the 1950s and 1960s will want you to demonstrate your ability to define and explain those causes rather than to express your personal feelings about the movement.

There's a kernel of commonsense wisdom, then, in some teachers' prohibition against using *I*. The problem is that there are times when *I* is exactly the *right* pronoun to use—when you're describing a personal experience, for example, or when you want to show that an observation truly is your own opinion. Rather than adhering rigidly to rules like this one that may or may not make sense in a specific situation, you can use your rhetorical sensitivity to make decisions as you write and revise.

Application

Think of several writing "rules," such as the one just discussed, that you've never understood or fully accepted. List as many of these rules as possible. Then choose one of the rules you listed and write a brief explanation of why you question it.

Group Activity

Bring your response to the previous application to class. Working with a group of classmates, discuss your lists, and select one writing rule that you agree may be questionable or too rigidly applied. To report your conclusions to the class, choose one person to record the group's answers to the following questions about that rule:

1. Why do the members of your group think that this writing rule may be questionable? Identify a situation when following this rule might not be preferable or wise.
2. What arguments in favor of this rule can your group identify? At what times would following this rule make good sense?

Be prepared to discuss your conclusions with your classmates.

THINKING—AND ACTING—LIKE A WRITER

As you've just seen, thinking commonsensically about writing can help you understand some of the basic conventions of writing. Later chapters will focus more specifically on ways to increase your rhetorical sensitivity and thus become a more *effective* writer. But you may also wish to improve your *efficiency* as a writer—your ability to manage your time well, to cope with the inevitable frustrations of writing, and to use all your personal energies and resources when you write. Can some commonsense thinking about writing help you in that respect as well?

Writing is a *process,* yet few people stop to think about how their writing process may affect the quality of their writing. Such analysis can prove illuminating, however. One of my students, for example, formulated an analogy that helped us all think very fruitfully about how the writing process works. "Writing," he said, "is actually a lot like sports."

Writing—like sports? Let's see what this comparison reveals about the writing process.

1. *Writing and sports are both performance skills.* You may know who won every Wimbledon since 1950, but if you don't actually play tennis, you're not a tennis player—just somebody who knows a lot about tennis. Similarly, you can know a lot about writing, but to demonstrate (and improve) your skills, you must *write.*
2. *Writing and sports both require individuals to master complex skills and to perform these skills in an almost infinite number of situations.* Athletes must learn specific skills, plays, or maneuvers, but they can never execute them routinely or thoughtlessly. Writers, like athletes, must be resourceful and flexible. You can learn the principles of effective essay organization, for instance, and you may write a number of essays that are, in fact, well organized. Nevertheless, each time you sit down to write a new essay, you have to consider your options and make new choices about your writing. This is a primary reason why writers cannot rely on formulas or rules but must instead use their rhetorical sensitivity to analyze and respond to each particular situation.
3. *Successful athletes and writers know that a positive attitude is essential.* You've read about athletes who "psych" themselves up before a game or competition, sometimes with the help of

a sports psychologist. But any serious athlete will tell you that's only part of what having a positive attitude means. It also means running five miles when you're already tired at three or doing twenty-five repetitions during weight training when you're exhausted and no one else would know if you did only fifteen. A positive attitude is also important in writing. If you approach a writing task with a negative attitude—"I never was good at writing"—you immediately create obstacles for yourself. Keeping a positive, open attitude is hard when you're a beginner—at tennis, skiing, or writing. But it's essential.

4. *To maintain a high level of skill, both athletes and writers need frequent practice and effective coaching.* This point is so obvious for sports that it hardly merits discussion. Without frequent practice and an experienced coach who can help the athlete evaluate his or her performance, an athlete's skills will inevitably slip. "In sports," a coach once said, "you're either getting better or getting worse." Without practice—which for a writer means both reading and writing—your writing skills will inevitably slip (and so will your confidence). Likewise, coaching is essential in writing because it's hard to distance yourself from your own work. Coaches—your writing instructor, a tutor in your writing center, or a fellow student—can help you gain a fresh perspective on your writing and make useful suggestions about revision as well.
5. *Successful athletes and writers continually set new goals for themselves.* This point is actually a variation of the coach's adage mentioned earlier. Athletes know that they are either getting better or getting worse, so they set new challenges for themselves and analyze their performance. They know that coaches can help them but that they are ultimately the ones performing. Successful writers know this too, so they look for opportunities to practice their writing. And they don't just evaluate their success by an instructor's grade or a supervisor's comment. Their writing is, they recognize, always work in progress.

Exploration

Freewriting, discussed as a strategy for invention in Chapter 5, is a technique used to generate and explore ideas. In case you are not familiar with freewriting, here is a description of it by Peter Elbow, the professor who first created this technique.

> To do a freewriting exercise, simply force yourself to write without stopping for [a certain number] of minutes. Sometimes you will produce good writing, but that's not the goal. Sometimes you will produce garbage, but that's not the goal either. . . . Speed is not the goal, though sometimes the process revs you up. If you can't think of anything to write, write about how that feels or repeat over and over "I have nothing to write" or "Nonsense" or "No." If you get stuck in the middle of a sentence or thought, just repeat the last word or phrase till something comes along. The only point is to keep writing.

Use this technique to freewrite about your attitude toward writing. Write for five or ten minutes, perhaps beginning with one of the following phrases:

- When I write, I feel . . .
- Writing means . . .
- Writing is like . . .

DEVELOPING A PORTFOLIO OF YOUR WRITTEN WORK

Successful athletes and writers share another common trait: both regularly monitor and evaluate their performance. You're probably aware that serious athletes videotape their performances; doing so enables them to pinpoint their strengths and weaknesses and set short- and long-term goals. Successful writers also develop ways to review and evaluate their progress. They don't videotape themselves writing, of course; rather, they review earlier writing projects to analyze and learn from previous efforts. Writers who save copies of their work as it progresses from rough draft to finished essay can observe their own writing as it grows and changes. Doing so can help them gain insights into the strengths and weaknesses of individual essays or reports, and it can also catalyze helpful insights about the writing process. Studying drafts of my own writing, for instance, helped me recognize an unproductive tendency to spend too much time on sentence-level changes when working on early drafts. Now I defer such changes until I am sure that I have a workable rough draft.

Because writing teachers recognize that writers can benefit a great deal from reviewing and reflecting on their own writing, many ask their students to keep copies of rough and final drafts of their writing in a *portfolio.* Your portfolio may take different forms; it may be a notebook or file folder, or you may keep your work on disk. What matters is that you keep both final and rough drafts of your work; you may even want to save your notes and plans so that you can have the fullest picture of your writing process. At various points throughout the term, your teacher may ask you to review the work in your portfolio, asking yourself questions like the following:

- Which of the essays contained in my portfolio represents my best work as a writer? Why?
- What general strengths and weaknesses can I observe in my work?
- Does a review of my written work indicate that I am more confident and successful working on some kinds of writing than on others?
- What can I learn about my writing process by analyzing my writing as it develops from rough to final drafts?
- How can I use what I have learned from reviewing my work to set both short- and long-term goals for myself as a writer?

Keeping a portfolio allows you to document and reflect on your development as a writer. Like athletes who take their own performance seriously enough to study past efforts, writers who keep a portfolio have a valuable opportunity to analyze their writing and their growth as writers.

BECOMING PART OF A COMMUNITY OF WRITERS

For many people, one big difference between writing and sports is that athletes often belong to teams, whereas writers, they think, work in lonely isolation—tucked away in a carrel at the library or seated at the kitchen table or computer with only books and notes as companions. But does writing actually require isolation and loneliness? Let's go back to the people described at the beginning of this chapter. Of all these individuals, only the government safety inspectors may actually write together—sitting together and jointly composing their list of problems. Like many in business, industry, and the professions, however, the consulting engineer and the department store manager work as part of one or more teams. Much of the time they compose alone, but their work is part of a group effort: their drafts will be responded to, and perhaps changed, by the rest of the group or the group leader. Several of the other writers, such as the psychiatric social worker and the students, talk extensively with friends and coworkers before and while writing. And the retired librarian takes advantage of an electronic bulletin board as he considers how the school board might best respond to a request to remove several books from a school library. Later, he and other school board members will work collaboratively to draft a response to the petition.

As these examples indicate, the romanticized image of the writer struggling alone until inspiration strikes is hardly accurate. Just consider all the varied activities involved in writing—from first getting an idea or an assignment to planning, drafting, and revising. Most writers actually alternate between periods of independent activity, composing alone at the desk or computer, and social interactions, meeting with friends, colleagues, or team members for information, advice, or responses to drafts. These writers may also correspond with others in their field, or they may get in touch with people doing similar work through their reading, library research, or electronic networks.

Finally, people who take their writing seriously are just like other people who share an interest. They like to develop social relationships or networks with others who feel as they do. They realize that these networks will help them learn new ideas, improve their skills, and share their interest and enthusiasm. Sometimes these relationships are formal and relatively permanent. Many poets and fiction writers, for instance, meet regularly to discuss work in progress. Perhaps more commonly, writers' networks are informal and shifting, though no less vital. A new manager in a corporation, for instance, may find one or two people with sound judgment and good writing skills to review important letters and reports. Similarly, graduate students working on their M.A. theses may meet informally but regularly over coffee to compare notes and provide mutual support.

Unfortunately, college life generally does not encourage the development of informal networks like these, especially among undergraduates. Students juggling coursework, jobs, family demands, and various civic and political activities can find it difficult to get together or to take the time to read and respond to one another's writing. For these and other reasons, many colleges and universities have established writing centers, places where you can go to talk with others about your writing. Find out if your campus has a writing center. (Your composition instructor will know.) If it does, be sure to take advantage of the opportunity to get an informed response to your work.

Application

If your campus has a writing center, make an appointment to interview a writing assistant (or tutor) about the services the center provides. You may also want to ask the writing assistant about his or her own experiences as a writer. Your instructor may ask you to present the results of your interview orally or to write a summary of your discussion.

Whether you have access to a writing center or not, you can still participate in an informal network with others who, like you, are working to improve their writing skills. Because you are in the same class and share the same assignments and concerns, you and your classmates constitute a natural community of writers. You can benefit a great deal by participating in group activities. Here, for instance, is a statement about the benefits of working in groups by Su Tay, Lisa Brame, Gretchen Clary, and Sean O'Donnel, students in Dr. Deborah Bosley's composition class at the University of North Carolina at Charlotte. "We believe that working in groups is very important. It gives us the chance to share our problems with group members, and it also exposes us to how other people handle the writing process. It helps us to recognize our strengths and weaknesses. It is motivating to know we are not alone in our problems."

The following guidelines can help you participate effectively in group activities. These suggestions apply whether you work with the same group of students all term or participate in a variety of groups.

Guidelines for group activities

1. Develop the Skills That Contribute to Effective Group Work.

Good teamwork doesn't come naturally; you may need to develop or strengthen the skills that will contribute to effective group work. As you work with others in your class, keep these suggestions in mind.

- *Remember that people have different styles of learning and interacting.* Some of these differences represent individual preferences: some students work out their ideas as they talk, for instance, while others prefer to think through their ideas before speaking. Other differences are primarily cultural and thus reflect deeply embedded social practices and preferences. Effective groups value diversity and find ways to ensure that *all* members can comfortably participate in and benefit from group activities.

- *Balance a commitment to "getting the job done" with patience and flexibility.* When you participate in group activities, you usually have a limited amount of time to respond to a question or problem or to discuss work in progress. Responsible group members will recognize the need to "get the job done" but will also be flexible and patient.
- *Work with your peers to articulate group goals and monitor group processes.* To work together successfully, group members must take the time to clarify goals and procedures for particular tasks; otherwise, valuable time is wasted. Similarly, effective groups develop some means (formal or informal) of evaluating group activities. If you are part of a group that is meeting regularly, you might decide to begin all or some of your meetings by having each person state one way in which the group is working well and one way in which it could be improved. The time spent discussing these comments and suggestions could contribute to better group dynamics.
- *Deal immediately and openly with any problems in the group process, such as a dominating or nonparticipating member.* It's not always easy to discuss problems such as these openly, but doing so is essential to effective group work.

2. Be Ready to Assume Different Roles in Different Group Activities.

Sometimes you may function as your group's leader, either informally or formally by the group's (or your instructor's) decision. At other times you may act as a mediator or synthesizer, the person who helps the group reach a consensus. Or your main responsibility may be keeping the group on task so that you can achieve your goals in the time allotted. In effective groups, members assume the roles most appropriate to the specific task and situation, and they recognize the need for flexibility and variety.

3. Develop Ways to Encourage Productive Conflict.

"Two heads are better than one," the proverb reminds us—and that's because when two or more people get together to discuss an issue or solve a problem, they naturally have different ways of analyzing a topic or of approaching a problem. The diverse perspectives and strategies that people bring to a problem or task are one of the main reasons why group activities are so productive. Capitalize on these differences. Encourage the discussion of new ideas. Consider alternative approaches to your subject. Don't be afraid to disagree; doing so may enable your group to find a more creative solution to a problem, to discover a new and stimulating response to a question. Just be sure that your discussion remains both friendly and focused on the task at hand.

Not all conflict is productive, of course. If personality conflicts prevent effective discussion about the writing to be done or if you consistently spend a great deal of time arguing about procedural matters, such as when and how often to meet, your group is wasting time that could be better used for writing. Unproductive conflict erodes the effectiveness of your group; productive conflict enables your group to maximize your creativity and draw on all of your shared resources.

4. Be Realistic about the Advantages and Disadvantages of Group Learning Activities.

No method or strategy is perfect, and group learning activities are no exception. You'll discover that group learning does carry numerous benefits.

- Groups inevitably have greater resources than individuals.
- Groups can employ more complex problem-solving methods than individuals.
- Working in groups can help you learn more effectively and efficiently.
- Participating in group activities can be personally rewarding and can also help prepare you for on-the-job teamwork.
- By responding as writers and readers, groups can give members immediate responses to their writing and numerous suggestions for revision.

But there are potential disadvantages to group learning activities as well.

- Sometimes it can take longer to achieve consensus or solve a problem when people work in groups. (This is usually because the group members examine more options and look at the problem from more angles than a single individual would.)
- Individual group members may not always be prepared, or they may try to dominate or withdraw from discussion.
- Group members may not share responsibility for a project equitably.

Most of these problems can be avoided if you and the members of your group participate fully in group activities and respond to problems when they occur. Groups are, after all, a bit like friendships or marriages: they develop and change; they require care and attention. Problems can arise, but if you're committed to keeping the group going, alert to signs of potential trouble, and willing to talk problems out, you can all benefit from group work.

Group Activity

If your instructor has divided your class into groups, meet with the members of your group to discuss how you can most effectively work as a collaborative team. Begin your meeting by exchanging names and phone numbers; take time just to chat and get to know each other. You might also see if your group can formulate some friendly rules to guide group activities. (You might all pledge, for instance, to notify at least one other member if you can't make an out-of-class group meeting.) Try to anticipate some of the problems you may have working together, such as coordinating schedules, and discuss how to resolve them.

Activities for Thought, Discussion, and Writing

1. Now that you have read this first chapter and participated in at least one class discussion, it might be useful for you to set some goals for yourself as a writer. Make a list of several concrete goals you'd like to accomplish in your composition class this term; then write a paragraph or more discussing how you plan to achieve these goals.
2. Freewrite for five to ten minutes on one or more of the following topics:
   - your best writing experience
   - your worst writing experience
   - your feelings about writing in general
   - your strengths and weaknesses as a writer

   Save this freewriting. Your instructor may ask you to use it as the starting point for an essay.
3. Interview one or more students in your current or prospective major area. Ask questions like these to find out about student writing in this field:
   - What kinds of writing are students required to do in classes in this field? Is this writing similar to the writing students might do if, after graduation, they begin careers in this field? If not, how is it different?

- How is their writing evaluated by their professors?
- How well do the students interviewed feel that their composition classes prepared them for the writing they now do?
- What advice about writing would they give to other students taking classes in this field?

Your instructor may ask you to report the results of this interview to your group so that the group can summarize and present your collective findings to the class. Your instructor may also ask you—working alone or with classmates—to write an essay summarizing the results of your interview or of the class discussion of student writing.

4. After reflecting on your past experiences with group activities, freewrite for five to ten minutes in response to these questions:
   - How would you describe your experience with group activities in the past?
   - What factors contribute to making these group activities successful or unsuccessful?
   - What strengths do you feel you bring to group activities? What weaknesses?

   Your freewrite should give you valuable information that you can draw on when you work with others in your class. Your instructor may ask you to share your freewrites with other members of your group. The resulting discussion should produce some suggestions that will enable you to work together more productively and efficiently.

CHAPTER 2

UNDERSTANDING THE WRITING PROCESS

THINKING ABOUT WRITING: NONMAGICAL STRATEGIES VERSUS MAGICAL POWERS

Writing is hardly a mysterious activity, yet it is sometimes viewed as if it were. Many people, for instance, seem to think that those who write well possess a magical power or talent. According to this view, people are either born with the ability to write well or they're not, and those who do write well find writing easy. They just sit down and the words and ideas begin to flow.

My own experiences as a writer, and those of my students, indicate that this popular stereotype simply isn't accurate. Successful writers work as hard on their writing as anyone else—perhaps even harder. Unlike less accomplished writers, however, successful writers develop strategies that enable them to cope with the complexities of writing and thus to experience the satisfaction of a job well done.

Here are two essays, one by a student writer, Mary Kacmarcik, and one by a professor of English, Burton Hatlen. In different ways, Kacmarcik and Hatlen each discuss what it means to be a writer and comment on their own development as writers. They also each make the point that, as Hatlen says, "writing is a craft, which can be learned by anyone willing to work at it." As you read their essays, ask yourself the following questions:

- To what extent are your own assumptions about writing and experiences as a writer similar to those of Kacmarcik and Hatlen? How are they different?
- Can you recall specific experiences, such as those Kacmarcik and Hatlen describe in their essays, that played a critical role in your development as a writer or your understanding of writing?

Here is Mary Kacmarcik's essay.

A WRITER IS FORMED

The woman at the front of the room hardly resembled my idea of an English teacher. Her raggedy undershirt, heavy flannel jacket, disheveled pants, and braided, stringy hair gave her the appearance of having just returned from a backcountry expedition. And she was huge; she must have tipped the scales at well over two hundred pounds.

"My name is Harriet Jones," she said, "and this is English 111."

This was my introduction to college writing. Ten students had enrolled in this beginning composition class at Islands Community College. Like most of my classmates, I was returning to education after a period in the work force. I had spent one year at Western Washington University but had avoided writing classes. I discovered later, when I sent for my transcripts to apply to Oregon State University, that I had withdrawn from a writing course at Western. I have no memory of this. Did I drop it the first day, or did I struggle with an essay or two before giving up?

At any rate, I went to Alaska that summer to work in the seafood canneries. It was a trip I had planned with two friends during my senior year in high school. I expected to return to college in the fall with thousands of dollars in my bank account. The work was miserable, but I fell in love with remote Sitka, and I stayed. Time passed with adventures enough to fill a novel. I eventually landed a job I really wanted at Northern Lights Natural Foods, a small, family-owned natural foods store. That job inspired me to take a nutrition course at the community college. I realized during the course that some biology would help me understand nutrition, so I took biology the following semester. I began to consider a career in nutrition which led me to apply to the Department of Foods and Nutrition at OSU. I wasn't ready to leave Sitka, however; I would work one more year and take a few more classes on the side.

That is how I came to be sitting in Ms. Jones's class, preparing myself for a relationship with an English grammar handbook. We were to respond to short stories, an exercise in which my experience was limited to junior high school book reports. Although I have always been an avid reader, I had given little thought to characters, conflicts, plots, and settings. So those early essays were on topics that did not interest me. I had never heard of a comma splice either, but Ms. Jones assured us that any paper containing one would be promptly rewarded with an E grade. I would agonize over blank pages, afraid to begin, afraid of saying the wrong thing, afraid of committing some technical error. I somehow managed to fill up the pages and hand in those early essays. Fortunately, Ms. Jones encouraged us to revise after she had graded our papers.

It turned out that she was also very willing to talk with us about writing. I discovered that this formidable woman was actually a caring, humorous person. The writing did not instantly become easier, though. During the second term, we worked on longer papers that required some research. We also did in-class assignments such as freewriting and essay exams. By the end of the term, I had finally become comfortable with putting my ideas on paper.

The year with Ms. Jones was great preparation for my studies at OSU. I learned the importance of editing my work and following conventions. I gained confidence in stating my views. I also learned that teachers are human and that most of them enjoy discussing projects with students outside of class.

In thinking about my history as a writer for this essay, I realized that I have always been a writer--even when I felt unconfident and out of practice. Letters to aunts, uncles, and grandparents were my earliest writings outside of schoolwork, and they have been the main link between my parents' families on the East Coast and my nuclear family here in the Northwest. These letters followed a set format for years:

Dear Aunt ___________ (or Grandma),

How are you? I am fine. Thank you for the ___________.

Love,

Mary Ellen

My letters have matured with me, and I consider them a sort of journal except that I mail this journal off in bits and pieces instead of keeping it to read later. My letters describe what I have been doing, how I feel about things, and what I plan to do. When I lived in Alaska, letters were my link to family and friends in Washington.

Another early writing experience was an expanded form of passing notes in school. A friend and I wrote notes to each other that often went on for pages, much of it nonsense and gossip. We would work on these packets for days before exchanging them. Now I can see that we were flexing and developing our writing muscles as well as building our friendship through the sharing of ideas.

Currently, I write the newsletter for a club I belong to, an activity I volunteered for to gain experience and to stay involved with writing. I would like to combine writing with nutrition as a career. (I considered a major in journalism, but I have a strong desire to learn everything I can about nutrition.) I would like to help people improve their health by sharing this knowledge with them. I still think of myself as someone who is going to write someday. But I have been writing because I wanted to ever since I learned how.

MARY KACMARCIK

This is Professor Burton Hatlen's essay.

WRITING IS A CRAFT THAT CAN BE LEARNED, NOT AN EFFORTLESS OUTPOURING BY GENIUSES

A writer—that's what I would be when I grew up. I made that decision in 1952, when I was 16, along with what now seems to be half the people I knew at the time. We were all going to be "writers," whatever we meant by that.

I can't speak for my friends, but in my case, at least, being a writer meant living a certain kind of life. The setting would be Paris, *la rive gauche:* a sidewalk café. A man (with a beard, a beret dropping over his right eye, a turtleneck sweater, sandals, a pipe) is seated at a round table, a half-empty glass of red wine before him. There are other people around the table, but they are a little dim. And there is talk. Jung. Kafka. Anarchism. The decline of the West. But mostly there is that man. Me. Someday.

I didn't need anyone to tell me that the road from a dusty farming town in the Central Valley of California to that Paris café would be a long and difficult one. In fact, it was *supposed* to be long and difficult. "You must suffer, suffer"—so said a cartoon character of my youth to a would-be artist. And I had a real-life example of such suffering. When I was 10, my cousin brought her new husband, George, to town. George had actually been to Paris, and he was going to write a novel before returning there. Later, I heard my aunt tell my mother that she had read the manuscript of his novel. According to her, it was "filthy," and what was more, she whispered, she was sure George "drank." In any case, his novel remained unpublished and George never made it back to Paris. At some level I realized that his sad story augured ill for my own dreams of living the life of a writer in a 1950's version of Paris in the 20's.

Nevertheless, in 1956, after my junior year at Berkeley, I decided that if I was ever to become a writer, I'd better try to write. I spent five months working at various jobs, and when I had saved $500 I moved into a one-room apartment in San Francisco. By then the "renaissance" there was in full flower, and the city seemed to me a reasonable facsimile of Paris. In North Beach there were real cafés, where real poets—Kenneth Rexroth, Robert Duncan, Lawrence Ferlinghetti (who actually wore a beret)—sat around and talked. If location had anything to do with becoming a writer, San Francisco seemed the right place to be.

For three months, until my money ran out, I spent my evenings in North Beach and my days at the oilcloth-covered kitchen table in my apartment, writing. Or at least that's what I told myself I was doing. In fact, in those three months I managed to write only about three pages of what I called a novel. It was about a young man living alone in a San Francisco apartment, who looked into the sky one day, saw it split open, and went mad. I fussed for the first week or two over those pages, making sure that every word was *juste.* But I had never worked out a plot, and once the young man went mad, I didn't know what else to do with him.

I stopped writing, and devoted my days to reading—all of Dreiser, among other things. What I remember best about that time is not the few paragraphs I wrote, but the wonder I felt as I read the yellowing pages of my second-hand copy of *The "genius."*

In January I went back to Berkeley, and that spring, at the suggestion of one of my teachers, applied to graduate school. Over the next few years, the sidewalk café began to seem no more than an adolescent fantasy, and, before I knew it, I had become not a writer in Paris, but a teacher entangled in committee meetings and bureaucratic infighting.

What brought all this back to me was a conversation I had earlier this year with a one-time colleague of mine, the author of a respectable university-press book on Sir Thomas Browne and, in the days when we taught together, a tenured associate professor and a popular teacher of Shakespeare. A few years ago, at 44, he suddenly resigned his teaching position and moved to Boston, where, I heard later, he was working a couple of days a week as a waiter and spending the rest of his time writing. When I went to Boston last winter I looked him up.

We talked about his novel and my work. Then the conversation turned to our respective children, all of whom, we realized, had not only decided to become artists of one sort or another but, unlike us at their age, were actually *doing* so. I thought about the Paris café, and then I asked him what he had wanted to do with his life when he was 20.

"Actually," he said, "I wanted to live the way I'm living now—working at a nothing job that doesn't take anything out of me, and writing."

That was a pretty fair description of my own dream when I moved to that apartment in San Francisco. What had happened to it? I think the main reason that I never realized the dream was my mistaken notion of what it means to be a writer, which I had picked up partly from media images of Hemingway and Fitzgerald, Sartre and Camus, and partly from my teachers. Those influences had suggested that writing was something geniuses were somehow able to do without thinking about it; ordinary people dabbled at their peril. That writing is also a craft that can be learned, that a young person might decide to write and then systematically learn how to do so, was never so much as hinted at by anyone I knew. So, when the words for my novel did not automatically come pouring out of me, I had concluded that I must not be a writer.

In fact, I have over the years written enough poetry to make a good-sized book, and enough prose—if it were all gathered together—to make two or three. Yet I feel uncomfortable saying I'm a writer who teaches, preferring instead to see myself as a teacher who writes. Nevertheless, writing is clearly a major part of my life. Yes, I do feel some envy of my friend in Boston, who is at last doing what he dreamed of when he was 20. And no, I've never written that novel, because I still don't know how to go about it. If most of what I write is about other people's writing, that's all right, because through it I've found a way to share with others the wonder I felt 30 years ago as I read Dreiser.

Since then, I have gradually come to see that writing takes manifold forms, that the conception of writing as a hermetic mystery, which I picked up from my reading and my teachers in the 1950's, is not only wrong, but pernicious. It dishonors the writing that non-geniuses do and denies the hard work at the craft that is essential to all writing, even the writing of "geniuses." It caused my cousin's husband to decide that if he couldn't be a writer, he didn't want to be anything, and I think it caused me to waste several years chasing illusions.

The myth that real writing is the effortless outpouring of geniuses did not die in the 1950's. There is abundant evidence that it still persists—at least among my students, most of whom also dream that someone, someday, will find a spark of "genius" in what they write. As a teacher who writes (or a writer who teaches), I am becoming more and more convinced that it's my job to nurture the writer in every student, while at the same time making it clear that writing is a craft, which can be learned by anyone willing to work at it.

BURTON HATLEN

Exploration

Now that you have read Kacmarcik's and Hatlen's essays, reflect on your own assumptions about writing and your experiences as a writer. To do so, set aside at least a half an hour to respond (either by freewriting or jotting down notes) to the following questions:

- What are your earliest memories of learning to write?
- How was writing viewed by your family and friends when you were growing up?
- What role did reading play in your development as a writer?
- Can you recall particular experiences in school or on the job that influenced your current attitude toward writing?

- If you were to describe your history as a writer, what stages or periods in your development would you identify? Write a sentence or two briefly characterizing each stage or period.
- What images come to mind when you hear the term *writer*?
- What images come to mind when you think of yourself as a writer? (You may find it easiest to draw up a list of metaphors, such as "As a writer, I'm a turtle—slow and steady" or "As a writer, I'm a racehorse—fast out of the gate but never sure if I've got the stamina to finish.") Write at least two or three sentences that use images or metaphors to characterize your sense of yourself as a writer.
- What kinds of writing have you come to enjoy? To dislike?
- What do you enjoy most about the process of writing? What do you enjoy least?
- What goals would you like to set for yourself as a writer?

Application

Using the information generated by the previous exploration, write a letter to your classmates and teacher in which you describe who you are as a writer today—and how you got to be that way. You're writing a letter, so you don't need to worry as much about form and style as you would if you were writing a formal essay. Do keep in mind, however, that your classmates and teacher may actually read your letter, so write with this audience in mind.

Group Activity

Bring enough copies of your letter to class so that you can share it with members of your group. After you have all read one another's letters, work together to answer the following questions. Choose one person to record the group's answers so that you can share the results of your discussion with the rest of the class.

- To what extent are your attitudes toward writing and experiences as writers similar? List three to five statements about your attitudes toward and experiences as writers with which all group members can agree.
- What factors most clearly account for the differences in your attitudes toward writing and experiences as writers? List two or three factors that you agree account for these differences.

- Can you identify any common goals you would like to set for yourselves as writers? List at least three goals you can agree on.

MANAGING THE WRITING PROCESS

Writing is not a magical or mysterious process. Rather, it is a craft that can indeed be learned. But how do writers actually manage the writing process? Notice how differently the following six students say that they proceed.

> My writing starts with contemplation. I let the topic I have chosen sink into my mind for a while. Then I brainstorm on paper, coming up with words, phrases, and sentences that relate to my topic. It is usually during the brainstorming process that I find whether or not I have chosen the right topic. If I am not satisfied with my topic, I start over. Then I make a simple plan for my essay, and then I start on my rough draft. Peer responses, final drafts, and revisions follow, sometimes with more brainstorming in between.
>
> EDITH CASTERLINE

> I have to sit down with pen in hand and just write whatever comes out naturally. I then go back and work with what I've written.
>
> MICHELLE COLLUM

> I have to think my ideas out in detail before I begin drafting. Only then can I begin writing and revising.
>
> MARSHA CARPER

> When I write, I first brainstorm for an idea. This may take only a few minutes or days, depending on the kind of paper I'm working on. Once I get an idea, I then sit down and start writing. This seems to be the best way for me to get started. After I've written the rough draft I then go back and do some major revision. I revise and have others check for mistakes I might have missed, and then I type it out.
>
> DAVE GUENTHER

> As a writer, I am first a thinker and then a doer. I first think about my topic carefully, and then I write what I wish to say.
>
> GARY ETCHEMENDY

> I write by coming up with a sketchy rough draft and then filling it in or changing it.
>
> PAUL AUSTIN

On the surface, these students' writing processes seem to have little in common. Actually, however, all involve the same three activities: planning, drafting, and revising. These activities don't necessarily occur in any set order. Michelle Collum postpones most of her planning until after she has generated a rough draft, for example, whereas Marsha Carper plans extensively before she writes her first word. To be successful, however, all these writers must sooner or later think critically and make choices about words, ideas, and anticipated responses of readers. Then they must try out these choices either in their heads or on paper, evaluate the effects of these choices, and make appropriate changes in their drafts. Rather than being a magical or mysterious activity, then, writing is a process of planning, drafting, and revising.

Identifying composing styles

The preceding description of planning, drafting, and revising may make writing sound neater and more predictable than it actually is. Writing is, in fact, a messy and often unpredictable process. Even though all writers engage in planning, drafting, and revising, they do so in a variety of ways. Furthermore, no one approaches every writing task in the same way. (For this reason, it is more accurate to refer to writing *processes* rather than the writing process.) Instead, a writer will decide how to approach a writing assignment based on such factors as these:

- the nature and importance of the writing task
- the writer's own time schedule
- the amount of experience the writer has had with a particular kind of writing

Most successful writers do, however, have a typical or preferred way of managing the writing process. Many people find, in fact, that one of the following three styles of composing describes their preferred composing style.

1. *Heavy Planners.* These people, like Marsha Carper and Gary Etchemendy, generally consider their ideas and plan their writing so carefully in their heads that their first drafts are

often more like other writers' second or third drafts. As a consequence, they often revise less intensively and frequently than other students. Many of these students have disciplined themselves so that they can think about their writing in all sorts of places—on the subway, at work, in the garden pulling weeds, or in the car driving to and from school.

Some heavy planners write in this way because they prefer to; others develop this strategy out of necessity. Marsha Carper, for instance, says that she simply has to do a great deal of her writing "in her head" rather than on paper because she lives fifty miles from the university and must spend considerable time commuting. In addition, she's a mother as well as a student, and at home she often has to steal odd moments to work on her writing. As a result, she's learned to use every opportunity to think about her writing while she drives, cooks, or relaxes with her family.

2. *Heavy Revisers.* These students, like Michelle Collum and Paul Austin, differ greatly from the heavy planners just described. Heavy planners spend a great deal of time planning (either in their heads or in writing) before they begin to draft an essay. In contrast, heavy revisers need to find out what they want to say through the act of writing itself. When faced with a writing task, they prefer to sit down at a desk or computer and just begin writing.

   Heavy revisers often state that writing their ideas out in a sustained spurt of activity reassures them that they have something to say and helps them avoid frustration. These students may not seem to plan because they begin drafting so early. Actually, however, their planning occurs as they draft and especially as they revise. Heavy revisers typically spend a great deal of their writing time revising their initial drafts. To do so effectively, they must be able to read their work critically and be able, often, to discard substantial portions of first drafts.

As you've probably realized, in both of these styles of composing, one of the components of the writing process is apparently abbreviated. Heavy planners don't seem to revise as extensively as other writers. Actually, however, they plan (and, in effect, revise) so thoroughly early in the process that they often don't need to revise as intensively later. Similarly, heavy revisers may not seem to plan; in fact, though, once they write their rough drafts, they plan and revise simultaneously and often extensively.

3. *Sequential Composers.* A third general style of composing is exemplified by Dave Guenther and Edith Casterline. These writers might best be called sequential composers because they devote roughly equivalent amounts of time to planning, drafting, and revising. Rather than trying out their ideas and planning their writing mentally, as heavy planners do, sequential composers typically rely on written notes and plans to give shape and force to their ideas. And unlike heavy revisers, sequential composers need to have greater control over form and subject matter as they draft.

   Sequential composers' habit of allotting time for planning, drafting, and revising helps them deal with the inevitable anxieties of writing. Like heavy revisers, sequential composers need the reassurance of seeing their ideas written down; the resulting stack of notes and plans gives them the confidence to begin drafting. Sequential composers may not revise as extensively as heavy revisers, for they generally draft more slowly, reviewing their writing as they proceed. But revision is nevertheless an important part of their composing process; like most writers, sequential revisers need a break from drafting to be able to critique their own words and ideas.

Each of these three styles of composing has advantages and disadvantages. Heavy planners can be efficient writers; they spend less time at the desk or keyboard than do other writers. But heavy planners must have great mental discipline. An unexpected interruption when they are working out their ideas—a child in tears, a phone call—can cause even the most disciplined thinker to have a momentary lapse. Because so much of their work is done mentally, heavy planners are less likely to benefit from the fruitful explorations and revisions that occur when writers review notes and plans or reread their own texts. And because heavy planners put off drafting until relatively late in the composing process, they can encounter substantial difficulties if the sentences and paragraphs that had seemed so clearly developed in their minds don't look as coherent and polished on paper.

Heavy revisers experience different advantages and disadvantages. Because they write quickly and voluminously, heavy revisers aren't in danger of losing valuable ideas. Similarly, their frequent rereading of their drafts helps them remain open to new options that can improve their writing. However, heavy revisers must learn how to deal with emotional highs and lows that occur as they discover what they want to say through the process of writing itself. As noted earlier, heavy revisers must be able ruthlessly to critique their own writing, discarding large portions of text or perhaps starting over if necessary. Because they revise so extensively, heavy revisers must be careful to leave adequate time for revision or the quality of their work can suffer.

What about sequential composers? Because they plan to spend time planning, drafting, and revising—and do so primarily in writing, rather than mentally—they have more external control over the writing process than heavy planners and revisers do. Sequential composers are also unlikely to fool themselves into thinking that a quickly generated collection of ideas is an adequate rough draft or that a plan brainstormed while taking the subway is adequate preparation for writing. Sequential composers can, however, develop inefficiently rigid habits—habits that reflect their need to have external control over their writing process. They may, for instance, waste valuable time developing detailed written plans when they're actually ready to begin drafting.

Good writers are aware of their preferred composing style—and of its potential advantages and disadvantages. They take responsibility for decisions about how to manage their writing, recognizing the difference, for instance, between the necessary incubation of ideas and procrastination. Good writers are also flexible; depending on the task or situation, they can modify their preferred approach. A person who generally is a heavy reviser when writing academic essays, for instance, might write routine business memos in a single sitting because that is the most efficient way to get the job done. Similarly, heavy planners who prefer to do much of the work of writing mentally must employ different strategies when writing collaboratively with others, where a great deal of oral discussion is a necessity.

There is another way of managing the writing process—though it might best be described as management by avoidance.

4. *Procrastinators.* All writers occasionally procrastinate, but if you habitually put off writing a first draft until you have time only for a *final* draft (and this at 3 A.M. on the day your essay is due), your chances of success are minimal. Though you may have invented good reasons for putting off writing—"I write better under pressure"; "I can't write until I

have all my easier assignments done first"—procrastination makes it difficult for you to manage the writing process in an efficient and effective manner.

Is procrastination always harmful? Might it not sometimes be a period of necessary incubation, of unconscious but still productive planning? Here's what one thoughtful student writer discovered about her own tendency to procrastinate:

> For me, sometimes procrastination isn't really procrastination (or so I tell myself). Sometimes what I label procrastination is really planning. The trouble is that I don't always know when it's one or the other. . . .
>
> How do I procrastinate? Let me count the ways. I procrastinate by doing good works (helping overtime at my job, cleaning house, aiding and abetting a variety of causes). I procrastinate by absorbing myself in a purely selfish activity (reading paperbacks, watching TV, going to movies). I procrastinate by visiting with friends, talking on the telephone, prolonging chance encounters. I procrastinate by eating and drinking (ice cream, coffee, cookies--all detrimental). Finally, I procrastinate by convincing myself that this time of day is not when I write well. I'd be much better off, I usually conclude, taking a nap. So I do.
>
> Part of my difficulty is that I can see a certain validity in most of my reasons for procrastinating. There _are_ some times of day when my thoughts flow better. I have forced myself to write papers in the past when I just didn't feel fluid. Not only were the papers difficult to write, they were poorly written, inarticulate papers. Even after several rewrites, they were merely marginal. I would much rather write when I am at my mental best.
>
> I need to balance writing with other activities. The trouble is--just how to achieve the perfect balance!
>
> HOLLY HARDIN

Holly's realistic appraisal of the role that procrastination plays in her writing process should help her distinguish between useful incubation and unhelpful procrastination. Unlike students who tell themselves that they should never procrastinate—and then do so anyway, feeling guilty every moment—Holly knows that she has to consider a variety of factors before she decides to invite a friend to tea, bake a batch of chocolate chip brownies, or take a much-needed nap.

Analyzing your composing process

William Stafford, a noted poet, once commented that "a writer is not so much someone who has something to say as he is someone who has found a process that will bring about new things he would not have thought if he had not started to say them." Stafford's remarks emphasize the importance of developing a workable writing process—a repertoire of strategies that you can draw on in a variety of situations.

Attention to your writing process can pay big dividends for you as a writer, as the following comments by two students indicate:

> Thinking about--and experimenting with--my writing process has changed my idea of what writing is and how it is accomplished. As a process, writing is more like other kinds of work and less a visitation by the muses (as I once thought). I now know that anyone can write, not just those who are inspired.
>
> JIM HOGAN

> The process approach to writing has given me a new lease on life. Sorry to sound so dramatic, but before I learned about the writing process, I hated and feared writing. I felt I was a terrible writer and did what I could to avoid it. Now I actually welcome opportunities for writing. It is wonderful to know that I don't have to write a perfect paper on the first try and that all writers benefit from revision.
>
> TERRELL RATCHFORD

Much of this book is designed to help you achieve the confidence that Jim Hogan and Terrell Ratchford now feel about their writing. Part Two, for instance, presents specific practical strategies, and the following section focuses on general strategies you can use to manage the writing process.

Guidelines for analyzing your composing process

The following guidelines provide questions you can use to describe and evaluate your current composing strategies. Respond in writing to each of these questions.

1. What is your general attitude toward writing? How do you think this attitude affects the writing you do?
2. Of the descriptions of the four major composing styles in this chapter, which best describes the way you compose? If none seems to fit you, how do you compose?
3. How do you know when you are ready to begin writing? Do you have a regular "start-up" method or ritual?
4. How long do you typically work on your writing at any one time? Are you more likely to try to write an essay in a single sitting, or do you prefer to work on your writing over a number of days (or weeks)?
5. Has the availability of computers and word processing influenced your writing process? How?
6. What planning and revising strategies do you use? How do you know when you have spent enough time planning and revising?
7. What role do collaborative exchanges with others (such as conversations about your writing or responses to work in progress) typically play in your writing?
8. How do you procrastinate? (Be honest! All writers procrastinate occasionally.)
9. Are you aware of having preferred writing habits and rituals? What are they? Which would you describe as productive and supportive? Which interfere with or lessen the efficiency of your writing process?
10. Thinking in general about the writing you do, what do you find most rewarding and satisfying about writing? Most difficult and frustrating? Why?

Group Activity

Meet with classmates to discuss your responses to the composing process guidelines. Begin your discussion by having each person state two important things he or she learned as a result of completing the analysis. (Appoint a recorder to write down each person's statements.) Once all members of your group have spoken, ask the recorder to read these statements aloud. Were any statements repeated by more than one member of the group? Working as a group, formulate two conclusions about the writing process based on your discussion that you would like to share with the class. (Avoid vague and general assertions, such as "Writing is difficult.") Be prepared to discuss your conclusions with your classmates.

Keeping a writer's notebook

Many writers keep journals or notebooks, recording in them whatever seems useful at the time. Sometimes writers may focus on work in progress, jotting down ideas, descriptions, or bits of conversation. But writers also use their journals or notebooks to reflect on their own experiences as writers. Holly Hardin's discussion of procrastination was, in fact, an entry from her notebook. You may want to record your responses to this textbook's explorations and applications in your own writer's notebook. Your teacher may also ask you to include entries from your writer's notebook in your portfolio of written work (discussed in Chapter 1).

Whatever is recorded, a writer's notebook serves a single purpose—to help the writer—so if you keep a notebook, it should reflect your own interests and needs. Your notebook may be a nicely bound blank book or a spiral notebook, whatever seems most inviting to you. If you have access to a computer, you might want to take advantage of its speed and flexibility, keeping your notebook on disk and printing copies at regular intervals. The following guidelines indicate possible uses for your writer's notebook.

Guidelines for keeping a writer's notebook

Use your writer's notebook for the following purposes:

- to ask yourself questions
- to reflect on your writing process and on current writing projects
- to brainstorm in response to an assignment
- to record possible ideas for future writing projects
- to note details, arguments, or examples that might be useful in an essay
- to try out various introductions or conclusions
- to play with imagery or figurative language such as similes or metaphors
- to map out a plan for an essay
- to express your frustrations or satisfactions with your writing
- to make schedules for current writing projects
- to preserve random thoughts about work in progress
- to freewrite about an idea or a topic you're working on
- to copy phrases, sentences, or passages that impress you as particularly effective models for imitation or analysis

Application

If you are not already doing so, try keeping a writer's notebook for two weeks. At the end of this period, reflect on the following questions. Did keeping a notebook help you come up with ideas for writing? (Can you find two or three entries that you could possibly develop into an essay?) Has your notebook given you any insights into how you manage the writing process? Did you enjoy writing in your notebook?

Practicing effective time management

Effective time management can make the difference between completing a writing assignment on time (and being satisfied with your work) or having a frustrating, unproductive experience. Something as minor as being careful to organize your notes and drafts for a research paper can save you hours of confusion. Here are some suggestions to guide you as you plan for your writing.

Guidelines for managing your time

1. Begin a writing assignment as soon as possible after you receive it. You may just write down a few ideas, but you'll have focused your mind on your project, if only briefly, and thus will have taken a crucial first step in the writing process.
2. Establish a rough schedule for your writing. You don't have to write down your schedule—though that might help you keep on track. At some point fairly early in the writing process, however, you should consider your assignment in the context of the overall demands on your time. As you do so, ask yourself such questions as these:
   - What demands does this assignment make of me? What is likely to be most difficult for me about this assignment? What strengths do I bring to this assignment? How can I minimize my difficulties and build on my strengths?
   - How much time should I anticipate spending on planning, drafting, and revising? Is this schedule flexible enough to accommodate such potential problems as a false start or difficulty revising?

   You might not stick exactly to this schedule, but it will help you manage your time more effectively.

3. Develop some way to organize work in progress as you write. Doing so can save time and frustration as you plan, draft, and revise.

Group Activity

As students, you and your classmates understand better than anyone else the pressures that you face. Working with a group of classmates, generate at least three additional suggestions for effective time management when working on writing projects. (Be sure to select a recorder.) Be prepared to share your advice with classmates.

Developing realistic expectations for your writing

Try to be neither too easy nor too hard on yourself about your writing. Expect that your first drafts won't be as good as you'd like; you'll undoubtedly revise them. Expect to make some errors on your first drafts; you can correct them later. Expect that some kinds of writing will be easier for you than others. When you encounter a major problem, such as uncertainty about how to organize your essay or develop your ideas, ask your instructor, fellow students, or writing assistant for help. Most importantly, don't let your struggles with a particular essay or report stop your progress. One of the best ways to cope with writer's block is to relax, take a break, and let your unconscious mind work on the problem while you think about something else.

Developing productive writing habits and rituals

Scratch a writer and you'll discover a person with decided habits and rituals. Professional writers are often particularly conscious of their writing habits and rituals. All writers, however, have some predispositions that affect their writing. Some people write best early in the morning; others, late at night. Some require a quiet atmosphere; others find the absence of noise or music distracting. Some people can compose only by writing longhand; others can't imagine writing without a computer. People have different ways of telling themselves that they are ready to write. Clearing my desk of its usual rubble is one way that I tell myself it's time to get serious. Here is how two students, Holly Hardin and Tom Grenier, describe their start-up writing rituals. Holly relies on exercise to provide the mental and physical push she needs.

Exercise immediately before working on a paper seems to provide me mental, as well as physical, stimulation. After I run, I tackle a first draft with incredible PMA (positive mental attitude). The head of steam I build during my run (the natural "runner's high") tides me over to at least the second or third page of my first draft. Finishing most papers after that point is usually not a big problem. While I exercise, I spend as much time as I can thinking about new analogies or visualizing the paper's organization and flow. I think about the most basic message that I want my reader to get. If I were to summarize each paragraph in one sentence, I think to myself, what would the sentence say? Is there anything I can eliminate?

Sometimes I think about a chosen audience for the topic. If I were to tell them about the subject face-to-face would my message change? What would I say? What would they most easily understand?

Near the end of my run, I think about how good the paper will be--I hone my expectations. This cheerleading pushes me through the front door and straight to my desk. I can hardly wait to get started. I'm almost afraid the ideas I generated will escape me before I can corner them on paper.

I don't know whether the final product of this process is any better than it might otherwise have been, but it eases the pain of first-draft compositions. I produce a draft more confidently and more quickly than I would by sitting down and hacking away at it.

HOLLY HARDIN

As you'll see, Tom Grenier's approach is quite different.

Most of my writing begins at the kitchen sink. After the dishes are drying in the rack and the living room is in order, I head for my bedroom--where I do my writing--and make the bed, fold socks, empty the trash, and straighten anything that looks at all out of order. Throughout the final stage of this ritual I am spiraling inward toward my writing desk, the last place I clean. When the desk is bare except for a typewriter, a handbook, and two dictionaries (a paperback for quick spelling references and a hard cover for bigger jobs), I sit down and begin contemplating the task at hand. Following the premise that the mind will take up the discipline put on the body and surroundings, the

> process of organization moves from the outside inward until I'm sitting in front of the typewriter sharpening a pencil with my pocketknife. Cleaning house is also a good way to work out the "prewrite jitters" and let me think casually about what I want or need to write. With the house straight at a quiet hour, I start on the first drafts of an introductory paragraph. Now the process has moved out again in a form that I can store, mull over, scribble on, and type again in a new draft. I'm off!
>
> TOM GRENIER

Notice that Tom and Holly both emphasize the ways in which their particular rituals help them cope with what Tom calls the "prewrite jitters." Productive writing rituals like these are a positive way of pampering yourself—of creating the environment most conducive to writing.

WRITING WITH A WORD PROCESSOR

As a student, you are undoubtedly already aware that computers can do a great deal to ease the labor of writing. Those who find pen or pencil drafting a slow and uncomfortable process often marvel at the ease with which word processing enables them to generate text. Many writers report that composing at the computer encourages them to be creative and to revise more easily and effectively. And as companies produce increasingly sophisticated and powerful computers and software, word-processing programs offer a variety of options in addition to such traditional features as a spellchecker and a thesaurus. A program with window or split-screen capability, for instance, allows you to look at two sections of a text at the same time, and computer graphics programs allow you to include computer-generated charts, graphs, diagrams, and even artwork in your writing.

The following suggestions should make the process of writing with a word processor easier and more productive.

Guidelines for writing with a word processor

1. Experiment to Find Your Own Best Way of Using the Word Processor.

Some people reserve the computer for typing up and printing documents they have already written. They may make minor revisions at the computer, but they generally make major revisions on their printed texts and then enter the changes into the computer. Others actually compose at the computer. A writer might brainstorm at the computer, for instance, and then use the word-processing program's split-screen option to keep these notes on screen as a guide while writing. As you might expect, heavy revisers (people who prefer to generate ideas by writing) adapt particularly easily to composing at the keyboard. Take the time to explore the options available to you and find those best suited to your own needs.

2. **Recognize the Potential Limitations of On-Screen Revision.**

Computers can make revision easier and faster, but they have potential limitations as well. Sometimes writers can be seduced by the computer's ease of revision into focusing on minor stylistic changes instead of organization or development of ideas. Many writers find that to evaluate these more global aspects of their writing, they must work with hard copy. Because of the small size of the computer monitor's screen, it can be difficult to grasp the big picture—yet effective writing depends on just this ability.

When you print drafts of an essay to read and revise, be sure to save these earlier versions. You may decide that an introduction that you rejected in favor of a later version was best after all. Leaving a "paper trail" makes it easy to reinsert your original introduction.

3. **Take Advantage of the Special Features That Many Word-Processing Programs Provide.**

Some writers use their computers as glorified typewriters, primarily to ease the burden of producing neatly printed texts. But most computer programs offer a number of features that can make writing easier and more productive. I have already mentioned the window or split-screen option. Some programs allow you to write notes or directions that appear on-screen but not in the printed text; this feature allows you to interact with your own writing without cluttering up drafts with comments that must be deleted later. Your program's BLOCK and MOVE (or CUT and PASTE) function enables you to move sections of text easily, and the SEARCH function makes it possible to locate every instance of a word or phrase. You can use this function when editing to check that you've not overused a word or to correct a misspelled word used several times in a draft. Finally, if you are fortunate enough to have access to networked computers, you can benefit from electronic collaboration. Such networks enable you to get on-screen responses to work in progress; they also make group writing projects easier and more productive.

UNDERSTANDING THE SPECIAL DEMANDS—AND REWARDS—OF COLLABORATIVE WRITING

Earlier in this chapter, Professor Burton Hatlen challenged the assumption that writers are geniuses who work (and suffer) in isolation as they await their muse. Writing, Hatlen observes, is "a craft, which can be learned by anyone willing to work at it." And like other crafts, writing is best learned in interaction with others. Brainstorming with others about your ideas, planning and troubleshooting collaboratively, and getting responses to work in progress—these and other informal group activities can help you become a more effective and productive writer.

But what about more formal collaborative efforts—efforts that result in a group-authored essay or report? If you are like most students, you have considerably less experience with this kind of collaboration. Yet increasingly in business, industry, and the professions, individuals are collaborating in just this way. In the mid-1980s, for instance, Professor Andrea Lunsford and I conducted a survey of fourteen hundred members of seven professional associations, including engineers, city planners, chemists, and psychologists. Eighty-seven percent of the seven hundred professionals who responded to our survey indicated that they regularly wrote as members of a team or a group. Since 98 percent of these same individuals also rated writing in general as important or very important to the successful execution of their jobs, the writing they do as members of groups or teams matters a great deal to them. Studies completed since our survey have confirmed the growing importance of collaborative writing in the workplace.

There are practical reasons, then, for you to learn more about the process of writing collaboratively. As we move into what is sometimes called the Information Age, in which the generation and exchange of information will take precedence over the construction of material goods, individuals who can write effectively with others—in face-to-face meetings or through electronic networks—possess valuable communication skills. And there can be other benefits to collaboration: our survey respondents indicated that collaborative writing can be both intellectually stimulating and emotionally supportive. When a group works well together, one city planner reported, it becomes "as much a support group as a professional team."

Groups don't always work well together, however, as you are undoubtedly aware. If you've worked with others on civic, political, or church projects or in scholastic or extramural activities, you know that poor interpersonal communication or ineffective group dynamics can turn a potentially productive group effort into a frustrating, time-consuming tug-of-war.

Collaborative writers do face special demands. To work effectively, group members must have good interpersonal and group process skills and must be both willing and able to do their fair share of the work. Collaborative projects generally require more careful and explicit planning, coordination, and monitoring of efforts than individual projects. At times, the necessity of negotiating schedules and of managing such basic tasks as typing or photocopying can prove frustrating. Finally, melding a uniform style from the efforts of individual writers can be a challenge.

But the rewards of writing collaboratively with others can be substantial. Writers working collaboratively can, most obviously, take on projects that they would be unable to complete alone. If you and your group members wish to study a complex issue or problem, such as the adequacy of your university's counseling services or the impact of its minority student recruitment program, you *have* to work together. Only by sharing responsibilities and tasks can you hope to do justice to your topic in the time available to you. Additionally, when you collaborate with others, you can draw on everyone's interests and strengths. Groups can also benefit from the inevitable diversity of opinion and approach that occurs whenever people work together. Not all group members will have the same understanding of or response to your university's minority student recruitment program, for example. Working through these and other differences enables your group to examine all the issues at stake and thus can improve both your process of inquiry and the resulting essay or report.

There are no fail-safe, one-size-fits-all formulas that can guarantee a successful collaborative writing project. Just as your individual writing process varies—an essay for your history class comes together easily but a report for zoology takes three times as long as you expected—collaborative processes vary too. Commitment to the task at hand and to the group process, a flexible attitude, and respect for others can do a good deal to encourage effective collaboration. The following guidelines provide additional suggestions your group can use to respond effectively to the special demands of collaborative writing.

Guidelines for collaborative writing

1. Take Time at the Start of Your Project to Build Group Cohesion.

You probably already recognize the importance of beginning your project by developing a shared understanding of your assignment and discussing basic procedural and logistical issues. Less obvious, but equally important, is the need to build group cohesion and establish good interpersonal relations among members. Your group cannot be effective unless members feel both committed to and valued by the group. Take time when you first meet not only to discuss your project but also to get to know one another. Encourage members to discuss how they feel they can best contribute to your group effort. You may also find it helpful to discuss previous collaborative experiences; doing so can allow members to articulate anxieties or concerns about the group process.

2. Work Out Effective Meeting Procedures.

How your group handles meetings can make or break your collaborative effort. You need to be task-oriented, but you also need to be attentive to interpersonal and group dynamics. If your meetings are too informal and friendly, you may not accomplish what you need to do. Overly formal meetings, by contrast, can stifle creativity and foster boredom and tension. Your group should talk explicitly about how best to handle meetings; you should also recognize that a structure that's appropriate for an early meeting when you're just getting to know one another may be inappropriate as your project develops.

Once your project is under way, you should begin your meetings by establishing an agenda and agreeing on roles. One person may volunteer to run the meeting, for instance, while another agrees to keep notes. As your meeting progresses, stop now and then to review what you've accomplished and to ensure that members agree on important decisions. End your time together by discussing the meeting itself. Your goal in doing so should be to provide feedback the group can use to monitor its effectiveness. Asking each member to indicate one aspect of the meeting that worked well and one that might be improved provides a nonthreatening way for your group to fine-tune your meetings.

3. Know When You Should—and Shouldn't—Strive for Consensus.

Effective groups know the value of establishing a cooperative atmosphere. You don't want to waste everyone's time by bickering over how often you should meet or dealing with personal clashes between group members. Groups can, however, place such a high value on cooperation that they limit their group's effectiveness. Sometimes conflict can be productive.

When is conflict productive? In a study of student collaborative writing groups, Professor Rebecca E. Burnett discovered that productive conflicts encourage groups to "reexamine opinions, share diverse ideas, and discover creative solutions."* Your group cannot discover the most efficient way to divide responsibilities or to organize your essay unless you fully explore your options. As a group, you should strive to avoid conflicts that interfere with your group's effectiveness, but you should encourage the free play of ideas. Premature consensus on such issues as the approach you should take to your topic or the most effective way to introduce your essay can short-circuit the effectiveness of your decision making and limit the effectiveness of your group.

4. Develop Nonthreatening Ways to Deal with Problems in Interpersonal or Group Processes.

When interpersonal or group process problems occur, it's tempting to ignore them and hope they will disappear on their own. They rarely do. Difficult as this may be, groups must respond to problems when they occur, and they must do so in a way that promotes group solidarity and effectiveness, not diminishes it. But how? Active listening can resolve many difficulties. At times, apparent conflicts can be the result of miscommunication rather than substantial disagreement. By listening actively and resisting the impulse to evaluate or dismiss a statement, you can facilitate communication.

In other cases, explicit discussion of a conflict or problem may be necessary. When this occurs, attempt to avoid "you" statements that attack or discredit others. Rather than saying to another member, "You're not doing your share of the work," for instance, say, "I think we should look at who's done what so far. I've felt that I've done more than my share of the work, but I may not have a clear sense of what others have done." Doing so allows you to raise an issue that needs to be discussed without pointing a finger at any particular individual.

5. Expect the Unexpected.

Even with the best planning, most groups find that their process doesn't go quite as expected. One person's research may prove more time-consuming than anticipated, or it may uncover information that requires the group to rethink its approach to your topic. Illness or a family emergency may prevent members from completing work on time. As you organize and schedule your tasks, build in time for unexpected delays and problems. Recognize, too, that the group may have to redefine its goals or renegotiate the division of labor as you progress.

*Rebecca E. Burnett, "Substantive Conflict in a Cooperative Context: A Way to Improve the Collaborative Planning of Workplace Documents," *Technical Communication* 38 (1991):535.

Successful collaborative writing, like writing in general, depends on neither luck nor magic. Just as individual writers can learn more efficient, productive, and satisfying ways of managing the writing process, so too can those working on group projects learn how to work—and write—together.

Activities for Thought, Discussion, and Writing

1. You can learn a great deal about your own composing process by observing yourself as you write. To do so, follow these steps:
   - Choose an upcoming writing project to study. Before beginning this project, reflect on the project and its demands. How much time do you expect to spend working on this project, and how do you anticipate allocating your time? What challenges does this project hold for you? What particular strengths and resources do you bring to this project?
   - As you work on the project, use a process log to keep track of how you spend your time. Your log should include a record of when you started and ended each work section as well as a description of your activities and a paragraph commenting on your process. What went well? What surprised you? What gave you problems? What might you do differently next time?
   - After you have completed the project, draw on your prewriting analysis and process log to write a case study of this specific project. In developing your case study, consider questions such as these: To what extent was your prewriting analysis of your project accurate? How did you actually allocate your time when working on this project? What strategies did you rely on most heavily? What went well with your writing? What was difficult? Conclude by reflecting about what you have learned from this case study about yourself as a writer.
2. All writers procrastinate occasionally—some just procrastinate more effectively than others. After brainstorming or freewriting about your favorite ways of procrastinating, write a humorous or serious essay on procrastination.
3. Many interviews with professional writers have been published. You can learn a great deal about writing from reading these. Choose one of the following collections, and read two to five interviews. While reading them, try to think of the ways the statements these writers make might—and might not—apply to your own writing.

- *Writers at Work: The Paris Review Interviews.* First series. Edited by Malcolm Cowley. New York: Viking, 1958.
- *Writers at Work: The Paris Review Interviews.* Subsequent series edited by George Plimpton. New York: Viking, 1963, 1967, 1976, and 1981.
- *The Writer on Her Work.* Edited by Janet Sternburg. New York: Norton, 1980.
- *The Writer on Her Work, volume II: New Essays in New Territory.* Edited by Janet Sternburg. New York: Norton, 1991.
- *The Writer's Craft.* Edited by John Hersey. New York: Knopf, 1974.

4. The exploration and application on pages 35 and 36 encouraged you to reflect on your assumptions about writing and your experiences as a writer. Drawing on these activities and on the rest of the chapter, write an essay in which you reflect on this subject.

CHAPTER 3

UNDERSTANDING THE RHETORICAL SITUATION

Whenever you write—whether you are jotting a note to a friend or working on a lab report—you are writing in the context of a specific situation with its own unique demands and opportunities. A management trainee writing a memo to her supervisor faces different challenges than an investigative journalist working on a story for the *New York Times* or a student writing a research paper for a political science class. Successful writers know that they must consider the situations in which they write; they can't rely on formulas or blind luck when they compose. They know that they must use their rhetorical sensitivity—their understanding of the relationships among writers, readers, and texts—to help them make decisions as they write and revise.

In this chapter you will learn how to use your rhetorical sensitivity to analyze your specific writing situation. By asking yourself questions about this situation and by considering the three Aristotelian appeals (explained in the final section of this chapter), you can determine the most fruitful way to approach your topic and to respond to the needs and expectations of your readers.

LEARNING TO ANALYZE THE RHETORICAL SITUATION

Rhetoric, as introduced in Chapter 1, involves three key elements: a writer, a reader, and a text that makes communication possible. Even though you may write alone at your desk or computer, the act of writing inevitably involves you with all the elements of rhetoric. When you think about these elements, you are analyzing your rhetorical situation. Let's suppose, for instance, that for some time you've owed a close friend a letter. Probably without thinking about it too much, you are aware of certain aspects of this situation: your friend and you have a history of close communication; you want to continue your friendship and you know that it's important to stay in touch; a personal letter, rather than a phone call, is the medium of communication that you have chosen.

As you compose your letter, you will probably follow certain conventions of correspondence, such as dating your letter and beginning with a salutation (the "Dear So-and-so" line). The content of your letter may be influenced by less formal but still widely recognized conventions. You may begin by explaining your slowness in writing, falling back on the much-used phrasing "I know I should have written sooner, but . . ." You may feel a certain obligation to write at least a few paragraphs (unless you're writing on the back of a postcard) and to balance news of your own life with questions about your friend's.

In addition to these conventional features of correspondence, you will make other decisions while composing that are personal, creative, unique—but still influenced by your rhetorical situation. You will be aware of certain aspects of your own personality that you can count on your friend to appreciate and thus will feel free to display them—your sense of humor, perhaps. Either out of a wish to entertain your friend or just because expressing your humor comes naturally when you are at ease, you might weave jokes and humorous comments throughout your letter. Or because of your close friendship, you might allow yourself to express feelings of frustration or depression that you would hardly communicate in a more public document. In all of these cases, you are making decisions about your *text* that are influenced by what you know about your rhetorical situation.

Application

Imagine that you wish to write the following letters:

- a letter of application for a job
- a letter to a friend whose parent has recently died
- an entry to a radio station contest that asks for responses to the prompt "I should be a DJ for a night because . . ."

Keeping the elements of rhetoric in mind, spend a few minutes thinking about how you would approach these different writing situations.

- What is your role as writer and your purpose for writing in each situation?
- What image of yourself, or *persona,* would you wish to present in each letter, and how would you vary your language accordingly?
- How would the different readers of each letter influence the form and content of your writing?
- What other factors, such as format, would you need to consider in writing these letters?

Write a brief description of each situation, responding to the questions listed here.

Using your analysis to guide your writing

Most people don't consciously analyze the rhetorical situation when they write personal letters. They rely on commonsense rhetorical sensitivity to help them determine the most effective ways to present their ideas and to communicate with their readers. When you face the challenge of new and more difficult kinds of writing, however, as you do in college, it often helps to analyze your rhetorical situation consciously. Such analysis encourages you to consider each of the elements of rhetoric when you write.

The following guidelines provide questions you can use to analyze your rhetorical situation.

Guidelines for analyzing your rhetorical situation

Early in any writing project, you can lay a solid foundation by asking yourself the following questions:

WRITER

1. Why are you writing?
2. What do you hope your writing will accomplish? Do you want to convey information? Change the reader's mind? Entertain the reader?
3. How might your goals as a writer influence the eventual form and content of your essay?
4. What role does this rhetorical situation invite you as the writer to play? Is your role relatively fixed (as it is when you write an essay exam)? Or is it flexible to some extent?
5. What image of yourself *(persona)* do you want to convey to your readers? What "voice" do you want readers to "hear" when they read your writing?

READER

1. Who is the intended audience for your essay? How have you envisioned this audience? Is it more accurate or helpful to think of your readers as members of a specific audience (subscribers to a special-interest magazine, for instance) or as a general audience encompassing people with a wide range of backgrounds and interests?
2. What role do you intend for readers to adopt as they read this essay? What kinds of cues will you use to signal this role to readers?
3. If you do envision yourself as writing to a specific audience, do those readers have any demographic characteristics—perhaps their age, sex, religion, income, occupation, education, or political preference—that you need to consider?
4. How will your essay appeal to your readers' interests? Do you expect your audience already to be interested in the subject of your essay? Or do you need to create and maintain their interest?
5. How might the needs and expectations of your readers influence the form and content of your essay?

TEXT

1. If you are writing in response to an assignment, to what degree does the assignment specify or restrict the form and content of your essay? How much freedom, in other words, do you as the writer have?
2. What generic or stylistic conventions does your rhetorical situation require you to follow? Are these conventions rigidly defined (as in the case of lab reports) or flexible to some extent?

3. Does the nature of your subject implicitly or explicitly require that you provide certain kinds of evidence or explore certain issues?
4. Could you benefit by looking at models or other examples of the kind of writing your situation requires?

As these questions indicate, the process of analyzing your rhetorical situation challenges you to look both within and without. Your intended meaning—what you want to communicate to your readers—is certainly important, as is your purpose for writing. But unless you're writing solely for yourself in your journal or notebook, you can't ignore your readers or other situational factors. Analyzing your rhetorical situation helps you to respond creatively as a writer yet keeps you aware of limits on your freedom.

Setting preliminary goals

Before beginning a major writing project, you may find it helpful to write a brief analysis of your rhetorical situation, or you may simply review these questions mentally. This process of analyzing your rhetorical situation is an opportunity to determine your *preliminary* intentions or goals as a writer. (Your intentions will often shift as you write. That's fine. As you write, you will naturally revise your understanding of your rhetorical situation.) Despite its tentativeness, however, your analysis of your situation will help you begin writing with a sense of direction and purpose.

Here is an analysis of a rhetorical situation written by a student, Lynn Hansen. Also included is Lynn's essay so that you can see the relationship between her description of her rhetorical situation and her essay.

Here is Lynn's analysis of her rhetorical situation.

> I'm writing a review or travel essay on Burgdorf Hot Springs, a semiprivate resort thirty-five miles north of McCall, Idaho. My review might appropriately be published in a magazine like <u>Pacific Northwest</u>.
>
> Since Burgdorf offers only primitive accommodations and minimal development of the pool, I expect that the hot springs will attract a certain Bohemian type, so I'm aiming my review for such readers. I am also assuming that my audience will consist mainly of outdoor enthusiasts who appreciate the joys of wilderness hiking, camping, and backpacking. I recognize that a wide range of people read <u>Pacific Northwest</u>;

however, those who are already somewhat interested in hot springs and outdoor activities would be most likely to choose to read my essay. Others might read the essay in order to experience Burgdorf Hot Springs vicariously, so I'll try to make my essay interesting for a range of readers.

I want my persona to be pleasant, open, communicative, and appreciative of the fine experiences Burgdorf Hot Springs has to offer. I want my tone or "voice" to be friendly and engaging. I will concentrate in this essay on making the content of my review colorful, interesting, and easy to read. Because I feel that it is important to the success of my article that I convey feelings of adventure, mystery, and romance about the place I am reviewing, I will include some information on the rich historical background of Burgdorf. Since this is a travel review, I must also be sure to include basic information about the resort. The purpose of my review is to increase the audience's awareness that such places exist and to encourage those who are interested to explore and enjoy our natural wilderness areas.

Here is Lynn Hansen's essay.

BURGDORF HOT SPRINGS

You've opened your eyes at the first hint of light and rolled out of your sleeping bag to climb stiffly down from the loft. Shivering in the soft half-light of dawn, you look around the cabin for your towel, swim suit, and sandals, quickly get dressed, and then make a mad dash down the trail to the pool.

At the other end of the meadow, through the pine trees, you see steam rising from the pool and hanging heavy in the cool crisp air. The thought of your body (which is by now covered with goose bumps) easing into the hot water nearly makes you forget that you are walking through the wet grass at dawn in your bathing suit!

At last you are floating in the hot, pure mineral water, hovering at seven thousand feet above sea level. Every muscle relaxed, you forget tense and careworn thoughts of the world and its complicated affairs. All that is left is the blissful environment of sunrise sky, expansive mountains, and the peace and quiet that pervades the forests and wilderness lands of the Northwest.

Welcome to Burgdorf Hot Springs, a rustic, primitive hot-springs resort located thirty-five miles north of McCall, Idaho. The experience just described is common to hundreds of primitive and semiprivate geothermal water flows that can be found throughout the mountainous regions of Colorado, Oregon, Washington, Idaho, Utah, Montana, and Wyoming. The hot springs at Burgdorf is one of the oldest privately developed mineral-water resorts in Idaho. Much of what can be appreciated at Burgdorf--the large open-air pool, the quaint hand-built log cabins, the scenic meadows, the clear mountain streams, and an abundance of peace and quiet--has largely remained unchanged over the past thirty years.

Burgdorf Hot Springs, and indeed the entire surrounding territory, has a rich history which includes gold mining, trapping, ghost towns, and legendary folk heroes. Once sacred Indian ceremonial grounds, the land around the hot springs was first settled by an immigrant named Hans Burgdorf in the middle of the 1800s. During the height of the gold rush, Frank Harris (whose descendants still own Burgdorf) added to the already existing store and half-dozen cabins by building eight more log-and-chink cabins and an impressive three-story log hotel which was open for one summer and then closed due to lack of business. Today the hotel still stands in the meadow between the cabins and the pool. It is filled with handmade furniture and an enticing assortment of antiques, junk, and old photographs.

For the past sixteen years Frank Harris's great-great-grandson and great-great-granddaughter have been in control of the destiny of the hot springs. There were a few years in the seventies when a community of fifteen or so young people lived in the cabins year-round, and the hot springs were closed to the public. In 1975 the springs were reopened to the public but only for guests staying at three or four of the cabins. The resort's popularity has grown by word-of-mouth. In the past few years the number of permanent residents has dwindled, so more cabins have been made available for rental. As more people come to stay in the cabins and soak in the pool, the young Harrises have taken care to see that the tranquil atmosphere of the resort does not change.

Although it is possible to rent a cabin on a drop-in basis, it is best to write ahead for reservations. This must be done through the mail since there is no phone or electric service to Burgdorf. Requests for reservations should be addressed to Burgdorf Warden, Burgdorf Hot Springs, McCall, Idaho, 83611. Only cabin guests are allowed to use the pool, so be forewarned that a one-day trip to enjoy the pool is out of the question.

Costs for staying at Burgdorf are minimal ($5.00 per night per adult, $3.50 per child). Most of the cabins are one-room log structures with sleeping lofts. Each cabin is equipped with a table, a woodburning cook stove, an easy chair or two, a kerosene lantern, a good sharp axe, and all the dry wood you can use. Besides these necessities, an old broom and dustpan usually lean in the corner. You must provide your own cooking utensils, food, and water. Water is packed in from a clear mountain stream that runs a few hundred feet behind the cabins.

Many people come to Burgdorf, rent a cabin, and use the resort as a base camp for further explorations in the surrounding mountains. Visitors can hike to numerous lakes which afford excellent fishing, swimming, and huckleberry picking. Thirty miles up the road from Burgdorf lies the old mining town of Warren. A classical ghost town by modern standards, Warren has two open saloons and a post office. There are more things to see and do from Burgdorf than can be exhausted in a few days.

But speaking of exhausted, imagine yourself coming back from a ten-mile hike, covered with trail dust and sweat, dragging your aching feet up that final fifty yards to your cabin to stow your gear next to the wood box, shed clothes, boots and all, grab your towel and--

once again, there you are, blissfully floating over the white sand bottom in the clear warm turquoise water, watching the clouds turn rose pink as they hang effortlessly in the sky.

LYNN HANSEN

Exploration

To what extent does Lynn Hansen's essay achieve the goals she established for herself in her analysis of her rhetorical situation? To answer this question, first reread Lynn's analysis. In your own words, summarize Lynn's goals in terms of the key elements of rhetoric: writer, reader, text. Now reread Lynn's essay. Does Lynn fulfill the goals she established for herself? How? List at least five reasons why Lynn does or does not achieve these goals. Then find at least one passage in the essay that illustrates each of these five statements.

THINKING ABOUT READERS

If you look again at Lynn Hansen's description of her rhetorical situation on pages 61–62, you will notice that she carefully considers the expectations and interests of her audience, readers of *Pacific Northwest* magazine. Lynn recognizes that a small number of potential readers would seriously consider visiting Burgdorf Hot Springs and that an even smaller number might actually do so. Only a "certain Bohemian type," Lynn reasons, would be attracted to a rustic, undeveloped hot springs. But Lynn understands that those with no intention of vacationing at Burgdorf Hot Springs might nevertheless read and enjoy her review.

Some "armchair travelers" might read to experience a trip to the hot springs vicariously. Others might read her review simply because they enjoy reading essays about travel, just as some people enjoy reading mysteries or science fiction. Lynn also recognizes that those who read her review will have expectations based on previous reviews that they have read. They will expect her to provide enough information about Burgdorf Hot Springs so that they could plan a trip there if they wished to do so. They will also expect the review to be interesting, with vivid descriptions of the location, stories about the history of the hot springs, and other details that help them learn more about, and vicariously experience, this rustic, primitive resort.

How was Lynn able to develop such a rich, complex understanding of her readers? In part she drew on daily interactions with others; her knowledge of people told her that only a "certain Bohemian type" would actually visit Burgdorf Hot Springs. But Lynn also drew on her experiences as a reader. By reading other travel reviews, Lynn developed a strong intuitive understanding of the general form and style of such reviews. In analyzing her rhetorical situation, Lynn drew on the rhetorical common sense she has developed as a writer, reader, speaker, and listener.

Like Lynn, you have naturally developed considerable rhetorical common sense. As a student, for instance, you undoubtedly recognize the importance of teachers as readers of student writing. What students sometimes call "psyching out the teacher" is actu ally an example of rhetorical common sense in action. When you are working on an assignment for a class, whether an essay exam or a research paper, it makes sense for you to consider your teacher's expectations. Analyzing your teachers as readers involves more than considering their views on a particular subject, however; it includes understanding the values and intellectual commitments they share with other members of the academic community. These values and commitments, such as the preference that arguments should be supported by evidence that is substantial and appropriate to the discipline and topic, are discussed in greater detail in Chapter 10, "Understanding Academic Audiences and Assignments."

Your understanding of your readers' expectations and needs can help you make choices as you write. Lynn Hansen chose to begin her review in a dramatic way because she knew that she had to catch her readers' attention quickly. After all, readers of *Pacific Northwest* don't *have* to read her essay; they *choose* to do so. By addressing readers directly ("You've opened your eyes at the first hint of light and rolled out of your sleeping bag to climb stiffly down from the loft"), Lynn invites readers to stop flipping through their magazine and join the world of her essay. Her vivid description also reassures readers that this will be a good travel essay, one that will enable readers to visualize this remote resort in Idaho via the words on the page.

If Lynn were writing an in-class essay exam, her understanding of her teacher as reader would similarly influence her choices. Teachers may find all or some of their students' essays interesting, and they may learn new things from their students—I certainly do. Nevertheless, teachers read students' writing primarily to determine what students have learned about a subject and how effectively they can express this understanding to others. Teachers also often read under considerable time pressure;

a psychology teacher may take sixty essay exams home on Tuesday, knowing they must be returned on Thursday. A dramatic, attention-getting introduction, such as Lynn wrote for her review of Burgdorf Hot Springs, would irritate, not entertain, a psychology teacher reading an essay exam. Such a teacher would much prefer a concise introductory paragraph—one that clearly specified the writer's main point and indicated how the writer would support this point.

As these examples indicate, and as Chapter 9, "Understanding the Reading Process," further emphasizes, the relationship between writers and readers is dynamic, not static. Both writers and readers draw on the rhetorical sensitivity they have developed through writing, reading, speaking, and listening when they interact with a written text. Similarly, both writers and readers must anticipate and project as they attempt to create meaning through language.

Exploration

Suppose that Lynn Hansen had wanted to write an essay on Burgdorf Hot Springs not for readers of *Pacific Northwest* but for the Sunday supplement of a major East Coast newspaper such as the *New York Times*. What consequences might this different readership have for her rhetorical situation? How might she have to revise her essay in response to the interests and expectations of these readers? Write one or two paragraphs responding to these questions.

As a writer, your relationship with your readers is shifting and complex, not fixed and static; this relationship varies with your rhetorical situation. When you consider the expectations and interests of your readers, you naturally think *strategically,* asking yourself questions such as these:

- To what extent are my readers interested in and knowledgeable about my subject?
- What formal and stylistic expectations will my readers bring to my essay?
- What other aspects of my readers' situations might influence how they respond to my essay?
- How can I use my understanding of my readers' expectations and interests when I make decisions about the content, form, and style of my essay?

By asking yourself questions such as these—by thinking strategically about your writing—you can build on the rhetorical sensitivity you have already developed as a speaker, listener, reader, and writer.

Application

Introductions often help signal the relationship the writer intends to establish with readers. The following excerpts introduce two different discussions of stress, both designed for a general audience. The first excerpt is from the first chapter of a book titled *The Work/Stress Connection: How to Cope with Job Burnout.* The second is from the section called "Work and Stress" in *The Columbia University College of Physicians and Surgeons Complete Home Medical Guide.* As you read these excerpts, think about the differing roles that they invite readers to assume.

> Sally Swanson, a thirty-eight-year-old mother of four, works as a bank teller in Des Moines, Iowa. Like many women, she feels the pressure of running a home, raising children, managing a job, and carving out leisure time for herself. "I did fine until we got a new supervisor last year," she says with an exhausted sigh. "Within two months I had started to burn out." Sally takes antacid pills several times a day. She worries that she may have an ulcer. "I feel as if he's looking over my shoulder all the time," she says. "He never has a good word to say to anyone. Sometimes the tension at the bank is so thick you could cut it with a knife."

> Particular kinds of work seem to cause special stress, and the effects of health are manifested in an all-too-common pattern: fatigue, insomnia, eating disorders, nervousness, feelings of unhappiness, abuse of alcohol or drugs. Stress is often related to the nature of the job or imposed irregularities. Rotating shift work, in which hours are erratic or inconsistent with the normal sleep cycle, produces both physical and mental stress by constantly upsetting circadian rhythms that control specific hormonal and other responses. Jobs that involve little variation but require constant close attention, for example, assembly-line work or jobs requiring repetitive tasks with dangerous equipment, seem to be particularly stressful. In one study in a sawmill, people who ran the equipment had much higher levels of stress-related hormones than workers who did not come in contact with machinery, even though their jobs also may have been boring and repetitive.

Now that you have read these two introductions, describe the writer-reader relationship established in each. What signals or cues do the authors provide for readers to enable them to recognize and adopt an appropriate role? Cite at least three examples of these signals or cues.

RESPONDING TO YOUR RHETORICAL SITUATION: ARISTOTLE'S THREE APPEALS

Analyzing your rhetorical situation can provide information that will enable you to make crucial strategic, structural, and stylistic decisions about your writing. In considering how to use the information gained through this process, you may find it helpful to employ what Aristotle (384–322 B.C.) characterized as the three appeals. According to Aristotle, when speakers and writers communicate with others, they draw on these three general appeals:

1. *logos,* the appeal to reason
2. *pathos,* the appeal to emotion
3. *ethos,* the appeal to the credibility of the speaker or writer

As a writer, you appeal to *logos* when you focus on the logical presentation of your subject by providing evidence and examples in support of your ideas. You appeal to *pathos* when you use the resources of language to engage your readers emotionally with your subject or appeal to their values, beliefs, or needs. And you appeal to *ethos* when you create an image of yourself, a *persona,* that encourages readers to accept or act on your ideas.

These three appeals correspond to the three basic elements of rhetoric. In appealing to *ethos,* you focus on the *writer's* character as implied in the text; in appealing to *pathos,* on the interaction of writer and *reader;* and in appealing to *logos,* on the logical statements about the subject made in your particular *text.* In some instances, you may rely predominantly on one of these appeals. A student writing a technical report will typically emphasize scientific or technical evidence, not emotional or personal appeals. More often, however, you will draw on all three appeals in your effort to create a fully persuasive document. A journalist writing an essay on child abuse might begin her discussion with several examples designed to gain the attention of her readers and to convince them of the importance of this issue (*pathos*). Although she may rely primarily on information about the negative consequences of child abuse (*logos*), she will undoubtedly also endeavor to create an image of herself as a caring, serious person (*ethos*), one whose analysis of a subject like child abuse could be trusted.

In the following example, Monica Molina, a sociology major, uses Aristotle's three appeals to develop strategies for an essay exploring her recent efforts to come to terms with her Mexican heritage. Monica had previously analyzed her rhetorical situation, so she had already thought about her goals for this essay. Here is Monica's analysis of her rhetorical situation:

> I'm writing this essay because I want to work through my feelings about my ethnic identity. Since coming to college, I've had many questions about who I am and who I want to be. My father is Mexican, but we never spoke Spanish at home, and I'm light-skinned enough to appear Anglo. My parents didn't encourage us to speak Spanish or learn about our Mexican heritage. Now that I'm at college I find myself drawn to other Chicano students, but I don't always feel like I fit in.
>
> I'm writing this essay for my composition class, so my readers are my teacher and other students. Our assignment is to write an essay on some aspect of our personal experience. I chose my topic because it's important to me, and also because I want other students to understand some of the conflicts that minority students can feel. Many students on campus don't seem very sympathetic to minority students; I've had people tell me that America is a melting pot and that we should just be like everyone else. I want my readers to see that it's not so simple.

As Monica's analysis of her rhetorical situation reveals, Monica began working on her essay with a general sense of her goals as a writer. Nevertheless, Monica still found it difficult to move from general goals to specific strategies. For this reason, Monica decided to analyze her essay in terms of Aristotle's three appeals. Here is Monica's analysis of these appeals:

> Logos: If I were writing this essay for a sociology class, I'd probably use statistics, research studies, and other sources to make my point. But this is a different kind of essay, one about my experiences. I need to use the kind of examples that will help readers see the issues I'm facing. And I need to find ways to connect my examples so readers can understand what I'm

trying to say. In a sociology essay my main point would be obvious because I'd state it at the start of my essay. That wouldn't work for an essay like this.

<u>Pathos:</u> I've got to get readers to connect emotionally with my essay; otherwise, they won't care about my experience or the issues I'm facing. Ideally, my examples will help do this. I hope that even people who haven't experienced what I have will be able to identify with the kinds of questions I raise in the essay. Everyone grows up in a family, after all, and I'm not the only college student to feel confused about who I am.

<u>Ethos:</u> If readers feel that I'm lecturing them or preaching to them, they'll be put off. So I want to seem relaxed and friendly. But I also want my readers to know that this is a serious subject for me. I want readers to see that I understand how complicated the issues are. I also want it to be clear how much I love and respect my father, even though I sometimes wish he'd encouraged us to learn more about Mexico and to connect with that part of our heritage.

Here is the final version of Monica Molina's essay. As you read this essay, notice how she draws on the three appeals as she analyzed them.

BETWEEN CULTURES

Opening the door and peering curiously around the room full of brown faces, I felt nervous and awkward. My fears were soon eased, however, as cheerful voices welcomed me to an Oregon State University Hispanic Student Union meeting. Although I wasn't sure what the meeting would be about, I felt suddenly comfortable--almost like I was among family. But then some students in the corner began speaking in Spanish, their crescendo building with excitement as they shared a story. Soon it seemed that everyone was adding bits of information. I sat quietly, just getting the gist of what they were saying. Then everyone broke into laughter. Everyone but me, that is; I had missed the punchline.

* * * * *

Spanish sounds like a song to me, one that is beautiful and rich, but one I can't quite catch the words to. I ache for the foreign sounds to roll off my tongue, but instead only a few words stumble out, flat and anglicized. I studied Spanish for three years in high school, and for one year in college, but learning a language in a classroom from textbooks is different from hearing it spoken by your parents at home. My father is Mexican, and his native language is Spanish. But he has never spoken anything other than English with my mother, sisters, and me.

I was surrounded by Anglo culture as I grew up, and I assimilated easily, not even knowing what I was missing. Educated in mainstream schools and raised in a predominantly white neighborhood, I accepted the images I saw on television and in the movies. Most of the time, I took it for granted that we would speak English at home. When my friends learned that my father was Mexican and asked me if I spoke Spanish, or if we spoke it at home, I always answered "no," feeling a sudden sense of confusion and loss.

At times as I was growing up, I wondered why my father never spoke Spanish with us. Recently, I decided to ask him about it. My dad seemed surprised by my question and replied that he didn't know; perhaps it was because he was too busy to teach us. He didn't seem to want to talk about this subject. I could tell that he didn't understand why I asked the question or what it might mean to me. I didn't push my question, for I realized that it really doesn't matter why my father didn't speak Spanish with us. What matters is how I feel about this now--now that I realize I know only the Anglo side of my heritage and not the Mexican side. What matters is my desire to connect with my father's culture, with the Mexican heritage that has been ignored and silenced.

When I was a child, I asked innocent questions about life in Mexico that annoyed my father, questions like "Do they have ice cream in Mexico?" My dad would shake his head in disbelief at these questions and not even answer. Now I realize that the questions reminded him too much of snobby Anglos asking if the water was OK to drink in Mexico. My father must have found it hard to realize how little I knew about Mexican culture. Moreover, he probably felt there was no point in teaching us about a culture we would never embrace as our own.

My father struggled to learn to speak English and to make a place for himself in this country. But my father's English reminds my mom, sisters, and me that he is different from us. Dad's English is distinct in that he has created his own pronunciations and vocabulary. His words and phrases have become part of our family language, and we sometimes tease him about them. One of his favorite phrases is "You crazy!"; now we all say that to each other. We also mimic the exasperated way he says "What?!" Sometimes my father realizes that we are teasing him and laughs, but other times he gets angry. His anger reminds me how easy it is to forget his struggles with English and with Anglo culture, just as it is hard for my father to sense my need to connect with his Mexican way of life.

As a fifth grader, I remember my father coming to me with business letters to check for grammar and spelling. As I gently explained to my dad why a tense was wrong or a word misspelled, I knew it must be hard for him to ask his daughter for help. My father's lack of English skills coupled with my limited knowledge of Spanish highlighted the gap between our Anglo and Mexican cultures. I felt this gap most strongly when my dad called his family in Mexico. Calling home was a pretty big event, and my mom would tell us to be quiet so dad could hear. We would sit listening to the unfamiliar language, fascinated with the quick sounds and changes in expression. After my father hung up, we would rush to him and ask what he had said.

As a teenager, and now as a college student, I have made attempts to learn about my father's culture. Sometimes I try to explain my longing to connect with my Mexican heritage to my father, but he doesn't seem to understand why this is important to me. He also doesn't understand why some people would question my identification with Mexico and its cultural heritage. When I told my dad that people sometimes ask whether I am Mexican and are surprised when I say "yes" since I can't speak Spanish very well, he says it's none of their business and "to hell with them." Lately I'm beginning to think that my father may be right. Other people may worry if I don't fit into predetermined ethnic categories. But I think I can identify with both Mexican and Anglo cultures as long as I define what that means for me.

* * * * *

I come home from another Hispanic Student Union meeting, excited about the possibility of attending my first MECHA (Movimiento Estudiantil Chicano de Azatlan) conference. Entering my house, I notice that the answering machine light is on and push the button. My father begins the message he has left for me. Because his voice is so familiar, I don't usually hear my father's accent. But today it rings out as a reminder of the ways in which we're both similar and different. As I listen to my dad telling me what time he'll pick me up for a quick trip home, I think of how different my world is from his. My father came to a new country and had to work hard to support a family; he had to believe that he was gaining more than he was giving up. Because my father has struggled, I have more opportunities. In some ways, my success will be his. But unlike my father, I may not have to choose between two cultures. For me, gaining something new may not have to mean leaving something else behind.

Exploration

In what ways does Monica Molina's essay draw on the three appeals as she analyzed them? Write one or two paragraphs responding to this question. Be sure to include at least two or three examples in your analysis.

The strategies described in this chapter—analyzing your rhetorical situation and employing Aristotle's three appeals—are grounded in commonsense principles of communication, principles that date back at least to the time of Plato and Aristotle. Understanding these principles and knowing how to apply them will enable you to respond effectively in a variety of writing situations.

Activities for Thought, Discussion, and Writing

1. The following letter from the U.S. Committee for UNICEF is typical of many letters requesting charitable contributions for worthwhile causes. Using this letter as evidence or data, try to determine the assumptions the writer or writers made about this rhetorical situation. (Though Hugh Downs, a popular television personality, signed this letter, he may not have actually composed it.) After you have listed these assumptions, indicate ways in which these assumptions may have influenced the form or con-

tent of the letter. What assumptions about the readers, for example, may have led the writer to introduce the letter as he or she did?

Dear Friend:

In the ten seconds it took you to open and begin to read this letter, three children died from the effects of malnutrition somewhere in the world.

No statistic can express what it's like to see even one child die that way . . . to see a mother sitting hour after hour, leaning her child's body against her own . . . to watch the small feeble head movements that expend all the energy a youngster has left . . . to see the panic in a dying tot's innocent eyes . . . and then to know in a moment that life is gone.

But I'm not writing this letter simply to describe an all-too-common tragedy.

I'm writing because, after decades of hard work, *UNICEF*—The United Nations Children's Fund—*has identified four simple, low-cost techniques which, if applied, have the potential to cut the yearly child mortality rate in half.*

These methods don't depend on solving large-scale problems like increasing food supply or cleaning up contaminated water. They can be put into effect before a single additional bushel of wheat is grown, or before a single new well is dug.

They do depend on *what you decide to do* by the time you finish reading this letter. You see, putting these simple techniques to work requires the support of UNICEF's projects by people around the world. In our country, it means helping the U.S. Committee for UNICEF contribute to that vital work.

With your help, millions of children will be given the chance of a lifetime—the chance to live—to grow up healthy and strong. Without your help, more children will continue to die painfully, slowly and needlessly—children like the nine who have died in the past 30 seconds.

The first method is called *"oral rehydration."* Most children who die of malnutrition don't starve to death—they die because their body weight has been severely lowered by germs that cause diarrhea.

Simple medicines can stop such illness in our own country. But in the developing countries, there are no such medicines—and children may develop a new infection every six weeks. Until recently, there was no easy way of stopping the symptom and saving their lives.

But now, it's known that a mixture of sugar, salt and water in the right proportions will stop the critical loss of fluids and salts that leads to death. The cost of this "miracle" cure—less than ten cents a dose. But for want of that simple mixture, five million children die each year.

With your help, the U.S. Committee for UNICEF can assist UNICEF's projects to provide "oral rehydration salts" to mothers in developing countries around the world—and to teach families how to make the mixture on their own, to save the lives of children.

The second breakthrough method of saving children is to provide *worldwide immunization* against six childhood diseases: measles, polio, TB, tetanus, whooping cough and diphtheria. Together, these diseases kill three and a half million children each year in developing countries—the vast majority of them are malnourished youngsters with little resistance to disease.

It used to be hard to keep vaccines stable in their long journeys from laboratories to remote, often tropical places where children needed them most. But within the last year and a half, a measles vaccine has been developed that does not require refrigeration. The result: measles can now join smallpox on the list of child-killing diseases that have been wiped out—permanently.

The cost of this new measles vaccine is less than ten cents a dose. With it, *the lives of one and a half million children can be saved this year alone.* But without it, they will continue to die—like the child who has died of measles in the past 30 seconds.

With your help, the U.S. Committee for UNICEF can assist in UNICEF's work to deliver the new measles vaccine—and vaccines to fight the five other major child-killers—to youngsters who need them so badly in the developing world.

The third and fourth breakthrough methods of saving children's lives are even simpler. They require no medication at all. But they do require a worldwide education campaign—to promote *breast-feeding* among mothers, instead of the tragic trend toward bottle-feeding in developing lands, and to provide mothers with simple *paper growth charts* to detect the "hidden malnutrition" that can leave a child irreparably retarded in mind and body.

With your help, the U.S. Committee for UNICEF can assist UNICEF in mounting the massive educational campaign needed to teach parents these basic ways of preventing malnutrition—and can save the lives of children for years to come.

There you have it: four easy ways of saving the lives of millions of children for years to come.

Now it's time for you to decide what you're going to do about it.

I know you receive appeals for many good causes. But I can't think of a single cause more important than the life of a child. And in a very real sense, the life of a child somewhere in the world can be drastically changed by what you decide to do right now. You see, UNICEF's good work is supported entirely by voluntary contributions. That means your help does make a critical difference.

That's why I'm asking you to take a moment now to send a gift of \$20, \$50, \$100, \$500—as much as you possibly can—to the U.S. Committee for UNICEF in the enclosed reply envelope.

Your gift is tax deductible to the extent allowed by law. And by the time you fill out next year's tax returns, there will be one or more healthy, living children in the world as a result of the gift you send today. You will have given those kids the chance of a lifetime. And I hope that will make you feel very proud, indeed.

We're counting on your help. My personal thanks and best wishes.

Sincerely,

Hugh Downs

2. Lynn Hansen and Monica Molina did a good job, you'll probably agree, in anticipating the expectations and interests of their readers. In writing their essays, they focused not just on content (what they wanted to say) but also on strategy (how they might convey their ideas to their readers). Not all interactions between writer and reader are as successful. You may have read textbooks that seemed more concerned with the subject matter than with reader's needs and expectations. Or you may have received direct mail advertising or other business communications that irritated or offended you. Find an example of writing that in your view fails to anticipate the expectations and needs of the reader and write one or two paragraphs explaining your reasons. Your teacher may ask you to bring your example and written explanation to class to share with your classmates.
3. The following advertisements (Figures 3-1 to 3-4) are from popular magazines. Analyze the ways in which these advertisements draw on Aristotle's three appeals: *logos, pathos,* and *ethos.*

THE NEW TRADITIONALIST.

SHE STARTED A REVOLUTION — WITH SOME NOT-SO REVOLUTIONARY IDEALS.

She was searching for something to believe in — and look what she found. Her husband, her children, her home, herself.

She's the contemporary woman who has made a new commitment to the traditional values that some people thought were "old-fashioned."

She wasn't following a trend. She made her own choices. But when she looked over the fence she found that she wasn't alone.

In fact, market researchers are calling it the biggest social movement since the sixties.

The quality of life she has chosen is the embodiment of everything that Good Housekeeping has always stood for. The values she is committed to are the values we represent — the Magazine, the Seal, the Institute.

Who else can speak to the new traditionalist with that kind of authority and trust?

Who is more committed to helping her live the life she has chosen?

That's why there has never been a better time for Good Housekeeping.

AMERICA IS COMING HOME TO
GOOD HOUSEKEEPING

Figure 3-1

John's losing his hair. His mission: get it back.

ASAP!
But how?
Weaving? No.
Transplant?
Not for him.
A hairpiece?
Never, never.
What John really wants is his *own* hair back.
And now he's learned, **for male pattern baldness, only *Rogaine*® has been proven to regrow hair.**

Rogaine® Topical Solution (minoxidil 2%) works in part by prolonging the growth of hair, which grows in cycles. With more hairs growing longer and thicker at the same time, you may see improved scalp coverage.

After one year, over three fourths of men reported some hair regrowth.

Dermatologists conducted 12-month clinical tests. After 4 months, 26% of patients using *Rogaine* reported moderate to dense hair regrowth, compared with 11% of those using a placebo (a similar solution without minoxidil — the active ingredient in *Rogaine*). After 1 year, 48% of the men who continued using *Rogaine* in the study rated their regrowth as moderate to dense. Thirty-six percent reported minimal regrowth. The rest (16%) had no regrowth.

Side effects were minimal: 7% of those who used *Rogaine* had itching of the scalp.

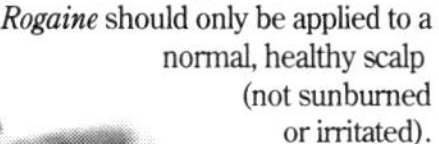

Rogaine should only be applied to a normal, healthy scalp (not sunburned or irritated).

Make it part of your normal routine.

Studies indicate that *at least 4 months of twice-daily treatment* with *Rogaine* are usually necessary before there is evidence of regrowth. So why not make it part of your normal routine when you wake up and go to bed, like brushing your teeth.

As you'd expect, if you are older, have been balding for a longer period, or have a larger area of baldness, you may do less well.

Rogaine is a treatment, not a cure. So further progress is only possible by using it continuously. Some anecdotal reports indicate that if you stop using it, you will probably shed the newly regrown hair within a few months.

Get your free Information Kit, plus a $10 incentive to see a doctor.

Why wait? Find out whether *Rogaine* is for you. Call **1-800-000-0000** today for a free Information Kit about the product and how to use it. **And because *Rogaine* requires a prescription,** we'll include a list of nearby *dermatologists or other doctors experienced in treating hair loss,* and a $10 incentive to visit a doctor soon.

Call

1 800 000-0000

for your free *Rogaine* Information Kit and a $10 incentive to see a doctor.

We'll also send you a list of nearby doctors experienced in treating hair loss.

Rogaine®
TOPICAL SOLUTION minoxidil 2%

See next page for important additional information.

Figure 3-2

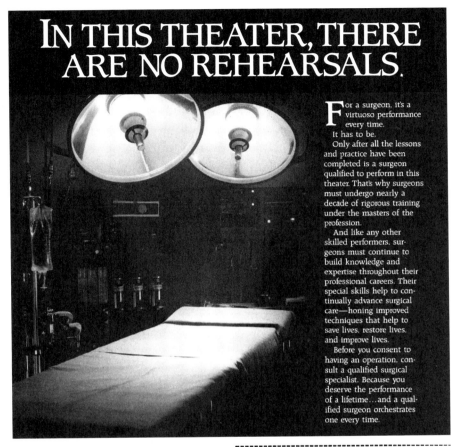

IN THIS THEATER, THERE ARE NO REHEARSALS.

For a surgeon, it's a virtuoso performance every time.

It has to be.

Only after all the lessons and practice have been completed is a surgeon qualified to perform in this theater. That's why surgeons must undergo nearly a decade of rigorous training under the masters of the profession.

And like any other skilled performers, surgeons must continue to build knowledge and expertise throughout their professional careers. Their special skills help to continually advance surgical care—honing improved techniques that help to save lives, restore lives, and improve lives.

Before you consent to having an operation, consult a qualified surgical specialist. Because you deserve the performance of a lifetime...and a qualified surgeon orchestrates one every time.

GET THE FACTS ABOUT SURGICAL CARE

You can learn more about how to find a qualified surgeon, basic surgical procedures, when to seek additional consultation or a second opinion, and other issues related to your good health through a series of free brochures prepared by the American College of Surgeons. Simply fill out the coupon and mail today.

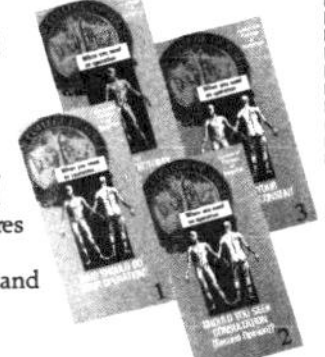

Mail information request to:

American College of Surgeons
55 East Erie Street
Chicago, IL 60611-2797

Name ____________________

Address ____________________

City/State/ZIP ____________________

Dept. BH-4

Figure 3-3

Hannah Dean
English professor

Spring lectures
Syllabi for the academic year
Lesson plans
My grandchildren's Christmas lists
WordPerfect
Aldus Persuasion
Student grade records
A scene I wrote for my theater group
Research notes for my book
Outline for my book
The beginning chapter of my book
My husband's sketches
Overheads for a lecture
Minutes from our sailing club meeting
Calculations for the *Mal 95* (my boat)
Navigation notes
Letters to candidates
Letters to my daughter
My entry in the annual Bad Hemingway contest

Lisa Wallen
Producer's assistant

Project plans
Storyboards
QuarkXPress
Shooting locations, February '93
Poems I'm working on
Shooting schedules
Shooting list
A movie treatment I'm writing
A cyberpunk novel on disk
A list of actors
Lists of crew, agency contacts, etc.
Salaries of actors, crew, etc.
My checkbook and budget
Notes from a poetry class
Production budgets
Master list of actors on video
Request for grant
QuickMail
Illustrations of cats

Figure 3-4

CHAPTER 4

WRITERS READING

Writing, like speaking, is a basic form of human communication, a powerful means of self-expression and dialogue with others. Effective writers use their rhetorical sensitivity—sensitivity developed through reading, writing, speaking, and listening—to help them analyze their rhetorical situation and make appropriate choices when they write. Here is how Mary Ann Firmin, a student at Oregon State University, explains the importance of analyzing the rhetorical situation when you write:

> Think of an orchestra playing without the conductor--that is how writers write when they don't understand their rhetorical situation. Without the conductor there are still musicians producing music; when writers don't understand the rhetorical situation there are still writers producing words. But with a conductor, the orchestra produces music that speaks to the audience because the conductor has a clear vision of how the music should sound and can blend the musicians into a group that has a controlling purpose. When writers understand their rhetorical situation, they can use all the elements of writing to have the greatest persuasive effect on the audience. It is difficult to describe how this happens, but the proof is in the product. When you have a conductor, the music can move

people. When you understand your rhetorical situation, your words can change people.

MARY ANN FIRMIN

In Chapter 3 you learned to ask yourself questions about your rhetorical situation and to use the results of your analysis to set preliminary goals and make effective choices as a writer. In this chapter you will continue to learn more about the rhetorical situation, but you will do so from the perspective of the reader. By reading to understand not just what writers say but *how* and *why* they say it—by reading like a writer—you can learn how to make your own writing more effective.

READING LIKE A WRITER

An analogy may help you understand how reading can contribute to your development as a writer. Consider the musicians described by Mary Ann Firmin. To develop their skills, musicians practice often, but they also listen to both live and recorded music. When they do so, they listen not simply to be moved by the music, to experience it, but also to discern how the performers achieve particular effects. They listen actively, participating in the music but also asking questions about technique and style. When they play, they draw on this knowledge and experience as they develop their own performance.

Like musicians, effective writers know that they can learn a great deal about how writing works by reading. Reading and writing are, after all, so interconnected that they are, in effect, two sides of the same coin. As Professor Deborah Brandt has said, "Learning to read is learning that you are being written to, and learning to write is learning that your words are being read."* By learning to read others' writing more critically and sensitively, by looking for clues to how other writers have analyzed and responded to their rhetorical situations, you can gain valuable insights about how writing works. You can improve your ability to read your own writing as well.

In a general sense, you have already been reading like a writer, for although you undoubtedly acquired some of your current knowledge about writing from formal instruction in English classes, much that you know you have gained by reading. You may never have

*Deborah Brandt, *Literacy as Involvement: The Acts of Writers, Readers, and Texts* (Carbondale, Ill.: Southern Illinois University Press, 1990): 5.

taken a class in short-story writing, for instance, yet simply by reading stories you have some understanding of how stories work. You can develop your innate rhetorical sensitivity as a reader by consciously asking yourself questions while you read—by becoming what student Joanne Apter calls a "noticing" reader. "Once I started reading like a writer," Joanne commented in a journal entry, "I began to notice new things—the shape of a sentence, the power of just the right word. Good writing didn't seem so mysterious or so impossible."

Like Joanne Apter, you can become a "noticing" reader. If you find an essay particularly interesting and effective, for instance, stop to ask yourself why. You might consider the writer's *persona* or voice and the role it plays in the essay. You might reread the essay looking for clues that reveal how the writer has envisioned the intended audience. Or you might focus on how the writer has used certain generic and stylistic conventions and reflect on why these conventions are appropriate given the writer's goals and situation. By focusing not just on what writers say but on what writers *do*, you can learn how other writers have responded to their rhetorical situation, and you can apply that knowledge when you work on your own writing.

ANALYZING TEXTUAL CONVENTIONS

When you read, you engage in silent conversation with the writer. As Chapter 9, "Understanding the Reading Process," emphasizes, your role in this conversation is active. You don't simply decipher or decode a writer's messages: rather, you use your own knowledge and experience to understand, interpret, and evaluate texts. As a reader you are not free, however, to interpret texts according to arbitrary or random whims. Textual conventions—agreements between writers and readers about how to construct and interpret texts—play an important role in keeping writers and readers on track so that their conversation doesn't turn into a pitched argument or a free-for-all.

The phrase *textual convention* may be new to you, but you can understand it easily if you think about other uses of the word *convention*. For example, *social* conventions are implicit agreements among the members of a community or culture about how to act in particular situations. At one time in America, for example, it was acceptable for persons who chewed tobacco to use spittoons in such public places as restaurants and hotel lobbies. (British writer Charles Dickens complained bitterly of this practice when he visited the United States.) Now this behavior is no longer acceptable; this particular social convention has changed over time.

If social conventions represent agreements among individuals about how to act, textual conventions represent similar agreements about how to write and read texts. Just as we tend to take our own social conventions for granted, so too do we tend to take for granted those textual conventions most familiar to us as readers and writers. When we begin a letter to our parents by writing "Dear Mom and Dad," for instance, we don't stop to wonder if this greeting is appropriate; we know from our experience as writers and readers that it is. When we read a text from another time or culture, we can sometimes see more clearly than in our own writing the extent to which such texts depend on shared understandings between writers and readers. Here, for instance, is a letter written in the twelfth century by two brothers studying in France asking their parents to send them money:*

> To their very dear and respected parents M. Martre, knight, and Mme. his wife, M. and N., their sons, send greetings and filial obedience. This is to inform you that, by divine mercy, we are living in good health in the city of Orléans and are devoting ourselves wholly to study, mindful of the words of Cato, "To know anything is praiseworthy," etc. We occupy a good and comely dwelling, next door but one to the schools and market-place, so that we can go to school every day without wetting our feet. We have also good companions in the house with us, well advanced in their studies and of excellent habits—an advantage which we as well appreciate, for as the Psalmist says, "With an upright man thou wilt show thyself upright," etc. Wherefore lest production cease from lack of material, we beg your paternity to send us by the bearer, B., money for buying parchment, ink, a desk, and the other things we need, in sufficient amount that we may suffer no want on your account (God forbid!) but finish our studies and return home with honor. The bearer will also take charge of the shoes and stockings which you have to send us, and any news as well.

In both form and content, this letter differs considerably from one that any contemporary student might write; it reveals a good deal not only about the conventions of writing in the Middle Ages but also about the life of the nobility at that time.

*Les Perelman, "The Medieval Art of Letter Writing," in *Textual Dynamics of the Professions: Historical and Contemporary Studies of Writing in Professional Communities,* Charles Bazerman and James Paradis, eds. (Madison: University of Wisconsin Press, 1991): 114–15.

Exploration

Reread the letter from the twelfth century and make a list of the textual features that seem unusual to you, such as the brothers' penchant for quoting ancient authors. After making this list, write one or two paragraphs discussing the shared assumptions and values that these features seem to draw on. (The citation of ancient authors, for instance, reveals a reverence for ancient authorities that characterized medieval culture but is much less pronounced in our own age.) Then write one or two sentences indicating the ways in which this letter differs from one you might write to your own parents.

As this example indicates, textual conventions are dynamic; they change over time as the assumptions, values, and practices of the writers and readers employing them change. Textual conventions are also situated. Two letters written today, one to your state senator and another to your closest friend, would have more in common with each other than with the letter written by the two brothers in the twelfth century. But they would differ in ways that reflect complex social understandings about what is and is not appropriate in a specific situation. Your letter to the senator would probably be fairly formal and would present a concise, well-supported position on a public policy issue. Your letter to your friend, however, might well be chatty and casual and refer to people and events familiar only to the two of you.

Because they play such a critical role in making communication between writers and readers possible, textual conventions are an important component of the rhetorical situation. When you think about the kind of writing that you are being asked to do, for instance, you are thinking in part about the textual conventions that may limit your options as a writer in a specific situation. Textual conventions do constrain writers. But writers also use textual conventions to signal their intentions and thus increase the likelihood that readers will respond appropriately to their ideas.

Some textual conventions are quite specific. Personal letters always begin with a greeting and end with a signature. Sonnets have fourteen rhymed lines, usually consisting of an octave (eight lines) and sextet (six lines) or three four-line quatrains with a closing couplet. Similarly, lab reports usually include the following elements: title page, abstract, introduction, experimental design and methods, results, discussion, and references. Someone writing a sonnet or a lab report can deviate from these textual conventions, but only at the risk of having readers misunderstand or reject their writing.

Other textual conventions are much more general. You may have read, for instance, that a well-written academic essay has qualities like these.

CHARACTERISTICS OF AN EFFECTIVE ACADEMIC ESSAY

1. An effective essay is well organized and well developed. It establishes its subject or main idea in the introduction, develops that idea in a coherent manner in the body, and summarizes or completes the discussion in the conclusion.
2. An effective essay is logical. It supports its main points with well-chosen evidence, illustrations, and details.
3. An effective essay is clear and readable. It uses words, sentences, and paragraphs that are carefully crafted, appropriate for the writer's purpose and subject, and free of errors of usage, grammar, and punctuation.

These statements summarize some of the most general conventions that govern academic essays. But because these statements are so general and apply to so many different kinds of writing, you may not know just what they mean in specific situations and in your own writing.

Seeing textual conventions in use

To help clarify how general textual conventions operate and to illustrate how you can analyze textual conventions, let's consider just one of the conventions cited above: the statement that an effective essay establishes its subject or main idea in an introduction (which often also serves to draw readers into the essay). This particular textual convention is learned early, for even young children introduce stories, if only (in Western cultures, at least) with *Once upon a time.* Furthermore, most writers and readers can easily understand why an essay needs an introduction. No one likes to be thrown into the middle of a discussion without any idea of the subject. Despite understanding the purpose of this convention, however, writers sometimes feel uncertain about what constitutes the best introduction for a specific essay.

Three articles by a well-known psychologist show how one writer tackled this problem (see Figures 4-1 to 4-3). All three articles were written by Dr. John H. Flavell, although the third was coauthored with two colleagues. All of the articles discuss research conducted by Flavell and his colleagues on the ability of young children to distinguish between appearance and reality, a distinction that Flavell argues is "worth studying because it is part of the larger development of our conscious knowledge about our own and other minds."

Figure 4-1 shows the introduction to the first article, "Really and Truly," which was published in *Psychology Today,* a popular magazine designed for members of the general public who are interested in learning about and applying principles of psychology in their own lives. The second article, "The Development of Children's Knowledge about the Appearance–Reality Distinction" (Figure 4-2), was published in *American Psychologist,* an academic journal sent to every member of the American Psychological Association, whose 60,000 members include psychologists and other behavioral and social scientists with quite a broad range of interests. The third article, "Development of the Appearance–Reality Distinction" (Figure 4-3), was published in *Cognitive Psychology,* a specialized academic journal for researchers in that field. As you read each essay's introduction, think about the impact that the different publications and intended audiences may have had on the form and content of each essay. Pay attention also to the format used to present each article.

Exploration

Read the introductions to Flavell's three articles, and write one paragraph characterizing the approach of each article. How would you describe the tone of each article and the kind of language used? What can you learn from your paragraphs about the differences among these articles?

Comparing and contrasting textual conventions

You need only glance at the first pages of Flavell's three articles to notice some striking differences. The first two pages of "Really and Truly," the *Psychology Today* article, have a great deal of white space and several large illustrations. The title doesn't actually state what the essay is about, but it does pique the reader's curiosity. The article begins informally with an attention-getting image: "It looks like a nice, solid piece of granite, but as soon as you squeeze it you know it's really a joke-store sponge made to

Really and Truly

UNTIL THEY ARE 4 OR 5, CHILDREN DON'T UNDERSTAND THE DISTINCTION BETWEEN APPEARANCE AND REALITY; WHAT YOU SEE IS NOT ALWAYS WHAT YOU GET.

BY JOHN H. FLAVELL

It looks like a nice, solid piece of granite, but as soon as you squeeze it you know it's really a joke-store sponge made to look like a rock. If I ask what it appears to be, you say, "It looks just like a rock." If I ask what it really is, you say, "It's a sponge, of course." A 3-year-old probably wouldn't be so sure. Children at this age often aren't quite able to grasp the idea that what you see is not always what you get.

By the time they are 6 or 7 years

PHOTOGRAPHS BY WALTER WICK

Figure 4-1

old, however, most children have a fair grasp of the appearance-reality distinction that assumes so many forms in our everyday lives. Misperceptions, misexpectations, misunderstandings, false beliefs, deception, play and fantasy—these and other examples of that distinction are a preoccupation of philosophers, scientists, artists, politicians and other public performers and of the rest of us who try to evaluate what they all say and do.

For the past half dozen years, my colleagues and I have been asking children questions about sponge rocks and using other methods to find out what children of different ages know about the difference between appearances and reality. First we give the children a brief lesson on the meaning of the appearance-reality distinction by showing them, for example, a Charlie Brown puppet inside a ghost costume. We explain and demonstrate that Charlie Brown "looks like a ghost to your eyes right now" but is "really and truly Charlie Brown," and that "sometimes things look like one thing

Continued on Page 42

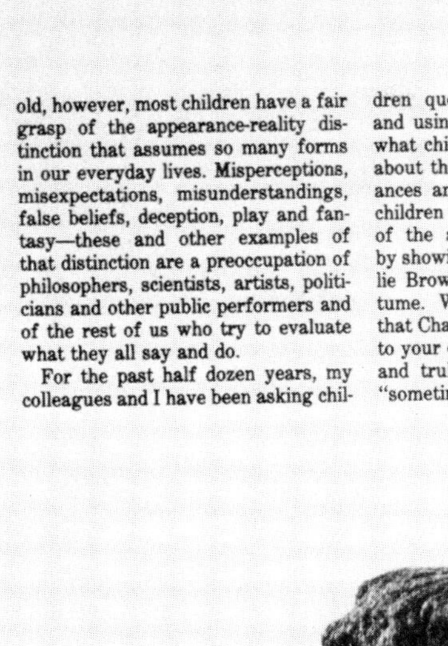

It looks like a rock, it feels like a sponge, but to a 3-year-old the distinction between appearance and reality can be quite confusing.

1985 APA Award Addresses

The Development of Children's Knowledge About the Appearance–Reality Distinction

John H. Flavell Stanford University

ABSTRACT: Recent research on the acquisition of knowledge about the important and pervasive appearance–reality distinction suggests the following course of development. Many 3-year-olds seem to possess little or no understanding of the distinction. They fail very easy-looking tests of this understanding and are unresponsive to training. At this age level, skill in solving simple appearance–reality tasks is highly correlated with skill in solving simple visual perspective-taking tasks. This and other findings are consistent with the hypothesis that what helps children finally grasp the distinction is an increased cognizance of the fact that people are sentient subjects who have mental representations of objects and events. It does so by allowing them to understand that the selfsame stimulus can be mentally represented in two different, seemingly contradictory ways: (a) in the appearance–reality case, how it appears to the self versus how it really is; and (b) in the perspective-taking case, how it presently appears to self versus other. In contrast to young preschoolers, children of 6 to 7 years manage simple appearance–reality tasks with ease. However, they have great difficulty reflecting on and talking about such appearance–reality notions as "looks like," "really and truly," and especially, "looks different from the way it really and truly is." Finally, children of 11 to 12 years, and to an even greater degree college students, give evidence of possessing a substantial body of rich, readily available, and explicit knowledge in this area.

Suppose someone shows a three-year-old and a six-year-old a red toy car covered by a green filter that makes the car look black, hands the car to the children to inspect, puts it behind the filter again, and asks, "What color is this car? Is it red or is it black?" (Flavell, Green, & Flavell, 1985; cf. Braine & Shanks, 1965a, 1965b). The three-year-old is likely to say "black," the six-year-old, "red." The questioner is also apt to get the same answers even if he or she first carefully explains and demonstrates the intended difference in meaning, for illusory displays, between "looks like to your eyes right now" and "really and truly is," and then asks what color it "*really* and *truly* is." At issue in such simple tasks is the distinction between how things presently appear to the senses and how or what they really and enduringly are, that is, the familiar distinction between appearance and reality. The six-year-old is clearly in possession of some knowledge about this distinction and quickly senses what the task is about. The three-year-old, who is much less knowledgeable about the distinction, does not.

For the past half-dozen years my co-workers and I have been using these and other methods to chart the developmental course of knowledge acquisition in this area. That is, we have been trying to find out what children of different ages do and do not know about the appearance–reality distinction and related phenomena. In this article I summarize what we have done and what we think we have learned (Flavell, Flavell, & Green, 1983; Flavell et al., 1985; Flavell, Zhang, Zou, Dong, & Qi, 1983; Taylor & Flavell, 1984). The summary is organized around the main questions that have guided our thinking and research in this area.

Why Is This Development Important To Study?

First, the distinction between appearance and reality is ecologically significant. It assumes many forms, arises in many situations, and can have serious consequences for our lives. The relation between appearance and reality figures importantly in everyday perceptual, conceptual, emotional, and social activity—in misperceptions, misexpectations, misunderstandings, false beliefs, deception, play, fantasy, and so forth. It is also a major preoccupation of philosophers, scientists, and other scholars; of artists, politicians, and other public performers; and of the thinking public that tries to evaluate what they say and do. It is, in sum, "the distinction which probably provides the intellectual basis for the fundamental epistemological construct common to science, 'folk' philosophy, religion, and myth, of a real world 'underlying' and 'explaining' the phenomenal one" (Braine & Shanks, 1965a, pp. 241–242).

Second, the acquisition of at least some explicit knowledge about the appearance–reality distinction is probably a universal developmental outcome in our species. This knowledge seems so necessary to everyday intellectual and social life that one can hardly imagine a society in which normal people would not acquire it. To

Vol. 41, No. 4, 418–425

Figure 4-2

cite an example that has actually been researched, a number of investigators have been interested in the child's command of the distinction as a possible developmental prerequisite for, and perhaps even mediator of, Piagetian conservations (e.g., Braine & Shanks, 1965a, 1965b; Murray, 1968).

Third, knowledge about the distinction seems to presuppose the explicit knowledge that human beings are sentient, cognizing *subjects* (cf. Chandler & Boyce, 1982; Selman, 1980) whose mental representations of objects and events can differ, both within the same person and between persons. In the within-person case, for example, I may be aware both that something appears to be A and that it really is B. I could also be aware that it might appear to be C under special viewing conditions, or that I pretended or fantasized that it was D yesterday. I may know that these are all possible ways that I can *represent* the very same thing (i.e., perceive it, encode it, know it, interpret it, construe it, or think about it—although inadequate, the term "represent" will have to do). In the between-persons case, I may be aware that you might represent the same thing differently than I do, because our perceptual, conceptual, or affective perspectives on it might differ. If this analysis is correct, knowledge about the appearance-reality distinction is but one instance of our more general knowledge that the selfsame object or event can be represented (apprehended, experienced, etc.) in different ways by the same person and by different people. In this analysis, then, its development is worth studying because it is part of the larger development of our conscious knowledge about our own and other minds and, thus, of metacognition (e.g., Brown, Bransford, Ferrara, & Campione, 1983; Flavell, 1985; Wellman, 1985) and of social cognition (e.g., Flavell, 1985; Shantz, 1983). I will return to this line of reasoning in another section of the article.

How Can Young Children's Knowledge About the Appearance–Reality Distinction Be Tested?

The development of appearance–reality knowledge in preschool children has been investigated by Braine and Shanks (1965a, 1965b), Daehler (1970), DeVries (1969), Elkind (1966), King (1971), Langer and Strauss (1972), Murray (1965, 1968), Tronick and Hershenson (1979) and, most recently and systematically, by our research group. In most of our studies we have used variations of the following procedure to assess young children's ability to think about appearance and reality (Flavell, Flavell, & Green, 1983). First, we pretrain the children briefly on the meaning of the distinction and associated terminology by showing them (for example) a Charlie Brown puppet inside a ghost costume. We explain and demonstrate that Charlie Brown "*looks like* a ghost to your eyes right now" but is "*really and truly* Charlie Brown," and that "sometimes things look like one thing to your eyes when they are really and truly something else." We then present a variety of illusory stimuli in a nondeceptive fashion and ask about their appearance and their reality. For instance, we first show the children a very realistic looking fake rock made out of a soft sponge-like material and then let them discover its identity by manipulating it. We next ask, in random order: (a) "What is this *really* and *truly?* Is it *really* and *truly* a sponge or is it *really* and *truly* a rock?" (b) "When you look at this with your eyes right now, does it *look like* a rock or does it *look like* a sponge?" Or we show the children a white stimulus, move it behind a blue filter, and similarly ask about its real and apparent color. (Of course its "real color" is now blue, but only people who know something about color perception realize this.) Similar procedures are used to assess sensitivity to the distinction between real and apparent size, shape, events, and object presence.

How Do Young Children Perform on Simple Appearance–Reality Tasks?

Our studies have consistently shown that three- to four-year-old children presented with tasks of this sort usually either answer both questions correctly, suggesting some ability to differentiate appearance and reality representations, or else give the same answer (reporting either the appearance or the reality) to both questions, suggesting some conceptual difficulty with the distinction. Incorrect answers to both questions occur only infrequently, suggesting that even the children who err are not responding randomly. There is a marked improvement with age during early childhood in the ability to solve these appearance–reality tasks: Only a few three-year-olds get them right consistently, whereas almost all six- to seven-year-olds do (Flavell et al., 1985).

Some illusory stimuli tend to elicit appearance answers to both questions (called a *phenomenism* error pattern), whereas others tend to elicit reality answers to both (*intellectual realism* pattern). The intellectual realism pattern is the more surprising one, because it contradicts the widely held view that young children respond only to what is most striking and noticeable in their immediate perceptual field (Flavell, 1977, pp. 79–80; for a review of other research on intellectual realism, see Pillow & Flavell, 1985). If the task is to distinguish between the real and apparent properties of color, size, and shape, phenomen-

Editor's note. This article is based on a Distinguished Scientific Contribution Award address presented at the meeting of the American Psychological Association, Los Angeles, California, August 1985.

Award addresses, submitted by award recipients, are published as received except for minor editorial changes designed to maintain *American Psychologist* format. This reflects a policy of recognizing distinguished award recipients by eliminating the usual editorial review process to provide a forum consistent with that employed in delivering the award address.

Author's note. The work described in this article was supported by National Institute for Child Health and Human Development (NICHD) Grant HD 09814. I am very grateful to my research collaborators, Eleanor Flavell and Frances Green, and to Carole Beal, Gary Bonitatibus, Susan Carey, Sophia Cohen, Rochel Gelman, Suzanne Lovett, Eleanor Maccoby, Ellen Markman, Bradford Pillow, Qian Man-jun, Marjorie Taylor, Zhang Xiao-dong, and other colleagues and students for their invaluable help with this research.

Correspondence concerning this article should be addressed to John H. Flavell, Department of Psychology, Jordan Hall, Building 420, Stanford University, Stanford, CA 94305.

Development of the Appearance–Reality Distinction

John H. Flavell, Eleanor R. Flavell, and Frances L. Green
Stanford University

Young children can express conceptual difficulties with the appearance–reality distinction in two different ways: (1) by incorrectly reporting appearance when asked to report reality ("phenomenism"); (2) by incorrectly reporting reality when asked to report appearance ("intellectual realism"). Although both phenomenism errors and intellectual realism errors have been observed in previous studies of young children's cognition, the two have not been seen as conceptually related and only the former errors have been taken as a symptom of difficulties with the appearance–reality distinction. Three experiments investigated 3- to 5-year-old children's ability to distinguish between and correctly identify real versus apparent object properties (color, size, and shape), object identities, object presence–absence, and action identities. Even the 3-year-olds appeared to have some ability to make correct appearance–reality discriminations and this ability increased with age. Errors were frequent, however, and almost all children who erred made both kinds. Phenomenism errors predominated on tasks where the appearance versus reality of the three object properties were in question; intellectual realism errors predominated on the other three types of tasks. Possible reasons for this curious error pattern were advanced. It was also suggested that young children's problems with the appearance–reality distinction may be partly due to a specific metacognitive limitation, namely, a difficulty in analyzing the nature and source of their own mental representations.

The acquisition of knowledge about the distinction between appearance and reality is a very important developmental problem for at least two reasons.

1. The distinction arises in a very large number and variety of ecologically significant cognitive situations. In many of these situations, the information available to us is insufficient or misleading, causing us to accept an apparent state of affairs (appearance) that differs from the true state of affairs (reality). We are variously misled or deceived by the information we receive from or concerning people, objects, actions, events, and experiences. The deceit may be deliberately engineered by another person; the person intentionally misleads us—through the use of lies, facades, dis-

This research was supported by NICHD Grant HD 09814. We are most grateful to the children, teachers, and parents whose cooperation made these studies possible. We are also much indebted to Ellen Markman, Marjorie Taylor, Carole Beal, and numerous other colleagues and students for their useful suggestions over the course of this project. Finally, we thank Rochel Gelman and two anonymous reviewers for their helpful critiques of this article.
Please send requests for reprints to Dr. John H. Flavell, Department of Psychology, Stanford University, Stanford, CA 94305.

Figure 4-3

guises, and other artifices. Very often, however, there is no intention to deceive. The time or distance seemed longer to us than it really was; the sun looks like it moves around the earth but it really does not; it appeared that S–R theory could explain language development but the reality turned out (appeared?) otherwise. The last two examples make it clear that all systematic pursuit of knowledge presupposes at least some awareness of the appearance–reality distinction (Carey, in press): "the distinction which probably provides the intellectual basis for the fundamental epistemological construct common to science, "folk" philosophy, religion, and myth, of a real world "underlying" and "explaining" the phenomenal one" (Braine & Shanks, 1965a, pp. 241–242). Although we may not know that appearances have in fact deceived us in any specific cognitive situation, we do know as a general fact that such deception is always possible. That is, although always susceptible to being deceived by appearances, we have acquired the metacognitive knowledge that appearance–reality differences are always among life's possibilities. There are also many situations in which we are aware of an existing appearance–reality discrepancy. In the above examples, for instance, we may subsequently discover the discrepancy of which we were initially unaware. Dreams constitute a frequent case in point: the events seem real during the dream; we know they were apparent rather than real when we wake up. We also deliberately create or seek out appearance–reality differences as well as discover them. Examples are as diverse as pretense and other forms of play, fantasy, the creation of imaginary or possible worlds (by philosophers, scientists, other adults, and children), magic, tricks, costume parties, jokes, tall tales, metaphor, and the arts (e.g., drama). Some differences between appearance and reality are unwanted and painful; for instance, the apparently "sure-fire" investment (financial or emotional) that really is not. Others, however, are sought after and pleasureful; good magic shows and well-crafted "whodunits" are two examples.

2. The development of knowledge about the distinction between appearance and reality is probably a universal development in human beings. The distinction seems so necessary for everyday adaptations to the human world that one can scarcely imagine a society in which normal children would not acquire it. Developments that are both ecologically significant and universal within the species seem particularly worthy of scientific investigation.

How might young children think and act if, as seems likely, their knowledge about the appearance–reality distinction were not as fully developed as our own? In situations where appearance and reality differ they might not consistently attend to both and keep the difference between them clearly in mind, even when evidence is available to indicate look like a rock." Addressing readers directly, the writer quickly establishes the contradiction that the article will explore: "If I ask what it appears to be, you say, 'It looks just like a rock.' If I ask what it really is, you say, 'It's a sponge, of course.' A 3-year-old probably wouldn't be so sure." The final sentence of the first paragraph clearly indicates the main subject that the essay will explore, but its revision of a popular saying—"what you see is not always what you get"—ensures that the reader's interest will be maintained.

The second article, published in *American Psychologist,* features little white space and no illustrations or photographs. It does state prominently that this essay is an APA Award Address; readers of this journal would recognize the importance of this award. The title is straightforward but complete and easy to understand. The article begins not with an attention-getting introduction but with an abstract, which summarizes the findings of the research reported in the article. The first paragraph of the article opens with a concrete incident but quickly moves to a more theoretical discussion: "At issue in such simple tasks is the distinction between how things presently appear to the senses and how or what they really and enduringly are, that is, the familiar distinction between appearance and reality."

The final article, which appeared in *Cognitive Psychology,* the most specialized of these publications, presents the most cramped and least inviting first page. The title is abbreviated. As with the *American Psychologist* article, an abstract summarizes the article. The article itself begins abruptly with a general statement: "The acquisition of knowledge about the distinction between appearance and reality is a very important developmental problem for at least two reasons." The numbered paragraphs that follow this statement are dense; the authors use a number of technical terms, such as *ecologically significant cognitive situations* and *S-R theory,* without defining them.

Analyzing these first few pages supplies important clues about these three publications and the expectations shared by their writers and readers. One fact is clear from these introductory pages: the less specialized the publication, the greater the expectation that the writer will attempt to interest readers in the article. People who subscribe to *Psychology Today,* the most general and popular of these journals, often don't have a clear purpose when they read; they're broadly interested in psychology, but they may read only the articles that pique their curiosity. A writer who hopes to be read will consequently attempt to gain the attention of these readers.

Readers of *American Psychologist* are, like Flavell, all professionals in that field. Because psychology is such a broad field with so many subdisciplines, Flavell can't assume that everyone who subscribes to the journal will be interested in his essay. Not even all the readers who subscribe to *Cognitive Psychology,* a more specialized journal that publishes only research in Flavell's area, will read the article by Flavell and his colleagues, though proportionately more are likely to do so.

Given this situation, why doesn't Flavell attempt to gain the attention and interest of readers in the introductions to these more specialized journals, as he does in his *Psychology Today* article? As you may have already realized, readers of *American Psychologist* and *Cognitive Psychology* read with different purposes and in different ways than readers of *Psychology Today.* They read these journals not so much for pleasure or curiosity but because they want to keep up with advances in their field. Most readers of these two journals probably subscribe to many professional publications. They don't have the time to read every article in these journals, so they skim the tables of contents, noting articles that directly affect their own research or have broad significance for their field. Reviewing an article's abstract helps these psychologists determine not only if but *how* they will read an article. Some will read only an article's conclusion, for instance; others will be more interested in how an experiment was designed and conducted.

These psychologists would find an engaging introduction like that of the *Psychology Today* article a waste of time. Instead, they want a straightforward, to-the-point approach. Their needs are best met by an abstract that allows them to judge for themselves if they should read an article. Furthermore, whereas most readers of *Psychology Today* would discard issues after reading them, readers of *American Psychologist* and *Cognitive Psychology* would probably save theirs. They know that an essay that seems unimportant today may need to be read later. They don't read articles in these journals just once, as readers of popular magazines like *Psychology Today* probably do. They may reread important articles a number of times as they work on similar studies or experiments.

Although these three articles report the same research, they differ dramatically in structure, tone, language, and approach to readers. Textual conventions play an important role in these differences. As shared agreements about the construction and interpretation of texts, textual conventions enable readers and writers to communicate successfully in different rhetorical situations.

Application

Answer the following questions about the introductions to the three Flavell articles to analyze further the differences and similarities among these three excerpts.

1. What kinds of examples are used in these excerpts? What function do they serve?
2. What relationship is established in each article between the writer and the reader? What cues help signal each relationship?
3. How do the abstracts of the *American Psychologist* and *Cognitive Psychology* articles differ? How do you account for these differences?
4. How would you characterize the styles of these three excerpts? Point to specific features that characterize each style. What is the effect of these stylistic differences?
5. What assumptions does Flavell make in each article about what readers already know? Try to point out specific instances that reflect these assumptions.
6. How would you describe the *persona,* or image of the writer, in each article? What specific factors presented contribute to the development and coherence of this *persona*?

Putting it all together: understanding the demands of academic writing

Some textual conventions are easy to identify. After reading just a few lab reports, you recognize that this form of writing adheres to a set format. Other textual conventions are less easy to discern and to understand. When you first read the introductions to Dr. Flavell's three essays, for instance, you may have noticed that the introduction to the *Psychology Today* essay differed considerably from the introductions to the other two, which were published in scholarly journals. You may not, however, have noted the differences between the latter two introductions.

To recognize and understand these differences, you need some knowledge not only of the journals in which the essays were published but also of the readers of these journals. The authors' decision to use technical terms, such as *phenomenism* and *S-R theory,* in the introduction to the *Cognitive Psychology* essay reflects their recognition that readers would not only understand these terms but would expect them. Furthermore, using such terms subtly informs readers that the writers are insiders, privy to the terminology used by those in this field.

As this example indicates, recognizing and understanding textual conventions can require considerable knowledge not only of the forms of writing but also of the situations of writers and readers. When you join a new community of writers and readers, as you do when you enter college, you can find it difficult to understand the demands of the writing you are expected to complete. Look again, for instance, at the characteristics of an effective essay on page 88. When you first read these characteristics, they probably made sense to you. Of course, essays should be well organized, well developed, and logical.

When you sit down at your desk or computer to begin working on an essay for a history, sociology, or economics class, however, you may find it difficult to determine how to embody these characteristics in your own writing. Just what will make your analysis of the economic impact of divorce on the modern family logical or illogical, you might ask yourself. What do economists consider to be well-chosen evidence, illustrations, and details? And does your economics teacher value the same kind of logic, evidence, and details as your American literature teacher?

Exploration

Freewrite for five or ten minutes about your experience thus far with academic writing. What do you find productive and satisfying about such writing? What seems difficult and frustrating? Does your ability to respond to the demands of academic writing vary depending on the discipline? Do you find writing essays about literature easier, for instance, than lab reports and case studies? What do you think makes some kinds of academic writing harder or easier for you?

Part Three of *Work in Progress,* "Connections: Writing, Reading, and Reasoning," will address these and other issues. You already know enough about rhetoric and the rhetorical situation, however, to realize that there can be no one-size-fits-all approach to every academic writing situation. To respond successfully to the challenge of academic writing, you must explore your rhetorical situation; you must also draw on the rhetorical sensitivity you have gained as a reader, writer, speaker, and listener.

A rhetorical approach to writing suggests a number of commonsense strategies that you can use when writing in an academic context. For writing to be successful, rhetoric emphasizes, you must have something to say, something to communicate with others. There is thus no substitute for direct critical engagement with the subject matter of your courses. As Chapter 10, "Understanding Academic Audiences and Assignments," emphasizes, your teachers share an intellectual commitment first to the concept of education as inquiry and then to their own discipline. When teachers read your writing, they are looking for evidence that you have *learned* (not simply memorized) something.

Becoming critically engaged with a subject and communicating the result of that engagement with others are not necessarily the same thing, however. What can you do when you are unfamiliar with the textual conventions of academic writing in general or of a particular discipline? A rhetorical approach to writing suggests that one important way to learn about textual conventions is to read examples of the kind of writing you wish to do. Discussing these models with an insider—your teacher, perhaps, or an advanced student in the field—can help you understand why these conventions work for these readers and writers. Forming a study group with others in your class or meeting with a writing assistant in your writing center can also help you increase your rhetorical sensitivity to the expectations of your teachers and the conventions of academic writing.

Finally, a rhetorical approach to writing encourages you to think *strategically* about writing, be it personal, professional, or academic, and to respond creatively to the challenges of your rhetorical situation. As a writer, you have much to consider: your own goals as a writer, the nature of your subject and the writing task, the expectations of your readers, the textual conventions that your particular situation requires or allows for. The rhetorical sensitivity you have already developed can help you make appropriate choices in response to these and other concerns. But you will also need to draw on other resources—textual examples; discussions with teachers, writing assistants, and other students—as you work on a variety of writing tasks. As a writer, you are not alone. By reaching out to other writers, in person or through reading their work, you can become a fully participating member of the academic community.

Application

Arrange to interview a teacher in another course you are taking this term, preferably one in which you have done some writing, so that you can learn more about your teacher's expectations of student writing. You may wish to ask some or all of the following questions:

- What do you look for when you read students' writing? (Or how would you characterize effective student writing in your discipline?)
- In your experience, what is the difference between an A and a C student essay (or lab report or case study) in your discipline?
- What are the major weaknesses or limitations of the writing produced by students in your classes?
- What advice would you give to students in an introductory class in your field who want to understand how to write more effectively?
- Do you think your discipline values particular qualities in student writing not necessarily shared by other fields, or is good writing good writing no matter what the discipline?
- Could you suggest some examples I could read that would help me understand the conventions of effective writing in your discipline?
- How would you characterize the differences between effective student writing and effective professional writing in your field?
- What role do you see yourself as playing when you read student writing?
- Is there anything else you can tell me that would help me better understand the kind of student writing valued in your discipline?

After your interview, write a summary of your teacher's responses. In addition, write at least two paragraphs reflecting on what this interview has taught you about academic writing.

Group Activity

Once you have completed your interview and written your summary, meet with a group of students. Begin by reading your summaries out loud. Then working together—be sure to appoint a recorder—answer these questions:

- Can you find at least three statements or beliefs shared by all the people interviewed?
- What were some major points of disagreement? Did some faculty members feel, for instance, that good student writing is good student writing whatever the discipline, while others believed that their discipline valued particular qualities in student writing?

- What surprised you in the interviews? Agree on at least two examples, and briefly explain why you were surprised.
- What did these interviews help you understand about academic writing? Include at least three statements that reflect your group's discussion of your interviews.

Be prepared to share the result of your discussion with the rest of the class.

Activities for Thought, Discussion, and Writing

1. Now that you have completed Part One of *Work in Progress,* take a few moments to summarize what you think you have learned about writing. What have you found particularly useful about taking a rhetorical approach to writing? What questions or concerns do you still have?
2. From a newspaper or a magazine, choose an essay, an editorial, or a column that you think succeeds in its purpose. Now turn back to the guidelines for analyzing your rhetorical situation on pages 59–61 and answer the questions *as if you were the writer.* To answer the questions, look for evidence of the writer's intentions in the writing itself. (To determine what image or *persona* the writer wanted to portray, for instance, look at the kind of language the writer uses. Is it formal or conversational? Full of interesting images and vivid details or serious examples and statistics?) Answer each of the questions suggested by the guidelines. Then write a paragraph or more reflecting on what you have learned from this analysis.
3. Writers can follow appropriate textual conventions and still not be successful. Most textbooks follow certain conventions, such as having headings and subheadings, yet undoubtedly you have found some textbooks helpful and interesting, while others have seemed unhelpful and boring. Choose two textbooks—one that you like and one that you dislike—and make a list of at least four reasons why the former is successful and the latter is not.
4. Working with a group of students, write an essay that summarizes and reflects on what you have learned about academic writing as a result of completing the application on pages 100–1 and the group activity on pages 101–2.

PART TWO

PRACTICAL STRATEGIES FOR WRITING

CHAPTER 5

STRATEGIES FOR SUCCESSFUL INVENTION

Writing is a complex, dynamic process, one that challenges you to draw on all your resources as you compose. As a writer, you don't need to wait in frustration at your desk or computer for inspiration to strike. By analyzing your rhetorical situation and by reflecting on your previous writing experiences, you can respond effectively and efficiently to the demands of writing.

Experienced writers are pragmatists. They understand that different writing tasks call for different approaches, so they develop a repertoire of strategies they can employ depending on the situation. Experienced writers are also flexible and adaptable; they recognize that their writing may take unpredictable twists and turns. They know they may have to work their way through moments of frustration or difficulty to achieve the insights that make writing worthwhile. And they know, too, that they needn't work alone. Both informally and formally—through conversation with friends and family members as well as through collaboration with classmates, writing assistants, and teachers—successful writers benefit from the support and insights of others who share their interest in writing.

Writing, like thinking, is too complex and situated a process to be reduced to rules or formulas. But even though writing can't be reduced to a set of recipelike directions, it does involve activities that you can understand, practice, and improve. As noted in Chapter 2, the writing process generally involves planning, drafting, and revising. Successful writers employ a variety of strategies as they work on these activities. The chapters in Part Two present a number of these strategies.

Read the chapters in Part Two with a writer's eye. Which of these strategies do you already use? Could you use these strategies more effectively? What other strategies might extend your range or strengthen your writing abilities? As you read about and experiment with these strategies, remember that your needs and preferences as a writer and the situation in which you are writing should influence your assessment of their usefulness.

UNDERSTANDING HOW INVENTION WORKS

Like many people, you may feel that the activity of discovering ideas to write about is the most mysterious part of the writing process. Where do these ideas come from? How can you draw a blank one minute and suddenly know just the right way to support your argument or describe your experience the next? Is it possible to increase your ability to think and write creatively?

Writers and speakers have been concerned with questions such as these for centuries. The classical rhetoricians, in fact, were among the first to investigate this process of discovering and exploring ideas. The Roman rhetoricians called this process *inventio,* for "invention" or "discovery." Contemporary writers, drawing on this Latin term, often refer to this process as *invention.* Invention is part of the larger activity of planning, discussed further in Chapter 6. Because of the importance of invention, however, this chapter will focus specifically on this process of discovering and exploring ideas.

In practice, invention usually involves both individual inquiry and dialogue with others. In writing this textbook, for instance, I spent a great deal of time thinking and working alone. I even experienced a few moments of what might be described as inspiration. For instance, the original outline for this textbook came to me while my husband and I were camping. (I'd been reading a novel, but I quickly grabbed the note card I was using as a bookmark and wrote my ideas down.) As my long list of acknowledgments in the prefatory note to instructors indicates, however, I could not have written this book without the help of many people. In the earliest stages of this project—long before I had written an outline or decided on a title—I spoke with textbook editors as well as with colleagues who had already written textbooks. They helped me understand the intricacies of writing a textbook and the rhetorical situation to which a textbook generally responds. Once I had an outline, I spent many hours talking with both students and fellow composition instructors. By reading articles and books on the teaching of writing, I expanded these conversations. My silent but intense dialogues with these writers were just as important as face-to-face conversations in helping me refine my ideas and troubleshoot potential problems.

Most people don't write textbooks. But most writers—whether they are working on essays, reports, or research papers—generate and explore ideas not only by sitting quietly and thinking or by brainstorming at the computer but by reading, conducting research, and exchanging ideas with friends and colleagues. The following strategies will enable you to invent more successfully, whether you're working alone or talking about your writing with classmates or friends.

USING INFORMAL METHODS OF DISCOVERING AND EXPLORING IDEAS

You may already use several of the methods of discovering and exploring ideas that are described in this chapter: freewriting, looping, brainstorming, and clustering. These methods are informal, natural mental activities. You don't need extensive training or practice to learn to brainstorm or cluster, for instance. Yet these methods can help you discover what you know—and don't know—about a subject. They can also enable you to explore your own ideas and to formulate productive questions that can guide you as you plan, draft, and revise your writing.

Most writers find that some of the following methods work better for them than others. That's fine, but be sure you give each method a fair chance. You may surprise yourself. Here, for instance, is a journal entry by Joanne Novak, a student in Professor Robert Irkster's composition class at St. Cloud State University, describing how her experience with the informal methods of invention taught her something new about writing.

> I began the process of using the informal methods thinking it was a waste of time because I just simply was not in the mood to write. I intended to try each of the informal methods to prove that they didn't work for me. I chose a topic I'd been thinking of writing

about and tried freewriting. It was a jumbled mess. At that point I had trouble looping because I was embarrassed by the unorganized words that appeared on the paper, but I finally did come up with a shallow summarizing sentence. It sounded good, but it wasn't from the heart. It was something I knew I should feel. From the summarizing sentence I used the brainstorming method and came up blank.

Feeling confident that my theory was correct and the text was wrong, I decided to prove it by clustering. As suggested, I put my topic in the center of the page and just drew in whatever came to mind around the outside. I saw some organization to this method. That started ideas coming faster than I could write. I jotted down a few words so I could remember the main idea, and before I knew it I was writing so small I could hardly form the letters as I was running out of space.

I returned to brainstorming, which worked this time, and I ended up with a long list of things to write about. It was amazing. I reread my freewriting and found a few more ideas. I was shocked. I've always believed that I had to be in the mood to write or I couldn't come up with ideas. Now I see that that belief has in fact inhibited my writing.

JOANNE NOVAK

Like Joanne Novak, you may discover that the informal methods of invention can be a productive means of discovering and exploring ideas.

Freewriting

Introduced in Chapter 1, freewriting is the practice of writing as freely as possible without stopping to criticize or censor your ideas. This strategy is a simple but powerful means of exploring important issues and problems. Freewriting may at first seem *too* simple to achieve very powerful results: the only requirement is that you must write continuously without stopping. But freewriting can help you discover ideas that you couldn't achieve through more conscious and logical means. Because you generate a great deal of material when you freewrite, freewriting is also an excellent means of coping with the nervousness that all writers feel at the start of a project. (Freewriting can, by the way, be done quite effectively on the computer.)

Freewriting is a potentially powerful strategy you can use in a variety of writing situations. If you are writing a research paper for your political science class on low voter turnout, you could employ freewriting as a means of exploring and focusing your own ideas. Here is one student's freewriting on this issue.

> I just don't get it. As soon as I could register I did--it felt like a really important day. I'd watched my mother vote and my sisters vote and now it was my turn. But why do I vote; guess I should ask myself that question--and why don't other people. Do I feel that my vote makes a difference? There have been some close elections but not all that many, so my vote doesn't literally count, doesn't decide if we pay a new tax or elect a new senator. Part of it's the feeling I get. When I go to vote I know the people at the polling booth; they're my neighbors. I know the people who are running for office in local elections, and for state and national elections--well, I just feel that I should. But the statistics on voter turnout tell me I'm unusual. In this paper I want to go beyond statistics. I want to understand <u>why</u> people don't vote. Seems like I need to look not only at research in political science, but also maybe in sociology. (Check journals in economics too?) I wonder if it'd be okay for me to interview some students, maybe some staff and faculty, about voting--better check. But wait a minute; this is a small college in a small town, like the town I'm from. I wonder if people in cities would feel differently--they might. Maybe what I need to look at in my paper is rural/small town versus urban voting patterns.

This student has not only explored her ideas but also identified a possible question to which her paper will respond and sources she will draw on as she works on her project.

You can employ freewriting to investigate complex academic issues, such as the causes of low voter turnout. But freewriting can also help you explore your personal experience, enabling you to gain access to images, events, and emotions that you have forgotten or suppressed. If you were writing an essay about your sense of family—how you developed this sense, what it is, and what it means to you now—freewriting could help you recall details and images that would lend a rich specificity to your essay. Here, for example, is my own freewriting about my sense of family. (You may understand this freewriting more easily if you know that I grew up in a family of twelve children, two of whom died in infancy.)

> Family. Family. So strong. So many children. Ten. But really twelve. Brian and Anthony dead, both babies. The youngest kids don't even remember—they know but don't remember. Odd. Our own family so enormous, but so little extended family. Mom's parents dead—I do remember Nana, though—one sister. Dad's parents dead too, one sister. Some of my brothers and sisters don't remember any grandparents. Older kids spread out. Leni and Robin in Florida. Sara in Virgina. Andy in Mass. Younger kids closer: Laurie, Shelley, Jeff, Robbie, Julie—all in Ohio, close to Mom and Dad. Me in Oregon, the farthest. Have I forgotten anyone? The list, run down the list. (Memory: amazing friends with how quickly I could say the names, but only in order.) Leni, Lisa, Andy, Sara, Jeff, Robin, Michelle, Laurie, Julie, Robbie. The photo from last summer's reunion: thirty people, Mom and Dad, brothers, sisters, spouses, children. Could be a photo of a company's annual picnic—but it isn't. Families like this just don't exist any more. When did it change? People used to smile at us when we all went out and ask how many. Now a friend with four children tells me people are shocked at the size of her family. I have no children, but I have family. Family—an invisible web that connects.

My brief freewrite did more than generate concrete images and details; it gave me a new insight into my sense of family. Rereading my freewriting, I am surprised at the strong sense of loss that appears as I comment on my infant brothers' deaths and those of my grandparents. I also notice a potential contradiction between my strong sense of family and my recent experience of living a great distance from my family.

Looping

Looping, an extended or directed form of freewriting, alternates freewriting with analysis and reflection. Begin looping by first establishing a theme or topic for your freewriting; then freewrite for five or ten minutes. This is your first loop. After you have done so, reread what you have written. In rereading your freewriting, look for the center of gravity or "heart" of your ideas—the image, detail, issue, or problem that seems richest or most intriguing, compelling, or productive. Write a sentence that summarizes this understanding; this sentence will become the starting point of your second loop. In looking back at my previous freewriting, I can locate several potential starting points for an additional loop. I might, for instance, use the following question to begin another freewriting session:

> What does it mean that my family includes a number of people—my brothers and grandparents—that my younger brothers and sisters never knew, can't remember?

When you loop, you don't know where your freewriting and reflection will take you; you don't worry about the final product. My final essay on my sense of family might not even discuss the question generated by my freewriting. That's fine; the goal in freewriting and looping is not to produce a draft of an essay but to explore your own ideas and to discover ideas, images, and sometimes even words, phrases, and sentences that you can use in your writing.

Application

Freewrite for five minutes, beginning with the word *family.* Then stop and reread your freewriting. What comments most interest or surprise you? Now write a statement that best expresses your freewriting's center of gravity or "heart." Use this comment to begin a second loop by freewriting for five minutes more.

After completing this second freewriting, stop and reread both passages. What did you learn about your own sense of family? Does your freewriting suggest possible ideas for an essay on some subject connected with your family? Finally, reflect on the process itself. Did you find the experience of looping helpful? Would you use freewriting and looping in the future as a means of generating and exploring your experiences and ideas?

Brainstorming

Like freewriting and looping, brainstorming is a simple but productive invention strategy. When you brainstorm, you list as quickly as possible all the thoughts about a subject that occur to you without censoring or stopping to reflect on your ideas. A student assigned to write an essay on child abuse for a sociology class would brainstorm by listing everything that comes to mind on this subject, from facts to images, memories, fragments of conversations, and other general impressions and responses. Later, the student would review this brainstorming list to identify ideas that seem most promising or helpful.

To brainstorm effectively, take a few moments at the start to formulate your goal, purpose, or problem. Then simply list your ideas as quickly as you can. Don't stop to analyze or criticize; that activity will come later. You are the only person who needs to be able to decipher what you've written, so your brainstorming list can be as messy or as neat as you like. You can also brainstorm at the computer.

Brainstorming can enable you to discover and explore a number of ideas in a short time. Not all of them will be worth using in a piece of writing, of course. The premise of brainstorming is that the more ideas you can generate, the better your chances of coming up with good ones. Suppose that after freewriting about my family, I decided to explore the possibility of writing an essay about the potential contradiction between my sense that family is "an invisible web that connects" and the fact that I live so far away from my family. In the five minutes after I wrote that last sentence, I used brainstorming to generate the following list of ideas and suggestions:

- Think about role of place (geography) and family.
- the house on Main St.—home since the 4th grade
- Mom's letters: so important in keeping us all in touch!
- images: Laurie, Shelley, and Sara all with new babies at Julie's wedding
  Andy pulling the same joke on me for 30 years
  the old house on Corey St. Why do I always remember the kitchen?
  my sadness at missing Robin's, Shelley's, and Laurie's weddings because we were in Oregon
  the wonderful, friendly, comfortable chaos at our reunion (the grandkids getting confused by all the aunts and uncles)
- Am I fooling myself? Is the tie I feel with my family as strong as I think it is? Greeting-card sentiments versus reality?
- special family times: birthdays, Christmas, cooking and baking together. How to evoke these without making it all seem sentimental and clichéd?
- Maybe it's the difficult times that keep families together. The hard times that (especially when you're a teenager) you think you'll never get beyond

- Families change over time. So does your sense of family. How has mine changed?

I certainly would have a long way to go before I could write an essay about my sense of family, but even this brief brainstorming list of ideas and questions has raised important issues I'd want to consider.

Application

Reread your earlier freewriting about your sense of family, assigned on page 111, and then choose one issue or question you'd like to explore further. Write a single sentence summarizing this issue or question, and then brainstorm for five to ten minutes. After brainstorming, return to your list. Put an asterisk (*) beside those ideas or images that hadn't appeared in your earlier freewriting. How do these ideas or images add to your understanding of your sense of family?

Clustering

Clustering shares a number of features with freewriting, looping, and brainstorming. All four strategies emphasize spontaneity. The goal of all four is to generate as many ideas as possible so that you can discover both what you know and what you might want to explore further. Clustering differs from brainstorming, freewriting, and looping, however, in that it uses visual means to generate ideas. Because clustering is nonlinear, some writers find that it frees them from their conventional patterns of thinking and enables them to explore their ideas more deeply and creatively.

To begin clustering, choose a single word or phrase as the starting point or stimulus for your discovery. If you are responding to an assigned topic, choose the word that best summarizes or evokes that topic. If your assignment is broad and you are unsure of your topic or thesis, choose a word that seems suggestive or fruitful. Place this word in the center of a page of blank paper, and circle it. Now fill in the page by expanding on or developing ideas connected with this central word. Don't censor your ideas or force your cluster to assume a certain shape. Simply circle your key ideas and connect them either to the first word or to other related ideas. Your goal in clustering is to be as spontaneous and as natural as possible.

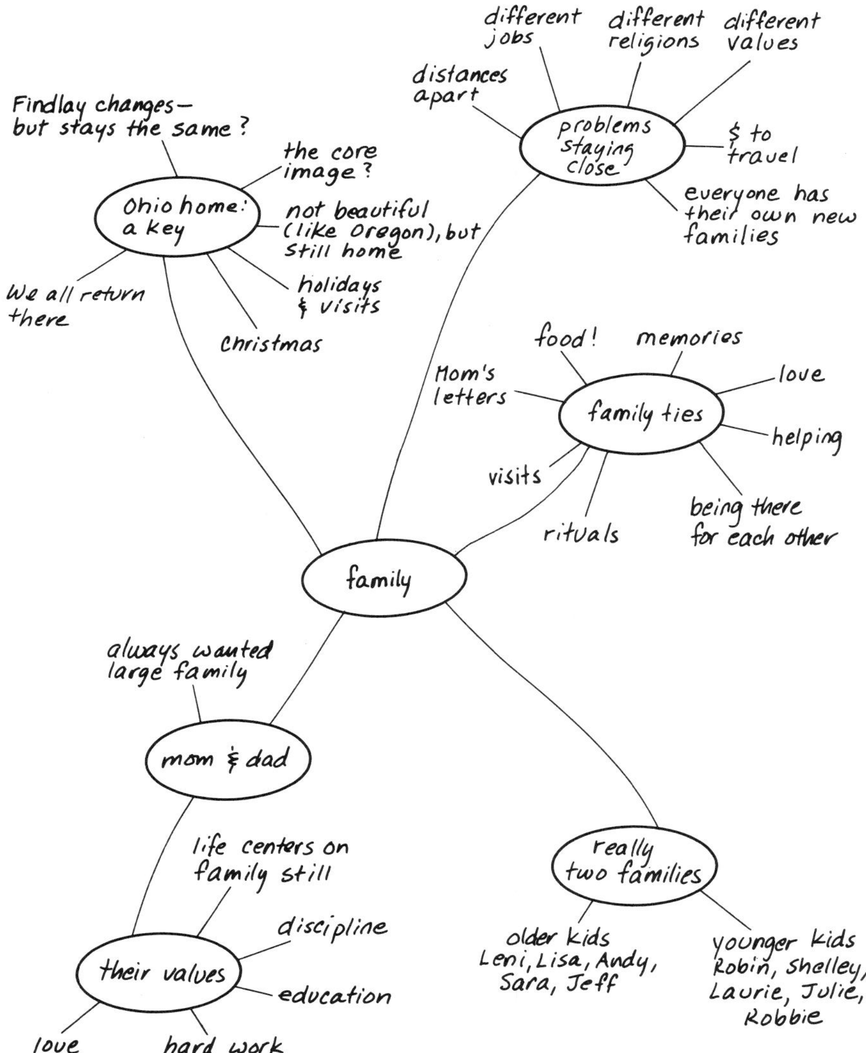

Figure 5-1

Figure 5-1 presents a cluster that I created shortly after freewriting and brainstorming about my sense of family. Notice that even though I wrote this only a short time later, the cluster reveals new details and images. As with brainstorming, looping, and freewriting, after clustering you must distance yourself from the material you've generated so that you can evaluate it. In doing so, try to find the heart or center of gravity of the cluster—the idea or image that seems richest and most compelling.

Application

Drawing on your experience freewriting, looping, and brainstorming about your sense of family, choose a word to use as the center of a cluster. (If you wish, just use the word *family.*) Without planning or worrying about form, fill in your cluster by branching out from this central word. Just include whatever comes to mind.

Group Activity

Meet with classmates to discuss the informal methods of discovering and exploring ideas that you have employed in the preceding applications. Begin your discussion by having group members briefly describe the advantages and disadvantages they experienced when they experimented with freewriting, looping, brainstorming, and clustering. (Appoint a recorder to summarize each person's statements.) Then, as a group, discuss your responses to these questions:

1. How might different students' preferences for one or more of these strategies be connected to different learning and composing styles?
2. What influence might such situational factors as the nature of the assignment or the amount of time available for working on an essay have on the decision to use one or more of these strategies?

Be prepared to discuss your conclusions with your classmates.

USING FORMAL METHODS OF DISCOVERING AND EXPLORING IDEAS

The informal methods of discovering and exploring ideas have a number of advantages. They are easy to employ, and they can help you generate a reassuringly large volume of material when you're just beginning to work on a paper. These strategies also help you become interested in and committed to your work in progress. Sometimes, however, you may find more formal and systematic methods of discovering and exploring ideas helpful. The strategies discussed in this section—the journalist's questions, tagmemics, and the topical questions—provide a variety of questions you can use to explore a topical issue, consider it from diverse perspectives, and generate ideas about it. Because they *systematically* probe a topic, these strategies can help you discover not just what you know about a topic but also what you *don't* know and thus alert you to the need for additional reading and research.

The journalist's questions

The journalist's questions—who, what, when, where, why, and how—are perhaps the easiest to understand and apply of the formal methods of discovering and exploring ideas. If you have taken a journalism class or written for your school or community newspaper, you know that journalists are taught the importance of answering these six questions in articles they write. By answering these questions, journalists can be sure that they have provided the most important information about an event, issue, or problem for their readers.

You may find the journalist's questions particularly useful when you are describing an event or writing an informative essay. Suppose that your political science instructor has assigned an essay on political conflict in Haiti. Using the journalist's questions as headings, you could begin working on this assignment by asking yourself the following questions:

- *Who* is involved in this conflict?
- *What* issues most clearly divide those engaged in this dispute?
- *When* did the troubles in Haiti begin, and how have they developed over time?
- *Where* does the conflict in this country seem most heated or violent?
- *Why* have Haitians found it so difficult to resolve the situation?
- *How* might this conflict be resolved?

Although you might discover much the same information by simply brainstorming, using the journalist's questions ensures that you have covered all these major points. Furthermore, using the journalist's questions as headings automatically organizes information as you generate it, whereas a brainstorming list would need to be analyzed, unscrambled, and reorganized.

Tagmemics

The name for this method of discovering and exploring ideas may sound strange or formidable, but tagmemics, the method presented by Richard Young, Alton Becker, and Kenneth Pike in *Rhetoric: Discovery and Change,* is not difficult to understand and apply. The basic principle underlying tagmemics can be easily stated: an object, experience, or idea can be viewed as a particle (a static unit), a wave (a dynamic unit changing over time), or a field (a unit seen in the context of a larger network of relationships). Each of these perspectives encourages you to ask different kinds of questions about your subject (represented here as X).

- particle perspective: What is X?
- wave perspective: How has X changed over time?
- field perspective: How does X relate to ______?

If you view something as a *particle,* you focus on it as a *static* entity. For example, if you were exploring ideas for a sociology paper on the transformation of the American nuclear family, you could use a particle perspective to ask questions like the following:

- What does the term *nuclear family* mean?
- Who formulated the term *nuclear family*?
- What features characterize the nuclear family?

If you look at a subject from the *wave* perspective, you view it as *dynamic* or *changing over time.* The wave perspective would encourage you to ask such questions as these:

- How long has the nuclear family characterized family structure in America?
- When did the nuclear family begin to change?
- What factors have caused the nuclear family to change?
- How might these factors affect the American family in the future?

Finally, if you look at a subject from the *field* perspective, you ask questions about the way that the subject functions as *part of a larger network of relationships.* This perspective would encourage you to ask questions like the following:

- How are changes in the structure of the American family related to other changes, such as those in the work force, organized religion, the educational system, and divorce rates?
- What are the consequences of changes in the nuclear family for American life in general? For politics? For social services? For education?

Tagmemics is a formal method of discovering or exploring ideas because its three perspectives of particle, wave, and field encourage you to examine your subject *systematically.* Don't be intimidated by the formality of tagmemics; adapt this method to meet *your* needs. Sometimes, for instance, you may use the three perspectives of tagmemics to determine how you might best approach or limit a general subject or problem, such as the breakdown of the nuclear family. In other cases, you may use tagmemics to generate a long list of details, examples, and ideas in support of a clearly defined thesis.

Application

Choose a subject of interest to you, such as the impact of computers on business, the debate over the importance of preserving wilderness lands, or the increasing commercialization of college football. (Alternatively, you could continue to explore what the term *family* means to you.) Using the journalist's questions and tagmemics, systematically explore the subject you have chosen.

Once you have employed each of these methods, take a few moments to reflect on this experience. To what extent did each strategy help you organize and systematically review what you already know, and to what extent did each define what you still need to find out?

The topical questions

The last formal method of discovering and exploring ideas is based on the topics of classical rhetoric. In his *Rhetoric,* Aristotle describes the topics as potential lines of argument or places (*topos* in Greek means "place") where speakers and writers can find evidence or arguments. Aristotle defined twenty-eight topics, but the list is generally abbreviated to these five: definition, comparison, relationship, circumstance, and testimony.

The classical topics represent natural ways of thinking about ideas. When confronted by an intellectual problem, we all ask such questions as these:

- What is it? (definition)
- What is it like or unlike? (comparison)
- What caused it? (relationship)
- What is possible or impossible? (circumstance)
- What have others said about it? (testimony)

Aristotle's topics build on these natural mental habits.

You may use these questions to discover and explore ideas about a subject. To do so, simply pose each question in turn about your subject, writing down as many responses as possible. You may also find helpful the following list of topical questions, adapted by Edward P. J. Corbett from the work of Richard L. Larson. These questions, from Corbett's *The Little Rhetoric and Handbook,* are organized according to subject matter.*

QUESTIONS ABOUT PHYSICAL OBJECTS

1. What are the physical characteristics of the object (shape, dimensions, materials, etc.)?
2. What sort of structure does it have?
3. What other object is it similar to?
4. How does it differ from things that resemble it?
5. Who or what produced it?
6. Who uses it? For what?

QUESTIONS ABOUT EVENTS

1. Exactly what happened? (who? what? when? where? why? how?)
2. What were its causes?
3. What were its consequences?
4. How was the event like or unlike similar events?
5. To what other events was it connected?
6. How might the event have been changed or avoided?

QUESTIONS ABOUT ABSTRACT CONCEPTS (e.g., DEMOCRACY, JUSTICE)

1. How has the term been defined by others?
2. How do you define the term?

*Edward P. J. Corbett, *The Little Rhetoric and Handbook* (Glenview, Ill.: Scott, Foresman, 1982): 38–39.

3. What other concepts have been associated with it?
4. What counterarguments must be confronted and refuted?
5. What are the practical consequences of the proposition?

QUESTIONS ABOUT PROPOSITIONS (STATEMENTS TO BE PROVED OR DISPROVED)

1. What must be established before the reader will believe it?
2. What are the meanings of key words in the proposition?
3. By what kind of evidence or argument can the proposition be proved or disproved?
4. What counterarguments must be confronted and refuted?
5. What are the practical consequences of the proposition?

Like the other formal methods for discovering and exploring ideas, the topical questions can help you pinpoint alternative approaches to the subject or probe one subject systematically, organizing what you know already and identifying gaps that you need to fill.

Application

Use the topical questions to continue your investigation of the same subject that you explored with the journalist's questions and tagmemics.

What new information or ideas did the topical questions generate? How would you compare this method to the other two formal strategies?

INVENTING COLLABORATIVELY: LEARNING WITH AND FROM OTHERS

Invention includes not only individual inquiry, such as that stimulated by freewriting, brainstorming, or tagmemics, but dialogue with others. Much of this dialogue occurs naturally as you go about your daily affairs. While riding the bus or subway home after class, for instance, you might talk over a writing assignment with a friend. Or you might brainstorm about an essay topic with your spouse or roommate after dinner. The ideas you gain through such exchanges can contribute a great deal to your understanding of your subject.

This section presents two strategies you can use to learn with and from others as you write—group brainstorming and group troubleshooting—that build on the informal exchanges you already have with friends, classmates, and family members.

Group brainstorming

You have already experimented with brainstorming alone, so you are aware of its basic procedures and benefits. You can also brainstorm as part of a group, however. In fact, Alex Osborn, the person generally credited with naming this technique, originally envisioned brainstorming as a group, not an individual, activity. Osborn believed that the enthusiasm generated by the group helped spark ideas. You will not be surprised to learn, then, that those who regularly write with teams or groups cite increased intellectual stimulation and improved quality of ideas as major benefits of collaboration.

Group brainstorming can be used for a variety of purposes. If your class has just been assigned a broad topic, for instance, your group could brainstorm a list of ways to approach or limit this topic. Or your group could generate possible arguments in support of or opposition to a specific thesis.

Because more than one person is involved, group brainstorming is more complicated than brainstorming alone. When working in a group, follow this procedure.

Guidelines for group brainstorming

1. Carefully define the problem or issue to be addressed at the start of your group session.
2. Appoint someone to act as a recorder. This person can write group members' ideas on the board or on a piece of paper, ready to be reproduced and distributed to group members later.
3. Encourage group members to contribute freely and spontaneously to the discussion. Don't stop to discuss or evaluate ideas; your goal is to generate as many ideas as possible.

Group troubleshooting

Group troubleshooting is a simple but often productive means of helping group members identify and resolve writing problems by discussing work in progress with peers who respond with questions and advice. To troubleshoot effectively, your group should follow this procedure.

Guidelines for group troubleshooting

1. Decide how much time to spend on each person's writing, and appoint a timekeeper to enforce these limits.
2. Begin by having the writer describe the issue or problem he or she would like discussed. The writer also should try to identify particular questions for group response. These questions may be very general. ("This is what I'm planning to do in my essay; can you think of any problems I might run into?" "Do you have any suggestions about how I might develop my thesis?") Or the questions might be quite specific. ("I've only been able to think of two potential objections to my thesis; can you think of others?" "I like these four ideas, but I don't think they fit together very well. What could I do?")
3. Let the writer facilitate the resulting discussion. If the writer needs a moment to write an idea down, for example, he or she should ask the group to pause briefly. The writer should feel free to ask group members to clarify or elaborate on suggestions.
4. Try as group members to respond to the writer's request for assistance as carefully and fully as possible.

You will probably find group troubleshooting most productive in the early stages of writing when you are still working out your ideas and determining your approach to your subject.

CONDUCTING RESEARCH

What does it mean to conduct research? You may think immediately of searching for articles and books in the library, and libraries certainly are a valuable source of information about many subjects. But research is actually a much more common activity in all of our lives. You are conducting research, for instance, if you spend an afternoon visiting electronics stores to examine and try out compact disk players so you can decide which model you should purchase. You are conducting research if you read *Bride's* magazine to help you plan your own or a friend's wedding. You are conducting research if you write to the chamber of commerce of a city to which you might move to request information about local businesses, property values, and taxes. And you are conducting research if you volunteer to work with a committee of concerned citizens charged with investigating the adequacy of your community's services for the homeless.

As these examples indicate, we all conduct research to make decisions and become better informed about the world around us. Research, then, is a natural human activity. Like developing your rhetorical sensitivity, sharpening your research ability is largely a matter of extending and refining skills you already command. As a student, you may need to learn certain techniques, such as using your library's database or designing bias-free questionnaires, but it is helpful to keep in mind that you already understand many basic research methods.

In-depth coverage of research methods and related issues, such as using source materials and documenting sources, is outside the scope of this book. You may wish to consult a college writing handbook if you need further information on these subjects. The rest of this chapter will provide a number of useful suggestions about conducting research, however. Additionally, Part Three, "Connections: Writing, Reading, and Reasoning," focuses on a number of issues directly related to research. Much of your research in college involves reading; Chapter 9, "Understanding the Reading Process," will help you develop the critical reading skills necessary for effective research. You can't conduct effective research unless you understand your assignment and have developed strategies that enable you to analyze and argue effectively: Chapter 10, "Understanding Academic Audiences and Assignments," and Chapter 11, "Understanding Academic Analysis and Argument," discuss these issues.

Perhaps the most important thing to understand when you conduct research is that the question you want to answer—your purpose—should govern your inquiry. You will undoubtedly begin with a general topic that interests you, but your research will be more efficient once you have turned the topic into a goal-driven question. If you are investigating the media's coverage of the AIDS crisis, you will proceed differently than if you are investigating the adequacy of AIDS services provided in your community. The nature of your project will also influence how you conduct research. If you are simply following up leads in an essay because you find the subject interesting, you may limit your research to a brief examination of the essay's bibliography. If you are embarking on a major research project, you will naturally employ a more extensive, systematic review of relevant materials.

When you conduct research, as when you write, you are engaged in a process that can vary depending on the situation. Just how much time you spend on library research as opposed to other methods of inquiry, such as observation, interviews, and questionnaires, may vary considerably. If you are writing an essay on images of women in rock videos, for instance, you will probably begin by spending some time closely watching a sample of videos. Then, depending on the kinds of questions you want to investigate, you might go to the library to seek out other writer's arguments on the subject or set up a group viewing with several others and distribute a questionnaire on their responses. By contrast, if you want to investigate the historical causes of ethnic conflict in the former Yugoslavia, chances are that you will need to rely almost exclusively on your library's print and electronic resources.

Conducting research can be one of the most satisfying parts of the writing process—but not if it is approached as a dreary hunt for evidence. Bad experiences have left some students with a view of research as a dry and tedious process of locating published authorities whose words and ideas are to be strung together in their essays like beads in a necklace. In actuality, conducting research—like the formal and informal methods of invention discussed earlier in this chapter—is a crucial and creative way of generating and exploring ideas; research is thus best understood as a kind of invention, not the retrieval of static information. Although you should respect the achievements of the authors of the essays, reports, and studies that you read, conducting research is more like a conversation than a lecture, and your role is active, not passive. Scholarly research is an ongoing, collaborative activity. One scholar presents his or her findings, only to be answered by another; a third responds to both. Your job is to enter that conversation, whether by reading various researchers' works and coming to informed conclusions about them or by contributing original research of your own.

Library research

The library need not be your only research resource, but for most academic writing, as you already know, it is an indispensable one. The following brief guidelines cannot tell you how to master your library and understand all its research materials but are offered as useful suggestions.

Guidelines for conducting library research

1. *Learn how to use your college or university library.* If you are familiar with the process of conducting library research, this step will involve little more than observing where materials are located in your library and discovering what special services, such as computerized databases, are available to you. But if you are less experienced at research, take the time to

get to know your library. Many academic libraries offer tours or educational programs for students. Take advantage of these if they are available.

2. *Establish an appropriate search strategy.* Before going to the library to do research for a project, even a minor one, you should work out a search strategy. Such a plan ensures that you will consult appropriate sources; it also helps you avoid frustration and wasted time. Often, for instance, you will want to get a broad overview of your subject before you read more specialized studies. Determining what materials to consult for this overview might be the first step in your search strategy. In other cases, especially when you already have some knowledge of your subject and have been assigned or have developed a specific, goal-driven question, you may consult specialized materials from the start. The important thing is to have a plan—to figure out what you need to know and how best to locate that information. If you have difficulty establishing an appropriate search strategy, ask a reference librarian for help.
3. *Build in time for unexpected delays and difficulties.* You may be surprised and frustrated when you discover that books you had counted on finding in the library are checked out or that a resource you had expected to be helpful is not. Be sure to budget not just adequate but *extra* time for research in case you run into unexpected difficulties.
4. *Recognize the importance of evaluating sources.* Not every book or essay you find in the library is accurate, up-to-date, and authoritative. When you conduct research, you must evaluate the usefulness and authoritativeness of your sources. To do so, ask yourself questions like the following:
   - Who is the author? Is he or she a recognized expert in the field? Have other sources referred favorably to this author's work?
   - Who published this? Does this publisher (whether of books or periodicals) have a solid reputation in the field?
   - To whom is the author writing? Is this a work intended for general readers or specialists?
   - When was this published? If it was not published within the past three to five years, is it still current or outdated? How rapidly is information in this field changing?
   - How relevant is this work to my topic? Have I skimmed a book's table of contents and preface or reviewed an article's introduction, section headings, and conclusions to determine if it merits a more careful reading?

At times, especially at the start of a research project, you may not be able to answer these questions because you just don't know enough about your subject. When that occurs, you have several options. The first is to consult the reference librarian. Large academic libraries generally have one or more librarians who specialize in each of the major disciplines and thus are especially well qualified to help you. If your library doesn't have specialized reference librarians, consult one of the general reference librarians. A second option is to discuss your sources with your instructor. After you have completed some preliminary research, for instance, you might ask your instructor's advice about the appropriateness of your sources and your search strategy. Finally, you can follow up leads in works you have already read. When researchers cite other scholarly works, they are not only acknowledging their use of the ideas of others but also indicating those whose work seems important to them. By consulting studies cited in footnotes or bibliographies, you can discover the researchers best qualified to comment on the work you are trying to evaluate.

Field research and interviewing

Research can—and often should—involve much more than consulting materials in your library. Such materials are indispensable for most academic writing, but don't overlook the possibilities afforded by other forms of information gathering, such as interviews, questionnaires, and firsthand observation. If you are writing an essay on sexual harassment on college campuses, for instance, you will probably find it helpful to do some library research to get a broad perspective on the issue—national trends, the history of the present controversy, illustrative incidents from campuses other than your own, and so forth. But you might find it especially helpful to interview an administration or faculty member who is involved in setting or enforcing your own school's policy on the issue, as well as individuals who have publicly opposed that policy. You might distribute a questionnaire to other students designed to measure their opinions on the issue (asking, for instance, how they would define sexual harassment; how important an issue they feel it is at your school; what, if any, policy they would like to see enforced; and so on). You might want to spend some hours closely observing the behavior of male and female students in a social setting, such as a bar or a party. Even if these sources of information do not play a major role in your essay, they will enrich your understanding of your subject and encourage you to consider it from a variety of perspectives.

There are other advantages to these forms of research—sometimes known as *field research* because they take you out of the library and put you directly in the field. Many students find that field research helps them build enthusiasm for and commitment to their subject. The face-to-face, interactive quality of this kind of research can have the same invigorating effect that many writers find in working collaboratively. Finally, field research affords the motivation—and the satisfaction—of knowing that you are doing original work, in effect *creating* new information that no one before you has compiled in quite the same way.

This is not to say library research is unnecessary. Even professional field researchers are careful to keep up with the work of other scholars, to compare their own findings with others', and to place themselves within the ongoing scholarly conversation we've referred to. Effective mastery of library research skills gives you access to the broadest, most comprehensive perspective on any topic. But, depending on the topic you've chosen and the questions you are asking about it, field research can help you arrive at a fascinatingly detailed and particular *local* perspective on a subject.

Interviews can often provide information unavailable through other kinds of research. Sometimes you may wish to consult an expert on the subject you are studying; on other occasions you may interview individuals in order to gain local perspectives on your issue, firsthand accounts of relevant experiences, or other information. A good interviewer is first of all a good conversationalist—someone who is able to draw out the person being interviewed. Interviews are more formal and time-pressured than most conversations, so be sure that you do not underestimate the importance of carefully preparing for and conducting them. Here are some suggestions to follow if you wish to interview someone for your writing.

Guidelines for field research and interviewing

1. Call or write to request an interview in advance. Carefully explain why you want the interview, how long it will take, and what you hope to accomplish.
2. Come prepared with a list of written questions.
3. If you wish to tape the interview, remember to ask permission first.
4. Take notes during the interview, even if you use a tape recorder. Your notes will help refresh your memory when you don't have time to review the entire tape; they can also help you identify the most important points of discussion.

5. Be flexible. Don't try to make the person you are interviewing answer all your prepared questions if he or she doesn't find some of them appropriate or interesting. If your interviewee shows more interest in a question than you had anticipated or wants to discuss a related issue, just accept this change in plans and return to your list of questions when appropriate.
6. Develop a variety of questioning techniques. People are sometimes unable or unwilling to answer direct questions. Suppose that you want to write about your grandmother's experiences during World War II. If you simply ask her what life was like then, she may not respond very fully or specifically. Less direct questions—"Where did you live during the war?" "What effect did rationing have on how you ate?" "Did Grandpa have to fight?"—may elicit more detailed answers.

Questionnaires

Distributing a questionnaire can be a good way to get a quick X ray of the attitudes, beliefs, and experiences of a large number of people. For instance, as a part of the preparation of this third edition of *Work in Progress,* I sent a questionnaire to a number of my former students, asking them about their experiences with writing since graduation. (See the epilogue for excerpts from some of the responses I received.) For one of your writing assignments, you may find it helpful to question a sample of your fellow students on their career plans, their reading habits, their favorite candidates for the next presidential election, or their opinions on your school's policy on hate speech.

Once again, a detailed discussion of the design and interpretation of questionnaires is beyond this book's scope. In some disciplines that deal extensively in questionnaire and poll data, such as sociology and political science, these matters are addressed in depth. For the purposes of an English class, it may be best to use questionnaires as a rough indicator of broad trends of thought and a source of differing perspectives on an issue or a topic rather than as a "scientific" measurement of the general population's views. The guidelines presented here are simply intended as basic suggestions. They assume that you have already decided on a topic to ask about and have devised a way to distribute your questionnaires to an appropriate number of representative people and to collect them when completed.

Guidelines for designing and using questionnaires

1. Treat the drafting of your questionnaire as you would any important writing project—in other words, keep your audience in mind and be prepared to do more than one draft to make sure your questions are clear, easily answerable, and directed toward getting the information you seek.
2. Keep in mind that the longer and more difficult a questionnaire is, the fewer responses you are likely to have returned. Yes/no and multiple-choice questions are the easiest to answer but restrict your respondent's freedom to give complex answers. Essay-style questions yield more nuanced answers but ask more work of your respondent and hence are best kept to a minimum.
3. Show a draft of your questionnaire to some friends or your writing group before copying and distributing it. Seek feedback on the clarity and "user friendliness" of your questionnaire.
4. Include all appropriate demographic questions in addition to questions about your primary subject. You may or may not need to have your respondents put their name on their questionnaires; unless the name is vital, make clear that they have the option of remaining anonymous. You may want to ask for other personal characteristics, such as sex, income, marital status, age, or education, depending on the questions governing your research. If you are asking about attitudes toward sexual harassment, for instance, you may well want to be able to note differences between the answers given by men and women. Or if you are gathering opinions about the homeless, your respondents' income levels may be relevant.
5. Whether or not you ask your respondents to give their names, you should write an explanation on the questionnaire of its purpose and the use you have in mind for it and ask them to check off *yes* or *no* to indicate whether you have permission to quote them.
6. Distribute more copies than you need to have returned. Anticipate a return rate well below 100 percent.

Unless you are administering your questionnaire under tightly controlled conditions, you will not generate scientifically verifiable data. There are still good reasons for using questionnaires. Responses to questionnaires can prompt you to consider multiple perspectives on an issue; they can also provide illustrative examples and voices to bring into your essay. (If, in the course of an essay arguing for more child-care facilities on your campus, you are able to quote directly from statements made by single parents who are full-time students, your questionnaire will have contributed a good deal to your essay's impact.)

Observation

Finally, don't overlook the kinds of information available through close observation of the various communities to which you have access. In disciplines such as sociology and anthropology, there are long and rich traditions of ethnographic research in which "participant-observers" living in and moving among various communities attempt to observe and interpret social customs and patterns of behavior. Ethnographers have gathered research data in twelve-step groups, day-care centers, crack houses, corporate boardrooms, and boxing arenas.

Although you will probably not undertake full-scale ethnographic research, you can generate stimulating questions and gather interesting material for your writing assignments through close observation of various communities. If you are writing a paper on the effectiveness of your college or university's student government, you might not only interview members of that government (and those who have criticized it) but also observe a variety of meetings—from the student senate to various subcommittees and working groups. You may already participate in activities that could contribute to your understanding of an issue. If you work as a restaurant waitperson, you might study the tipping practices of men and women to gain insight into gender differences and their social implications. As with other forms of field research, observation can enrich your understanding by generating questions and exposing you to multiple perspectives on a subject. A student who suspects that her student government is ineffective may find that observing a number of meetings challenges, and thus complicates, her understanding.

This chapter has described a number of strategies you can use to discover and explore ideas. Your preferred composing style, the nature of your subject, and the situation in which you are writing will influence your choice of strategies. In deciding how to generate ideas for an essay, take a pragmatic, goal-oriented approach. Don't waste time freewriting if you already have lots of ideas and a sense of how you want to approach your subject. Instead, see if you can develop a workable plan—as discussed in the next chapter—and then start writing. You may decide to stop and freewrite later, but then you'll have a clear purpose and thus will use your time more effectively. In some instances, even making a plan may seem unnecessary. If you're full of ideas and just want to write, you may want to explore your ideas by writing a draft and seeing, in effect, what you think. That's fine, too. Just remember that *all* of these methods of invention require you to evaluate the ideas you have generated, whether they take the form of a brainstorming list, a cluster, or a first draft.

Activities for Thought, Discussion, and Writing

1. Early in this chapter you used freewriting, looping, brainstorming, and clustering to investigate your sense of family. Continue your exploration of this topic by drawing on the formal methods of invention. Then write an essay in which you explore just what the word *family* means to you.
2. Observe some of your classmates working together on group brainstorming. Don't participate in the group activities; simply observe the group interaction, making notes about what you see. You may find it helpful to record how often each member of the group participates in the discussion, for example. Pay attention, too, to group dynamics. Is the group working effectively? Why or why not? What could group members do to ensure more effective interaction? Summarize the results of your observations in a report to group members. Be sure to suggest several ways the group could work more effectively in the future.
3. Choose one of the strategies discussed in this chapter that you have not used in the past. Experiment with the strategy as you work on your current writing assignment. If there is time, discuss this experiment with some of your classmates. Then write a brief analysis of why this strategy did or did not work well for you.

CHAPTER 6

STRATEGIES FOR SUCCESSFUL PLANNING AND DRAFTING

Planning is an important part of the writing process. As the discussion of differing composing styles in Chapter 2 indicated, people plan in different ways, depending on how they prefer to compose. Some develop detailed written plans; others rely primarily on mental plans to guide them as they draft and revise. Still others plan by freewriting a draft of their essay and determining their goals by rereading and reflecting on their own written text. Other factors can affect the process of planning, such as the time available or the complexity of the writing task.

People plan in different ways and at different times in the writing process, but planning always involves the following related activities:

- analyzing your rhetorical situation
- discovering and exploring ideas
- establishing a controlling purpose
- developing a workable plan

Earlier chapters have already discussed strategies you can use to analyze your rhetorical situation and to discover and explore ideas. This chapter will focus on the remaining two activities in the list: establishing a controlling purpose and developing a workable plan. It will also present a number of strategies for effective drafting.

UNDERSTANDING THE PROCESS OF PLANNING

You may find it helpful to think of planning as involving cycles or waves of "play" and "work." When you are discovering and exploring ideas, for example, you are in a sense playing. When you freewrite, loop, brainstorm, or cluster, your major goal is to be creative—to push your ideas as far as you can without worrying about how useful they may turn out to be later. Even more formal methods of invention, such as tagmemics or the topical questions, encourage mental play and exploration.

Most people can't write an essay based on a brainstorming list or thirty minutes of freewriting, however. At some point, they need to settle down to work, considering questions like those presented in the following guidelines.

Guidelines for planning your essay

1. What main point do I want to make in this essay? How does this main point relate to my purpose—to what I want this essay to *do* for readers?
2. Who might be interested in reading this essay?
3. How might my readers' expectations influence the form and content of this essay?
4. How can I structure my essay to communicate my ideas most effectively to readers?
5. What textual conventions might I need or want to draw on in this essay?
6. What kinds of examples and details should I use to support my main point?

Questions such as these require you to work on your ideas—to determine just what point you not only want to make but *can* make in your essay, to decide if you have all the information you need to support your assertions. These planning activities generally require more discipline than the informal or formal play of invention. Because much of the crafting of your essay occurs as a result of these activities, however, this work can be intensely rewarding.

Exploration

How do you typically plan when you are working on a writing project? Do you rely on written plans, or do you use other means to determine goals and strategies for your writing? How might you make your process of planning more efficient and productive? Freewrite for five or ten minutes in response to these questions.

ESTABLISHING A CONTROLLING PURPOSE

The planning activities discussed in this chapter are *goal-oriented* activities. You can't establish a controlling purpose or a workable plan for your essay without having at least a tentative sense of the goals you hope to achieve by writing. These goals may change as you work on your essay, but they represent an important starting point or preliminary set of assumptions for guiding your work in progress.

How can you determine appropriate goals for your writing? Whether you are writing a brief memo to your supervisor, a term paper for your history class, or an application for your first job, you can best understand and establish goals for writing by analyzing your rhetorical situation. This process, described in Chapter 3, encourages you to ask questions about the elements of rhetoric: writer, reader, and text. Once you have analyzed your rhetorical situation, you should have a clearer understanding not only of your reasons for writing but also of the most appropriate means to communicate your ideas to your readers.

Your *controlling purpose* for an essay reflects your essay's topic but differs from it in important ways. Unlike your topic, your controlling purpose is both action- and content-oriented. Your controlling purpose reveals not just what you want to write about but also the point you intend to make and the effect you wish to have on your readers. It is an *operational* statement of your intentions. Suppose that you are writing a guest editorial for your campus newspaper. "What are you going to write about?" a friend asks. "Library hours," you reply. You have just stated your topic—the subject you're going to write about—but this statement doesn't satisfy your friend. "What about library hours? What's your point?" "Oh," you say, "I'm going to argue that students should petition the vice president for academic affairs to extend the library hours. Current hours just aren't adequate." This second statement, which specifies not only the point you want to make but also its desired effect on readers, is a good example of a clearly defined controlling purpose.

If you and your friend had time for a longer conversation, you could elaborate on the rhetorical situation for this guest editorial. You could discuss your own intentions as the *writer* more clearly, and you could note how you intend to anticipate and respond to *readers'* needs and interests. Your friend might be able to give you good advice about how your *text* should reflect one of the most important features of editorials—brevity. Your friend may be too busy for such extended conversation, however. Your controlling purpose briefly and succinctly summarizes the goals you have in writing this guest editorial.

An effective controlling purpose limits the topic you will discuss and helps you clarify and organize your ideas. Once you have established a controlling purpose, you should be able to develop a number of questions that can guide you as you work on your writing. Here are some of the questions you might ask in response to the controlling purpose in the previous example.

- What arguments will most effectively support my position?
- How can I focus my discussion so that I can make my point in the limited space typically given to editorials?
- Do I know enough about the reasons why current library hours are limited? Should I interview the director of the library or the vice president for academic affairs?
- Am I correct in assuming that other students find current hours a problem? Should I talk with a number of students to get their reactions to this problem?
- Should I conduct research to find out how our library's hours compare with those at similar colleges and universities?
- Assuming that current library hours are a problem—and I'm convinced they are—how can I persuade students to go to the trouble of signing a petition?
- Given my rhetorical situation, how formal should my language be? And what image of myself should I try to create in my editorial?

As this example indicates, establishing a controlling purpose encourages you to be pragmatic and action-oriented. You may revise your controlling purpose as you work on your essay. In the meantime, you can use the insights gained by formulating and analyzing your controlling purpose to set preliminary goals for writing.

Once you have established a preliminary controlling purpose, you can test its effectiveness by asking yourself the questions listed in the following guidelines. (Or you may wish to discuss these questions with classmates or members of your writer's group.) If you can't answer one or more of these questions, you may not have analyzed your rhetorical situation carefully enough or spent adequate time discovering and exploring ideas.

Guidelines for evaluating your controlling purpose

1. How clearly does your controlling purpose indicate what you want this essay to do or to accomplish? Is your controlling purpose an *operational* statement of your intentions, not just a description of your topic?
2. How realistic are these intentions, given your rhetorical situation, the nature of the assignment, and your time and page limitations?
3. How might you better prepare yourself to accomplish this controlling purpose? Should you do additional reading or clarify your ideas by talking with others or by spending more time discovering and exploring ideas?
4. In what ways does your controlling purpose respond to your understanding of your rhetorical situation, particularly the needs and expectations of your readers?
5. What questions, like those listed on page 135, does your analysis of your controlling purpose indicate that you need to consider as you work on your writing?

Application

For an essay you are writing for this or another course, use the questions listed here to evaluate your current controlling purpose. Then write a paragraph evaluating the effectiveness of your controlling purpose and suggesting ways to improve it. Finally, list the questions your evaluation indicates you need to consider as you work on this essay.

In some cases, you may be able to establish a controlling purpose early in your writing process. In many other instances, however, you will have to nurture your controlling purpose by thinking about your rhetorical situation and by employing informal and formal methods of invention. You will, in other words, think and write your way into understanding what you want to say. You may even decide that the best way to determine your controlling purpose is to write a rough draft of your essay and see, in effect, what you think about your topic. This strategy, which is sometimes called *discovery drafting,* can work well as long as you recognize that your rough draft will need extensive analysis and revision.

You should always view any controlling purpose as preliminary or tentative, subject to revision. After you have worked on an essay for a while, your controlling purpose may evolve to reflect the understanding you have gained through further planning and drafting. You may even discover that your controlling purpose isn't feasible. In either case, the time you spend thinking about your preliminary controlling purpose is not wasted, for it enables you to begin the process of organizing and testing your ideas.

FORMULATING A WORKABLE PLAN

A plan is a written representation that enables you to explore and organize your ideas and establish goals for your writing. Plans can take many forms. Some writers develop carefully structured, detailed plans. Others find that quick notes and diagrams are equally effective. The form that a plan takes should reflect your own needs, preferences, and situation.

As mentioned earlier, writers don't always make written plans. A very brief writing project or one that follows clearly defined textual conventions (such as a routine inventory update for a firm) may not require a written plan. Nevertheless, as a college student, you will often find written plans helpful. Plans are efficient ways to try out your ideas. Developing a plan—be it a jotted list of notes or a formal outline—is also a good way to engage your unconscious mind in your writing process. Finally, many students find that by externalizing their goals, by putting them on paper or on-screen, they can more effectively critique their own ideas, an important but often difficult part of the writing process.

There is no such thing as an ideal one-size-fits-all plan. An effective plan is a *workable* plan—a plan that works for you. Plans are utilitarian. They are meant to be used—and revised. In working on an essay, you may draw up a general plan only to revise this plan as you write. Nevertheless, by enabling you to begin drafting, your first plan has fulfilled its function well.

BOBBIE'S PIZZA	PIZZA-IN-A-HURRY	PIZZA ROMA
$4.00 close limited hours delivery charge pizza OK but not great; little variety	$6.55 coupons crust thin and soggy tastes like frozen pizza	$6.10 best pizza! unusual sauce two kinds of crust more toppings

Figure 6-1

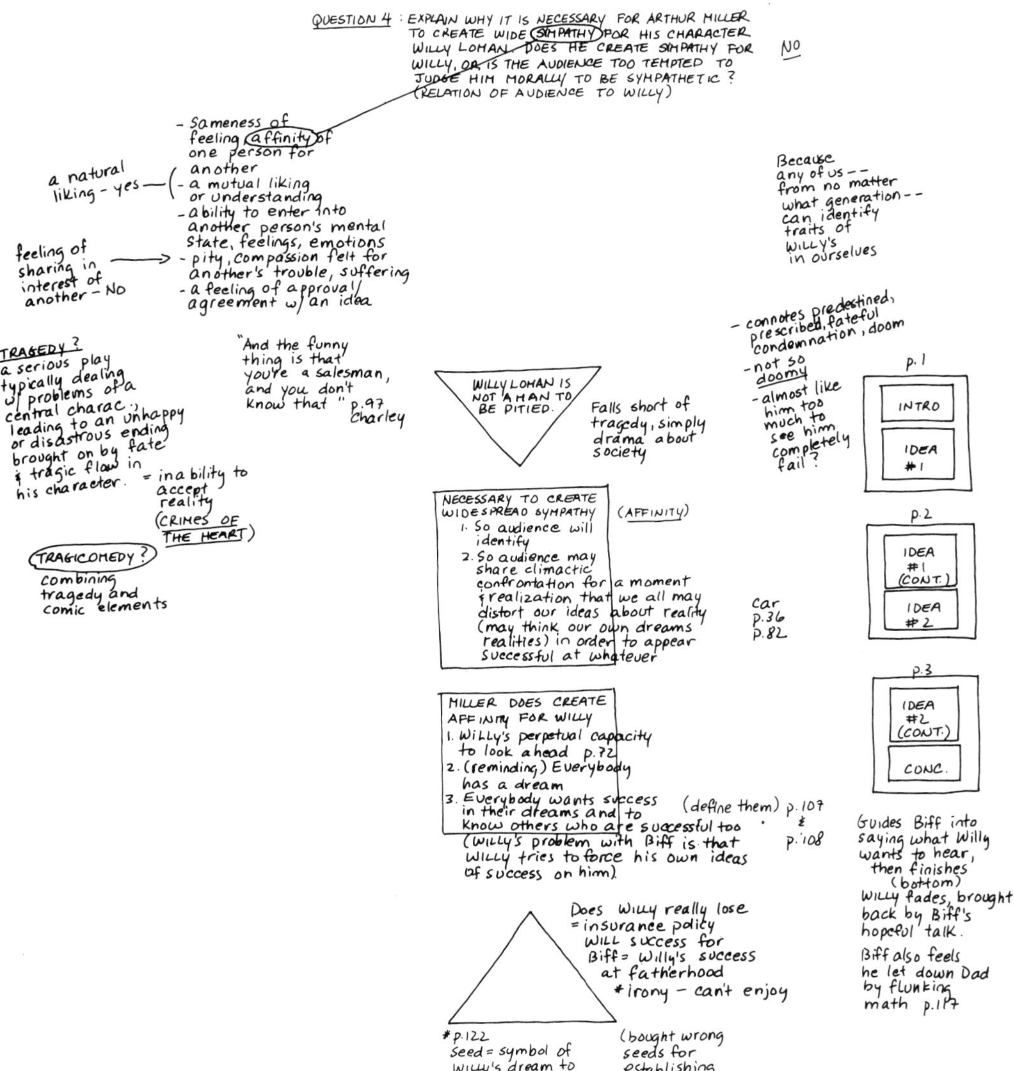

Figure 6-2

You may better understand how plans work by examining three students' actual plans. These plans vary significantly, yet each fulfilled the author's needs. The first plan (Figure 6-1 on page 137), is by Lisa DeArmand, a freshman majoring in business. It is a plan for a brief essay reviewing three popular pizza parlors near campus. As you can see, Lisa's plan, which consists of little more than a few notes about each pizza parlor, is both brief and simple. But in this case it was all that Lisa needed. Lisa had already analyzed her rhetorical situation, and she had recognized that the most effective way to organize her essay would be to compare the three restaurants. She also had detailed notes about these restaurants, including interviews with students, which she planned to use in her essay. Because Lisa had such a clear mental image of what she wanted to say and how she wanted to say it, she didn't need a complex or highly detailed written plan.

Now look at the second plan (Figure 6-2). This is a plan by Dodie Forrest, a junior English major, for a take-home midterm in an American drama class. This plan is much more complex than the one for the pizza parlor review. It includes two diagrams that helped Dodie visualize how the essay might be organized, several quotes from the play that Dodie thought were important, reminders to herself, definitions of terms, and many general comments about the play. Dodie's task was more complex than Lisa's, so it makes sense that her plan should be more complex. Her task was also more open-ended. The question that Dodie was required to answer was this: "Explain why it is necessary for Arthur Miller to create wide sympathy for his character Willy Loman in *Death of a Salesman*. Does he create sympathy for Willy, or is the audience too tempted to judge him morally to be sympathetic?" Dodie used her plan to help explore her ideas and to determine the best organization for her essay. Although probably no one but Dodie could develop an essay from the various diagrams and notes she created, the plan fulfilled Dodie's needs—and that's what counts.

Here is a third plan, this one by Dave Ross, a returning student intending to major in natural resource economics. Dave began by writing about the "feel" he wanted his essay to have, then developed a detailed plan.

This will be a personal essay about my experiences working at Urban Ore, a business that sells salvaged building materials. I want the reader to share my pleasure at working among all that great recyclable junk. The interesting "finds," the colorful characters, my own satisfaction at organizing the chaos. The essay should feel <u>crowded</u> with odds and ends, just like the salvage yard is: strange bits of description, stories, humorous observations. I guess "funky" is the word.

I. Description of the yard.

-- Among one-family underclass homes, rusting railroad tracks, corrugated sheet metal auto body shops: a weedy, dusty scrapyard surrounded by eight-foot cyclone fence, filled with doors, windows, kitchen cabinets, lamps, toilets, sinks, bathtubs, faucets, pipes, bricks, stoves, coils of wire.

-- A real business: this junk generates nearly $200,000 a year in sales to construction workers, contractors, or just weekend fixer-uppers.

II. People working there.

-- Joe, the owner: Urban Studies Ph.D., abstract painter, two-time candidate for mayor.

-- Webb, looks like Jerry Garcia but with a rhino's strength.

-- Charles, lives on brown rice and has a passion for snakes.

-- Vagrant cats and a German shepherd named Ripthroat who melts when you scratch his butt.

III. Me working there.

-- My first big job, organizing the windows and doors. First big rush of satisfaction: being able to tell a customer exactly where to find the bottom half of a double hung window, 36″ by 28″.

-- First Law of Urban Ore: "The more organized we are, the more we sell." But that's not the only reason I liked doing it. Bringing order out of chaos. An artist of the junkyard.

IV. Treasure Island: Found among the weeds and blackberry brambles: Art Deco bathroom tiles, mint-condition platform heels, bottles of all shapes and colors, a Three Stooges coffee mug (think of more).

V. Not all fun. Sometimes punishing work.

-- No electricity, heat, running water or toilet. Only one shack, crowded when it rains.

-- Winter: cold, stiff hands, wet gloves. Summer: pounding sun, dust.

-- rusty nails, metal or glass edges

-- hauling cast-iron bathtubs, six-burner ranges: hernia city!

VI. Conclusion: honest, constructive work and creative in its way. Great when a customer found just what he/she wanted--or something they'd never dreamed of.

```
    -- One evening, local skid-row types formed a band
with stuff they'd found lying around.  Played "Working
on the Chain Gang"--sounded pretty bad, but a lot of
spirit.  A certain strange beauty amid the disorder--
sums up Urban Ore for me.
```

Dave's plan is more detailed than Lisa's; it is also more clearly organized than Dodie's. Dave's approach to planning probably reflects his preference for detailed, well-organized plans. It also reflects the nature of the essay he had envisioned: he wanted to include such a profusion of material that a detailed plan would help ensure a coherent structure. Dave probably couldn't have worked efficiently from a freer, less clearly organized plan, like Dodie's; Dodie might find Dave's more structured approach equally difficult.

Plans play an important role in writing. They help you explore, organize, and try out your ideas; they also enable you to set goals for your writing. You might think of plans as notes, reminders, or directions that you write to yourself. No one else needs to be able to understand your plans, just as no one else needs to be able to shop from your grocery list. Through experimentation, you should be able to arrive at a style of planning that works for you.

Exploration

What kinds of plans do you typically draw up? Do you formulate detailed, carefully structured plans, or do you prefer to develop less structured ones? Do you use diagrams or other visual elements in planning? Can you think of one or more suggestions that might enable you to develop more useful plans?

Use these questions to think about your plans. Then spend ten minutes writing down your most helpful observations about them.

Group Activity

Meeting with a group of classmates, take turns reading your responses to the previous exploration. After each person has read, work together to answer these questions. (Be sure to appoint a recorder.)

1. What planning strategies do the members of your group most often employ?
2. How often do group members develop written plans? What kinds of plans do you most often develop? How formal and

detailed are your plans, for instance? Do group members often use diagrams and other visual means to plan their writing?

3. Did any group members suggest planning strategies that other members think they might like to experiment with? If so, briefly describe these strategies and explain why group members believe they might be useful.
4. Make a list of three conclusions about planning with which all group members can agree. Make another list of at least three suggestions on how group members can plan more efficiently and productively.

Be prepared to share the results of your discussion with your classmates.

DEVELOPING EFFECTIVE STRATEGIES FOR DRAFTING

Drafting—inscribing words on paper or composing at your computer—is only part of the writing process. You actually begin writing an essay when you first spend ten minutes freewriting or brainstorming in response to an assignment. Revision, too, often occurs before you complete a rough draft: if you make a list of possible titles for an essay, cross out two, and circle one as your best current choice, you have revised. Drafting is nevertheless an important component of the writing process, for it is through drafting that you create a text that embodies your preliminary intentions. Once you have a rough draft, you can begin the rewarding process of developing and refining your ideas through revision.

Overcoming resistance to drafting

When you first sit down at your desk or computer to begin drafting, it can be hard to imagine the satisfaction of completing a rough draft. Indeed, just picking up pen or pencil or beginning to type at the computer can seem impossible; suddenly you can think of a hundred things you'd rather do. All writers experience some resistance to drafting; productive writers, however, have developed ways to overcome this resistance.

Many writers rely on rituals, such as those described on pages 47 and 48, to help them deal with what Tom Grenier calls the "prewrite jitters." There are other strategies you can use to overcome resistance to drafting. If you've already spent time discovering and exploring ideas and making one or more tentative plans, you will have the reassuring knowledge that you're not starting from scratch. Reading through early notes and plans is a very effective way to begin a drafting session. You may find yourself turning hasty notes and fragments into full sentences or grouping them into paragraphs—drafting before you know it.

Another way to motivate yourself to start drafting is simply to remind yourself that you're only working on a draft; it doesn't have to be perfect. When you begin drafting, your initial goal should simply be to *get the words down.* If you can't think of a way to open your essay, for instance, don't try to do so; simply begin writing a section that you are ready to write. As you reread what you've written, you'll eventually discover an introduction that works for you.

Many writers find it helpful to discuss their ideas with others when they're having trouble getting started. If you do this, be sure to have pen and paper ready so that you can write down important points that come up in your discussion. If no one is available to discuss your writing, try composing a letter to someone you know and trust about your difficulties. Such a letter might begin like this: "Dear Mom, I need to draft a report for my biology class, but I just can't get started. I'm supposed to be writing about _______, but the only thing I'm sure I want to say about this subject right now is . . ." Before you know it, you're off and running!

Managing the drafting process

Once you get past the initial hurdle of getting started, you'll probably experience the drafting process as a series of ebbs and flows. You may write intensely for a short period, stop and spend time reviewing what you've written, make a few notes about how you might best proceed, and then draft again more slowly, pausing now and then to reread what you've written. The process of rereading your text as it develops is an important part of the drafting process. Research shows not only that experienced writers reread their writing often while drafting but that they reread with an eye toward such major concerns as the extent to which their draft responds to the needs and expectations of readers. Chapter 8, "Strategies for Successful Revision: Revising for Structure and Style," will present a number of strategies you can use to strengthen your ability to read work in progress. Here are some suggestions that should help make the *process* of drafting more efficient and productive.

Guidelines for drafting

1. Don't Try to Correct—or Perfect—Your Writing as You Draft.

When you are drafting, your goal should be to get enough words on paper so that you can reflect on and revise your writing. The easiest way to produce a rough draft is to work at an even pace so the momentum of drafting helps you move steadily toward your goal. Stopping to worry whether a word is spelled correctly or to fiddle with a sentence can interrupt your momentum and throw you off balance. Furthermore, most writers find that it's easier to delete unnecessary or repetitive material when they revise than to add new material. When drafting, your goal should be to get words written, not to make decisions more appropriate to revision. If you can't quite articulate an argument or formulate an example, write yourself a note and keep drafting. When you return to your draft, you can fill in these gaps and omissions.

2. Try to Keep in Touch with Your "Felt Sense," Your Awareness of What Your Writing Is Doing, as You Draft.

When drafting, you naturally attend to many things. You stop and reread the words on the page. You reflect about your topic and assignment; you think about your readers. If you are an effective writer, you look at what you have written not just to see what is on the page or on-screen but also what is *not* there or *might be* there. Some writers call this kind of attention to their writing as it develops keeping in touch with their "felt sense" as writers.*

You might think of "felt sense" as inspiration—and it is, in the sense that many writers, if interrupted while drafting, would find it difficult to articulate why they are writing a particular sentence or paragraph. The ability to develop "felt sense" does not require magical or mysterious gifts, however. Rather, writers develop "felt sense" when they are deeply immersed in their writing—when they are intensely involved not only with meaning (what they want to say) but with their entire rhetorical situation.

To develop and maintain your "felt sense" while drafting, you need to draft for long enough periods—an hour, minimally, but longer if possible—so that you can become immersed in your writing. And though you are of necessity writing words, sentences, and paragraphs, you need to keep one eye on such global issues as the appropriateness of your organization while drafting. Reflecting on con-

*As Professor Sondra Perl notes in "Understanding Composition" (*College Composition and Communication,* 31 [1980]: 363-69), "the term 'felt sense' has been coined and described by Eugene Gendlin, a philosopher at the University of Chicago" (365).

cerns such as these—asking yourself questions like "Where am I going; am I still following my plan?" or "Will readers be able to understand the example I just wrote; do I need to elaborate on it?"—and jotting down notes about your current thoughts are good ways to keep in touch with your "felt sense" as you draft.

3. When Drafting at the Computer, Remember to Take Advantage of the Full Capabilities of Your Word-Processing Program.

As discussed in Chapter 2, most writers find that the ease with which they can enter and change text on a computer makes composing less frustrating and more productive. But if you are using your computer only to enter and change text, you are not taking advantage of its full range of options. One useful word-processing feature allows you to write invisible notes that appear on-screen but not on your printed text. If you are drafting quickly and wish to maintain your momentum but want to remember a question or an idea, you can simply insert comments as you write and return to them in a later drafting session. Another common word-processing feature, the split screen or windows option, enables you to work with two texts at the same time. You might place a freewrite, outline, or plan in one window and write your draft in the other. Or you might keep your introduction in view as you write later sections.

You can employ your program's BLOCK and MOVE (or CUT and PASTE) option to move text from one file to another; this option enables you, for instance, to transfer sections of freewriting directly into your draft. You can also use this option to move paragraphs or sections within a file to see the effect of changes that you might wish to make. If you do so, however, save and copy the file that you are working on, making changes only on the copy. Be sure to title your files so you can follow your essay's development; you might title various drafts of an argument "arg. 1," "arg. 2," "arg. 3," and so on. Do not delete any of these files until you are sure that your essay is complete.

As you use these various features of your word-processing program, remember to protect your work by saving frequently, making backup copies of your drafts and printing hard copies in case disk or computer problems occur.

4. Develop a Repertoire of Blockbusting Strategies.

All writers experience moments when the words just won't come. Experienced writers don't just sit and bemoan their fate when this occurs. Instead, they draw on a repertoire of blockbusting strategies, including the following:

- Lower your standards. If you can't find the right words to express your ideas, get them down in any form you can. Write enough to remind yourself of the point you want to make; then keep going.
- Stop trying to draft and instead spend ten minutes employing your favorite inventional strategy, such as freewriting or brainstorming.
- Switch to some writing task that you can do. If you can't determine how best to organize the body of your essay, for instance, spend some time revising your introduction or reading some background material on your subject. Or switch to another project you need to complete.
- Change strategies. If you've been trying to develop a written plan for your essay, try diagramming, clustering, or doodling instead.
- Talk out your ideas. Find a friend to talk with, or talk into a tape recorder. Begin by saying, "I've been trying to work on my essay, but I'm blocked. What I want to do is . . ."
- Take a few minutes to describe the difficulty you're experiencing; then take a break from writing to do something that will give you satisfaction—exercising, cooking, or some other activity that you enjoy.

5. Learn When—and How—to Stop Drafting.

Ideally, you will come to a natural stopping point, a moment when you feel you've solved a problem you've been wrestling with or concluded the section of your essay you've been working on. At this point it's a very good idea to take a few moments to jot down not just what you think you've accomplished in that drafting session but also what you need to do when you return to your writing. You may also wish to pose a few questions to yourself. "What's the best transition into this next major section of my essay?" you might write. "Which of the examples I've gathered should I use next?" If you're like many writers, your subconscious mind will reflect on these questions and present appropriate answers to you when you next sit down to draft.

6. Draft When You're Not Drafting.

You can draw on your mind's subconscious ability to see connections and to resolve problems through the process of incubation. When you incubate ideas, you stop thinking consciously about them and just let them develop in your mind while you relax, sleep, or occupy yourself with other projects. As a result of this period of incubation, you will often spontaneously recognize how to resolve a problem or answer a question.

You can't draw on your mind's subconscious powers, however, if you don't build time for incubation into your drafting process. And don't confuse productive incubation with procrastination. Procrastination means avoiding or denying the writing process; incubation means recognizing and using the fluctuations of the process to your advantage.

Exploration

How do you typically draft an essay? How long do your drafting sessions usually last? What do you do when you run into problems while drafting? Could one or more of the suggestions presented here enable you to draft more productively? How might you best implement these suggestions?

Spend five or ten minutes freewriting in response to these questions.

Group Activity

Meeting with a group of classmates, take turns reading your responses to the previous exploration. After each person has read, work together to answer these questions. (Be sure to appoint a recorder.)

1. What drafting strategies do the members of your group most often employ?
2. How do group members overcome resistance to drafting? How long do drafting sessions typically last? How do you keep in touch with your "felt sense" while drafting?
3. Did any group members suggest drafting strategies that other members think they might like to experiment with? If so, briefly describe these strategies and explain why group members believe they might be useful.
4. Make a list of three conclusions about drafting with which all group members can agree. Make another list of at least three suggestions on how group members can draft more efficiently and productively.

Be prepared to share the results of your discussion with your classmates.

ORGANIZING AND DEVELOPING YOUR IDEAS

The noted British writer E. M. Forster once said: "How can I know what I think until I see what I say?" By working through drafts of work in progress, you gradually learn what you think about your subject. As you move from drafting to revising—an evolutionary process that proceeds differently with each writing project—you also become increasingly engaged with issues of style and structure. The question "What do I think about this subject?" becomes less important; the question "How can I best present my ideas to my readers?" more so.

This section presents guidelines for organizing and developing your ideas that respond to this second question. As you read these guidelines, remember that they are suggestions only. Remember also that your responses to these suggestions should be based on your understanding of your assignment, purpose, and rhetorical situation.

Guidelines for organizing and developing your ideas

1. Check to Determine if You Need to Expand or "Unpack" Code Words That Mean a Great Deal to You But Not to Your Readers.

If you've spent time employing various invention strategies, begin your drafting session by reviewing the material you've already generated, looking for ideas and details you can use in your draft but also ones that need to be more fully developed. Often in rereading these explorations (and early drafts of work in progress), writers realize that they've relied on what Professor Linda Flower calls "code words," words that convey considerable meaning for the writer but not necessarily for readers.* Learning to recognize and expand or "unpack" code words in your writing can help you develop your ideas so that their significance is clear to readers.

Here is a paragraph from a freewrite a student did when first asked to write an essay about what the word *family* means to her. Rereading the freewriting at the start of her drafting session, she recognized a number of code words, which she underlined.

> When I think of the good things about my family, Christmas comes most quickly to mind. Our house was filled with such <u>warmth and joy</u>. Mom was busy, but she was <u>happy</u>. Dad seemed less absorbed in his work. In

*Linda Flower, *Problem-Solving Strategies for Writing,* 4th ed. (Fort Worth, TX: Harcourt Brace, 1993): 147.

> the weeks before Christmas he almost never worked late at the office, and he often arrived with brightly wrapped presents that he would tantalizingly show us--before whisking them off to their hiding place. And at night we did fun things together to prepare for the big day.

Words like *warmth* and *joy* undoubtedly evoke many strong connotations for the writer; most readers, however, would find these terms vague. By looking for code words in her freewriting, this writer realized that in drafting she would have to provide readers with a number of concrete, specific details that enable them to visualize what she means.

2. Recognize the Importance of Sharing Your Controlling Purpose with Your Readers.

Earlier in this chapter, I emphasized the importance of establishing a controlling purpose for your writing. One way to help organize a draft is to share this controlling purpose with your readers. How you can most effectively do so depends on a number of situational factors. If you are working on a take-home essay examination for your history class, for example, you may wish to include a *thesis statement,* a single sentence that states the main idea of your essay, in your introduction. You may also decide to preview the main lines of argument you will use to support your position. After all, your instructor is going to be reading many essay exams—and reading not for enjoyment but to evaluate your understanding of the subject. You don't want your instructor to have to hunt for your main point.

In other situations, including a specific thesis statement in the first paragraph of your essay may not be necessary or even desirable. If you are writing an essay about what the word *family* means to you, you might decide that you don't want to reveal the main point of your essay at the start. Instead, you might begin with a specific, detailed example that will create interest in your essay and show, rather than tell, what *family* means to you.

Readers quickly become irritated if they feel they're reading unorganized, disconnected prose or if their expectations about how a certain kind of writing should be organized are violated. For these reasons, sharing your intentions with readers and providing cues about how you will achieve them is essential. By analyzing your rhetorical situation and by studying how others engaged in similar writing tasks have fulfilled this obligation to readers, you can determine strategies to use to keep in touch with your readers.

3. Take Advantage of Conventional Methods of Organizing Information When Appropriate.

When you begin drafting, you don't have to come up with an organizational structure from scratch. Instead, you can draw on conventional methods of organization, methods that reflect common ways of analyzing and explaining information. Suppose that you have been studying recent political and economic changes in Eastern Europe and must write an essay about some aspect of this topic. Perhaps in your reading you were struck by the different responses of Russian and Czech citizens to economic privatization. You could draw on conventional methods of *comparing and contrasting* to organize your analysis. Or perhaps you wish to discuss the impact that severe industrial pollution in Russia could have on the development of a Western-style economy. After *classifying* the most prevalent forms of industrial pollution, you could discuss the consequences of this pollution for Russia's economy.

As these examples indicate, your subject may naturally lend itself to certain methods of organization. In some cases, you may be able to use a single method of organization—such as comparison, definition, cause and effect, or problem-solution—to organize your entire essay. More often, however, you will draw on several methods of organization to present your ideas. In considering how you can best draw on conventional methods of organizing information, remember that you should not impose these methods formulaically or in an overly rigid manner. Begin thinking about how to organize your draft by reflecting on your goals as a writer and your rhetorical situation. If your analysis suggests that one or more methods of organizing information represent commonsensical, logical ways of approaching your subject, use them in drafting. But remember, form should grow out of meaning, not be imposed on it.

PLANNING AND DRAFTING COLLABORATIVELY

The preceding discussion of planning and drafting has encouraged you to take a pragmatic, flexible approach to these activities. The discussion of planning emphasized, for instance, that although all writers must plan at some point in their writing process, they may do so in diverse ways, depending on their task and situation. When you are writing alone, you are relatively free to choose how you wish to plan and draft an essay, and the process of making decisions about your writing can often remain implicit and fluid. But in general, people writing in teams or groups must relinquish some of the autonomy and flexibility they have when they write alone. Most of those who write collaboratively find that they gain more than they lose, however, for groups can be particularly effective in generating ideas and developing plans, and the final product of such efforts often reflects the enhanced quality of ideas that is one of the primary advantages of collaborative inquiry.

Nevertheless, the necessity of coordinating and evaluating a collaborative writing project, of attending to group process issues, and of negotiating such potential problems as differing schedules or word processing programs does pose special challenges for writers working in groups and teams. The following guidelines provide suggestions your group can use as you work to plan and draft a collaborative essay or report.

Guidelines for collaborative planning and drafting

1. Take Advantage of Multiple Roles and Perspectives in the Planning Process.

When you plan collaboratively, you naturally draw on group members' varied experiences and perspectives. Researchers who have studied collaborative planning have identified several strategies that can maximize the effectiveness of this process. After studying student groups engaged in collaborative planning, for instance, Professor Rebecca Burnett discovered that students in the most effective groups regularly assumed a variety of roles as they worked together. Sometimes they initiated ideas; in other instances they served as questioners, clarifiers, or recorders. As they worked together, they demonstrated a task-oriented, problem-solving approach to planning.

Good questions are the heart of the collaborative planning process. To encourage her students to ask productive questions—questions that challenge them to look at their topic from multiple perspectives—Professor Burnett developed the following "questions for collaborative planning." Your group may want to use these questions at various points in your planning; if you do so, remember that they are designed to stimulate discussion rather than to limit or constrain it.*

*Rebecca E. Burnett, "Benefits of Collaborative Planning in the Business Communication Classroom," *Bulletin of the Association for Business Communication* 53.2 (1990): 12.

QUESTIONS FOR COLLABORATIVE PLANNING

CONTENT QUESTIONS

- What more can we say about ___________?
- What additional information might we include?
- Have you considered including (excluding) ___________?
- Don't you think we should include (exclude) ___________?

PURPOSE/KEY POINT QUESTIONS

- What do you see as our main point (purpose)?
- What did you mean by ___________? Could you clarify the point about ___________?
- I can't quite see why you've decided to ___________. Could you explain why?
- I see a conflict between ___________ and ___________. How will we deal with it?

AUDIENCE QUESTIONS

- Who is our intended audience? Why is this the appropriate audience?
- What does the reader expect to read [learn, do]?
- How will our reader react to ___________? Connect ___________ to ___________?
- What problems [conflicts, inconsistencies, gaps] might our reader see?

QUESTIONS RELATING TO CONVENTIONS OF ORGANIZATION AND DEVELOPMENT

- How can we explain ___________?
- How will we organize (develop, explain) this?
- What support (or evidence) could we use? What examples could we use?
- How does this (convention) let us deal with ___________?

QUESTIONS RELATING TO CONVENTIONS OF DESIGN

- Have you considered using ___________? How do you think it would work?
- Couldn't we also try ___________?
- How does this [convention] let us deal with ___________?
- Why do you like ___________ better than ___________ as a way to present this information?

SYNTHESIS/CONSOLIDATION QUESTIONS

- How does ____________ relate to [develop, clarify] ____________?
- Given our purpose and audience, should we use ____________?
- Is there a conflict between using ____________ and ____________?
- Why do you think ____________ is a good way to explain our key point to this audience?

As you may have realized, the kinds of questions that Professor Burnett encourages writers engaged in collaborative planning to ask one another are also good questions for you to ask yourself when you are working alone. The experience you gain planning collaboratively can thus strengthen your general writing abilities.

2. Develop a Shared Vision of Your Task, But Be Prepared to Fine-Tune That Vision as Your Work Progresses.

As your group moves from exploring your ideas to planning and drafting, you need to develop a shared understanding of your task and of the strategies you will employ to respond to it. Such an understanding should grow naturally out of your discussions and should balance a concern for efficiency—for making decisions and assigning responsibilities—with the need to have full and candid dialogues on important issues. The nature of this understanding will inevitably change as your work progresses. Your group might begin your project assuming that you will present a strong argument for or against a specific issue, for instance, only to discover through reading and discussion that your views are more complex. Recognizing this shift in position immediately can save you valuable time and reduce frustration.

3. Supplement Individual and Group Memory with Such Written Communications as Summaries of Meetings and Individual and Group Progress Reports.

When your group is engaged in an intensive, task-oriented discussion, it can seem tedious to make written notes summarizing your meeting. Yet both individual and group memory can be surprisingly brief—and varied. To ensure that all group members have the same understanding of your group's decisions, take turns keeping notes during your meetings. Conclude each meeting by reviewing (and, if necessary, revising) these notes, which should then be reproduced and distributed.

To facilitate communication among members, you may find it useful to share regular progress reports. Members can also use such interim communications to raise questions about current research or writing and to note issues for group discussion. At several points during your project, you may find it helpful to devote all or part of a meeting to generating a group progress report that both summarizes what you have accomplished and lists tasks that still need to be completed.

4. Take the Time Needed to Nurture and Maintain a Collective "Felt Sense" of Your Writing as It Develops.

When writers are immersed in work in progress, they are able to draw on their "felt sense" to make decisions as they write. When you write collaboratively, you need to nurture and maintain a collective "felt sense." There are several strategies that your group can use to do so. You might begin some of your group meetings, for instance, by having each member freewrite for five minutes in response to questions such as these: "What are we trying to achieve in this essay or report? What is working well in our current draft? What seems rough or awkward?" Or you might each respond in writing to the guidelines for analyzing your rhetorical situation on page 59. Discussing group members' freewriting or their responses to questions about your rhetorical situation should enable you to articulate—and, if necessary, negotiate—a collective "felt sense" of your evolving text.

As your writing develops, you may occasionally find it useful to have one group member read your text aloud while others listen and make notes. The person reading should read the entire text without stopping; others should take notes quietly. Each group member should read his or her comments before you begin a general discussion of your responses. This activity can help you develop a holistic grasp of your text as it evolves and can generate responses you can use as you write and revise.

5. Avoid a "Cut and Paste" Approach to Drafting.

Collaborative writers often find it efficient to have group members take responsibility for drafting different sections of the text. This approach can work well—as long as you avoid a "cut and paste" approach to drafting. Such an approach assumes that once you have developed an outline or organization for your writing, individual members will work only on the portions of the text for which they are responsible. This approach has several negative consequences. The "cut and paste" approach to drafting makes it difficult for group members to develop a shared "felt sense" about work in progress. Group members may also develop such a strong sense of individual ownership of their writing that they resist changes to their drafts.

Although group members may initially assume responsibility for different sections of your text, you should begin not only to exchange but also to revise one another's drafts as soon as possible. (As when you work on your own writing, be sure to keep a clear paper trail of all changes made, in case you wish to return to an earlier version.) Doing so will encourage group ownership of your text and make the process of developing a coherent and unified style much easier. It will also give you a head start on revising the final draft of your essay or report.

6. Make the Fullest Use of the Electronic Technologies Available to You.

Electronic technologies, if available, can greatly simplify the process of writing collaboratively. Word-processing programs enable group members to reproduce and revise texts without the burden of frequent retyping and photocopying. If group members use the same word-processing program, you can exchange work in progress on disk; you can also use most programs' hidden-text feature as a means of commenting on work in progress.

With access to networked computers or E-mail, your options increase: you can send summaries of meetings, progress reports, and other communications, including drafts, electronically. Some networked computers have group authoring systems, software programs designed to facilitate the process of collaborative writing. If your computer lab has such a program, take the time to learn it; doing so will pay off in the long run.

7. Build in Regular "Reality Checks" Designed to Elicit and Resolve Any Difficulties Involving Your Group Process.

As the discussion of collaborative writing in Chapter 2 emphasized, whenever humans work together, interpersonal and group process problems can occur. If not addressed immediately, such problems can derail even a well-conceived, clearly organized group project. The best way to prevent such problems from occurring is to make regular "reality checks" a recurring feature of your group effort. To do so, reserve time in meetings to discuss your collaborative process in a friendly, nonevaluative manner. You might conclude meetings, for instance, by freewriting about your group effort or about that particular meeting. Or you could respond to specific questions, such as the following:

- What in our group process is working well?
- How might we improve the productivity and efficiency of our collaborative effort?
- What about our group effort do I find personally satisfying?
- What changes might make the group process more satisfying for me?
- Are there any issues, such as workload or deadlines, that we need to discuss and perhaps renegotiate?

If you regularly take time to share your freewriting or responses to questions such as these, your group should be better prepared to identify and resolve interpersonal or group process problems.

This chapter has discussed a number of strategies for successful planning and drafting. Throughout, it has emphasized the importance of being self-reflective, flexible, and goal-oriented and of asking yourself questions before and while you write. Whether you write alone or with others, writing is a process of thinking critically and making choices, trying these choices out, and then evaluating their effects and making necessary adjustments. Planning and drafting are essential components of this process.

Activities for Thought, Discussion, and Writing

1. Think of a time when you simply couldn't get your writing going. What did you do to get beyond this block? How well did your efforts work—and why? After reflecting on your experience, write an essay (humorous or serious) about how you cope with writer's block.
2. Choose a writing assignment (for this or another class) that you have just begun working on. After reflecting on your ideas, develop and write a workable plan for this essay. While drafting the essay, keep a record of your activities. How helpful was your plan? Was it realistic? Did you revise your plan as you wrote? What can you learn about your writing process from this experience? Be prepared to discuss this experience with members of your group or with your class.
3. Interview a person working in the field you hope to enter after graduation to discover how he or she plans and drafts on-the-job writing. How do your interviewee's profession and work schedule influence his or her preferred methods of planning and drafting? How often does this person write alone or as a member of a group or team? What does this person see as the advantages and disad-

vantages of planning and drafting alone versus doing so as part of a team or group? Does the person rely on any technological aids to make these activities easier, such as using a tape recorder for dictation or using a computer network? Write an essay summarizing the results of your interview.

CHAPTER 7

STRATEGIES FOR SUCCESSFUL REVISION: MANAGING THE REVISION PROCESS

In the broadest sense, revision occurs throughout the writing process. If you write a tentative first sentence for an essay, decide that it doesn't work, and cross it out, you have revised. Although revision can occur at any time, you will probably revise most intensively after you have written a rough or working draft. At this point, you have managed to articulate at least a preliminary statement of your ideas. Revision challenges you to look at this statement from a dual perspective. You must read your work with your own intentions in mind. But you must also read your work from your reader's perspective.

Reading thus plays a crucial role in revision. When you read over your work, you attempt to discover strengths you can build on and weaknesses you can remedy. Consequently, you must think about not just what is actually in your text but also what is *not* there and what *could be* there. You must read the part (the introduction, say, or several paragraphs) while still keeping in mind the whole.

As a writer, you should have a healthy respect for the demands of revision, but you should not be overwhelmed by it. By studying both your own writing process and the products of that process (the essays and other papers that you write), you can develop an awareness of your strengths and weaknesses that will enable you to revise both more effectively and more efficiently. As you write and revise, and as you read and respond to the work of others, you'll discover that revising can be the most rewarding part of the writing process. For when you revise, you have the satisfaction of bringing your ideas to completion in an appropriate form.

Here is how Ellen Goodman, a popular columnist, describes the satisfaction of revising.

> What makes me happy is rewriting. In the first draft you get your ideas and your theme clear, if you are using some kind of metaphor you get that established, and certainly you have to know where you're coming out. But the next time through it's like cleaning house, getting rid of all the junk, getting things in the right order, tightening things up.
>
> *ELLEN GOODMAN*

You don't have to be a professional writer to feel the same sense of satisfaction. Christine Hoekstra, a junior English major, describes her experience of revision in very similar terms.

> Revision is an extremely important part of the writing process for me now. It's really the part of writing where I feel the bulk of the work gets done--where the story takes shape, the essay is created. I couldn't imagine writing without revising.
>
> CHRISTINE HOEKSTRA

For writers like Ellen Goodman and Christine Hoekstra, revision is the heart of the writing process.

Chapters 7 and 8 will enable you to experience the satisfaction of successful revision. Chapter 7 focuses on revision as a process, an activity. It answers questions like the following:

- What is revision? How does revision differ from proofreading or correcting mistakes?
- How can I use responses to work in progress to help establish priorities for revision?
- How can I learn to read work in progress more objectively so that I can recognize strengths and weaknesses?
- How can I develop strategies that will help me revise more effectively and efficiently?

Chapter 8 discusses ways to improve your essay's structure and style. Together, Chapters 7 and 8 should help you understand why writers like Ellen Goodman and Christine Hoekstra can't imagine writing without revising.

REVISING THROUGH RE-VISION

You can learn a great deal about revision just by considering the word itself. *Revision* combines the root word *vision* with the prefix *re-*, meaning "again." When you revise, you "see again": you develop a new vision of your essay's shape or of the most emphatic way to improve the flow of a paragraph to help readers understand your point.

Revision is very different from proofreading, an activity that generally occurs at the end of the writing process. When you proofread, you are concerned mainly with correctness. Does your essay have any errors of grammar, punctuation, or usage? Are your words spelled correctly? Do you need to fix any obvious problems of word choice or sentence structure? Proofreading is the tidying up that concludes the writing process.

Exploration

Using the preceding distinction between revision and proofreading, think back to some of your writing experiences. When, and for what reasons, have you revised your work rather than just proofread it? How would you characterize these revision experiences? Were they satisfying? Frustrating? Why? Freewrite for five or ten minutes about these revision experiences.

Unlike proofreading, revision is most typically a process of discovery where much more than correctness is at stake. Because it generates growth and change, revision sometimes requires you to take risks. Often these risks are minor. If you spend three or four minutes attempting to find just the right words to clarify an idea, for instance, you've only lost a little time if you're unsuccessful. Sometimes, however, when you revise, you make large-scale or global decisions with potentially more significant consequences.

After writing the first draft of an essay, for instance, Matt Brown, a freshman physics student, met with members of his group to talk about his writing. He was unhappy with his draft, which argued that newspaper carriers work too hard and are paid too little, given the difficulty of their work. The members of his group were sympathetic to Matt's problems, but they couldn't help teasing Matt a bit. After all, how serious are a newspaper carrier's problems in the overall scheme of things?

Gradually, Matt recognized that he needed to take a different approach to his material. He realized that he could more effectively encourage his readers to empathize with carriers by writing a humorous essay, one that pointed out the problems carriers face but did so in a lighthearted manner. Once he made this decision to revise his approach to his topic, Matt found that he was able to write and revise more quickly with much less frustration. In his case, taking the risk of trying a new approach paid off.

BENEFITING FROM RESPONSES TO WORK IN PROGRESS

As Matt Brown's experience indicates, you can draw on the responses of others to help you re-see your writing. Talking with others about your writing can also provide crucial social support. You may write alone a good deal of the time, but writing does not have to be a lonely process.

When you ask others to respond to your writing, you are asking for feedback. Sometimes students confuse feedback with criticism. When you give writers feedback, you are attempting to help them see their writing in fresh and different ways. Providing feedback is thus not a negative process, and its goal is not to criticize but to help writers gain additional perspectives on their writing.

Responses to work in progress can take a number of forms. Sometimes you may find it helpful to ask others to describe your writing for you. In *Sharing and Responding,* Professors Peter Elbow and Pat Belanoff present a number of questions you can use to elicit descriptive responses to work in progress:*

> *Sayback:* Ask readers: "Say back to me in your own words what you hear me getting at in my writing."
>
> *Pointing:* Ask readers: "Which words or phrases stick in mind? Which passages or features did you like best? Don't explain why."
>
> *Summarizing:* Ask readers: "What do you hear as my main point or idea (or event or feeling)? And the subsidiary ones?"
>
> *What's Almost Said or Implied:* Ask readers: "What's *almost* said, implied, hovering around the edges? What would you like to hear more about?"
>
> *Center of Gravity:* Ask readers: "What do you sense as the source of energy, the focal point, the seedbed, the generative center for this piece?"

*Peter Elbow and Pat Belanoff, *Sharing and Responding* (New York: Random House, 1989): 64–66.

On other occasions, you may find more analytical responses helpful. You might ask readers to comment on the organization of your essay or the extent to which it attempts to anticipate and respond to the needs and interests of readers. Or you might ask readers to play what Professors Elbow and Belanoff call "believing and doubting."

> *Believing and Doubting:* Ask readers: "Believe (or pretend to believe) everything I have written. Be my ally and tell me what you see. Give me more ideas and perceptions to help my case. Then doubt everything and tell me what you see. What arguments can be made against what I say?"

How can you determine what kind of feedback would be most helpful to you? If you think commonsensically about your writing—about where you are in your composing process, how you feel about your draft, and the kind of writing you are working on—you can make appropriate decisions. If you have just completed an early and rough draft of an argument, for instance, you might find descriptive feedback most helpful. After you have worked longer on the essay, you might invite more analytical responses.

As a student, you can turn to many people for feedback. Some of these individuals, such as your instructor and classmates, can approach your writing as insiders. They know the assignment you are working on and the standards for evaluation. Others, such as your writing assistant, friends, or family members, must approach your writing as outsiders. The differences in the situations of these potential respondents will influence how they respond; these differences should also influence how you use their responses. No matter who the person responding to your writing is, you must ultimately decide how to interpret and apply his or her comments and criticisms.

Friends and family members

You can certainly ask friends and family members to read and respond to your writing, but you should understand the strengths and weaknesses they bring as readers. One important strength is that you trust them—otherwise, you wouldn't ask them to read your writing. Unless you spend time filling them in, however, friends and family members won't understand the nature of your assignment or your instructor's standards for evaluation. This lack of knowledge, as well as their natural desire to see you do well, may cause them to be less critical of your work than other readers might be.

Despite these potential problems, friends and family members can provide useful responses to work in progress. When you are considering getting such responses, keep these suggestions in mind.

Guidelines for responses from friends and family

- Choose the person you ask to read your work carefully. Is this person a competent writer? Have you benefited from this person's response in the past?
- Recognize that this person can't fully understand the assignment or situation, even if you take some time to explain it. Take this lack of knowledge into consideration when evaluating his or her comments.
- Draw on family members' and friends' strengths as outsiders. Rather than asking them to respond in detail to your essay, for instance, ask them to give a general impression or a descriptive response. You might also ask such readers to tell you what they think is the main idea or controlling purpose of your essay. If they can't identify one, or if their understanding differs substantially from your own, you've gained very useful information about your essay.
- Ask your friends or family to read your work aloud to you *without having first read it silently themselves.* When you read your own work, you unconsciously compensate to reflect your intentions. Listening to someone else read your work can help you hear problems that you couldn't detect through more conventional analysis. If your reader falters over a phrase or has to read a sentence several times before it makes sense, that may indicate a problem of style or logic.
- Don't rely solely on the response of a friend or family member. Try to get at least one other informed response to your work.

Classmates

If you have been getting responses to your writing from fellow students, you know how helpful their reactions and advice can be. Here is a comment by education major Karen Boaz about her experience with peer response:

> At first, I was wary of peer response to my writing. I was afraid of criticism and of exposing something as personal as writing to my classmates. Peer response turned out to be one of the most valuable aspects of my writing class. The members of my writing

group were genuinely interested in my ideas, and they gave responses and suggestions I could really use.

Because your classmates know your instructor and the assignment as insiders, they can provide particularly effective responses to your writing. Students participating in writing groups typically form strong bonds; they genuinely want group members to do well, to develop as writers. Yet group members can often read work in progress more objectively than family members and friends can. When student writing groups function well, they provide a helpful balance of support and constructive criticism.

To ensure that *your* writing group works well, follow these guidelines.

Guidelines for responses from your writing group

ADVICE FOR WRITERS

- Learn to distinguish between your writing and yourself. Try not to respond defensively to suggestions for improvement, and don't argue with readers' responses. Instead, use these responses to gain insight into your writing.
- Prepare for group meetings by carefully formulating the questions about your work that you most need to have answered.
- Always bring a *legible* draft to class.
- Be sure that the draft you bring is a working draft, not a jumble of brainstorming ideas, freewriting, and notes.
- Provide information that will enable readers to understand your goals for your writing. If you are addressing your essay to a specific group of readers—members of a certain organization, for example, or readers of a particular magazine—inform classmates about your rhetorical situation.
- Remember that your fellow students' responses are just that: responses. Treat your readers' responses to your essay seriously, for they are a potentially powerful indication of the strengths and weaknesses of your essay. But maintain your own authority as the writer. What all this means, finally, is that your readers' responses may be useful evidence about the effectiveness of your essay, but you must always decide how to interpret these responses—what to accept and what to reject.

ADVICE FOR READERS

- Follow the golden rule: respond to the writing of others as you would like them to respond to your work.

- Don't attempt to "play teacher." Your job is not to evaluate or grade your classmates' writing, but to respond to it.
- Take your cue from the writer. If the writer asks you to summarize an essay's main point, don't launch into an analysis of its tone or organization.
- Remember that the more specific and concrete your response is, the more helpful it will be.

You don't need to be an expert to provide helpful responses to work in progress. You simply need to be an attentive, honest, supportive reader.

Group Activity

Take five minutes to think about responses to your work that you have received from classmates. Freewrite for five or ten minutes about these experiences, and then draw up a list of statements describing the kinds of responses that you have found most helpful in the past.

Bring this list to class, and meet with a group of classmates. Begin by having each group member read his or her list. Then, working together, write a series of suggestions for helpful peer response. (You can draw on comments made in this chapter, but if you do, use your own words to state your suggestions.) Have one student record your group's suggestions. You may wish to copy these recommendations and distribute them to group members to guide future peer responses.

Writing assistants (peer tutors)

When students go to a campus writing center, they sometimes misunderstand the writing assistant's role and situation. They may regard writing assistants as editors trained to correct their writing. Or they may consider writing assistants to be faculty aides standing in for "real" instructors who are unavailable or too busy to meet with students. Neither view is accurate.

Writing assistants are neither editors nor substitute instructors. Rather, writing assistants are good writers who work well with other students. Like your classmates, your writing assistant's main job is to *respond* to your writing, not to analyze or critique it extensively. But unlike your classmates, your writing assistant has been formally trained in peer response methods. Because writing assistants work with many students, they have also read and responded to a broad range of writing.

Before you meet with a writing assistant, you should reread your writing and identify some goals for your conference. Then when you meet with your writing assistant, discuss these goals. You may also want to provide background information about your assignment. Finally, don't expect your writing assistant to do your work for you—the writing assistant's job is to respond and advise, not to correct or rewrite your essay.

Your instructor

Because your instructor is such an important reader for your written assignments, you want to be certain that you make good use of any written comments he or she provides. Use the following suggestions to help yourself benefit fully from these comments.

Guidelines for using your instructor's responses

- Read your instructor's written comments carefully. They are the clearest, most specific indication you have of the degree to which you have fulfilled the assignment.
- Read your instructor's comments *more than once.* When you first read them, you'll be reading mainly to understand your instructor's general response to your writing. That's a useful reading but does little to help you set goals for revision. Later, read the comments again several times. In these later readings, see if you can use these comments to help you establish priorities for revision.
- Recognize the difference between your instructor's local and global comments. Local comments indicate specific questions, problems, or errors. For example, *awkward sentence* is a local comment indicating some stylistic or structural problem with a specific sentence. Global comments address broader issues, such as your essay's organization or the effectiveness of your evidence. The global comments in particular can help you set large-scale goals for revision.
- Meet with your instructor if you don't understand his or her comments. Even if you do understand the comments, you may wish to meet to discuss your plans for revision.

Friends, family members, classmates, writing assistants, instructors—all can provide helpful responses to work in progress. None of these responses should take the place of your own judgment, however. Nor should you automatically accept responses (whether criticism or praise) as accurate. Your job as the writer is to *interpret* and *evaluate* these responses, using them along with your own assessment of your rough draft to establish goals for revising.

BUILDING OBJECTIVITY TOWARD WORK IN PROGRESS

As the person who must finally evaluate your own writing as well as interpret the responses of others, you need to develop strategies for objectively viewing your own work in progress. Building such objectivity enables you to achieve the distance necessary to make the hard decisions that revision sometimes requires. The following suggestions should help you develop this objectivity.

Guidelines for revising objectively

1. Plan at Least a Short Break Between Writing and Revising.

It's difficult to critique your rough draft if you've just finished composing it. Your own intentions are still too fresh for you to be able to read your words as they are, not as you intended them to be. Student Audrey Meier, for instance, wrote in her journal about the importance of letting work in progress "sit a while":

> I can only do so much good thinking and writing at any one time. I need to work as hard as I can for a reasonable amount of time -- say, two to three hours. But then I need to let go, shift gears. I call this the "baking" part of my writing process -- it's when I put papers in my mental oven for a while. The result is almost always a better paper.

2. Prepare Mentally for a Revising Session.

Taking a break from your essay before revising can help you distance yourself from work in progress. But you also need to consider how you can best prepare for—and begin—revising. You may find it helpful to review your assignment and your rhetorical situation before you reread your draft. As you do so, ask yourself questions like these:

- To what extent does my draft respond to this assignment?
- To what extent does my draft respond to my rhetorical situation as I have analyzed it?

- What state is my draft in? In other words, how rough or near completion is my draft?
- What goals should I establish for this revising session, and how should I fulfill them? What should I work on first?

By preparing mentally before you begin revising, you will make the most efficient and most productive use of your time.

3. Revise Work in Progress from Typed or Printed Copy.

We all grow used to our own handwriting, no matter how awkward or homely our scrawl. Even the letters on a computer screen can become overfamiliar after staring at them for hours while drafting. Perhaps for this reason, you, like many writers, may find that you're less critical of handwritten or electronically displayed texts than you are of typed or printed drafts. To counteract this tendency, you may find it helpful to type your essays or print them out as you write and revise. (If you compose at the computer, you're one step ahead.) Once your words appear in type, you can often see problems that were invisible before. Revising from typed or printed copy can not only help you detect local stylistic problems but can also help you recognize global problems of organization and development.

Although some writers prefer to revise on-screen, many people find it easier to revise on hard copy, enter these revisions into the computer, and then print the results. Marsha Carper, a student who revises on the computer, describes this strategy as follows: "When I revise, I make the changes on the printout, then type them in and print another copy. I read this, then make more changes, and continue this process until I am satisfied with the product or I have run out of time." Whether you revise using a hard copy or working on-screen, be sure to save copies of all stages your essay goes through.

4. Use Descriptive Outlines to Help You "X-Ray" Your Draft.

Familiarity may not always breed contempt, but it can make it difficult for you to evaluate your writing objectively. To gain distance from work in progress, you may find it helpful to "x-ray" your draft by developing what Professor Kenneth Bruffee calls a "descriptive outline."* To construct a descriptive outline, indicate the content and purpose of each paragraph in your essay—in other words, what each paragraph in your essay *says* and what it *does* for readers. To illustrate how you might use descriptive outlining when you revise, here

*Kenneth A. Bruffee, *A Short Course in Writing: Composition, Collaborative Learning, and Constructive Reading,* 4th ed. (New York: HarperCollins, 1993): 51.

is an essay by Rosie Rogel exploring what the word *family* means to her. (She wrote this essay in response to activity 1 on page 131.)

MEMORIES

My earliest memories are in Spanish. This seems a bit odd to me because I no longer think in Spanish; English has long since prevailed in that department. But, nonetheless, scattered images of my family replay themselves word for word in my first language. It's always been soothing for me to hear my parents speak Spanish--those soft rolling R's can calm me even today. These early childhood flashbacks have acted as a basis for what my concept of a family truly is.

The word family causes my mind to flood with emotions and sensations straight out of my childhood. Images of my mother, the matriarch of the small kingdom she and my father chose to create, fill my mind. My mother's approval and support have always been very important to my sisters and me. When we were small and contemplating behaving poorly, one stern glance in our direction was (usually) enough to temper the three-girl storm threatening to break. I recall somersaulting down the grassy hill behind our home with my sisters, dizzy with delight at the incredible feeling of freshly cut grass against our skin. I remember warm summer mornings when I'd brush my grandmother's hair in the early morning sun. I'd stand on a chair, on the tips of my daintily painted pink toes. How I loved to brush those thick locks. Before the brush reached the ends of her hair, I'd pull it up and into the sun to admire the shimmering fan of black strands, lightly threaded with silver, that I had created. I remember my daddy trying to get me excited about my first day of kindergarten and how his strong, callused hand knitted softly in mine miraculously seemed to transfer his courage to me. These memories emerge from some sweet corner of my mind, whispering to me just what the word _family_ means. It means comfort, security, warmth, and happiness.

When I was small, my family was my entire world. As in most families, the threads of our lives are entwined together. I learned everything I know about relationships with other human beings from them. My interaction with them has been the foundation for my ability to relate to the rest of the world--whether I saw the world as good or bad largely depended on how my parents taught me to view it. Thanks to my parents, I saw the world as a beautiful garden with hundreds of flowers just waiting to be admired and examined--each one different and each one equally important.

My definition of the word _family_ stretches much farther than simply those people one lives with who are related (or not). As I got older, my family stretched to include close friends. To me, a family member is someone who loves me unconditionally. It makes almost no difference to me whether he or she is a blood relation. My definition of the word _family_ also includes the human race as a whole. We are family because we are here, together. I believe our humanity makes us family.

The word _family_, in every sense, is extremely important to me because of the huge impact our family (or lack of family) has on who it is we become. What we learn from the people who gave birth to us and raised us is something we'll carry with us always. Unfortunately, not everyone is lucky enough to be born among stable, loving families. There are those who are not, and entire communities are suffering because of it. This is where my far-stretching sense of the word _family_ comes in.

The concept of the family unit has, of late, been furiously discussed in the media and in politics. The traditional, "typical" American family doesn't really exist anymore. To me, whether a family has one mother or one father (or two mothers, for that matter) doesn't matter. If there is love, acceptance, and trust swirling around, then it qualifies as a family. With these basic human needs met, a child can grow up, perhaps remembering somersaulting sisters, black-silver strands shimmering in the sun, or a reassuring hand-hold, to make a family of his or her own.

ROSIE ROGEL

When Rosie Rogel asked members of her writing group to respond to this essay, they praised its vivid and moving examples, but they also indicated that the essay seemed to shift gears midway and that it covered quite a number of issues. To get a clearer sense of how her essay worked, Rosie decided to construct a descriptive outline. As she did so, she wrote comments she could use to establish priorities for revision; these appear in parentheses following her analysis of each paragraph.

Paragraph 1

What it says: This paragraph describes the importance of Spanish and of my earliest memories to my concept of family.

What it does for readers: This paragraph provides information readers need to know to understand my experience of family, and it emphasizes the importance of my early childhood experiences.

(I like the way this paragraph emphasizes the importance of my heritage, but I wonder if the last sentence could be stronger.)

Paragraph 2

What it says: This paragraph presents a number of images and examples of my family life.

What it does for readers: By presenting vivid and concrete images, this paragraph will, I hope, create interest in my family and give readers a sense of what my family was like when I was growing up.

(I like this paragraph; my writing group also said this was one of the strongest paragraphs in the essay.)

Paragraph 3

What it says: This paragraph discusses several issues, such as the importance of my family to my development as a person and what I learned from my family.

What it does for readers: This paragraph continues to give readers information about what family means to me.

(This paragraph could be more focused. Also, I had a hard time determining what this paragraph does for readers.)

Paragraph 4

What it says: This paragraph presents my definition of family.

What it does for readers: This paragraph presents a new element in my understanding of family. Since most readers are likely to think of family as including their parents, sisters, brothers, etc., this paragraph asks readers to expand their understanding of family.

(I can see that this is quite a jump from the earlier paragraphs; this must be one of the places where my writing group started to feel I was switching gears.

The early part of my essay is personal and concrete; this almost feels like it's from a different essay.)

Paragraph 5

What it says: This paragraph develops my argument that it's important to think of family as more than simply the people who are directly related to us. But it also goes back to the earlier topic of how much impact my immediate family had on me.

What it does for readers: ??

(I wanted this paragraph to bring together the early part of my essay, which focuses on my own experiences, and the expanded idea of family that I introduce in paragraph 4, but I'm not sure it really does this.)

Paragraph 6

What it says: This paragraph argues that the traditional American family doesn't exist.

What it does for readers: This paragraph raises a new issue and asks readers to agree with my position about this issue.

(Now that I'm summarizing each paragraph, I can see that this paragraph, like paragraphs 4 and 5, raises another new topic. Although the last sentence tries to remind readers of the first part of the essay, this paragraph doesn't really draw the essay together.)

After developing her descriptive outline, Rosie was able to see the kinds of shifts in purpose and tone that had concerned her readers. She also recognized that her draft attempted to cover too many issues; she couldn't both develop a rich and vivid portrait of her family and support several arguments about the nature and role of family in society today. By summarizing not only what each paragraph in her essay said but also what it did for readers, Rosie was able to establish priorities for revision.

Application

Choose an essay that you are currently working on, and develop a descriptive outline for each paragraph. Once you have done so, exchange essays with a classmate and construct a similar outline for your classmate's essay. After you have completed this activity, compare the outlines of your essays. To what extent do your outlines coincide? To what extent do they differ? Did this exchange enable you to better understand the strengths and weaknesses of your essay? If so, in what ways?

REVISION IN ACTION: A CASE STUDY

What kinds of changes do writers make as they revise? The following case study, which chronicles the development of an essay by Kira Wennstrom, a first-year biology major, should give you a clearer, more concrete understanding of how revision works.

Kira's assignment was relatively broad and open-ended; it specified only that Kira should write an essay describing some personal experience and explaining the significance of that experience. Kira had few problems coming up with a topic. During the previous summer she had cared for two children while their mother was in the hospital. The experience had taught her a great deal about herself and about the bond between parents and children. She wanted to explore her experience further and to share what she had learned with others.

Kira describes herself as a heavy planner, and her self-assessment seems accurate. She did much of the planning for this essay in her head, rather than on paper. She thought for several days about her experience, and she also discussed it with friends and classmates. By the time Kira sat down to write the first draft, reproduced below, she had thought through her ideas so carefully that she was able to write using only a brief list of major ideas as a guide.

Kira's first draft is reprinted here. Its paragraphs are numbered for ease of reference. Also included are some of the written comments that members of Kira's writing group made in response to her draft.

Kira's first draft

(1) While my friends swam and tanned at the lake, I ran a household with two incredibly rambunctious and mildly accident-prone children. However, I think in the long run my time was better spent than that of my peers.

1st ¶ seems a bit weak, Kira.

(2) When Josh and Timmy's mother had to go into the hospital, she asked me if I would be willing to stay with the boys until she could come home. I quickly accepted. However, the few days I had planned on became two weeks, and there was work and trouble and responsibility I never imagined.

Do you really want to emphasize these negative factors so strongly?

(3) Since the children were only five and eight, I couldn't leave them alone in the house; I had to be there or be with them 24 hours a day. In addition to the normal precautions of making sure I knew where they were, I also had to worry about their father. He and the boys' mother had divorced several years ago, and there were still problems with custody.

Nice concrete details in these ¶'s Kira, but do you need them all?

(4) I spent my days as a housewife: planning meals, doing laundry, cleaning house. I handled all the typical minor emergencies. There were scraped knees to be washed and bandaged, fights to be settled, Kool-Aid to be cleaned out of the carpet, and once or twice I had to rescue pots and pans from the sandbox to cook dinner.

The sentence structure flows smoothly here, & during the rest of the essay, too.

(5) My evenings were spent preparing meals and dishes and settling disputes as to who was going to bed when and whose turn it was to choose the TV channel. After things settled down and the kids were in their rooms,

I was finally left alone to read or watch the Tonight Show before I hit my own pillow, exhausted. However, my nights were seldom complete without being awakened to check out at least one scary noise or to deny a request for a midnight snack.

(6) I had agreed to care for the kids knowing that it wouldn't be all fun, but I never dreamed the amount of laundry two active children can go through. I did a load of wash almost every other day, and was just barely keeping up. I was also amazed by the complexities of working out a simple dinner schedule. There was no single entree that both boys liked. They would sooner have starved, I think, than eat anything that didn't come in a wrapper, a can, or a box. Gradually, as the days passed, however, I began to realize what it is about parenting that makes my mother's eyes bug out at the end of the day. I loved those children terribly.

whew—this feels abrupt!

(7) I discovered that perhaps the hardest part of parenting is the loss of privacy. I never had a moment to myself, completely to myself, when I could just let my mind catch up to the rest of me. Having always been used to spending hours alone and enjoying my own company, I found it incredibly difficult

sometimes to force a smile when one of the boys interrupted a quiet minute with yet another demand on my time. I learned to treasure the ten or so minutes of silent darkness between the time I shut off the light and the time I went to sleep.

(8) My own mother, whom I telephoned with great regularity, seemed to find enormous delight in the fact that I was going through the same thing that she had been trying (and failing) to explain for seventeen-odd years. She gave me marvelous advice and brilliant suggestions on how to cope with the whole mess and then, I am sure, hung up the phone and laughed her socks off in utter vindictiveness. But I can forgive her this, because although I didn't realize it then, what I was experiencing would prove invaluable.

(9) I look at mothers, especially mine, with better understanding now, with less scorn. I look at children with a little more appreciation. I use my time alone more carefully now; I spend it wisely, now that I know how crucial it is. Most of all, I value my freedom more highly than ever because I know what it is to lose that freedom. As much as I cared about those children, it's not time yet to give up my claim

Now that I've read your essay twice, Kira, I can see that you want to balance the work of caring for Josh & Timothy with your love of them. Develop more fully?

esp. nice sentence structure

your conclusion might have more impact if you helped readers to my life. I understand now how important it is to live for yourself before you live for anyone else.

understand how much you came to love Josh & Timmy.

Kira was fortunate when she began revising. Her first draft had many strengths which members of her writing group had acknowledged. But they had suggestions for improvement as well. A number of them commented in their closing notes to Kira that her abrupt shift in paragraph six to a strong statement of her love for Josh and Timmy confused them since it conflicted with her previous emphasis on all the "work and trouble" involved in caring for the two boys. This potential contradiction also made it difficult for Kira's readers to grasp the significance of her final paragraph; several commented that they weren't sure, finally, what point she was trying to make in this paragraph.

After Kira thought about her readers' responses to her draft, she met with a writing assistant to establish the following priorities for revision:

-- work on intro
-- most important: try to show more clearly why Josh and Timmy meant so much to me, despite all the work
-- see if all that housekeeping detail needs to stay; cut some?
-- play with style a bit

Although Kira's list is (quite appropriately) informal, it nicely identifies several ways that she could improve the focus, organization, and content of her essay. It's not possible to show all the stages that Kira's draft went through, for this process involved many scribbles, inserts, and crumpled papers. But the final draft, reprinted below, demonstrates that Kira's analysis enabled her truly to revise her essay, to "see again" how she could most effectively make her point. Here is Kira's revised essay with comments in the margin pointing out some of her most important changes.

Kira's final draft

THE BOYS OF SUMMER

(1) Few teenagers get the chance to be parents, and for those who do, it's usually too

late to change their minds. One summer, though, I was given the opportunity to become a mother--without the lifetime commitment.

New introduction gets the reader's attention.

(2) When Josh and Timmy's mother had to go into the hospital, she asked me if I would be willing to stay with them until she could come home. I quickly accepted, envisioning a few days of playing "mommy" to the kids whose babysitter I had been for about two years. However, my visions of happy homemaking paled when the few days became two weeks and the trouble and responsibility of being a parent began to hit home.

(3) Since the children were only five and eight, I couldn't leave them alone in the house; I had to be with them twenty-four hours a day. While my friends swam and tanned at the lake, I spent my days as a housewife: planning meals, doing laundry, cleaning house. I handled all the minor emergencies that seem to follow little boys around like shadows. There were fights to be settled, Kool-Aid to be cleaned out of the carpet, and once or twice pots and pans to be rescued from the sandbox to cook dinner.

Revised paragraph consolidates details on situation from three draft paragraphs.

(4) My days were whittled away with meals, dishes, and mountains of laundry. I did a

load of wash almost every other day and just barely kept up. I was also amazed by the complexities of working out a simple dinner schedule. There was no single entree that both boys approved of, and it was like walking hot coals to try to serve anything new. They would sooner have starved, I think, than eat anything that didn't come out of a wrapper, box, or can. Most of all, though, I missed my privacy. Because the children were so dependent on me, I never had a moment to myself. I sometimes found it very difficult to force a smile when one of the boys interrupted a quiet moment with yet another demand on my time.

Concise and balanced paragraph combines details on routine work from three draft paragraphs.

(5) As the days passed and I became more proficient at running my little household, I began to realize a very surprising thing. Despite the trouble they caused, despite the demands they made, my two charges were becoming very special people to me--people who needed me.

Paragraph prepares readers for the shift from responsibilities to emotions.

(6) I remember taking the boys to the beach one afternoon and buying them a corn-dog-and-soda lunch with Gummi worms for dessert. Josh, who was older than Timmy, loved the lake and delighted in swimming out just past the dock where the water was especially cool. Timmy was afraid to follow his

New dramatic scene shows readers Kira's deep feelings for the boys.

brother and sat beside me on the sand, sucking on his last Gummi worm and looking wistfully out to where Josh was laughing and diving. After half an hour of this, Timmy touched me on the arm and said, "Take me to Josh, Kira."

(7) "Are you sure, Timmy?"

(8) "Mm-hm. But hold on tight to me."

(9) So I held on tight to him, and we waded into Rainy Lake's cool green water. When we got out past the point where Timmy could touch bottom, he locked his arms around my neck and pressed his face against my shoulder, but he didn't ask me to take him back. As we neared the spot where Josh was playing, I called, and he swam over to us. We splashed each other and giggled, and Timmy clutched me with one hand and Josh with the other. Their bodies were slick like seals, warm against me in the chill lake water. Together we swam out to where none of us could touch bottom, and they held on to me to keep afloat. They trusted me to keep them safe, and I would have drowned before I broke that trust. I loved them.

(10) Because I loved them, the children had a hold on me like nothing else I know. Simply by going out to play each day, they gave me more hours of worry than I like to admit.

Every time one of them was late coming home, I imagined all the dreadful things that might be happening--an angry dog, a child molester, a car accident--until he walked through the door, perfectly safe and wanting supper. When one of them was angry or hurt, I hurt. They were children, and it's so hard to be a child sometimes. Almost as hard as being a mother.

Paragraph adds detail that helps clarify Kira's feelings.

(11) My own mother, whom I telephoned with great regularity, seemed to find enormous delight in the fact that I was going through the same things she had been trying (and failing) to explain to me for seventeen-odd years. She gave me marvelous suggestions on how to cope with the demands of my new family and then, I am sure, hung up the phone and laughed her socks off in utter vindictiveness. But I can forgive her this because, although I didn't know it then, what I was experiencing was invaluable.

Effective new transition connects paragraphs.

(12) I look at mothers, especially my own, with better understanding now, with less scorn. I look at children with a little more appreciation. I use my time alone more carefully now; I spend it wisely, now that I know how crucial it is. Most of all, I value my freedom more highly than ever because I know what it is to give up that

Conclusion now has greater impact and complexity.

freedom. As much as I cared about those children, it's not time yet to let others make such claims on my life. I understand now how important it is to live for yourself before you live for anyone else.

KIRA WENNSTROM

Kira's revision, I'm sure you'll agree, is successful. She combined and deemphasized the details about how hard she worked—details that misdirected some of her readers and were also somewhat repetitive. Kira added paragraph 10 to explain her feelings for Josh and Timmy. And the scene at the beach, another important addition, gave concreteness and immediacy to these feelings. The resulting essay is a penetrating exploration of the rewards, and the demands, of caring for children.

REVISING COLLABORATIVELY

As the preceding discussion emphasized, revision is primarily a process of discovery and change. Although you may revise more intensively and self-consciously as you approach your final deadline, revision occurs throughout the writing process. While working on the conclusion of an essay, for instance, you may suddenly see a more effective way to organize your major arguments. While the idea is still fresh in your mind, you quickly reorganize the body of your essay and then continue drafting your conclusion.

When you write collaboratively, the revision process generally needs to be more explicit, self-conscious, and public than when you write alone: you would hardly reorganize the body of a collaborative essay or report without consulting others in your group first. But what you lose in flexibility and autonomy you gain in other ways. Most notably, your group can draw on members' diverse perspectives to develop a richer, more detailed vision of your text's strengths and weaknesses. When your group meets to discuss alternative ways of organizing your essay, for instance, you can consider more options—and evaluate them more fully—than when you write alone. Group members can also function both as a sample audience for your writing and as a peer response and support group. And once you articulate a shared understanding of the changes that need to be made, you can distribute tasks according to individuals' strengths and interests.

One group member might agree to revise your essay's transitions so that they are more consistent and fluid, for example, while another rewrites the conclusion and a third checks all references to be sure they are accurate and in the correct form.

The following guidelines present suggestions your group can use as you revise a collaboratively written essay or report.

Guidelines for collaborative revision

1. Recognize That Interpersonal and Group Process Issues Are as Important as You Near the Completion of Your Project as They Are at the Start.

As your deadline approaches, your group will naturally become increasingly task- and product-oriented. That's fine, but to get the task done—to produce an effective essay or report—you need to remain sensitive to interpersonal and group process issues. In particular, you need to be able to distinguish between writing problems and those growing out of interpersonal clashes or ineffective group dynamics. As Professor Karen Spear observes in *Sharing Writing:*

> When groups bog down, it is frequently because members assume they have exhausted the task when it's more likely that they haven't developed a strategy for dealing with it. . . . The ability to step back from the immediate problem to examine group procedures, note evasions or abrupt changes of subject, encourage participation, express feelings, integrate various points of view, summarize, devise alternative approaches—these are the ways in which a group fulfills its tasks.*

2. Maximize Your Group's Resources by Drawing on a Variety of Revision Strategies.

There are a number of strategies your group can employ as you move from drafting to revising. Early in your writing process, for instance, you may trade initial drafts and revise one another's writing. This strategy, recommended in Chapter 6, encourages group ownership and "felt sense" of your text. But there are other strategies your group may draw on, depending on your situation and purpose. Once you have a complete draft of your essay or report, for instance, you may decide that all members of your group should revise a particularly important part of your text, such as the introduction or the conclusion, so that you can try out and evaluate a variety of approaches. At other times, you may choose to work together in group revision sessions. To do so, have one group member function as secretary

*Karen Spear, *Sharing Writing: Peer Response Groups in English Classes* (Portsmouth, NH: Boynton/Cook, 1988): 27.

while others suggest changes. (Access to a computer—or, better yet, networked computers—facilitates this process.) As your deadline nears, one or two members may take responsibility for a final revision to ensure consistency of style and tone. There is no one-size-fits-all way to approach the task of collaborative revision. Instead, your group should use strategies that are appropriate for your particular situation and purpose.

3. Remember the Importance of Keeping in Close Contact as You Revise Work in Progress.

However you negotiate responsibilities as you revise work in progress, develop ways to keep all group members thoroughly informed about the status of your text and the work that remains to be done. The closer you get to your final deadline, the more careful you need to be to ensure the fullest and most up-to-date exchange of information. Whether you use electronic technologies, photocopying, phone calls, meetings, or all of these, the time spent keeping in touch can prevent larger problems from developing.

4. Establish Explicit Goals for All Revision Sessions.

Whenever your group engages in revision activities, you should articulate specific, concrete goals; doing so will help keep you on track and enable you to make the best use of your time. If you agree to exchange rough drafts, for instance, you should decide whether members will simply comment on or revise one another's writing. Similarly, if you are engaged in a group revision session, you should begin by determining the issues you will focus on. As when you write alone, it is generally more efficient to consider global issues involving organization, focus, and content before spending time on such local concerns as sentence structure and word choice. Whether you are evaluating your current draft's organization or looking at the stylistic effectiveness of your essay's introduction, establishing clear goals will ensure a productive work session rather than an unfocused and frustrating free-for-all.

5. Develop Procedures You Can Use to Resolve Disagreements as You Revise Your Text.

As has been emphasized in earlier discussions of collaborative writing, when you write with others, you want to maximize productive conflict—the kind of conflict that enhances your group's creativity and effectiveness—but minimize interpersonal and procedural disagreements. It may make sense for your group to spend several hours exploring possible ways to reorganize your report. A two-hour argument about the stylistic effectiveness of your introduction is much less likely to be productive.

When does it make sense to encourage debate about work in progress, and when should you encourage—and perhaps even require—consensus? In part you can draw on common sense as you make decisions: the more consequential the issue you are discussing, the more sense it makes to encourage lengthy and freewheeling debate. But common sense is not always an infallible guide; for this reason, you may find it helpful to establish ground rules that members can refer to as you revise your collaboratively written text.

You might agree, for instance, that any member can call for a time-out if he or she feels that the discussion has become unproductive. During your time-out, your group should remind itself of the goal of your discussion, review your progress so far, set new goals—including, if necessary, a time limit—and then continue. Particularly when you are discussing such local issues as sentence structure and word choice, you may find it helpful to allow members to call for a vote on a particular issue that they feel has been adequately discussed. If several members have been arguing about the wording of a sentence, for instance, one might call for a vote on this question. If a majority agrees on one version, that would constitute consensus, and you would move to another issue.

If your group establishes these or other procedures, remember that your purpose is to encourage the fullest, most productive discussion of your options as you revise work in progress. If you take a rigid, legalistic approach to resolving disagreements, you risk creating or exacerbating interpersonal or group problems and stifling the kind of productive conflict that is one of the major benefits of collaborative writing.

Activities for Thought, Discussion, and Writing

1. To study your own revision process, number and save *all* your plans, drafts, and revisions for a paper you are currently writing. (You could also use materials from a recently written essay if you're between assignments.) After you have completed the paper, go back and review these materials, paying particular attention to the kinds of revisions you made. Can you describe the revision strategies that you followed? Can you identify ways for you to improve the effectiveness of this process? Your instructor may ask you to write an essay discussing what you have learned as a result of this analysis.

2. In her discussion of revision, Ellen Goodman said that for her, revision is "like cleaning house." Take ten or fifteen minutes to make your own list of possible analogies for revision. (Is revision for you like tuning a motor or pruning a plant, for instance?) Later, return to this list and decide which analogy best expresses your process of revising. Develop this analogy in one or two paragraphs.
3. Interview two other students in your class about their revision strategies. How do their revision strategies reflect their preferred composing styles? How are their strategies similar to and different from your own? How do these students *feel* about revising, and how do their feelings compare with your own? Can you apply any of the strategies they use in your own writing? What can you learn from these interviews about how revising works and about how you can improve your own revising process? Your instructor may ask you to write an essay summarizing the results of your interviews.

CHAPTER 8

STRATEGIES FOR SUCCESSFUL REVISION: REVISING FOR STRUCTURE AND STYLE

As the previous chapter observed, revision is a process of discovery, one that challenges you to "see again" your writing. When you revise—whether you are restructuring your essay, playing with word choice, or fine-tuning your sentence structure—you are always concerned with the creation of *meaning*. As you work to produce this meaning, you must balance two related objectives: self-expression and communication. When you revise, you attempt to articulate your own ideas as clearly and as fully as possible. If you hope to communicate these ideas to others, however, you must be equally attentive to the expectations and interests of your readers.

Revision is a demanding but rewarding process. Chapter 7 presented suggestions that should enable you to manage the process of revision more effectively and efficiently. Chapter 8 continues this discussion of revision, by providing strategies for improving the structure and style of your writing. These strategies are designed to help you evaluate, and then revise, your work in progress.

As you read this chapter, remember that decisions about structure and style, even about a single word, always require that you consider *context*. If you want to decide whether a particular sentence is awkwardly written, for instance, you must look not just at that sentence but also at the paragraph of which it is a part. From the moment you first begin thinking about an essay until you make your last revision, you must be an analyst and decision maker. Even though some decisions you make may seem minor, together they determine the character and the effectiveness of your writing.

ASKING THE BIG QUESTIONS: REVISING FOR FOCUS, CONTENT, AND ORGANIZATION

When you revise a draft, begin by asking yourself the big, important questions—questions about your essay's focus, content, and organization. These questions are big because they challenge you to consider the degree to which your essay has fulfilled its most significant goals. If you discover—as writers often do—that your essay has not achieved its original purpose or that your purpose evolved as you wrote, you will make major changes in your draft, changes that will significantly affect the meaning of your essay.

Asking the big questions first is a *practical* approach to revising. You will only waste your time if you spend half an hour revising a paragraph that you will eventually delete because it doesn't contribute to your essay's main point. Furthermore, once you are confident that the overall focus, content, and organization of your essay are satisfactory, you will be better able to recognize less significant, but still important, stylistic problems.

Use the questions in the following guidelines to assess the effectiveness of your draft's focus, content, and organization.

Guidelines for evaluating your focus, content, and organization

FOCUS

- What do I hope to accomplish in this essay? How clearly have I defined my controlling purpose? How have I communicated this controlling purpose?
- How does my essay represent an appropriate response to my rhetorical situation? If it is an academic essay, how does it fulfill the requirements of the assignment?
- Have I tried to do too much in this essay? Or are my goals too limited and inconsequential?
- How does my essay respond to the needs, interests, and expectations of my readers?

CONTENT

- How does my essay develop or support my controlling purpose? How does it fulfill the commitment stated or implied by my controlling purpose?
- What supporting details or evidence have I provided for my most important generalizations? Are these supporting details and evidence adequate? Do they relate clearly to my controlling purpose and to each other?
- What additional details, evidence, or counterarguments might strengthen my essay?
- Have I included any material that is irrelevant to my controlling purpose?

ORGANIZATION

- What overall organizational strategy does my essay follow?
- Have I tested the effectiveness of this strategy by outlining or summarizing my essay?
- What is the relationship between the organization of my essay and my controlling purpose?
- Is this relationship clear to readers? How? What cues have I provided to make the organization clear and easy to follow?
- To what extent does my essay follow the general conventions appropriate for this kind of writing?
- Could my introduction and conclusion be made more effective? How?

Only after you have answered these questions and used your answers to establish a general plan for revising should you focus on such issues as word choice and sentence structure.

To illustrate how you can analyze the effectiveness of your essay's focus, content, and organization, here is how one student, Todd Carpenter, used these questions to establish goals for revision. Todd was responding to the following assignment: "Write a two- to three-page argumentative essay on a subject of your own choice. Consider your instructor and your classmates the primary readers of your essay." Todd described his rhetorical situation in these terms:

> I am writing an argumentative essay for my composition class. I want to convince my readers--my instructor and my classmates--that our government should institute a national bottle law. Oregon is one of the nine states that currently have bottle laws, so most students in the class may already agree with me about this law's importance. (Since Oregon has had a bottle

bill for more than twenty years, students may not realize how important it is.) But because this is an essay for my writing class, I've got to present an unbiased view. Even if my instructor agrees that there should be a national bottle law, she won't give me a good grade unless I write an effective argument. In class, my instructor has stressed the importance of looking at both sides of the issue and presenting evidence for my views, so I'll try to do that here.

Here is Todd's rough draft.

WHY ISN'T THERE A NATIONAL BOTTLE LAW?

(1) Our country faces an important problem, yet it's one that few people take seriously--what to do with the bottles and cans we use daily. When thrown away, bottles and cans cause pollution, increase the volume of solid wastes, waste energy, and use up natural resources. To control these problems only nine states have adopted bottle laws. What a shame.

(2) If you're like me, you're tired of walking down streets and seeing fast-food wrappers, bottles and cans. Last week I went to the coast and found a beautiful isolated beach. It was great until I came upon some hamburger boxes and beer bottles. This happened with a bottle law. Think how much worse things would be if Oregon didn't have a bottle law.

(3) Bottle laws are important because they require recycling, and recycling reduces pollution and solid waste. Recycling aluminum reduces air emissions associated with aluminum production by 96 percent. Solid waste would reduce as aluminum and glass are eliminated from landfills. Also, a large per-

centage of the pollution on and around streets and highways is bottles and cans. If these cans and bottles were worth some money, people would be less likely to throw them away.

(4) Extracting aluminum ore requires twenty times as much electricity as recycling the metal. Therefore, if we recycled more aluminum then less aluminum would have to be extracted. This would save enough energy to provide electrical power for at least two million people annually.

(5) Bottle laws are currently effective in Oregon, Vermont, Maine, Michigan, Iowa, Connecticut, Delaware, Massachusetts, and New York. These laws work largely because of the legislation's support by the people. Of the Americans polled, 73 percent would support such bottle laws. Some people are getting tired of the environment being polluted and abused and now realize that this planet and its resources are finite. Aluminum is a natural resource and without recycling we will eventually run out.

(6) With all the people in favor and the obvious environmental reasons supporting it, one would think that a national bottle law would have started long ago. But some people just don't want to bother with saving their containers, and it is a lot easier to just throw them away, despite the fact that they're worth five cents each. Steel and aluminum companies unfairly attack bottle bill laws--and so do supermarkets. These biased efforts must be stopped now.

(7) Although 54 percent of the aluminum beverage cans made and used in the U.S. are recycled at more than twenty-five hundred recycling centers, this could be increased to as much as 90 percent by requiring a national bottle law. Instead of considering unions' and companies' losses for a basis of decision on the bottle law, we should consider the ecological gains. In the future, a few dollars saved will mean nothing compared to a polluted and destroyed environment society will face without recycling.

Using the questions about focus, content, and organization earlier in this chapter, Todd analyzed his draft. His analysis revealed that his essay would be more effective if he made several important changes. Here is Todd's analysis of his essay.

FOCUS

My essay needs to be focused on a single subject, and I think it is, but I don't indicate my controlling purpose clearly enough at the start of my essay. I can also see that paragraph 2 gets off track because it talks about litter in general, not just the need for a bottle law. I should revise or drop this paragraph. I also may need to drop the last sentence of paragraph six. It may get off track, too.

I tried to emphasize evidence in writing this draft, but I think I need to provide more. I need to talk more about the reasons why some companies and supermarkets attack bottle bills, and I should try to present their side of the issue also.

CONTENT

The focus questions already helped me see that I need to revise paragraph 2 and add more evidence. I also don't describe how bottle laws work--and I should.

ORGANIZATION

I think the basic organization of my essay is OK. I don't think that I have to make big changes in the structure of my essay. I just have to provide more information and take out some details that don't fit.

I'm not sure about my introduction and conclusion--maybe they could be better. I'll work on the rest of the essay and decide later.

By using the questions about focus, content, and organization to analyze his rough draft, Todd was able to set priorities for revising. His priorities included the following changes:

- stating his controlling purpose early in his essay
- cutting unnecessary material
- adding evidence in support of his position
- explaining how bottle laws work
- checking to be sure he's considered both sides of the argument

In analyzing his essay, Todd also realized that his introduction and conclusion might be made more effective. Given the importance of the other changes he needed to make, however, Todd was right to put off working on the opening and closing paragraphs. Once he has made the major changes his analysis calls for, he can look again at his introduction and conclusion.

Application

Here is the revised version of Todd Carpenter's essay. Read the essay carefully, noting the major changes that Todd made as he revised. Write down the two or three most important changes on a sheet of paper. Finally, reread the essay with this question in mind: How could this essay be improved further? Write down one or two suggestions for revision in response to this question.

WHY ISN'T THERE A NATIONAL BOTTLE LAW?

(1) What do you do with your empty cans and bottles? There are two choices, throwing them away or recycling. Throwing away an aluminum beverage con-

tainer wastes as much energy as filling a can with gasoline and pouring half out. Besides wasting energy, throwing away bottles and cans causes pollution, increases the volume of solid wastes, and uses up natural resources. To control these problems, only nine states have adopted bottle laws. The United States government should require every state to have a bottle law or institute a national bottle law.

(2) To understand how a bottle law can help, you must know how it works. When consumers buy canned or bottled beverages at the store, they pay deposits. This deposit can range from five to twenty cents per bottle or can. In order to get this deposit back, the bottles and cans must be returned to a supermarket after they are emptied. The supermarkets then return the bottles and cans to their manufacturers for either reuse or recycling.

(3) Recycling plays a significant role in reducing pollution and solid waste. Recycling aluminum reduces air emissions associated with aluminum production by 96 percent. Solid waste is also reduced as aluminum and glass are eliminated from landfills. Finally, a large percentage of the pollution on and around the streets and highways is bottles and cans. If these could be returned to supermarkets for cash, people would be less likely to throw them away.

(4) Extracting aluminum ore requires twenty times as much electricity as recycling the metal. Therefore,

if we recycled more aluminum, less aluminum ore would have to be extracted. This could save enough energy to provide electrical power for at least two million people annually.

(5) Bottle laws are currently effective in Oregon, Vermont, Maine, Michigan, Iowa, Connecticut, Delaware, Massachusetts, and New York. These laws work largely because the general public supports them. A recent poll of Americans revealed that 73 percent support bottle laws. This support undoubtedly results from people's concern about pollution and our planet's limited resources.

(6) Given the large number of people in favor of bottle laws, you might expect that we would already have a national bottle law. But a vocal minority of people don't want to bother with saving their containers, so they oppose such legislation. Some supermarket chains also lobby against bottle laws; they don't want to have to deal with all the cans that people would bring to them. I understand these individuals' concerns. Recycling bottles and cans does require extra effort from consumers and distributors. The larger economic and ecological issues indicate that this extra effort is worthwhile.

(7) Finally, steel and aluminum companies and metal workers' unions oppose bottle laws because they fear they would cause cuts in their production and therefore affect jobs and wages. EPA and General Accounting studies estimate, however, that a national

bottle law would produce a net increase of eighty thousand to one hundred thousand jobs, so these fears are misplaced.

(8) Although 54 percent of the aluminum beverage cans made and used in the U.S. are currently recycled at more than twenty-five hundred recycling centers, we could increase this to as much as 90 percent by requiring a national bottle law. Instead of worrying about the inconvenience and possible economic consequences of instituting a national bottle law, we should consider the ecological gains. In the future, a little time saved will mean nothing compared to a polluted and destroyed environment.

TODD CARPENTER

Application

Use the guidelines for evaluating your focus, content, and organization to evaluate the draft of an essay you are currently working on. Be sure to respond as specifically and as concretely as possible. After answering these questions, take a few moments to reflect on what you have learned about your draft. Then make a list of goals for revising.

KEEPING YOUR READERS ON TRACK: REVISING FOR COHERENCE

Most writers are aware that paragraphs and essays need to be unified—that they should focus on a single topic. You know, for instance, that if you interrupt a paragraph on the benefits of walking as a form of exercise with a sentence praising your favorite walking shoes, your readers will be confused and irritated. You may not be aware, however, that a paragraph or an essay can be unified and yet still present difficulties for readers. These difficulties arise when a paragraph or essay lacks coherence.

Writing is coherent when readers can move easily from word to word, sentence to sentence, and paragraph to paragraph. When writing is coherent, readers are often unaware that writers are giving them signals or cues that enable them to stay on track when they read; the writing just seems to flow. Writers have various means of achieving coherence. Some methods, such as *repeating key words and sentence structures* and *using pronouns to refer to nouns,* reinforce or emphasize the logical development of ideas. Another method is to *employ transitional words.* Words like *however, although,* and *because* function as directions for readers; they tell readers what to do as they read. A sentence beginning with "For example" tells readers, for instance, that this sentence will substantiate or exemplify a preceding point, not introduce a new idea or concept.

The following whimsical paragraph from an essay by Cullen Murphy titled "Going to the Cats" uses all of these means to help keep readers on track, progressing effortlessly from sentence to sentence. The most important means of achieving coherence are italicized.

> Every decade or so the United States of America crosses some portentous new threshold that symbolizes the nation's evolution from one kind of society into another. *It crossed one* after the Second World War, when for the first time in history American men bought more belts than they did suspenders. *It crossed another* in the mid-1950s, when the number of tractors on American farms for the first time exceeded the number of horses. *Now,* in the 1980s, the country faces a new demographic reality: the number of cats in American households is rapidly overtaking, if it has not already overtaken, the number of dogs. *According to* Pet Food Institute, a Washington-based trade association, *there were* about 18 million more dogs than cats in the United States as recently as a decade ago, *but* today *there are* 56 million cats and only 52 million dogs. *Actually,* because millions of unregistered dogs and cats—the illegal aliens of the animal kingdom—go uncounted, it may be that dogs still maintain a slight edge. *But* sales of dog food are holding steady, *whereas* sales of cat food have been increasing in recent years at an annual rate of five to eight percent. The trend is clear.

Most writers concern themselves with strengthening an essay's coherence *after* writing a rough draft and determining if the essay's focus, content, and organization are effective. At this point, the writer can attend to fine tuning, making changes that enable readers to move through the writing easily and enjoyably.

When you read work in progress to determine how you can strengthen its coherence, use your common sense. Your writing is coherent if readers know where they have been and where they are going as they read. Don't assume that your writing will be more coherent if you sprinkle transitions liberally throughout your prose. The logic of your discussion may not require numerous transitions; in such a case, adding them will only clutter up your writing. For example, the following excerpt from an article in *Sunset* magazine about choosing a liquid garden fertilizer proceeds logically from the introduction to a statement of the problem and a series of guidelines. The few explicit transitions, such as *in addition* in the first paragraph, easily keep readers on track.

> The attention-getting labels on liquid fertilizer bottles often seem like the late-night TV commercials of the gardening world. Competing with myriad packages on nursery shelves, they make every claim imaginable. In addition to basic nutrients, they tout everything from vitamins to hormones, extracts, and secret formulas supposed to give bigger blooms or better-tasting vegetables.
>
> How do you know what's best for your plants? From fertilizers, plants can receive nitrogen, phosphorus, potassium, and a variety of micronutrients, including iron, manganese, and zinc. Of these, nitrogen is usually the most important, and for a given price, the fertilizer with more nitrogen is a better value.
>
> Here are some guidelines for choosing liquid fertilizers. . . .

Instead of many unneeded transitions, the few necessary transitional phrases, the pronouns (such as *they* in the first paragraph), and the repeated key words (such as *fertilizer* throughout and *nitrogen* in the second paragraph) supply the logical connections a reader needs.

Revision for coherence proceeds more effectively if you look first at large-scale issues, such as the relationship among your essay's introduction, body, and conclusion, before considering smaller concerns. When you revise for coherence, follow these steps.

Guidelines for revising for coherence

- Read your essay quickly to determine if it flows smoothly. Pay particular attention to the movement from introduction to body and conclusion. How could you tighten or strengthen these connections?
- Now read your essay slowly, paying special attention to the movement from paragraph to paragraph. How do new paragraphs build on or connect with previous paragraphs? Would more explicit connections, such as transitions, help readers better understand the development of your ideas?
- Finally, read each paragraph separately. How do your word choice and sentence structure help readers progress from sentence to sentence? Would repeating key words or pronouns or adding transitions increase a paragraph's coherence?

EXPLORING STYLISTIC OPTIONS

"Proper words in proper places"—that is how Jonathan Swift, author of *Gulliver's Travels,* defined style. Swift's definition, though intentionally abstract, is accurate. The style of an essay or a story reflects all of the choices that a writer makes, from global questions of approach and organization to the smallest details about punctuation and grammar. In this sense, *all* of the decisions that you make as a writer are stylistic decisions.

As Swift's definition indicates, style is an elusive yet essential feature of texts. It is difficult to articulate—or consciously to control—all the decisions that influence a writer's style. Yet when proper words *are* in proper places, not only are readers able to follow the writer's ideas with comprehension and interest, but they also sense the person behind the words, the writer's presence.

We often associate style with the personal, referring, for instance, to a person's style of dress or style of interacting with others. And a writer's style does reflect his or her individual taste and sensibility. But just as people dress differently for different occasions, so too do writers vary their style, depending on the rhetorical situation. Just as you may choose to dress conservatively for a job interview, for instance, so too may you decide that in certain rhetorical situations, presenting a strong personal style—a style that calls attention to itself—is inappropriate. When you are writing an essay examination, for instance, you know that your instructor is primarily interested in your ability to write intelligently about a subject. A style that calls attention to itself might interfere with, not promote, communication.

Effective writers naturally vary their style depending on their rhetorical situation. As they do so, they are particularly attentive to the *persona* or voice they convey through their writing. Sometimes writers present strong and distinctive voices. Here, for instance, is the beginning of an essay on a Northwest rodeo, the Pendleton Round-Up. The essay is by Ken Kesey, author of *One Flew Over the Cuckoo's Nest.*

> My father took me up the Gorge and over the hills to my first one thirty-five years ago. It was on my fourteenth birthday. I had to miss a couple of day's school plus the possibility of suiting up for the varsity game that Friday night. Gives you some idea of the importance Daddy placed on this event.
>
> For this is more than just a world-class rodeo. It is a week-long shindig, a yearly rendezvous dating back beyond the first white trappers, a traditional powwow ground for the Indian nations of the Northwest for nobody knows how many centuries.

Kesey's word choice and sentence structure help create an image of the writer as folksy, relaxed, down-home, and yet also forceful—just the right insider to write about a famous rodeo.

In other situations, writers don't wish to present a distinctive personal voice. Here, for instance, is the introduction to an essay on student volunteerism in the 1990s published in *Rolling Stone.*

> There is a quiet phenomenon taking place on campuses across the country: a surge in volunteerism among a generation of Americans dismissed for their self-interest, apathy and nihilism. Nearly half of all Americans between the ages of 18 and 24 volunteer at least a day of their time during the course of a year, according to a 1992 Gallup survey.
>
> The percentage has been rising since 1988. Recent polls confirm a 1990 survey by the National Postsecondary Student Aid Study reporting that about a quarter of the nation's undergraduates volunteered an average of five hours a week for a community service program.

The authors of this article, students in Michael Shapiro's Advanced Reporting and Writing Course at the Columbia Graduate School of Journalism, have chosen to write in a relatively anonymous public voice, one that focuses attention on their subject rather than on the writers.

Application

From newspapers, magazines, or books that you are currently reading, choose one passage that presents a distinctive personal voice. Choose another passage that presents a more anonymous public voice. Then answer these questions in writing:

- How would you describe the *persona* or voice evoked by each passage?
- How does the author of each passage succeed in creating this *persona* or voice? (Cite specific examples to support your analysis.)
- How do you respond personally to each of these passages? Write several sentences explaining your response to each passage.

Work in Progress encourages you to adopt a rhetorical perspective on writing. If you think rhetorically, asking yourself questions about your rhetorical situation, you will naturally consider such major stylistic issues as the *persona* or voice you wish your writing to convey to readers. Look again at the guidelines for analyzing your rhetorical situation, presented on page 59. These guidelines pose questions that can help you determine the appropriate style for specific situations. You may also find it helpful to review the discussion of Aristotle's three appeals—*logos, pathos,* and *ethos* (pages 70–75). When you consider the degree to which you wish to draw on appeals to reason (*logos*), emotion (*pathos*), and your own credibility as writer (*ethos*), you are led to consider your own *persona* or voice and your relationship with readers.

UNDERSTANDING GENERAL PRINCIPLES OF EFFECTIVE PROSE STYLE

In addition to considering such major stylistic issues as the *persona* or voice they wish to convey to readers, writers must make a number of smaller but no less important stylistic decisions. Some of these decisions are made consciously. When you draft several sentences and study them to determine which provides the most effective transition from one paragraph to the next, you are consciously considering an aspect of style. Other decisions are only partly conscious. When you write a word, strike it out, and write another, you are making a stylistic choice—even if you are only partly aware of the reasons why you prefer the latter word over the former.

The choices you make as you draft and revise reflect not only your understanding of your rhetorical situation but also your awareness of general principles of effective prose style, principles that apply to much academic and professional writing. Perhaps the easiest way to understand these principles is to analyze a passage that illustrates effective prose style in action.

Since much of your current reading is of textbooks, here are two paragraphs from the first chapter of a textbook on psycholinguistics, *Psychology and Language,* by Herbert H. Clark and Eve V. Clark. As you read these paragraphs, imagine that you have been assigned to read them for a course in psycholinguistics, an interdisciplinary field that studies linguistic behavior and the psychological mechanisms that make verbal communication possible.

> (1) Language stands at the center of human affairs, from the most prosaic to the most profound. (2) It is used for haggling with store clerks, telling off umpires, and gossiping with friends as well as for negotiating contracts, discussing ethics, and explaining religious beliefs. (3) It is the medium through which the manners, morals, and mythol-

> ogy of a society are passed on to the next generation. (4) Indeed, it is a basic ingredient in virtually every social situation. (5) The thread that runs through all these activities is communication, people trying to put their ideas over to others. (6) As the main vehicle of human communication, language is indispensable.
>
> (7) Communication with language is carried out through two basic human activities: speaking and listening. (8) These are of particular importance to psychologists, for they are mental activities that hold clues to the very nature of the human mind. (9) In speaking, people put ideas into words, talking about perceptions, feelings, and intentions they want other people to grasp. (10) In listening, they turn words into ideas, trying to reconstruct the perceptions, feelings, and intentions they were meant to grasp. (11) Speaking and listening, then, ought to reveal something fundamental about the mind and how it deals with perceptions, feelings, and intentions. (12) Speaking and listening, however, are more than that. (13) They are the tools people use in more global activities. (14) People talk in order to convey facts, ask for favors, and make promises, and others listen in order to receive this information. (15) These actions in turn are the pieces out of which casual conversations, negotiations, and other social exchanges are formed. (16) So speaking and listening ought to tell us a great deal about social and cultural activities too.

These two paragraphs, you would probably agree, do embody effective prose style. They are clearly organized. Each paragraph, in fact, begins with a topic sentence which the rest of the paragraph explains. The paragraphs are also coherent. The authors use a number of means—especially repeating pronouns, key words, and sentence patterns—to help readers proceed easily through this explanation. But what most distinguishes these two paragraphs, what makes them so effective, is the authors' use of concrete, precise, economical language and carefully crafted sentences.

Suppose that the first paragraph were revised as follows. What would be lost?

> (1) Language stands at the center of human affairs, from the most prosaic to the most profound. (2) It is a means of human communication. (3) It is a means of cultural change and regeneration. (4) It is found in every social situation. (5) The element that characterizes all these activities is communication. (6) As the main vehicle of human communication, language is indispensable.

This revision communicates roughly the same ideas as the original paragraph, but it lacks that paragraph's liveliness and interest. Instead of presenting vivid examples—"haggling with store clerks, telling off umpires, and gossiping with friends"—the second, third, fourth, and fifth sentences state only vague generalities. Moreover, these sentences are short and monotonous. Also lost in this revision is any sense of the authors' personalities, as revealed in their writing. The original examples not only clarify how language is used but also convey to readers a sense of the authors' character and interests.

As this example demonstrates, effective prose style doesn't have to be flashy or call attention to itself. The focus in the original passage is on the *ideas* being discussed. The authors don't want readers to stop and think, "My, what a lovely sentence." But they do want their readers—students required to read their book for a course—to become interested in and engaged with their ideas. So they use strong verbs and vivid, concrete examples whenever possible. They pay careful attention to sentence structure, alternating sequences of sentences with parallel structures (sentences two, three, and four as well as sentences nine and ten) with other, more varied sentences. They take care that the relationships among ideas are clear. In both paragraphs, for example, the first and last sentences (which readers are most likely to remember) articulate the most important ideas. As a result of these and other choices, these two paragraphs succeed in being economical, yet also emphatic.

Exploring your stylistic options—developing a style that reflects your understanding of yourself and the world and your feel for language—is one of the pleasures of writing. The following sections review varied sentences, concrete language, and concise wording, all basic principles of effective style. As you read these guidelines, think of an essay you have written recently. How could you employ these suggestions to strengthen your essay?

Guidelines for revising your style

1. Vary the Length and Structure of Your Sentences.

Few students write only very short or very long sentences. Even so, the sentences they do use may seem randomly presented. Their rhythm may be awkward, or their length or structure may work against the ideas the writer is trying to express. Consider, for example, the sentences in the following paragraph from an essay urging students to use coupons when they shop.

> (1) Almost everywhere you look, there are coupons. (2) Daily newspapers are probably the best sources for coupons. (3) The <u>Oregonian</u> and the <u>Barometer</u> have

coupons every day. (4) The <u>Gazette-Times</u> has coupons too. (5) The Sunday <u>Oregonian</u> is loaded with coupons. (6) Some of the sources that are not so obvious may be coupon trader bins in groceries and flyers handed out in dorms. (7) The backs of store receipts and coupons on boxes or other items you have previously purchased are also common.

The sentences in this paragraph lack variety. Sentences two, three, four, and five are roughly the same length; they also are structured similarly. Because the information they express is so obvious—each simply indicates a possible source of coupons—these sentences seem repetitive. The final two sentences (six and seven) break this pattern, but they are awkward and hard to follow.

Revision could make this paragraph much more effective:

(1) You may be surprised by how easy it is to find coupons. (2) Daily newspapers, such as the <u>Oregonian</u>, the <u>Gazette-Times</u>, and the <u>Barometer</u>, are probably the best sources for coupons. (3) If you don't want to purchase a daily paper, the Sunday <u>Oregonian</u>, which is loaded with coupons, may be the next best choice. (5) Don't just look for coupons in newspapers, however. (6) You can also watch for special coupon bins in grocery stores and for flyers used to distribute coupons in dorms. (7) You can even discover coupons on the backs of store receipts or on the boxes or packages from other purchases.

You may have noticed that the revised version of this paragraph changes more than the length and structure of the sentences. The wording of the first sentence is now more emphatic. The final two sentences are more direct because they begin with *you,* the subject of the action. Finally, added transitions clarify the relationships among ideas in the paragraph. As this revision shows, even though you may be revising with a particular purpose in mind (in this case to vary the sentences), revision usually involves a multitude of changes.

When you revise, you generally want to achieve an appropriate variety of sentence lengths and structures, one that carries readers forward with a clear yet unobtrusive rhythm. The following paragraph from a student essay on salmon fishing illustrates this accomplishment.

> Picture yourself in a scenic river setting. The fall colors are at their peak, and shades of burnt red and copper gold brighten up the shoreline. The crisp, clean smell of fall is in the air, and a gentle breeze blows lightly against your face. Off in the distance you hear the sound of swift white water thundering over massive boulders until it gradually tames into slower-moving pools of crystal green. As you look out across the river, the smooth glassy surface is momentarily interrupted as a large salmon leaps free of its natural element.

You may at times want to use more dramatic sentence structures to emphasize a point. For example, here is the first paragraph of a chapter called "Some Biographical Statistics" from David James Duncan's novel *The River Why.*

> A fishing prodigy, like a musical prodigy, is perforce a solitary. Because of fishing I started school a year late; because of fishing I was considered a kind of mild-mannered freak by my schoolmates; because of fishing I grew up osprey-silent and trout-shy and developed early on an ability to slide through the Public School System as riverwater slides by the logjams, rockslides and dams that bar its seaward journey. It wasn't that I was antisocial; I simply suffered from that lopsidedness of character typical in prodigies. As young Mozart cared for nothing but keyboards, strings, and woodwinds, so I cared for nothing but lakes, rivers, streams and their denizens. Years before I could have put it into words, I realized that my fate would lead me beside still waters, beside rough waters, beside blue, green, muddy, clear, and salt waters. From the beginning my mind and heart were so taken up with the liq-

> uid element that nearly every other thing on the earth's bulbous face struck me as irrelevant, distracting, a waste of time.

Duncan's dramatic sentence structures use repetition and balance to emphasize his character's obsession with fishing.

2. When Appropriate, Use Specific, Concrete Language.

Look again at the two paragraphs from the psycholinguistics textbook on pages 202–203. One of the strengths of these two paragraphs is the authors' use of specific, concrete words and examples. Rather than writing that language "is a means of human communication," the authors say that language "is used for haggling with store clerks, telling off umpires, and gossiping with friends as well as for negotiating contracts, discussing ethics, and explaining religious beliefs." This sentence doesn't merely interest readers; it challenges them to pause and think about just how many ways they use language to communicate.

Specific, concrete words can give your writing power and depth. Such language isn't always appropriate, however. Sometimes you *need* to use abstract or general terms to convey your meaning. Abstract words—like *patriotism, love,* and *duty*—refer to ideas, beliefs, relationships, conditions, and acts that you can't perceive with your senses. General words designate a group. The word *computer* is general; the words *Leading Edge Model D* identify a specific machine within that group.

Effective writing usually interweaves the specific and the concrete with the abstract and the general. The sentences in the paragraphs on psycholinguistics, for example, move back and forth from specific and concrete to general and abstract words and statements. After specifying and describing various ways people use language to communicate, the writers close the first paragraph with a much broader statement: "As the main vehicle of human communication, language is indispensable." Good writers use general and abstract language when appropriate—and when you are writing about intellectual problems or ideas or emotions, such language often is appropriate. But skillful writers balance abstract generalities with concrete, specific words and examples that give their ideas force and vigor.

Some writers overuse abstract, general words. They may believe that these words sound more intellectual, formal, or official. Or they may assume that they should use abstract or general language when in fact specific, concrete words and examples would be more effective.

For instance, here is a paragraph from a student essay analyzing *Sports Illustrated.* Notice how vague much of the language is.

> Sports Illustrated's articles are informative because its writers try to get information which nobody else knows. The articles explain how the subject is unique and how the subject became popular and successful. Articles are rarely negative. Most are positive and explain the good things in sports rather than emphasizing the negative aspects, such as drugs.

This paragraph leaves readers with more questions than answers. What does this writer mean when he calls articles "informative"? What kind of information that "nobody else knows" are writers for *Sports Illustrated* able to get? Just what kinds of subjects does the publication cover? (Many magazines feature articles about subjects that are "unique," "popular," and "successful.") Does the magazine emphasize the human drama of competition, for example, or strategy, techniques, and statistics? Readers familiar with *Sports Illustrated* can probably use their prior knowledge to interpret this paragraph; others can only guess at the writer's intentions.

3. Reduce Wordiness.

Most readers are impatient. They are reading for a reason—*their* reason, not yours—and they are irritated if you waste their time with unnecessary words or flabby sentences. Consequently, when they revise, experienced writers read their work carefully to determine if they can prune unnecessary words and sentences.

In revising to eliminate wordiness, your goal is not necessarily to eliminate every possible word. Rather, your goal should be to ensure that *every word serves a purpose.* Words that are not strictly necessary can serve purposes of emphasis, rhythm, flow, or tone; the degree to which these are important to your writing is a question that can only be answered by considering your rhetorical situation and purpose.

Words and phrases that add unnecessary length to your sentences without serving any rhetorical purpose are known as *deadwood,* and deadwood turns up in the drafts of even the most experienced writers. The revision phase of your writing process is a good time to concentrate on finding deadwood and clearing it out. While rereading an early draft of the second chapter of this book, for instance, I noticed the following sentence:

> Rather than attempting to determine a sequence of activities that you always follow when you write, you should develop a range of strategies that you can employ at any point in the writing process.

It took only a few minutes to rid this sentence of its deadwood.

> Rather than following a rigid sequence of activities, you should develop a range of strategies that you can employ at any point in the writing process.

This revised sentence communicates the same idea as the original but uses significantly fewer words (twenty-six rather than thirty-four). Like me, you will often discover wordy sentences when you reread your drafts. Don't be surprised at such discoveries. When you're struggling to express ideas, you can't expect to worry about being concise at the same time. Knowing this, however, you should be particularly alert for deadwood—words that clutter up your sentences and lessen their impact—when you revise.

Sometimes you can eliminate deadwood by deleting unnecessary words; in other cases, you may need to revise your sentence structure. The following examples of sentences clogged with deadwood are from early drafts of this textbook; I have italicized the unnecessary words. My revisions follow the original sentence.

> As you *work to improve your* writing, you can *benefit a great deal from* drawing on your *own* commonsense understanding of how people in our culture use language.
> As you write, you can draw on your commonsense understanding of how people in our culture use language.

> Your discussion with your instructor will be most profitable (for both of you) if you *have already done a fair amount of preparation before* the conference.
> Your discussion with your instructor will be most profitable (for both of you) if you prepare for the conference.

> *One traditional way of viewing these disciplines is to see them as falling into* one of the following *major* categories: sciences, humanities, and social sciences.
> Most academic disciplines fall into one of the following categories: sciences, humanities, or social sciences.

These examples from my own writing emphasize that even experienced writers need to revise their writing to achieve an effective prose style. Placing "proper words in proper places" does require patience and commitment, but it is also one of the most rewarding parts of the writing process, for it ensures effective communication between writer and reader.

Activities for Thought, Discussion, and Writing

1. From an essay you are currently working on, choose a paragraph that lacks adequate coherence. Determine the main reasons why the paragraph lacks coherence. Then use the strategies discussed in this chapter to revise your paragraph.
2. From the same essay, choose two or three paragraphs that you suspect could be more stylistically effective. Using this chapter's discussion of style as a guide, revise these paragraphs.
3. Here is an essay written by Ian Frazier. Read this essay and then answer the questions that follow it.

TO MR. WINSLOW

On June 1st, in the afternoon, four teen-agers approached a forty-two-year-old drama teacher named Allyn Winslow on Quaker Hill, in Brooklyn's Prospect Park, and tried to steal his new mountain bike. When he resisted and rode away, they shot him four times with a .22-calibre pistol. He rode down the hill to the cobbled path leading to the Picnic House, fell off his bike, and died. The TV news that evening showed the bike on the grass, and his body, covered by a sheet, next to it. I recognized the spot where he lay. I take my daughter to the pond nearby to throw bread to the ducks. She and I had sat there, or near there.

I walked by the spot the next day. It was marked by a wad of discarded surgical tape and an inside-out surgical glove. The day after, when I went by there I saw a Timberland shoebox with a bouquet of flowers in it, and a glass wine carafe with more flowers. In the shoebox was a piece of lined paper on which someone had written in blue ink: "To the biker Mr. Winslow, May you be in a better place with angels on a cloud." These words echoed in the media as reporters quoted and misquoted them. Men and women were carrying microphones and TV cameras in the vicinity, and if you weren't careful they would interview you. About a week later, an American flag had been stuck into the ground next to the shoebox. There was a bunch of papers in a clear-plastic envelope, and the one on top said, "AVENGE THIS ACT OF COWARDICE." In and around the shoebox were notes addressed to Mr. Winslow and his wife and their two children; a blue-and-white striped ribbon; a ceramic pipe; a bike rider's reflector badge in the image of a peace sign; a red-and-white bandanna; a flyer from the Guardian Angels organization; and an announcement of an upcoming service to be held in his memory.

The following week, the accumulation around the shoebox had grown. The flowers in it and in the wine carafe were fresh—roses, peonies, yellow freesias. Someone had arranged many pinecones and sprigs of oak leaves in a circle on the perimeter. In the ground by the flag was a cross made of wood, bound with red ribbon and draped with a string of purple glass beads, and, near the cross, a photocopy of a newspaper photograph of Allyn Winslow. A Dover edition of Shakespeare's "Complete Sonnets" rested on a pedestal made of a cross-section of a branch from a London Plane tree. There were also several anti-N.R.A. stickers, a blue candle in a plastic cup, and a five of spades from a pack of Bicycle playing cards. Chunks of paving stones held down a poster showing the number of people killed in 1990 by handguns in various countries: thirteen in Sweden, ninety-one in Switzerland, eighty-seven in Japan, sixty-eight in Canada, ten thousand five hundred and sixty-seven in the United States. A girl visiting the park on a class picnic asked another girl, "Is he buried here?"

A week or two later, many of the items had vanished. Someone had burned the flag, but the charred flagpole remained. The cross, broken off at the base, lay on the ground. The plastic cup with the candle was cracked. The grass around the spot was worn down in a circle and littered with dried flower stems. The carafe had a big chip out of the top. The shoebox had begun to sag. The papers were gone, except for a rain-stained sign saying, "To Honor, To Mourn Allyn Winslow," and a pamphlet, "Verses of Comfort, Assurance and Salvation."

By mid-July, the shoebox was in pieces. There were a few rocks, two small forked branches stuck in the ground, the ashes of a small fire, and a "You gotta have Park!" button. By mid-August, the tramped-down grass had begun to grow back. I noticed a piece of red-and-white string and a scrap from the shoebox. By September, so little of the memorial remained that the spot was hard to find. A closer look revealed the burned patch, some red-and-white string now faded to pink, and flower stems so scattered and broken you'd have to know what they were to recognize them.

Just now—a bright, chilly fall day—I went by the place again. Color in the park's trees had reached its peak. In a grove of buckskin-brown oaks, yellow shot up the fountain of a ginkgo tree. A flock of pigeons rose all at once and glided to a new part of the Long Meadow, circling once before landing, like a dog before it lies down. A police car slipped around the corner of the Picnic House, a one-man police scooter rode down the path, a police helicopter flew by just above the trees. At first, I could find no trace of the memorial at all: grass and clover have reclaimed the bared dirt. I got down on one knee, muddying my pants. Finally, I found a wooden stake broken off about half an inch above the ground: the base of the memorial cross, probably—the only sign of the unmeasured sorrows that converge here.

IAN FRAZIER

- How would you describe the general style of this essay? Write at least three or four sentences describing its style.
- How would you describe the *persona* or voice conveyed by this essay? List at least three specific characteristics of the writer's *persona* or voice, and then indicate several passages that you think particularly exemplify these characteristics.
- Find at least three passages from this essay that you believe demonstrate the principles of effective prose style as discussed in this chapter. Indicate the reasons why you believe each passage is stylistically effective.
- What additional comments could you make about the structure and style of this essay? Did anything about the style of this essay surprise you? Formulate at least one additional comment about the essay's structure and style.

4. Find a brief article or essay that you think adheres to the principles of style discussed in this chapter. Bring a copy of this selection to class for discussion. Also bring a list of five specific reasons why you think the essay or article is well written.

PART THREE

CONNECTIONS: WRITING, READING, AND REASONING

CHAPTER 9

UNDERSTANDING THE READING PROCESS

READING ACTIVELY

Why do people write? To answer this question, Chapter 1 presented a number of representative writing situations: a psychiatric social worker recording clinical observations, a consulting engineer working with colleagues to draft a proposal, two students working together on an essay for their literature class, and a retired teacher writing her recollections of her parents and grandparents. These and other representative writing situations emphasize that whenever we write, we do so in a specific context or situation. Because each situation differs, effective writers draw on their rhetorical sensitivity to make a variety of choices, from global decisions about purpose and audience to local decisions about sentence structure and word choice.

Why do people read? Not surprisingly, people read for as many different reasons and in as many different contexts as they write. People read to gain information—to learn how to program their VCR or to make decisions about whether to attend a movie or purchase a new product. People read for pleasure: they immerse themselves in others' lives and worlds, from serious and humorous tales of romance, suspense, adventure, and travel to poems, fiction, diaries, essays, and social commentaries. People read to engage in extended "conversations" with others about issues or questions of importance to them, such as ecology, United States policy in the Middle East, or women's rights. In these and other instances, people read to enlarge their world, to experience new ways not only of thinking but also of being and acting.

As Chapter 4, "Writers Reading," emphasized, you can strengthen your abilities as a writer by learning to read others' writing more critically and sensitively. By focusing not only on what writers say but also on what writers *do,* you can learn how other writers have responded to their rhetorical situation, and you can apply that knowledge when you work on your own writing.

Reading and writing are thus mutually reinforcing processes. Perhaps the central reason why this is so is that both are acts of *composing,* of constructing meaning through language. When you first read an essay, for instance, you are engaged in a preliminary or "rough" reading. The process of grappling with an essay for the first time—of attempting to determine where the writer is going and why—is similar to the process of writing a rough draft. When you reread an essay to appreciate the strategies the writer has used or to critique the writer's arguments, you are revising your original reading, much as you revise a draft when you write.

Both writing and reading challenge you to construct or compose the meaning of a specific text; both also engage you in dialogue with others. Perhaps because writing requires the physical activity of drafting, you are generally aware of the active role you play as writer. You may be less aware of the "work" you do when you read a text. Nevertheless, reading is an equally active process. Here, for instance, are excerpts from the "Harper's Index" for January 1994. As you read, notice how you forge connections among these "exotica and telling facts." If you are like most readers, you will discover that certain themes or issues emerge from your reading.

HARPER'S INDEX*

A collection of exotica and telling facts from *Harper's* magazine

- Chances that a job created in the U.S. since the end of the recession is at Wal-Mart: 1 in 14
- Number of America's ten largest industrial companies that have created new jobs since the end of the recession: 1
- Amount IBM will spend this year on parties for its top employees: $20,000,000
- Amount Miller Brewing spends each year to promote its Thurgood Marshall Scholarship Fund: $300,000

*Figures cited are the latest available as of November 1993. "Harper's Index" is a registered trademark.

- Amount it spends each year to endow the scholarship: $150,000
- Number of fire bombings in Sacramento, California, since July for which the Aryan Liberation Front has taken credit: 5
- Chances that a Korean-owned business damaged during the L.A. riots in 1992 has not re-opened: 1 in 2
- Percentage of all immigrants to the United States during the 1980s who were receiving welfare in 1989: 4
- Rank of Ecuadorans, Italians, and Poles, among the largest illegal immigrant groups in New York State: 1, 2, 3
- Ratio of the number of New York City cabbies killed last year to the number of U.S. soldiers killed in Somalia: 6:5
- Percentage of Americans who do not know that Somalia is in Africa: 43
- Chances that an African lives outside of his or her country of birth: 1 in 18
- Number of Kuwaiti human-rights groups permanently banned last August by the Kuwaiti government: 6
- Ratio of the number of refugees in Iran to the number in Germany: 5:1
- Chances that a Briton would move to another country "if free to do so": 1 in 2
- Reward the town of Burns, Oregon, is offering anyone who can convince a medical doctor to move there: $15,000
- Chances that hospital care will save the life of a heart-attack victim who does not respond to on-site care: 1 in 200
- Amount spent each year on emergency hospital care for non-responsive heart-attack victims: $500,000,000
- Monthly fee charged by Courtscan, a Philadelphia company providing physicians with patients' litigation records: $79.95
- Estimated portion of the price of an eight-foot stepladder accounted for by litigation costs and insurance: 1/5
- Average percentage markup on an "economy" casket sold by a U.S. funeral home: 300
- Rank of January, among months in which the greatest number of Americans die: 1
- Ratio of January sales of health-club memberships to average monthly sales during the rest of the year: 3:2
- Hours the average Chinese worker must work to earn the price of an ice-cream cone at Beijing's new Baskin-Robbins: 7
- Cups of iceberg lettuce one must consume in order to satisfy the minimum daily requirement of any vitamin: 27.5
- Cups of spinach one must consume in order to satisfy the minimum daily requirement of any vitamin: 1.3

Exploration

Freewrite for five minutes about the experience of reading the "Harper's Index." What strategies did you find yourself using as you read this miscellany of "telling facts"? After freewriting, reread the index one more time and then list the major themes or issues that your reading stimulated. Reviewing this list, consider the extent to which your own background and experiences influenced your reading of this index.

Reading, like writing, is a *situated* activity: when you read, you draw not only on the words on the page but on your own experiences as well. The connections that you perceived among the first three items in the "Harper's Index," for instance, were undoubtedly influenced by your own economic and political views. Reading is situated in additional ways. Just as you approach different writing tasks in different ways, depending on your rhetorical situation, your approach to and experience of reading varies, depending on the specific relationship of writer, reader, and text. Without thinking, you naturally read the introduction to a psychology text differently than you read your current mystery or the sports page of your newspaper.

Application

Read the following texts. The first, "Girl," is a very brief short story set in the Caribbean, by the contemporary writer Jamaica Kincaid. The second presents the first two paragraphs of the introduction to Robin Lakoff's book *Language and Woman's Place,* a scholarly work that attempts "to see what we can learn about the way women view themselves and everyone's assumptions about the nature and role of women from the use of language in our culture."

GIRL

Wash the white clothes on Monday and put them on the stone heap; wash the color clothes on Tuesday and put them on the clothesline to dry; don't walk barehead in the hot sun; cook pumpkin fritters in very hot sweet oil; soak your little cloths right after you take them off; when buying cotton to make yourself a nice blouse, be sure that it doesn't have gum on it, because that way it won't hold up well after a wash; soak salt fish overnight before you cook it; is it true that you sing benna in Sunday school?; always eat your food in such a way that it won't turn someone else's stomach; on Sundays try to walk like a lady and not like the slut you are so bent on becoming; don't sing benna in Sunday school; you mustn't speak to wharf rat-boys, not even to give directions; don't eat fruits on the street—flies will follow you; *but I don't sing benna on Sundays at all and never in Sunday school;* this is how to sew on a button; this is how to make a button-hole for the button you have just sewed on; this is how to hem a dress when you see the hem coming down and so to prevent yourself from looking like the slut I know you are so bent on becoming; this is how you iron your father's khaki shirt so that it doesn't have a crease; this is how you iron your father's khaki pants so that they don't have a crease; this is how you grow okra—far from the house, because okra tree harbors red ants; when you are growing dasheen, make sure it gets plenty of water or else it makes your throat itch when you are eating it; this is how you sweep a corner; this is how you sweep a whole house; this is how you sweep a yard; this is how you smile to someone you don't like too much; this is how you smile to someone you don't like at all; this is how you smile to someone you like completely; this is how you set a table for tea; this is how you set a table for dinner; this is how you set a table for dinner with an important guest; this is how you set a table for lunch; this is how you set a table for breakfast; this is how to behave in the presence of men who don't know you very well, and this way they won't recognize immediately the slut I have warned you against becoming; be sure to wash every day, even if it is with your own spit; don't squat down to play marbles—you are not a boy, you know; don't pick people's flowers—you might catch something; don't throw stones at blackbirds, because it might not be a blackbird at all; this is how to make a bread pudding; this is how to make doukona; this is how to make pepper pot; this is how to make a good medicine for a cold; this is how to make a good medicine to throw away a child before it even becomes a child; this is how to catch a fish; this is how to throw back a fish you don't like, and that way something bad won't fall on you; this is how to bully a man; this is how a man bullies you; this is how to love a man, and if this doesn't work there are other ways, and if they don't work don't feel too bad about giving up; this is how to spit up in the air if you feel like it, and this is how to move quick so that it doesn't fall on you; this is how to make ends meet; always squeeze bread to make sure it's fresh; *but what if the baker won't let me feel the bread?;* you mean to say that after all you are really going to be the kind of woman who the baker won't let near the bread?

JAMAICA KINCAID

LANGUAGE AND WOMAN'S PLACE

Introduction

Language uses us as much as we use language. As much as our choice of forms of expression is guided by the thoughts we want to express, to the same extent the way we feel about the things in the real world governs the way we express ourselves about these things. Two words can be synonymous in their denotative sense, but one will be used in case a speaker feels favorably toward the object the word denotes, the other if he is unfavorably disposed. Similar situations are legion, involving unexpectedness, interest, and other emotional reactions on the part of the speaker to what he is talking about. Thus, while two speakers may be talking about the same thing or real-world situation, their descriptions may end up sounding utterly unrelated. The following well-known paradigm will be illustrative.

(1) *(a)* I am strong-minded.
(b) You are obstinate.
(c) He is pigheaded.

If it is indeed true that our feelings about the world color our expression of our thoughts, then we can use our linguistic behavior as a diagnostic of our hidden feelings about things. For often—as anyone with even a nodding acquaintance with modern psychoanalytic writing knows too well—we can interpret our overt actions, or our perceptions, in accordance with our desires, distorting them as we see fit. But the linguistic data are there, in black and white, or on tape, unambiguous and unavoidable. Hence, while in the ideal world other kinds of evidence for sociological phenomena would be desirable along with, or in addition to, linguistic evidence, sometimes at least the latter is all we can get with certainty. This is especially likely in emotionally charged areas like that of sexism and other forms of discriminatory behavior. This book, then, is an attempt to provide diagnostic evidence from language use for one type of inequity that has been claimed to exist in our society: that between the roles of men and women. I will attempt to discover what language use can tell us about the nature and extent of any inequity; and finally to ask whether anything can be done, from the linguistic end of the problem: does one correct a social inequity by changing linguistic disparities? We will find, I think, that women experience linguistic discrimination in two ways: in the way they are taught to use language, and in the way general language use treats them. Both tend, as we shall see, to relegate women to certain subservient functions: that of sex object, or servant; and therefore certain lexical items mean one thing applied to men, another to women, a difference that cannot be predicted except with reference to the different roles the sexes play in society.

ROBIN LAKOFF

Now that you have read these two texts, use the following questions to analyze your reading experience.

1. What were your expectations when you began to read each of these texts? Did you expect to find one or the other easier or more interesting to read? Why? To what extent did your expectations derive from your own previous experiences as a reader?
2. Each of these texts in a different way comments on the situation of women in society and the role that language plays in women's lives. How did your own assumptions and values about these issues influence your reading? Did you approach these texts as a sympathetic, accepting reader, for instance, or were you resistant to the general subject at the start? Why?
3. Just as writers often shift goals and strategies while writing, readers too sometimes revise their goals and strategies while reading. Did you find yourself doing so while reading either passage? Why? What caused these shifts, if they occurred?
4. As you read these two texts, were you aware that the authors' stance toward or relationship with readers differed? How would you describe each author's stance or relationship with readers? Similarly, did these texts invite you to play a different role as reader? How would you describe your role as you read these texts, and how did your awareness of this role influence your reading? Try to list several features of each text that encourage readers to adopt a particular role.
5. What three or four factors most influenced your ease or difficulty of reading these two passages? To what extent did the two texts require you to draw on different skills and different prior knowledge about the subject matter? Try to rank these factors in terms of the difficulty they posed for you as you read.
6. If you found reading one or both of these texts difficult or unenjoyable, can you imagine someone else who would find them easy and pleasurable to read? What values, knowledge, and skills would this person have—in what ways would this person differ from you? If you found one or both of these passages easy and enjoyable reading, can you identify the reasons why?

Now reread each of these two texts. To what extent does this second reading differ from your first—to what extent, in other words, do you find yourself revising your first reading? List several ways that the second reading differed from the first.

Group Activity

Meet with a group of classmates to discuss your responses to the preceding application. (Appoint a member of the group to act as a recorder so you can share the results of your discussion with the rest of the class.) Begin your discussion by comparing your answers to each of the six questions on page 221. As a group, formulate two or three responses to the following two questions:

1. In what ways do your answers to these questions differ?
2. What do these differences reveal about the nature of the reading process?

RECOGNIZING THE NEED FOR DIVERSE READING STRATEGIES

As a college student, you read many different kinds of texts for a wide variety of purposes. Sometimes you read primarily for information; you do so when you read your chemistry textbook or when you scan the screen of your library's circulation computer to determine what references are available for a current project. On other occasions, you read not simply to gain information or for main ideas but to engage in the process of inquiry. Professors David Bartholomae and Anthony Petrosky call this kind of reading "strong reading." To engage successfully in strong reading, students must understand that:

> Reading involves a fair measure of push and shove. You make your mark on a book and it makes its mark on you. Reading is not simply a matter of hanging back and waiting for a piece, or its author, to tell you what the writing has to say. In fact, one of the difficult things about reading is that the pages before you will begin to speak only when the authors are silent and you begin to speak in their place, sometimes for them—doing their work, continuing their projects—and sometimes for yourself, following your own agenda.*

Strong readers evaluate their reading in terms of what they are able to *do* with their reading.

If you are like many students, you may feel more confident reading for information or main ideas than engaging in a strong reading of

*David Bartholomae and Anthony Petrosky, *Ways of Reading: An Anthology for Writers*, 3d ed. (Boston: Bedford, 1993): 1.

an essay, poem, political treatise, or engineering, physics, or philosophical problem. Yet the ability to "make your mark on a book," rather than simply allowing it to "make its mark on you," represents one of the most important goals of a college education. Such engaged, critical reading is intrinsically satisfying, for it enables you to engage in genuine inquiry. Strong reading also naturally leads to, and benefits from, writing; one of the best ways to strengthen your writing ability is thus to become adept at strong reading.

Just as successful writers develop a repertoire of writing strategies they can draw on in various situations, successful readers develop a repertoire of reading strategies. The next section of this chapter presents a number of strategies you can use in a variety of reading activities. Whatever reading you do, the following general guidelines for effective reading should make that process easier and more productive.

Guidelines for effective reading

1. Recognize That Effective Readers Are Flexible Readers.

Effective readers understand that different reading situations call for different reading strategies; they also understand that their purpose in reading should help them determine how to approach a text. If you know that you will eventually engage in the strong reading of an essay, you might first employ such strategies as previewing and annotating to get the gist of the text and to understand the author's general values and assumptions. Later you will reread the essay, drawing upon a variety of reading and writing strategies to deepen your engagement with it.

2. Analyze a Text for Cues about Its Context or Situation.

Chapter 3 presents guidelines for analyzing your rhetorical situation as a writer; you can use the same guidelines to analyze the context or situation of an already published piece of writing. Before and while reading an essay, for instance, you can ask questions like these:

- *Questions about the author.* What did the author hope the essay would accomplish? How might the author's goals have influenced the form and content of the essay? What voice or image *(persona)* does the author project in this essay?
- *Questions about the reader.* Who is the intended audience for this essay—a general audience or an audience of specialists? What role does the writer invite readers to adopt as they read this essay? Does the writer assume that readers will already

know a great deal about this subject? What factors encourage or prevent me from assuming the role this writer invites me to adopt? What consequences does this have for my reading of this text?

- *Questions about the text.* When was this text published? By whom? To what specific or general situation, concern, or question might this text be a response? Does the situation in which the author wrote require that certain textual conventions be followed? If so, to what extent did these conventions shape the essay? Does the nature of the subject require that the author provide certain kinds of evidence or explore certain issues? Does the author fulfill this obligation? Have I read other examples of similar writing that can help me understand the goals and strategies of this text?

Your answers to these questions can help you understand the situation or context in which a text was written and thus approach it with a richer appreciation of its assumptions, goals, and strategies.

3. Develop Strategies That Allow You, When Appropriate, to Resist or Read Against the Grain of a Text.

To read critically and actively, readers sometimes choose to resist a text or to read "against the grain." For example, while reading an essay on abortion intended for a general audience, you might decide to consider the essay from the perspective of a health-care provider or from that of a woman who has experienced an abortion. How would those readers respond to the author's arguments and strategies? You might read the essay paying particular attention to issues that the author *doesn't* raise or examples that the author *doesn't* use. Or you might focus on the degree to which your own experience does or does not support the author's arguments. Such probing, resistant readings can help you determine not only what an essay says and does but also what it doesn't say and do and can thus provide an opening for fruitful questioning, analysis, and dialogue.

4. Recognize That Effective Reading Often Requires Rereading.

Effective readers understand that rereading a text provides an opportunity for them not only to appreciate the text more fully but also to understand their own reading strategies. In rereading an essay on abortion, for instance, you might notice that your agreement with the author's position caused you to downplay problems with some of the arguments. When you begin a second—or third or fourth—reading of the essay, you can bring your previous reading to bear, so that you can read with a fuller appreciation of not only the author's intentions but also of your own.

DEVELOPING A REPERTOIRE OF CRITICAL READING STRATEGIES

When you read critically, you read *actively*. You read not just to memorize facts or gather information but to evaluate, analyze, appreciate, understand, and apply. As a critical reader, you engage in a dialogue with the author. You don't automatically accept the author's perspective or arguments. Instead, you challenge the author and subject his or her ideas to careful examination.

To read critically, you need to develop a repertoire of critical reading strategies. The following discussion will introduce you to a number of strategies for critical reading and provide an opportunity for you to apply these strategies to a specific text, an article that calls for significant changes in the nature, structure, and goals of public schools.

Previewing

When you preview a text, you survey it quickly to establish or clarify your purpose and context for reading. In doing so, you ask yourself questions such as those included in the following guidelines.

Guidelines for previewing a text

1. Where and when was this text published? What do this source and date suggest about the accuracy, authority, and currency of this text?
2. What, if anything, do I know about the author of this text?
3. What can I learn from the title?
4. What can I learn by quickly surveying this text? Is the text divided into sections? If so, how do these sections appear to be organized? Can I easily perceive the gist or general approach the author is taking? What predictions about this text can I make on the basis of quickly surveying it? What questions can I now formulate to guide my subsequent reading of this text?
5. What is my personal response to the text, based on this preview of it?

Application

Using the guidelines just given, preview the following article, "The End of School," by George Leonard, reprinted from the May 1992 issue of *The Atlantic.* Be sure to answer all the questions for previewing a text.

THE END OF SCHOOL

School as we know it is doomed. And every attempt to improve—but fundamentally preserve—the present system will only prolong its death throes and add immeasurably to its costs, both financial and social. By the year 2010, if we are to survive as a democratic society, our children will have to learn in a variety of new ways, some of them already on the drawing board, some unforeseen. None of them will involve a teacher in the front of a classroom presenting information to twenty or thirty children seated at desks.

Ironically, the success of a highly publicized school-reform movement has most clearly revealed the failure of school to meet the challenges of these times. The movement began on April 26, 1983, with the publication of a report by the National Commission for Excellence in Education. *A Nation at Risk: The Imperative for Educational Reform* asked for a longer school day and year. It called for the assignment of "far more homework." It demanded higher standards for college admissions, more-rigorous grading, better textbooks, and a nationwide system of standardized achievement tests. Like most of the dozens of reform proposals from other organizations which followed, *A Nation at Risk* was preoccupied with course requirements at the high school level—four years of English, three of math, three of science, and so on. As if four rather than three years of English for students already turned off by the present system would really make much difference.

The interesting thing about the National Commission report (along with most of the other proposals) is that with all its talk of "fundamental" change, it proposed nothing really new. Let's ratchet up the present system, the report seemed to say. Let's get tough on students and teachers. Let's have the same, but better and more of it.

A Nation at Risk set off a firestorm of interest and approval. All three television networks did shows on education. Newsmagazines ran cover stories on the subject. Governors throughout the nation scrambled to get on the bandwagon and create their own commissions and task forces on school reform. Public-opinion polls showed a willingness, even an eagerness, to spend more on the schools. In an amazingly short time—as touted in the Department of Education's follow-up report,

The Nation Responds—the more-of-the-same movement was well under way.

No movement to improve the schools gets all it asks for, but this one got more than most. From 1978 to 1983 total spending per public school student, from kindergarten through high school, adjusted for inflation, had remained stable. From 1983, when *A Nation at Risk* was published, to 1991 per capita spending, adjusted for inflation, increased by 30 percent.

With what results? Blacks and Hispanics have shown some real improvement in reading and writing, and students in general have made small gains in math scores. But even with more and more teachers devoting up to half their time preparing pupils for achievement tests, today's students nationwide are scoring little better, or even worse, in reading and writing than did their predecessors. The painful truth is that despite the spotlight on schooling and the stern pronouncements of educators, governors, and Presidents, despite the frantic test preparation in classrooms all over the country and the increased funding, school achievement has remained essentially flat over the past two decades.

The failure of this well-intended, well-executed movement toward reform summons us to think the unthinkable: we can no longer improve the education of our children by improving school as we know it. The time has come to recognize that school is not the solution. It is the problem. Take a look:

- Clearly, human beings learn at different rates. This doesn't mean that slow learners are less intelligent than fast learners; they're just slower. Yet by and large, school as we know it forces everyone to learn at the same rate or be declared uneducable.
- When we human beings first emerged on this planet, our ability to cooperate gave us an advantage over larger and more powerful creatures. Throughout history we have worked together and learned together to further ourselves and our species. Today if you need help, you're likely to find a friend or a fellow worker who will bat the problem around with you, check out your ideas, offer suggestions. Yet for the most part school is set up to teach competition rather than cooperation.
- A certain amount of self-confidence and self-respect is an essential precondition to learning. Yet by and large, school is set up to humiliate publicly those who, for whatever reason, are unable to come up with the right answer when called upon.

Middle school and high school make it worse. The day is divided into periods of some forty minutes. You sit in a room with twenty or thirty other people with whom you are discouraged from talking over what you are hearing, listening to a presentation that's probably either too demanding or not challenging enough for you. Then a bell rings, and you go sit in another room, with twenty or thirty different people, listening to another presentation that's probably either more or less than you want, on another subject. The teacher in this room probably doesn't know what the teacher in the other room has said or done, nor will any of the teachers in still other rooms know what the other teachers have said or done. . . .

In spite of the best of intentions, the commissions, foundations, task forces, governors' conferences, national and state administrations, and departments of education have missed the point. Longer *bad* school days and years don't add up to a good education. Cranking up the assembly line a bit tighter, spending all year teaching to the achievement tests, might increase the scores a few points, but at the cost of whatever love of learning remains in our students' hearts. Raising graduation standards without radically improving the mode of instruction will only increase the dropout rate or worsen the cheating that is already rampant in our schools. The assumption that higher-quality textbooks, or teachers who "really know their subject matter," can set things right crumbles beneath the boredom, cynicism, and despair produced by the present system. Even if the top graduates from the most prestigious universities were to go into teaching, their best efforts would founder within an essentially unworkable system.

If all of this is true, then what is the alternative? The key to good education, almost totally overlooked by the putative reformers, is to be found by taking the viewpoint of the learner, and, more particularly, by focusing on the interaction between the learner and the learning environment. We can say that the effectiveness of any learning experience depends on the frequency, variety, quality, and intensity of that interaction. Unless the interaction is improved, any and all proposals to improve education are moot. With this premise in mind, one can easily see why school is doomed.

Start with the fact that the human being is a learning animal, pure and simple. What sets him or her apart from all other known forms of life is the ability to learn prodigiously from birth to death. By the time our children start to school, almost all of them have completed one of the most spectacular learning tasks on this planet: the mastery of spoken language *with no formal instruction whatever.* Rather than any kind of formal instruction, they have enjoyed a feast of high-intensity interaction with their learning environment, which in this case comprises all the adults and older children around them. Here are teachers who react immediately to success, permit approximations, and aren't likely to indulge in lectures—that is, the best kind of teachers. School as it is now constituted minimizes interaction and thus minimizes learning among our children, while yoking teachers to a frustrating, essentially impossible task.

What can we do? We must summon the courage to recognize that the present system is entirely inadequate to our present educational needs. We must move as swiftly as possible to end it. We must empower our educators to create interactive learning environments rather than merely presenting information to passive students. We must shift our national educational goals from improving school as it is to building something beyond it—call it metaschool.

A number of educational experiments that move us in the direction of metaschool are already under way. Albert Shanker points to the success of a secondary school in Cologne, Germany. There the Köln-Holweide school uses team teaching, cooperative learning, and peer tutoring to create a close-knit learning community for some 2,000 secondary school students from middle- and lower-income households. Teachers, rather than administrators, make all instructional decisions at this school. They work in teams of six to eight, keeping the same group of eighty-five to ninety students for their entire six years at the school, from the equivalent of our grade five to grade ten.

But these teachers don't hold forth from the front of the room. Actually, the room has no "front," no rows of desks lined up in the same direction. Instead, the students sit around tables, working with the same "table group" of five or six students, integrated by sex, ability, and ethnic origin, for at least a year. The table group is the basic unit of learning, the key to the school's success. Students are in constant interaction, helping one another learn. "If a student has a problem," the headmistress, Anne Ratzki, explained in an interview in *American Educator* magazine, "he doesn't have to wait for a teacher; he can ask his table group for help. If the group can't help, then the teacher will—but the first responsibility lies with the group."

The school day at Köln-Holweide is long, from 8:15 to 4:15, with a thirty-minute pause in the morning, an eighty-minute lunch period, and, for each student, generally one or two periods a day devoted to tutorial or project work or free learning. School closes early every Tuesday, so that students can take care of doctors' appointments, piano lessons, and other nonschool activities. What we would call homework is mostly taken care of in the tutorial or free-learning periods, during which other students or teachers can help out. The extended lunch period is time for sports in the gym, special lessons in such things as theater and ceramics, and dancing in a disco.

What are the results? A dropout rate of one percent, as compared with a West German average of 14 percent, and an astonishing 60 percent rate of admission to four-year colleges, as compared with a national average of 27 percent. And this despite the fact that Köln-Holweide's student body is far from an elite one. Best of all, the kids seem to enjoy their education. Parents report that they can't wait until the holidays end, so that they can get back to school. By ending frontal, lockstep teaching, maximizing interaction with the learning environment, and putting the natural human bonding drive to work for rather than against the educational process, Köln-Holweide travels a good distance past school as we know it and toward the metaschool that lies beyond.

Recent developments in computerized interactive multimedia can take us considerably further. The filmmaker George Lucas is one of a number of innovators who are devising tools for electronic learning. Lucas, the creator of the Star Wars and Indiana Jones sagas, is devoting a quarter of his time these days to long-term research and development in education. He hopes over the next few years to create a "curiosity-driven" demonstration project, perhaps an entire semester's eighth-grade curriculum, combining still and moving pictures, sound, and text, all computerized so that the learner can intervene and interact at any point along the way. . . .

When computers were first proposed as learning tools, some people were concerned that children would become little robots, plugged in to their machines, isolated from human contact. In most cases just the opposite has happened. Actually, the conventional classroom, not the computer, is the isolation cell, the lockup. Contemporary electronic technology, used not as an adjunct to the conventional classroom but as something entirely new, inspires cooperation, encourages learning teams, and builds student confidence.

Moreover, this technology can join students with a whole universe of information, allowing them to reach out to other learners and teachers all across the United States and overseas, and to link up with data bases that eventually will contain a goodly chunk of all human knowledge. When these connections are made, the classroom walls will dissolve, the egg-carton model of education will become a memory, and the schoolhouse will become, in effect, the whole world. Metaschool, a truly new educational entity, might well be born from an imaginative combination of highly interactive technology with the kind of nonfrontal, cooperative learning modeled at Köln-Holweide.

Education circles in the United States are astir with talk of something like this, something beyond school as we know it. But most of the talk thus far has led only to piecemeal experimentation: a model classroom here and there, a "school within a school." One exception can be found in Modesto, an agricultural town with a large Hispanic population in California's central valley. "We are not an extension of the past," says Charles Vidal, the principal of the Evelyn A. Hanshaw Middle School. "We're something entirely new and different—a new building, a new kind of teacher, a new educational concept, a new way of thinking of our kids. We don't call them students. We call them citizens."

At Hanshaw, which opened last September with 807 "citizens," 78 percent of them Hispanic, teachers work in teams, children sit around tables rather than in rows, and every room contains a computer lab, in which all the computers are linked into a network. From the beginning Vidal has sought to eliminate the textbook as a prime educational tool. Instead, teaching teams work out core subjects from which related knowledge develops. Social studies provides a core for history and English. Science serves as a springboard into math. During their two-year stay the citizens of Hanshaw must also do eight "exploratories" in such subjects as arts and crafts, home economics, and drama and chorus. The technology exploratory is made up of twenty-eight five-day segments in such specialties as pneumatics, robotics, hydroponics, and desktop publishing.

It's still too early to tell how this metaschool will work, but Vidal's aims are nothing if not ambitious. Hanshaw is made up of seven sub-schools, which are named for the seven California state universities, and during the year all the children are bused in for a visit to their school's namesake university. "During the visit," Vidal says, "I ask them to close their eyes and see themselves there."

As for the reform movement that began in 1983, even its most avid supporters are beginning to realize the futility of more-of-the-same measures for improving education. . . .

What's needed today is a willingness to think the unthinkable—that school as we know it is doomed—and the will to create something new to take its place. Only a consummate fantasist could argue that this can be done without a substantial initial investment of federal, state, and local money. Since all else in our national life follows from the development of our human resources, this is the most important long-term investment we could possibly make. The end of school could mean the beginning of an education that would tap the potential of all our children, and immeasurably increase individual fulfillment and national success as we enter a new millennium.

GEORGE LEONARD

Annotating

When you annotate a text, you highlight important words or passages and write comments or questions that help you establish a dialogue with the text or remember important points. Different individuals have different styles of annotating. Some people are heavy annotators; they highlight many passages and fill the margins with comments and questions. Others annotate more selectively, preferring to write few comments and to highlight only the most important passages or key words. In thinking about your own annotating strategies, remember that your purpose in reading should influence the way you annotate a text. You would annotate a text you are reading primarily for your information differently than you would an essay you are reading for an assignment or a poem you are reading for pleasure.

Many readers annotate directly on the text as they read. If you have borrowed the text or prefer not to mark up your own book, you can use a separate piece of paper or computer to copy important passages and to write questions and comments.

Use the questions in the following guidelines to help you improve or adapt your preferred method of annotating in different situations.

Guidelines for annotating a text

1. What is my purpose in reading this text? What do I need to annotate to accomplish this purpose?
2. Where does the writer identify the purpose and thesis or main idea of the text?
3. What are the main points, definitions, and examples in the text? Would it be useful to number the main points or make a scratch outline in the margin?
4. What questions does this text suggest to me?
5. Can I identify key words that play an important role in this writer's discussion? Does the text provide enough information so that I can understand these key words and appreciate their significance, or do I need to do additional reading or ask another reader for an explanation?
6. Can I identify passages that seem to play a particularly crucial role in this text? What is my response to these passages?
7. Can I identify passages where my personal experience and values or knowledge of the subject cause me to question the author's assertions, evidence, or method?

Application

Annotate "The End of School" (pages 226–31) as you would if you expected to write an essay responding to it for your composition class.

Summarizing

Students often underestimate the usefulness of writing clear, concise summaries of essays or books. Writing a summary allows you to restate the major points of a book or essay in your own words. Summarizing is a skill worth developing, for it requires you to master the material you are reading and make it your own. Summaries can vary in length, depending on the complexity and length of the material being summarized. Ideally, however, they should be as brief as possible.

Here are suggestions to follow as you write your own summaries.

Guidelines for summarizing a text

1. Reread the material, trying to identify the main ideas.
2. Highlight or number the main points if you have not already done so.

3. Generally stick to main points and leave out illustrations, examples, anecdotes, or evidence.
4. Before writing, try to form a coherent mental picture of the most important ideas.
5. State the main ideas in your own words, as briefly and clearly as you can.

Application

Following the guidelines just provided, write a brief summary of "The End of School" (pages 226–31).

Analyzing the argument of a text

Annotating, outlining, and summarizing can all help you determine the central informative or argumentative points made in a text. "The End of School," for instance, begins with a strong, even provocative assertion: "School as we know it is doomed." This main point constitutes the article's *claim,* and the statements, explanations, and examples throughout the article comprise the evidence or *supports* for this claim.

As Chapter 11, "Understanding Academic Analysis and Argument," points out, whenever you have a claim and a number of supporting statements, you have an argument. Rather than simply accepting an author's assertions and evidence, critical readers attempt to determine for themselves if the evidence provided supports the author's claim. Whether you are writing an argument—the focus of the discussion in Chapter 11—or reading an argument, you are engaging in reasoned inquiry. You are attempting to discover if there are good reasons why you should agree with one or more assertions. The questions included in the following guidelines for analyzing the argument of a text can help you determine if a writer's argument merits your assent.

Guidelines for analyzing the argument of a text

1. What is the major claim or thesis of this text? Is it explicitly stated at any point, or is it implicit, requiring you to "read between the lines"?
2. What interests or values may have caused this writer to support this particular thesis? (Information about the writer from other sources, as well as clues from the writing itself, may help you determine this.)

3. What values and beliefs about this subject do you bring to your reading of this text? How might these values and beliefs affect your response to the writer's argument?
4. Does the writer define key terms? If not, what role do these unstated definitions play in the argument?
5. What other assumptions does the writer rely on in setting up or working through the argument?
6. Consider the writer's appeal to *logos:* What kind of evidence does the writer present? Is the evidence used logically and fairly? Has the writer failed to consider any significant evidence, particularly evidence that might refute his or her claims?
7. Consider the writer's appeal to *pathos:* In what ways does the writer try to put the reader in a receptive frame of mind? Does the writer attempt to persuade the reader through inappropriately manipulative emotional appeals?
8. Consider the writer's appeal to *ethos:* How does the writer establish his or her credibility? What image or *persona* does the writer create for himself or herself? How do appeals to *ethos* contribute to the writer's arguments?

Application

Using the guidelines for analyzing the argument of a text, analyze the argument of "The End of School" (pages 226–31). Be sure to answer all of the questions for analyzing an argument.

Group Activity

By comparing your responses to the applications with those of your peers, you can gain a helpful perspective on the effectiveness of your critical reading strategies. You can also better understand how individual students' different purposes and practices influence their reading of and responses to texts.

Bring your responses to the previous applications in this section to class. (These include your preview, annotations, summary, and analysis of the argument of "The End of School.") Meeting with a group of peers, compare your responses to one or more of the applications, as directed by your instructor. After you have shared your responses, work together to describe briefly the extent to which your responses were similar or dissimilar. Then discuss what these similarities and differences have helped you understand about the process of critical reading, coming to two or three conclusions that you are prepared to share with your classmates.

READING TO WRITE: RESPONDING TO YOUR READING

Response is a natural part of the reading process. Some responses are fleeting. While reading an essay on changing demographics in America, for instance, you may find yourself wondering why the writer emphasizes the economic and political consequences of these changes but barely mentions their social and cultural implications. If on reflection you find that the writer's inattention to the social and cultural consequences of demographic change indicates substantial problems with his or her discussion, you may later write a more formal analysis of this essay in which you discuss the significance of changing demographics on American social and cultural life.

Because they are both acts of composing, reading and writing are complementary processes that together can help you not only deepen your understanding of a text but also increase your emotional and intellectual engagement with it. Writing can thus serve several important functions as you respond to your reading. You can use writing to explore a reading and your response to it; you can also express that understanding through writing.

The preceding section of this chapter presented a number of strategies you can use to read actively and critically. These strategies encouraged you to attend carefully to the text you are reading—to learn more about how it is structured and the kinds of evidence and arguments the writer relies on. As noted earlier, however, reading involves more than attention to the words on the page. These words represent the writer's intended meaning, but as a reader you construct your own understanding of a text. Your response to a text—the meaning that you make of it, what you *do* with it—is influenced by such factors as your personal interest in and previous knowledge of the text's subject and your familiarity with its textual conventions. Many individuals might enjoy reading a detective novel, for instance, but only those who have read a wide range of detective fiction and thus are familiar with the conventions of this popular form of writing can appreciate the differences between classic American hard-boiled detective mysteries (such as those by Dashiell Hammett) and the more intellectual and refined efforts of such writers as Great Britain's Agatha Christie. Similarly, if you have never given much thought to the ecological and economic importance of coastal wetlands, you will read an essay on this topic differently than if you have been actively involved in a campaign to protect wetlands in your area.

As a reader, your goal is to get the most out of your reading, to *do* the most with it. To do so, you need to pay attention to your initial response to a reading and to your own reading process. Whatever your response—from confusion to disagreement to boredom—you can use it to develop strategies for a second reading. One student who originally disagreed strongly with "The End of School" was able to explore her response by freewriting.

> Who does this Leonard guy think he is? The end of school: Everyone else is wrong about education--teachers who've spent years and years in the classroom are wrong about education--but he knows just what the solution is? I know that I have my own biases about schools; my mom's a high school principal and I know how hard she works, how much she cares. And I know that some good things are going on in her school. It really made me angry that Leonard was so negative right from the start about schools. It made me want to shout him down, prove him wrong. OK, I can admit that maybe I read with a chip on my shoulder; I didn't give him much of a chance. Still, everything Leonard says is so black and white, either-or. School as we know it is all bad; his model is all good. Some of the activities he describes in the German and California schools are new, but some aren't. When I was in high school some of my classes were team taught, and we used group work all the time. Why doesn't Leonard recognize changes that are already occurring? Maybe it's true that things like group work or team teaching can't work the way that Leonard thinks they should in a conventional school--but shouldn't Leonard explain why that's so? What does he get by taking such an extreme, all or nothing "end of school" approach? I guess I'll have to read a little more coolly if I want to understand what he's up to.

This student's freewriting enabled her not only to understand why she originally had such a strong negative reaction to Leonard's essay but also to pose a question for a second reading of the essay.

Just as you can learn a good deal about your strengths and weaknesses as a writer by reflecting on your writing process, so too can you gain by reflecting on your reading process. You may do so through brief informal responses, like that of the student just quoted, or through group discussions of readings; talking with others is one of the easiest and most productive ways of gaining multiple perspectives on your reading. You may also find it helpful to keep a reading journal. Whether you write in a notebook or use your computer, your reading journal should serve *your* purposes as a reader. The following guidelines for keeping a reading journal suggest some possible uses for your journal.

Guidelines for keeping a reading journal

Use your reading journal for the following purposes:

- to summarize a text you are reading
- to explore your personal responses to a text
- to relate a text to your own personal experience or to other texts that you have read
- to identify key terms or issues used in a text that you would like to learn more about
- to explore alternative readings of a text
- to "play" with a text by parodying the style or by pushing the ideas to their limit
- to engage in dialogue (serious or humorous) with the author of a text
- to pose questions for future reading, research, and writing
- to record passages that you find particularly effective (or ineffective) and explain why
- to analyze the reasons why you find various kinds of texts difficult or easy to read, boring or interesting, and so on
- to note textual conventions that strike you as unusual or difficult to understand
- to observe and analyze your own reading strategies
- to set goals for yourself as a reader

As you can see, you can use your reading journal not only to deepen your understanding of texts you are reading but also to reflect on and strengthen your reading process.

Activities for Thought, Discussion, and Writing

1. Analyze the first chapter of two textbooks you are reading this term (including this one, if you like). Do these textbooks share certain textual conventions? How do you think the writers of these textbooks have visualized their rhetorical situation? These text-

books are written for you and other students. How effective are they? How might they be more effective?

2. Earlier in this chapter you read "The End of School," by George Leonard. The readings at the end of this section also focus on education in America. These readings include: an editorial from a newspaper, a newspaper article, a professional essay, an opinion column from a weekly newsmagazine, a cartoon, and a poem. First skim the various texts; then read them more carefully. Afterward, answer the following questions:
   - As you skimmed these texts, what were your expectations? To what extent did the form of a text and its place of publication influence your expectations?
   - After reading each text more carefully, what was your response? To what extent did this response represent a deepening of or shift from your earlier expectations?
   - How did your own assumptions and values about education influence your reading of these texts?
   - How would you describe the author's stance or relationship with readers in each of these texts? What role did each text invite you to play as reader?
   - How did the fact that you were reading these texts together, rather than separately, influence your reading process? Did you find that you substantially revised your goals and strategies as a reader as you moved from text to text? In what ways? Did some of these texts invite or elicit stronger reading than others? Why or why not?
   - How did you respond to the content of these texts? Which texts did you find more or less persuasive? Why?
   - How did reading these texts influence your own views about education in America? Did you find that these texts established a coherent dialogue about education that you could easily enter, or did you find it harder to put these texts together in a coherent way? Why?
   - What other observations about reading or about the subject of education in America did these texts stimulate in you?
3. After reading the selections on education that follow this section, reread Leonard's "End of School." How has your reading of these additional texts influenced your response to and evaluation of Leonard's argument?
4. After reading the following selections, you will have read a number of texts that focus on education in America. Write an essay articulating your own views on this subject. Alternatively, write an essay that responds to one or more of the previous readings on education.

IT'S TIME TO GRADE PARENTS

OK, it's not an entirely serious suggestion. And there's scant belief here that either parents or schools will leap at the prospect of grading parental involvement.

But neither is it an entirely whimsical notion.

The importance of parents—and parental involvement—in boosting students' chances of school success is clear in both academic research and anecdotal evidence. Parents matter. More than the niftiest curriculum or the shiniest school facilities and, let us be clear, more than stratospheric school spending, parents matter.

And we're not just talking about gung-ho parents who are themselves academic high-rollers.

Researchers are confirming what many teachers already know—that the periodic classroom presence and the constant supervision at home by parents—even those who may not be literate or who may not yet speak English—usually boost children's school performance. The behavior tells the students that the parents value the teachers and what's going on in the classroom—and the child as well. It says that the parents see school as more than a glorified baby sitter.

Parental involvement, of course, takes many forms. And if schools ever start grading parents, they should use the broadest definition. Parents who never show their faces at parent-teacher-association meetings may still be doing honors work for their kids' education if they set up study areas at home and become as tough as Pharaoh's taskmasters in seeing that the homework gets done.

Listening and reading to your children daily could well beat a day or two reading in the classroom.

So there's no magic formula—though attending parent-teacher conferences (or telephoning when that is impossible) and responding to teachers' calls of concern would seem a skinny minimum.

If schools ever get into the parent-grading game, they'll need to do all they can to promote the different kinds of parental involvement. That will require adapting to the changed schedules and demands of today's changed families. (More single-parent families require child-care provisions if schools want anyone to attend their meetings.) Parents will have to be given clearly defined expectations on their roles in their students' education.

Overall, schools will have to be sincerely committed to parental involvement—even when parents have different ideas about how to educate junior. That hasn't always been the case in the past—or now.

In the end, grading parents might end some of the scapegoating that agitates much of today's education debate. Parents with abysmal marks on the parental-involvement line of their children's report cards might be less ready to blame the schools for their children's—and their own—failures.

SUNDAY OREGONIAN
September 5, 1993

CHALLENGES OUTSIDE CLASSROOM THREATEN U.S. TEENS, STUDY SAYS

WASHINGTON—American teen-agers are holding their own in school, even improving their math skills, but they face dramatic challenges outside the classroom that threaten to drag them down, according to a statistical portrait of today's youth.

"We cannot be satisfied with just holding our own. It's not good enough in this new global economy," Education Secretary Richard Riley said Tuesday after sitting in on a seventh-grade math and science class and watching eighth-graders learn how to solve problems through mediation.

Riley went to Hine Junior High School, just a few blocks from the U.S. Capitol, to release the Education Department's *Youth Indicators 1993: Trends in the Well-Being of American Youth.*

The 153-page study, filled with charts and tables, found that a much higher percentage of students are completing high school than in the 1950s and that college enrollment is at a record high. In 1991, 86 percent of high school seniors said they recognized the value of a good education.

But the study also shows that children today have a lot more to worry about than doing well in school.

"As children grow up, they must deal with the reality of violence, AIDS, drugs, the sheer drag of poverty," Riley told students, teachers and parents at the junior high.

Hine Principal Princess Whitfield said students are looking to the school as a haven from outside pressures. "It's a place where people care for them," she said. "A place where children can feel like children again."

Among the study's findings:

- Twenty-four percent of children lived in single-parent families. In 1970, only 11 percent did. Among black children, 57 percent live with only one parent. Riley said schools must find innovative ways to involve single parents in their children's education.
- Young people today are three times as likely to be murdered and twice as likely to commit suicide as teen-agers were in 1950, and the proportion of teens getting arrested has soared 30-fold over the same period. In 1990, 57 percent of Americans arrested for serious crimes were under 25, the report said.
- Eighty-eight percent of high school seniors said they have consumed alcoholic beverages sometime in their lives, with 51 percent having done so in the previous 30 days. But use of illegal drugs at least once has declined, from 65 percent in 1980 to 41 percent in 1992. Sixty-two percent of the 1992 seniors said they smoked cigarettes at least once, 28 percent in the previous 30 days.

The report said science scores for 9- and 13-year-olds were about the same in 1990 as they were in 1970, but fell for 17-year-olds. Proficiency in math was "significantly higher" in 1990 than it had been in 1978.

The study found no overall improvement in youths' reading skills from 1971 to 1990, but "increases in the scores of black and Hispanic 17-year-olds suggest improvements were made in the education of our less-advantaged students."

"American youth are getting the message that you aren't born smart, you get smart by studying and stretching your mind," Riley said. "They are increasingly aware that being a high school dropout is the dead-end road to failure."

Michael Calhoun, a ninth-grader at Hine, said the biggest challenge he faced was violence. "Too many kids are getting involved with drugs," he said, "and it's just a mad house," but school is safe.

Colicchio Proctor, president of the Hine Parent-Teacher Association and mother of a ninth-grader, said she makes a concerted effort to keep her son busy. "If you stay involved, if you keep him involved, it keeps him from being on the streets," she said.

Riley said the median income of young men has been "in a nose dive" since 1970. "Unless we educate these young men, unless we give them some economic hope, we have little chance of stemming the violence or creating two-parent families that can provide the economic wherewithal for these children," he said.

In 1991, 85 percent of 25- to 29-year-olds had graduated from high school and 23 percent had completed four years of college, the study said. That's up significantly from 1950, when 53 percent had completed high school, and 8 percent had graduated from college.

Outside of the classroom, the report found that religion is becoming less important to youths. Thirty-one percent of high school seniors reported attending religious services once a week, down from 43 percent in 1980.

Among extracurricular activities, athletics remained the most popular, with 52 percent of high school sophomores participating in 1990. Academic clubs gained in popularity over the decade, but interest in music and hobby clubs declined.

CAROLE FELDMAN
Associated Press

GUN CRAZY

In the early fifties, when I went to Fordham Prep, a small high school in the Bronx run by a band of intrepid Jesuits, the only violence was an occasional cuff delivered by a faculty member to the head of a particularly dim-witted student. It was a small school, attended mostly by the sons of blue-collar families. Many of us, including me, were first-generation immigrants, but we had no difficulty mastering English as a second language without the benefit of a federally funded program. We were there to apply ourselves and to do what we were told.

So we were profoundly shaken when we heard that an algebra teacher in a nearby public high school had been shot and killed by a student. In that bygone Truman-Eisenhower era, such crimes were unheard of in any school. The murder weapon was a zip gun. A zip gun was of home manufacture, consisting of a piece of ordinary pipe, a wooden handle kept in place by string or wire wrapping, and a rubber-band-like firing mechanism similar to a slingshot's. The thing was wildly inaccurate and unpredictable, so the teacher was incredibly unlucky to have fallen victim to it.

It is a testament to our rising standard of living that today's high-school kids don't have to depend on such crudely unreliable weaponry. When I was in high school, handguns were rare and next to unobtainable. But, progress being what it is, the 1993 high schooler has a car, a CD player, and an Uzi. A Louis Harris poll published last week tells us that, among pupils in grades six through twelve, nine percent have taken a shot at another human being and eleven per cent have had a shot taken at them by another human being. Nearly sixty per cent said they would know where to get a gun if they needed one. Not surprisingly, more than a third of the children attending our Sarajevo-like institutions of instruction believe there is a good possibility that they will die before they reach threescore and ten. Fifty-five per cent of these young academic-combat veterans also said they would like to see metal detectors installed at school entrances. This Dodge City, check-your-guns-at-the-door approach to the problem might go some way to achieving a cease-fire in the classroom, but it wouldn't silence the gunfire out-of-doors.

Patrick Daly, a Brooklyn elementary-school principal, was killed in crossfire last December when he was out on the street looking for a missing student. How can young people keep their minds on quadratic equations when they know that something similar could happen to them when they come down the front steps after school? The more advanced centers of education are now training their pupils to deal with the kind of battlefield conditions that prevail in, say, Somalia or the former Yugoslavia. To be prepared for a life of scholarship, students are now being taught to use condoms and to ignore the crump of distant artillery. The militarily challenged child is also being taught how to apply a tourniquet without depositing bodily fluids on hard-to-come-by textbooks.

In my day, Mother packed a banana in your lunchbox, and you had to use that as a pistol to fake it when attempting a heist or a mugging. Today, it seems, the box contains Teflon-coated .38-calibre specials along with the trail gorp. This is certainly an advance of a sort, for at least today's students no longer have to depend on zip guns.

NICHOLAS VON HOFFMAN
The New Yorker

AGAINST THE GREAT DIVIDE

I always notice one thing when I walk through the commons at my high school: the whites are on one side of the room and the blacks are on the other. When I enter the room, I think I'm at an African nationalist meeting. The atmosphere is lively, the clothes are colorful, the voices are loud, the students are up and about, the language is different and there's not a white face to be seen. But the moment I cross the invisible line to the other side, I feel I've moved to another country. There are three times as many people, the voices are softer, the clothes more subdued. Everyone's sitting or lying down, and one has as much chance of seeing a black student as a Martian.

The commons is a gathering spot where students relax on benches and talk with friends. They also buy candy and soda, watch TV and make phone calls. It's a place where all sorts of things happen. But you'll never find a white student and a black student talking to each other.

After three years, I still feel uncomfortable when I have to walk through the "black" side to get to class. It's not that any black students threaten or harass me. They just quietly ignore me and look in the other direction, and I do the same. But there's one who sometimes catches my eye, and I can't help feeling awkward when I see him. He was a close friend from childhood.

Ten years ago, we played catch in our backyards, went bike riding and slept over at one another's houses. By the fifth grade, we went to movies and amusement parks, and bunked together at the same summer camps. We met while playing on the same Little League team, though we attended different grade schools. We're both juniors now at the same high school. We usually don't say anything when we see each other, except maybe a polite "Hi" or "Hey." I can't remember the last time we talked on the phone, much less got together outside of school.

Since entering high school, we haven't shared a single class or sport. He plays football, a black-dominated sport, while I play tennis, which is, with rare exception, an all-white team. It's as if fate has kept us apart; though, more likely, it's peer pressure.

In the lunchroom, I sit with my white friends and my childhood friend sits with his black ones. It's the same when we walk through the hallways or sit in the library. If Michael Jackson thinks, "It don't matter if you're black or white," he should visit my high school.

I wonder if proponents of desegregation realized that even if schools were integrated, students would choose to remain apart. It wasn't until 1983 that St. Louis's voluntary city-suburban desegregation program was approved. Today, my school has 25 percent black students. While this has given many young people the chance for a better education, it hasn't brought the two races closer together.

In high school, I've become friends with Vietnamese-Americans, Korean-Americans, Iranian-Americans, Indian-Americans, Russian-Americans and exchange students from France and Sweden. The only group that remains at a distance is the African-Americans. I've had only a handful of black students in all my classes and only one black teacher (from Haiti).

In its effort to put students through as many academic classes as possible and prepare them for college, my school seems to have overlooked one crucial course: teaching black and white students how to get along, which in my opinion, would be more valuable than all the others. It's not that there haven't been efforts to improve race relations. Last fall, a group of black and white students established a program called Students Organized Against Racism. But at a recent meeting, SOAR members decided that the separation of blacks and whites was largely voluntary and there was little they could do about it. Another youth group tried to help by moving the soda machine from the "white" side of the commons to the "black" side, so that white students would have to cross the line to get a Coke. But all that's happened is that students buy their sodas, then return to their own territory.

Last summer, at a youth camp called Miniwanca in Michigan, I did see black and white teens get along. I don't mean just tolerate one another. I mean play sports together, dance together, walk on the beach together and become friends. The students came from all races and backgrounds, as well as from overseas. Camp organizers purposely placed me in a cabin and activity group that included whites, blacks, Southerners, Northerners and foreigners, none of whom I'd met before.

For 10 days, I became great friends with a group of strangers, at least half of whom were black. One wouldn't know that racism existed at that idyllic place, where we told stories around campfires, acted in plays and shared our deepest thoughts about AIDS, parents, abortion and dating. Everyone got along so well there that it was depressing for me to return to high school. But at the same time, it made me hopeful. If black and white teenagers could be friends at leadership camp, couldn't they mix in school as well?

Schools need to make it a real priority to involve whites and blacks together as much as possible. This would mean more multicultural activities, mandatory classes that teach black history and discussions of today's racial controversies. Teachers should mix whites and blacks more in study groups so they *have* to work together in and out of school. (Students won't do it on their own.) And most important, all students should get a chance to attend a camp like Miniwanca. Maybe the Clinton administration could find a way to help finance other camps like it.

As it is now, black and white teenagaers just don't know one another. I think a lot about my friend from childhood—what he does on weekends, what he thinks about college, what he wants to do with his life. I have no answers, and it saddens me.

BRIAN JARVIS
Newsweek

PARA TERESA[1]

A tí-Teresa Compeán
Te dedico las palabras estás
que explotan de mi corazón[2]

That day during lunch hour
at Alamo which-had-to-be-its-name
Elementary

[1]For Teresa. [All footnotes were written by the author.]
[2]To you, Teresa Compean, I dedicate these words that explode from my heart.

my dear raza
That day in the bathroom
Door guarded
Myself cornered
I was accused by you, Teresa
Tú y las demás de tus amigas
Pachucas todas
Eran Uds. cinco.[3]

Me gritaban que por que me creía tan grande[4]
What was I trying to do, you growled
Show you up?
Make the teachers like me, pet me,
Tell me what a credit to my people I was?
I was playing right into their hands, you challenged
And you would have none of it.
I was to stop.

I was to be like you
I was to play your game of deadly defiance
Arrogance, refusal to submit.
The game in which the winner takes nothing
Asks for nothing
Never lets his weaknesses show.

But I didn't understand.
My fear salted with confusion
Charged me to explain to you
I did nothing for the teachers.
I studied for my parents and for my grandparents
Who cut out honor roll lists
Whenever their nietos'[5]names appeared
For my shy mother who mastered her terror
to demand her place in mother's clubs
For my carpenter-father who helped me patiently with my math.
For my abuelos que me regalaron lápices en la Navidad[6]
And for myself.

Porque reconocí en aquel entonces
una verdad tremenda
que me hizo a mi un rebelde

[3]You and the rest of your friends, all Pachucas, there were five of you.
[4]You were screaming at me, asking me why I thought I was so hot.
[5]Grandchildren's.
[6]Grandparents who gave me gifts of pencils at Christmas.

Aunque tú no te habías dado cuenta[7]
We were not inferior
You and I, y las demás de tus amigas
Y los demás de nuestra gente[8]
I knew it the way I knew I was alive
We were good, honorable, brave
Genuine, loyal, strong

And smart.
Mine was a deadly game of defiance, also.
My contest was to prove
beyond any doubt
that we were not only equal but superior to them.
That was why I studied.
If I could do it, we all could.

You let me go then,
Your friends unblocked the way
I who-did-not-know-how-to-fight
was not made to engage with you who-grew-up-fighting
Tú y yo, Teresa[9]
We went in different directions
Pero fuimos juntas.[10]

In sixth grade we did not understand
Uds. with the teased, dyed-black-but-reddening hair,
Full petticoats, red lipsticks
and sweaters with the sleeves
pushed up
Y yo conformándome con lo que deseaba mi mamá[11]
Certainly never allowed to dye, to tease, to paint myself
I did not accept your way of anger,
Your judgements
You did not accept mine.

But now in 1975, when I am twenty-eight
Teresa Compeán
I remember you.
Y sabes—

[7]Because I recognized a great truth then that made me a rebel, even though you didn't realize it.

[8]And the rest of your friends/And the rest of our people.

[9]You and I.

[10]But we were together.

[11]And I conforming to my mother's wishes.

Te comprendo,
Es más
Te respeto
Y, si me permites, te nombro hermana.[12]

INÉS HERNÁNDEZ-ÁVILA
Con Razón Corazón

[12]And do you know what, I understand you. Even more, I respect you. And, if you permit me, I name you my sister.

CHAPTER 10

UNDERSTANDING ACADEMIC AUDIENCES AND ASSIGNMENTS

As a student in college, you need to understand the textual conventions of academic writing. These conventions are not arbitrary—though they may at first seem confusing to you. Rather, they respond to and reflect the academic rhetorical situation. Like other textual conventions, they represent agreements between writers and readers about the construction and interpretation of texts. This chapter describes the values and expectations of an important group of academic readers—your instructors. It also shows you, as a writer, how to analyze academic writing assignments. The next chapter focuses on two important skills required in all academic writing: analysis and argument.

UNDERSTANDING YOUR AUDIENCE: STUDENTS WRITING, INSTRUCTORS READING

Because your instructors are the primary readers of the writing you do in college, you need to understand their values and goals for you and other students. No matter what their discipline, your instructors are members of an academic community. As such, they share a number of intellectual commitments and values. Perhaps the most central of these is the commitment to the ideal of education as inquiry. Your instructors—in business, liberal arts, agriculture, engineering, and other fields—want to foster your ability to think, write, and speak clearly and effectively. Consequently, when they read your papers and exams, your instructors are looking both for your knowledge of a specific subject and for your ability to think and write with sophistication.

Although they might disagree about specifics, those who teach in colleges and universities generally agree about what it means to be a well-educated, thoughtful, knowledgeable person. They believe, for instance, that perhaps the worst intellectual error is oversimplifying. They want their students to learn how to go beyond obvious and stereotypical analysis and arguments to deeper understandings. Thus a historian might urge students to recognize that more was at stake in the American Civil War than freeing the slaves, and an engineer might encourage students to realize that the most obvious way to resolve a design problem is not necessarily the best.

Most college instructors want their students to be able to do more than memorize or summarize information. They want to develop their students' abilities to analyze, apply, question, and evaluate information read and discussed in class. College instructors also want their students to be able to consider issues from multiple perspectives. They tend to believe that nearly every issue or problem has at least two sides. Because most intellectual issues are so complex, college instructors believe that to explore an idea adequately, you must often limit the issue, question, or problem under discussion. They also believe that arguments should be supported by substantial and appropriate evidence, not emotional appeals or logical fallacies. Various disciplines accept different kinds of evidence and follow different methodologies to ensure that conclusions are as accurate and meaningful as possible. But all share the conviction that people arguing a point should support their assertions with more than just an "in my opinion."

The habits of thinking that your college instructors are committed to helping you acquire are intrinsically rewarding. The knowledge that you can analyze a complex issue or problem, work through various arguments, and develop your own position on a subject brings both intellectual and emotional satisfaction and confidence. These same habits of thinking also bring extrinsic rewards, for they are—as chief executive officers in business and industry emphasize—precisely the habits of mind required to succeed in positions of responsibility in any field. And they also enable you to participate effectively in civic affairs at the local, regional, and national levels.

Exploration

Freewrite for five or ten minutes about your experiences so far as an academic writer. What has frustrated or confused you? What has excited you? What questions do you have about the academic rhetorical situation and the conventions of academic writing?

What *do* instructors look for when they read students' writing? Most broadly, your instructors want writing that demonstrates learning and a real commitment to and engagement with the subject being discussed. They want writing that reveals that you are making connections between the issues discussed in class and your life and personal values. And they want writing that adheres to the standards of clear thinking and effective communication that they share as members of the academic community. Specifically, most instructors would agree that they hope to find qualities such as those listed here in their students' papers.

CHARACTERISTICS OF EFFECTIVE STUDENT WRITING

Effective college writing:

- addresses a limited but significant topic
- establishes a meaningful context for the discussion of this topic
- presents a sustained and full discussion, given the limitations of the topic, the time to do the assignment, and the page length
- follows a clear pattern of organization
- discusses sources (if included) fairly and effectively
- provides adequate details and evidence for generalizations
- uses appropriate, concise language
- avoids serious errors of grammar, punctuation, and usage

The following essay, written by Tessa McGlasson for a class in European history, meets these criteria. This essay was written in response to the following assignment for a take-home midterm exam: "What does Francesco Guicciardini's biography of Lorenzo de' Medici reveal about the realities and ideals of fifteenth-century Italy?" Tessa's instructor, Professor Lisa Sarasohn, presented students with excerpts from the biography that Guicciardini, a Florentine historian, wrote shortly after Medici's death. These excerpts are included here. Read both the excerpts from Guicciardini's biography and Tessa's essay with care. As you read, note how Tessa uses these excerpts to support her conclusions about "the ideals and realities of the late fifteenth century" in Italy.

A PORTRAIT OF LORENZO DE' MEDICI

The city was in a state of perfect peace, the citizens of the state united and bound together, and the government so powerful that no one dared to oppose it. Every day the populace delighted in spectacles, feasts and novel diversions. The city was sustained both by its abundant supplies and its flourishing and well-established business enterprises; men of talent and ability were rewarded through the recognition and support given to all letters, all arts, all gifts. And finally when the city was in a state of profound tranquility and quiet within, and at the height of glory and reputation without—as a result of having a government and a head of the greatest authority, of having recently extended its dominion, of having been in great part responsible for the salvation of Ferrara and then of King Ferrante, of controlling completely Pope Innocent, of being allied with Naples and Milan, and of being a kind of balance for Italy as a whole—something happened which turned everything upside down, to the confusion not only of the city but of all Italy. And this was the fact that in the said year, Lorenzo de' Medici, having had a long illness, finally on the 8th day of April, 1492, passed from this life.

This death was marked out as one of the greatest consequence by many omens: a comet had appeared a short time before; wolves had been heard to howl; a mad woman in Santa Maria Novello had cried out that an ox with fiery horns was burning up the whole city; some lions had fallen into a fight and the most beautiful had been killed by the others; and finally a day or two before his death lightning had struck at night the lantern of the dome of Santa Liparate [Reparata] and knocked down some enormous stones, which fell toward the house of the Medici. . . .

Lorenzo de' Medici was forty-three years old when he died, and . . . although he was so young and supposedly under the control of Messer Tommaso Soderini and other elders of the state, nevertheless, in a short time he gained such strength and reputation that he governed the city in his own way. Since his authority multiplied every day and then reached its height through the political crisis of 1478 and later on his return from his successful mission to Naples, he continued until his death to govern the city and to arrange matters entirely according to his own will, as if he were the sole and absolute master. . . .

There were in Lorenzo many and most excellent virtues; there were also in him some vices, due partly to nature, partly to necessity. He possessed such great authority that one could say that in his time the city was not free although it abounded in all the glory and felicity that a city can have; free in name, but in fact and in truth tyrannized over by one of its citizens. His deeds, although they can be censured in part, were very great nonetheless, and so great that they win much more admiration from careful consideration of the facts than from mere hearsay, because they are lacking in those feats of arms and in that military art and discipline for which the ancients are so famous. This was due not to any fault of his but to the age. . . .

No one, even among his adversaries and those who maligned him, denies that there was in him a very great and extraordinary genius. To have governed the city for twenty-three years, and always with increasing power and glory, is such proof of it that anyone who denies it is mad; especially since this is a city most free in speech, full of the most subtle and restless talents. . . . Proof also is the friendship and great reputation he enjoyed with many princes both inside and outside Italy. . . . This reputation sprang from nothing else than knowing how to keep the friendship of these princes with great dexterity and skill. Proof also to those who heard him was his public and private discourse, full of acumen and subtlety, by which in many times and places . . . he gained very great advantage. Proof also are the letters dictated by him, full of such art that one could not ask for more; these seemed the more beautiful inasmuch as they were accompanied by a great eloquence and a most elegant style.

He desired glory and excellence beyond that of anyone else, and in this he can be criticized for having had too much ambition even in regard to minor things; he did not wish to be equalled or imitated by any citizen even in verses or games or exercises, turning angrily against any who did so. He was too ambitious even in great affairs, inasmuch as he wished in everything to equal or emulate all the princes of Italy. . . . In general, however, such ambition was praiseworthy and was responsible for making his renown celebrated everywhere, even outside Italy, because he strove to bring it about that in his time all the arts and talents should be more excellent in Florence than in any other city of Italy. Chiefly for the sake of letters he refounded in Pisa a university of law and the arts. . . . And therefore there always taught in Pisa in his time, with the highest salaries, all the most excellent and famous men of Italy, whom he did not spare expense or trouble to secure. And similarly there flourished in Florence the studies of the humanities. . . . He showed the same favour to vernacular poetry, to music, architecture, painting, sculpture, and all the fine and mechanical arts, so that the city was overflowing with all these graces. These arts developed all the more because he, being most versatile, could pass judgment on them and distinguish among men, with the result that all strove with one another in order to please him more. Of advantage also was the boundless generosity with which he showered pensions on talented men and supplied them with all the tools necessary to their arts. For example, when he wanted to create a Greek library, he sent Lascaris, a most learned man who taught Greek in Florence, as far as Greece to seek out ancient and good books.

The same liberality preserved his renown and his friendship with the princes outside Italy, since he neglected no show of magnificence, even at the greatest expense and loss, by which he might influence great men. And so, through such display and lavishness, his expenditures multiplied in Lyons, Milan, Bruges, and in various centres of his trade and his company, while his profits diminished from being neglected by incompetent agents. . . . His accounts were not well kept because he did not understand commerce or pay enough attention to it, and as a result his affairs more than once fell into such disorder that he was on the point of bankruptcy, and it was necessary for him to help himself out both with money from his friends and with public funds.

FRANCESCO GUICCIARDINI

AN ANALYSIS OF GUICCIARDINI'S
BIOGRAPHY OF LORENZO DE' MEDICI

The late fifteenth century, when Lorenzo de' Medici ruled Florence, was a prosperous, progressive era for that city, and indeed all of Italy. A more enlightened way of thinking had arrived, and human activity strove to use this new light to illuminate everything that was good and right. But in any rapidly progressing time period there are less desirable elements which come hand in hand with the good. This document reveals much information about the clash of human ideal and human reality in fifteenth-century Florence.

The first paragraph of Guicciardini's biography sets forth the overlying cultural and political climate of the period: the city was flourishing and "in a state of perfect peace." What we think of as the Renaissance was under way; "recognition and support" was fully given to the arts and letters, and the citizens enjoyed "spectacles, feasts, and novel diversions" every day. Florence had risen to become one of the most powerful cities on the Italian peninsula under the Medici by the time Lorenzo took power despotically after his father's death in 1469. He ruled Florence "in his own way" and "according to his own will, as if he were the sole and absolute master." Medici traveled to Naples in 1479 and made friends with its king, Ferrante. Since Ferrante was allied with the pope, this shrewd move earned Florence two worthy allies at once and ended the city's ongoing wars with the papal states. This resulted in Medici's "controlling completely Pope Innocent" and "of being allied with Naples." Another alliance existed with Milan. Since we know that city-state alliances were constantly shifting during these years, the first paragraph takes on a fleeting, one-moment-in-time sort of quality; indeed it should, since it is describing only where Florence was in early April of 1492, at the time of Lorenzo de' Medici's death.

The second paragraph of the biography reveals another interesting characteristic of this period--that is the increasing importance being placed upon the relationship between humans and the universe. People had begun to believe that the events in the universe affected humans, and vice versa. Medici's death was apparently "marked out as one of greatest consequence by many omens." Included in these are astrological and meteorological signs (the comet and lightning), signs from the animal kingdom (howling wolves and fighting lions), and strange, inexplicable behaviors of other humans (the mad woman's ravings). Everything in the universe was believed to be connected somehow to everything else, and this assumption rests behind much of the advancement made in the era.

The ideals and realities of the late fifteenth century are illustrated clearly in this manuscript by the personality and actions of Lorenzo de' Medici himself. "There were in Lorenzo many and most excellent virtues," we are told, among them a "very great and excellent genius." He was a great diplomat: he knew "how to keep the friendship of these princes with great dexterity and skill." He spoke and wrote eloquently: his discourse "full of acumen and subtlety" and his letters in a "most elegant style." Medici was highly educated and patronized the arts in every way. He paid well for "all the most excellent and famous men of Italy" to teach at his university in an effort to make Florence a center for all types of learning--great evidence of the "civic pride" and love of liberal education so valued in the Renaissance. Like an ideal noble, Medici patronized talented people with "boundless generosity." The study of the classics was important to him, as shown by his quest for the best Greek books. These traits and passions were considered ideal by fifteenth-century Florentines as well as other Italians.

With Medici's position of power, however, came opportunities for corruption and greed. Guicciardini points out that "there were also in him some vices." The absolute power of his rule invited tyranny, and Guicciardini admits that no matter how "tranquil" and "glorious" Florence was, it "was not free." Medici was intensely ambitious and egotistical: he "did not wish to be equalled" and "turned angrily against" anyone who tried. He was often overly extravagant, and his lavishness cost him dearly. Contrary to his status as the ideal "Renaissance prince," matters of commerce escaped his understanding, and so he ignored and neglected them, letting his greed and vanity take over and eventually bring him to "the point of bankruptcy." We further are told that to "help himself out," he took money from "public funds." Although in other sources about him we read mostly about his idealized genius and virtue, this document points out some of Medici's real-life faults as well.

With any despotism or other form of absolute government comes the unlimited power of tyranny and all its opportunities for immoral human behavior. Likewise, with the ideal must come a dose of reality. Lorenzo de' Medici and his life as detailed in this document represent the grand, honorable, civilized elements of fifteenth-century Florence. Guicciardini's biography also reminds us that anything involving humans is always far from perfect. Italy's fifteenth century, and indeed the entire Renaissance, was no exception.

TESSA McGLASSON

Group Activity

Working with a group of classmates, discuss how Tessa McGlasson's essay demonstrates the characteristics of effective student writing listed on page 251. Locate at least one specific example of each characteristic in Tessa's essay. Appoint a recorder to write down the results of your discussion, which your instructor may ask you to present to the class.

LEARNING TO ANALYZE ACADEMIC WRITING ASSIGNMENTS

Understanding your instructors' values and goals as members of the academic community can enable you to respond more appropriately to the demands of academic writing. In addition to understanding these values and goals, however, you must know how to analyze the assignments given to you by instructors. Such analysis is crucial, for assignments (whether presented orally or distributed in writing) provide concrete indications of instructors' expectations. You can improve your understanding of your academic assignments by analyzing each assignment, identifying its assumptions, developing strategies to increase your commitment to it, and making action-oriented plans that you can use as you work on the assignment.

Analyzing the assignment as presented by your instructor

All assignments are not alike. Sometimes instructors present students with broad, unstructured topics. Such assignments are usually relatively brief and open-ended. A political science instructor might ask you to write a twenty-page research paper discussing an important political consequence for America of the Vietnam War. Or a psychology instructor might ask you to write a four- to six-page essay exploring how your family background has influenced your current attitudes about marriage or parenthood. With broad assignments like these, you must often determine not only the specific topic but also the approach to take in analyzing and presenting your material.

In other instances, instructors develop quite limited or specific assignments. Such assignments may substantially restrict your freedom of choice in regard to a topic; they may also include a format or sequence of steps or activities that you must follow. Other assignments may fall in a middle ground between these two extremes.

Whether your instructors give you broad or limited assignments, the words they use to describe these assignments, especially certain key words, can tell you a great deal about their intentions. These key words—*define, analyze, evaluate, defend, show, describe, review, prove, summarize, classify*—are usually action verbs. They are crucial in essay examination questions because you must quickly determine how to respond to a topic, but they are important in any writing assignment. An assignment that asks you to *summarize* Freud's Oedipal theory, for instance, is quite different from one that asks you to *criticize* or *evaluate* it. To summarize Freud's Oedipal theory, you need to recount its major features. Criticizing this theory challenges you to identify its strengths and weaknesses and to provide evidence for your assessment.

Identifying the assumptions behind an assignment

To complete an assignment effectively, you need to know more than whether it is broad or limited. You need to know the criteria your instructor will use to evaluate the assignment and the processes and resources you can best use as you work on it. Some instructors provide information about these and related matters for students. If your instructor provides such suggestions, study them with care. If you don't understand how to act on your instructor's suggestions, make an appointment to speak with your instructor. Discussing your assignment with other students in your class is another helpful way to test your understanding.

Not all instructors provide this kind of information about assignments, however. Sometimes they think that the criteria for evaluation and the processes and resources students might best use to complete an assignment are so obvious that they need not be stated explicitly. Some instructors believe that students learn more effectively when they take full responsibility for all aspects of an assignment. For this reason, these instructors want students to discover for themselves how they can best work on an assignment and the features that characterize a successful response to an assignment.

Whenever you are presented with an assignment, you need to "read between the lines," for even detailed suggestions cannot tell you exactly what processes and resources you should use as you work on an assignment. One way to begin this process of reading between the lines is to think about the ways your assignment relates to the objectives, class discussions, and readings for a course. Your instructor may not comment specifically on this connection, but you can be sure that one exists. Asking yourself the questions in the following guidelines should help you recognize such connections and analyze the assumptions inherent in an assignment.

Guidelines for identifying the assumptions behind an assignment

1. How does this assignment reflect the objectives of this course?
2. What general analytical and argumentative strategies does my instructor emphasize during class discussions? In discussions of readings, what organizational, stylistic, and logical qualities does my instructor praise or criticize? How might this assignment represent my instructor's effort to help me develop the critical abilities he or she emphasizes in class?
3. How much class time has my instructor spent on discussions of readings or on activities related to the content or form of this assignment? What has the instructor emphasized in these discussions or activities? How do these discussions and activities relate to this specific assignment?
4. Does this assignment call for a specific type of writing? How can I use my experience with previous writing assignments to help me complete this assignment?
5. To what extent does this assignment require me to follow the methodology and format characteristic of this discipline?
6. If this is one of several assignments for this course, can I apply comments my instructor has made in response to earlier essays to my current project?

If you find it difficult to answer these questions, you may want to meet with your instructor to discuss your assignment. This conference will be most useful (for both of you) if you prepare ahead. Before seeing your instructor, ask yourself the questions listed here. Try rewriting the assignment in your own words, and then draw up a plan describing how you intend to complete it. Come to the conference prepared with your plan and with a list of specific questions, if possible. Most instructors are happy to discuss assignments with students, especially students who have prepared carefully for the conference. Don't expect your instructor to give you a step-by-step list of dos and don'ts for an assignment, however. What you want to clarify—and what an instructor will be glad to discuss with you—is your general understanding of and approach to the assignment.

Building commitment to an assignment

Most academic writing is, by definition, *required* writing—writing done to fulfill a requirement. As a student, you are inevitably aware that you are writing not necessarily because you want to but because you have to. These conditions may make it hard for you to feel a strong sense of "ownership" of your writing. Furthermore, even if you're genuinely interested in your topic, you may feel so pressed by deadlines and other demands that all you can think is "I've just got to get this essay out of the way so I can get ready for biology lab." All writers face these problems, including those who write on the job. Successful writers know, however, that they can't write well unless they are interested in and committed to their subjects. Consequently, they develop strategies to help them build this interest and commitment so that they can transform a required assignment (whether a research paper or a report for the boss) into a question or problem they care about and feel challenged to resolve.

This is not to suggest that you must become passionately absorbed in and excited by every writing assignment. That would be unrealistic. But if you can't find some way to interest yourself in an assignment, to view it as an intellectual challenge you want to meet, you're going to have trouble getting beyond stale formulas. Some students in this situation simply put off working on their assignments for so long that they must complete them in a desperate, chaotic frenzy. They then blame their poor performance and low grades on their last-minute effort. There are better ways to respond to the challenge of required writing assignments.

You can, for instance, try to build your interest by using invention strategies—strategies explained in Chapter 5, such as freewriting, looping, brainstorming, and clustering or the more formal journalist's questions, tagmemics, and topical questions. Keeping a writer's journal or notebook may also help you generate interest in a topic that at first doesn't seem compelling. Suppose, for example, that your economics instructor has asked you to write an essay on some topic connected with the Great Depression of the 1930s. At first you might not find this subject very interesting. After all, the depression occurred decades ago. You'd rather evaluate one of the current administration's economic policies. But after brainstorming, freewriting, or writing in your journal, you find that you keep coming back to a single image: the much-reproduced photograph of a businessman in a topcoat selling apples on a street corner. Did this actually happen? How often? How representative is this image of the depression as a whole? Suddenly you've got a series of related questions—questions that you care about and that can help you limit and focus your topic.

When you are building commitment to an assignment, you are looking for reasons to *want* to write, reasons to "own" the assignment your teacher has given you. Not only can talking with your teacher about an assignment help you understand the assignment, but it can also make you care more strongly about it. You can also employ the following guidelines to turn a required assignment into an interesting challenge that you want to complete.

Guidelines for generating interest in and commitment to an assignment

1. Use Freewriting, Brainstorming, Journal Writing, or Other Informal Kinds of Writing to Explore What You Already Know About Your Assignment.

Freewriting and brainstorming can help you discover images, questions, contradictions, and problems that turn required assignments into questions you want to answer. You may also find it helpful simply to write or list what you already know about a subject; you may be reassured to discover that you have a surprisingly large fund of information on your subject.

2. Use the Same Strategies to Explore How You Feel about an Assignment.

You may find it helpful to freewrite or brainstorm about your feelings about an assignment. While writing in her journal about a required assignment in a journalism class, for instance, Holly Hardin noted that she didn't want to work on a story about whether quarters or semesters are more conducive to learning because it was "just another dead issue." Once she understood the source of her resistance, Holly realized that she should see if her assumption was in fact correct. After interviewing several faculty members on campus, Holly discovered to her surprise that they held widely varying views on this subject. "Once I found a point of conflict," Holly wrote in a later journal entry, "I found a reason to write. From that point on the story was not just easy to work on but interesting."

3. Work Collaboratively with Other Students in the Class.

Any assignment can seem overwhelming—something to put off rather than to begin—when you're sitting alone in your room or the library thinking about it. A much more productive strategy is to meet with other students in the class to discuss your understanding of the assignment and the processes and resources you are employing to respond to it. I'm not talking about a gripe session, or *only* a gripe session. You may want to spend a few moments commiserating with one another about how busy you are and how many assignments you need to do, but you should keep your primary goal in focus. By talking about your assignment and about your current efforts to respond to it, you want both to generate enthusiasm for this project and to help each other complete it more effectively.

If you are enrolled in a course in a discipline that you have found difficult in the past, you may wish to form a study group of students who will meet on a regular basis. Simply meeting together can provide discipline and intellectual and emotional reinforcement that you can use to your advantage. Your discussions and responses to works in progress can also help stimulate both your interest in the subject and your ability to respond successfully to assignments.

Exploration

Think back to an academic writing experience that was difficult or frustrating for you. To what extent did this problem result from your inability to build a genuine commitment to the assignment? How might you have responded more effectively to this problem? Freewrite for five or ten minutes about this experience.

Preparing to do an assignment

Analyzing ways to prepare for an assignment may seem like an obvious suggestion, but surprisingly often, students don't heed it. Sometimes they may lack commitment to the assignment. Other times they may be simply overwhelmed by all the conflicting demands of academic work. Whatever the motive, the consequence is the same: their writing often suffers.

You need not make elaborate preparations for doing all your assignments, but soon after you receive an assignment, you should be able to answer the questions in the following guidelines.

Guidelines for getting started on an assignment

- What is the purpose of the assignment?
- What demands does this assignment make of me?
- How much time should I reserve for research?
- How much time should I reserve for planning, drafting, and revising?
- How will my work for other courses and my personal responsibilities influence my time schedule for completing this assignment?
- What is likely to be most difficult for me about this assignment? How can I anticipate and resolve the potential difficulties?
- What strengths do I have going into this assignment? How can I build on these strengths to make my job easier?

- Do I need to build commitment to the assignment so that I will be better motivated to develop and stick to a plan?
- Am I likely to need help with this assignment? Should I schedule a conference with my instructor or writing assistant?

These are commonsensical questions, questions that many students ask themselves automatically. They may never write out their answers, but they keep them in mind as they juggle course requirements, schedule their time, and prepare to work on their assignments.

Activities for Thought, Discussion, and Writing

1. Interview either an instructor whose class you are taking this term or an instructor in your major area of study. Ask this person to describe his or her understanding of the goals of undergraduate education and the role your particular class or field of study plays in achieving these goals. Discuss the special analytic and argumentative skills required to succeed in this course or field. Ask what advice this person would give to someone, like yourself, who is taking a class in this field or planning to major in it. Be prepared to report the results of this interview to your group so that the group can present its collective findings to the class. Your instructor also may ask you to write an essay summarizing and commenting on the results of your interview.
2. Choose a writing assignment that you are currently working on for this or another course. Using the suggestions in this chapter, analyze this writing assignment. Begin by analyzing the assignment as it is presented by your instructor. Then look for the assumptions behind the assignment, developing strategies to help you build commitment to the assignment, and finally prepare to get started using the questions in the chapter.

   After you have completed the assignment, try to determine if the analysis did or did not make your work easier or more productive. Would you follow this process again?
3. Write an essay about the differences between your expectations of what college would be like and your experiences so far. What have you learned about yourself, and about college, as a result?

CHAPTER 11

UNDERSTANDING ACADEMIC ANALYSIS AND ARGUMENT

As a student, you must respond to a wide range of writing assignments. For your American literature class, you may have to write an essay analyzing the significance of the whiteness of the whale in *Moby Dick,* whereas your business management class may require a group-written case study. You may need to write a lab report for your chemistry class and critique a reading for sociology.

Although these assignments vary considerably, a close look reveals that they, like most academic writing assignments, draw on two related skills: analysis and argument. Strengthening these two important academic skills will enable you to respond more effectively to the demands of academic writing.

DEVELOPING EFFECTIVE STRATEGIES FOR ANALYSIS

Analysis is the activity of separating something into parts and determining how these parts function to create the whole. When you analyze, you examine a text, an object, or a body of data to understand how it is structured or organized and to assess its validity and usefulness. Most academic writing, thinking, and reading involve analysis. Literature students analyze how a play is structured or how a poem achieves its effect; economics students analyze the major causes of inflation; biology students analyze the enzymatic reactions that comprise the Krebs cycle; and art history students analyze how line, color, and texture come together in a painting.

As these examples indicate, analysis is not a single skill but a group of related skills. An art history student might explore how a famous painting by Michelangelo achieves its effect, for instance, by *comparing* it with a similar work by Raphael. A biology student might discuss future acid-rain damage to forests in Canada and the United States by first *defining* acid rain and by then using *cause-and-effect* reasoning to predict worsening conditions. A student in economics might estimate the likelihood of severe inflation in the future by *categorizing* or *classifying* the major causes of previous inflationary periods and then *evaluating* the likelihood of such factors influencing the current economic situation.

Different disciplines naturally emphasize different analytic skills. But whether you are a history, biology, or business major, you need to understand and practice this crucial academic skill. You will do so more successfully if you establish a purpose and develop an appropriate framework or method for your analysis.

Establishing a purpose for your analysis

Your instructors will often ask you to analyze a fairly limited subject, problem, or process, such as Mrs. Ramsey's role in Virginia Woolf's *To the Lighthouse,* feminists' criticisms of Freud's psychoanalytical theories, or Gregor Mendel's third law of genetics, the law of dominance. Such limited tasks are necessary, your instructors believe, because of the complexity of the material being analyzed. Books have been written on Woolf's masterpiece and Freud's theories, so you can hardly examine these subjects completely in a brief essay or a research paper. Even though you are analyzing a limited topic, however, the general purpose of your analysis is much broader; it is to clarify or better understand the material being examined. When you analyze a limited topic, you are like a person holding a flashlight in the dark: the beam of light you project is narrow and highly focused, but it illuminates a much larger area.

Recognizing this larger purpose of analysis can help you make important decisions as you plan, draft, and revise. If your instructor has assigned a limited topic, for instance, you should ask yourself why he or she might have chosen this particular topic. What might make it an especially good means of understanding the larger issues at hand? If you are free to choose your own topic for analysis, your first questions should involve its overall significance. How will analyzing this topic improve your understanding of the larger subject, process, or problem? As you write, ask yourself regularly if your analysis is leading you to rethink or understand your topic more deeply. If you can answer yes to this question, you are probably doing a good job of analysis.

Even though the general purpose of your analysis is to understand the larger subject, process, or problem, you still need to establish a more specific purpose to provide direction for your writing. Imagine, for instance, that your Shakespeare instructor has asked you to write an essay on the fool in *King Lear.* You might establish one of these specific purposes for your analysis.

- to explain how the fool contributes to the development of a major theme in *King Lear*
- to discuss the effectiveness or plausibility of Shakespeare's characterization of the fool
- to clarify the role the fool plays in the construction of the plot of *King Lear*
- to agree or disagree with a particular critical perspective on the fool's role and significance

Establishing a specific purpose for your analysis helps you define how your analysis should proceed. It enables you to determine the important issues you should address or the questions you should answer. A student analyzing the effectiveness of Shakespeare's characterization of the fool would address different questions, for example, than one who is agreeing with a particular critical perspective on the fool's role and significance.

There are no one-size-fits-all procedures you can follow to establish a purpose for your analysis. Sometimes your purpose will develop naturally as a result of reading, reflection, and discussion with others. In other instances, you may need to draw on the invention strategies described in Chapter 5. Such informal and formal methods of invention as freewriting, brainstorming, tagmemics, and the topical questions can help you explore your subject and discover one or more fruitful questions that can guide your analysis. You may need to write your way into an understanding of your purpose by composing a rough draft of your essay and seeing, in effect, what you think about your topic. Writing and thinking are dynamically interwoven processes.

Developing an appropriate method for your analysis

Once you have a purpose, how do you actually analyze something? The answer depends on the subject, process, or problem being analyzed; it also depends, in academic writing, on the discipline within which the analysis is done. The students studying *To the Lighthouse* and Mendel's third law may both use such analytic processes as definition, causal analysis, classification, and comparison to analyze their subjects. But the exact form of the processes each uses—the way each organizes the analysis and the criteria each uses to evaluate it—may well differ. Despite these disciplinary differences, both students must establish some method for analysis if they are to succeed.

There are no hard-and-fast rules for establishing such a method. In general, however, you should look to the methods of inquiry characteristic of the specific discipline for guidance. The questions presented in the following guidelines can help you develop an appropriate method for your analysis.

Guidelines for developing an appropriate method for your analysis

- How have your instructors approached analysis in class? Do they rely on a systematic procedure, such as case-study or problem-solving methodology, or does their analysis vary, depending on the subject under discussion?
- What kinds of evidence and examples do they draw on? What criteria seem to influence their choice of evidence and examples?
- What kinds of questions do your instructors typically ask in class discussions? Why might people in the discipline view these as important questions?
- What kinds of answers to these questions do your instructors accept or praise as effective? Why might people in this discipline value these kinds of responses to questions?

If, after considering these questions and reflecting on your experience in a class, you continue to have difficulty settling on an appropriate method for analysis, meet with your instructor to discuss this problem. You might ask your instructor to recommend student essays or professional articles that you can read. Analyzing these articles and essays can help you understand the analytical methods used by people writing in the field.

RESPONDING TO THE DEMANDS OF ACADEMIC ARGUMENT

What do you think of when you read the word *argument*? Do you imagine two journalists disagreeing heatedly about political issues on shows like *Crossfire*? Or do you think of formal debates, like those at forensic competitions or in courts or state legislatures? These are all examples of arguments, but they do not represent the full range. Argument is not limited to debates or angry confrontations, nor does it necessarily involve the heated exchange of opinions. Argument occurs whenever people make judgments, whenever they present good reasons for their beliefs and actions. If you and your roommate spend an hour thoughtfully exploring the issues raised by the controversial practice of surrogate motherhood, you are not adversaries but rather partners in inquiry—two friends exploring a complex legal, ethical, and moral question.

As this example indicates, debate is not the only possible model for argument. The debate model of argument can actually pose problems for students writing in the context of the academic rhetorical situation. Think about the terminology used in debate: opponents "attack" their "adversaries," hoping to "demolish" their arguments in order to "win" the judge's assent and claim "victory" in the "contest." This model of argument may prevail in forensic and political debates, but it hardly seems appropriate for academic analysis and argument. Your teachers are not interested in whether you can "attack" or "demolish" your opponents; rather, they value the ability to examine an issue or a problem dispassionately and from multiple perspectives. Their commitment is not to winning but to clear reasoning, substantial evidence, and well-developed arguments. Academic argument is best conceived of as conversation and dialogue—as inquiry—not as debate.

Exploration

Spend five or ten minutes freewriting in response to the following questions.

- In the past, what have you associated with the word *argument*? How have you responded to the word?
- How may these associations or responses have influenced your attitude toward written arguments?
- If you have adhered in the past to the debate model of argument, how might you benefit by viewing argument as inquiry and dialogue rather than debate?

Academic argument complements and builds on analysis. The art history student who analyzes Michelangelo's painting by comparing it with Raphael's might decide that Michelangelo's style owes more to sculpture than Raphael's does. This comparative analysis would form the foundation of an argument to this effect. If the instructor finds this student's discussion effective, it will be because the student has provided good reasons in support of his or her major assertions.

As explained in Chapter 10, most college instructors are committed to objective, reasoned argument. In their personal lives, they may have deeply held religious, political, or personal beliefs that influence their thinking and actions—beliefs that they accept "on faith." As members of the academic community, however, they encourage students to adopt a questioning, inquiring approach toward issues and ideas. Consequently, in academic argument you cannot simply assert that something is or is not true, valid, effective, or just; you must provide appropriate evidence for your assertions.

Whether you are interpreting the symbolism of Hester Prynne's scarlet A in *The Scarlet Letter* or evaluating the merits of competing proposals for a business class, you are arguing—presenting good reasons why others should or should not agree with your conclusions. To prepare a successful academic argument, you need to determine what is at stake in an argument, what evidence is appropriate, and what counterarguments are possible.

DETERMINING WHAT'S AT STAKE IN AN ARGUMENT

You can't argue by yourself. If you disagree with a recent legislative decision reported in your morning newspaper, you may mumble angry words to yourself at breakfast—but you'd know that you're not arguing. To argue, you must argue with someone. Furthermore, the person with whom you wish to argue must agree with you that an assertion raises an arguable *issue*. If you like rap music, for example, and your friend, who prefers jazz, refuses even to listen to (much less discuss) your favorite tape, you can hardly argue with your friend's preference. You'll both probably just wonder at the peculiarities of taste.

Similarly, in academic argument you and your reader (most often your instructor) must agree that an issue is worth arguing about if you are to argue successfully. Often this agreement involves sharing a common understanding of a problem, process, or idea. A student who writes an argument on the symbolism of Hester Prynne's scarlet A in *The Scarlet Letter,* for example, begins from a premise, one she believes will be shared by the teacher, that Hester's A has significance for the meaning or theme of the novel.

All argument, in this sense, begins from shared premises. There is, however, an important distinction between the kind of casual arguments you have with family and friends and academic arguments. Academic arguments, unlike casual arguments, must be structured so that they focus on a limited issue or topic. In a late-night discussion with friends, you may easily slip from a heated exchange over the cause of the national budget deficit to a friendly debate about the best way to remedy bureaucratic inefficiency. In an academic argument, however, you must limit your discussion not just to a single issue but to a single *thesis*. It is not enough, in other words, to decide that you want to write about nuclear energy or the need to protect the wilderness. Even limiting these subjects—writing about the Three Mile Island nuclear reactor or the Forest Service Land Management Plan for the White Mountain National Forest in New Hampshire—wouldn't help much. That's because your thesis must be an assertion—something, in other words, to argue about.

A clear, adequately limited thesis is vital for argument because it indicates (for you and for your reader) what's at stake. For this reason, many instructors and writers suggest that academic arguments should contain an explicit thesis statement, a single declarative sentence that asserts or denies something about the topic. The assertion "The United States Forest Service's land management plan for the White Mountain National Forest fails adequately to protect New Hampshire's wilderness areas" is an example of a thesis statement.

Thesis statements serve important functions for writers and readers. Developing a clear, limited thesis statement can help ensure that a writer stays on track and includes evidence or details relevant to the main point rather than extraneous or only loosely related information. Readers—especially busy readers like your college instructors—also find thesis statements helpful. A limited, clearly worded thesis statement in the introduction of your essay reassures your readers that your essay will be more than a mishmash of loosely connected ideas and examples. Also, once your readers clearly understand the main point you wish to make in your essay, they can read your writing both more critically and more efficiently.

Here is the first paragraph of an essay written for a class on Latin American history. The student's thesis statement is underlined. Notice how this statement clearly articulates the student's position on the topic, the role of multinational and transnational corporations in Central America.

> Over the past fifty years, Latin American countries have worked hard to gain economic strength and well-being. In order to survive, however, these countries have been forced to rely on multinational and transnational corporations for money, jobs, and technological expertise. <u>In doing so, they have lost needed economic independence and have left themselves vulnerable to exploitation by foreign financiers</u>.

A clear thesis statement can help both writer *and* reader stay on track as they "compose" an essay.

Application

Look back at the rough and revised drafts of Todd Carpenter's essay, "Why Isn't There a National Bottle Law?" on pages 191–97. Reread both drafts and then answer these questions.

- The rough draft does not contain a clear thesis statement, but the revised draft does. What is the thesis statement in the revised draft? Does this thesis statement help make Todd's essay easier for you as a reader to follow?
- Todd's analysis of his rhetorical situation, presented on pages 190–91, demonstrates his awareness of the academic rhetorical situation and of the demands of academic analysis and argument. Todd notes, for instance, that "even if my instructor agrees that there should be a national bottle law, she won't give me a good grade unless I write an effective argument. In class, my instructor has stressed the importance of looking at both sides of the issue and presenting evidence for my views, so I'll try to do that here." Review Todd's rough and revised drafts, paying particular attention to the ways in which the revised draft responds to these concerns. List at least three of these changes, and write a brief explanation of why they increase the effectiveness of Todd's essay as an academic argument.
- Suppose that Todd were writing an essay on this subject not for his instructor but for members of an ecological group whom he hopes to convince to support this effort. How might

Todd revise his argument to meet the needs and expectations of these readers, who are likely to support the idea of a national bottle law but may not necessarily view it as a priority for their particular organization?

If you are like many writers, you will at times have to think—and write—your way into a thesis. You may know the subject you want to discuss, and you may have a tentative or *working* thesis in mind from the start. Often, however, you will find that only by actually writing a rough draft, by marshaling your ideas and ordering your evidence, can you finally determine exactly what thesis you can support. In situations like this, you will revise your thesis as you write to reflect your increased understanding of your topic and your rhetorical situation.

UNDERSTANDING THE ROLE OF VALUES, ASSUMPTIONS, AND BELIEFS IN ARGUMENT

When you argue, you give reasons and provide evidence for your assertions. The student arguing against the Forest Service plan might warn that increased timber harvesting will reduce access to the forest for campers and backpackers or that building more roads will decrease wildlife. This writer might also show that the Forest Service has failed to anticipate some problems with the plan and that cost-benefit calculations are skewed to reflect logging and economic-development interests. These are all potentially good reasons for questioning the proposed plan, but notice that these reasons necessarily imply certain values or beliefs. The argument against increasing the timber harvest and building more roads, for instance, reflects the assumption that preserving wildlife habitats and wilderness lands is more important than the economic development of the resources.

Is this student's argument flawed because it appeals to values and beliefs? Of course not. When you argue, you can't avoid making some assumptions, nor can—or should—you suppress your own values and beliefs. Your values and beliefs enable you to make sense of the world; they provide links between the world you observe and experience and yourself. They thus play an important role in any argument.

Suppose that you and a friend are getting ready to leave your apartment to go out for dinner. You look out the window and notice some threatening clouds. You say, "Looks like rain. We'd better take umbrellas since we're walking. I hate getting soaked." "Oh, I don't know," your friend replies. "I don't think it looks so bad. It usually rains in the mornings in summer. I think we should risk it." Brief and informal as this exchange is, it constitutes an argument. Both you and your friend observed something, analyzed it, and drew conclusions—conclusions backed by reasons. Although you each cite different reasons, your conclusions may most strongly reflect your different personal preferences. You're generally cautious, and you don't like getting caught unprepared in a downpour, so you opt for an umbrella. Your friend is more of a risk taker.

If your individual preferences, values, and beliefs shape a single situation like this where only getting wet is at stake, imagine how crucial they are in more complicated and contested situations—situations where the central issue is not whether clouds will bring rain but whether a controversial proposal is right or wrong, just or unjust, effective or ineffective. Argument necessarily involves values and beliefs, held by both writer and reader. These values and beliefs cannot be denied or excluded, even in academic argument, with its emphasis on evidence and reasoned inquiry. The student arguing against the Forest Service plan cannot avoid using values and beliefs as bridges between reasons and conclusions. And not all of these bridges can be explicitly stated; that would lead to an endless chain of reasons. The standards of academic argument require, however, that the most important values and beliefs undergirding an argument be explicitly stated and defended. In this case, then, the student opposing the Forest Service plan should at some point state and support the belief that preserving wildlife habitats and wilderness lands should take priority over economic development.

It's not easy to identify and analyze your own values and beliefs, but doing so is essential in academic argument. Values and beliefs are often held unconsciously, and they function as part of a larger network. Your opinions about the best way for the government to respond to unemployed individuals reflect values and beliefs you hold about the family, the proper role of government, the nature of individual responsibility, and the importance of economic security. Thus if your political science instructor asks you to argue for or against workfare programs (programs requiring welfare recipients to work at state-mandated jobs in exchange for economic support), you need to analyze carefully not just these workfare programs but also the role your values and beliefs play in your analysis.

The following guidelines for analyzing your values, assumptions, and beliefs should enable you to respond more effectively to the demands of academic argument.

Guidelines for analyzing your values, assumptions, and beliefs

1. Use the Informal Methods of Invention, Described in Chapter 5, to Explore Your Values, Assumptions, and Beliefs about a Subject.

Once you have a general topic, and certainly by the time you have developed a controlling purpose or thesis, you should explore your values, assumptions, and beliefs about your topic. Your goal here is to discover *why* you believe what you believe; to do so, you need to consider more than rational, logical arguments: you need to tap into your experiences and emotions. Freewriting, looping, brainstorming, and clustering are excellent ways to gain access to the network or web of assumptions, values, and beliefs that encourage you to adopt a particular stance toward an issue.

2. After Exploring Your Values, Assumptions, and Beliefs, Consider the Degree to Which They Enable You to Argue Effectively about a Subject.

Exploring your own assumptions, values, and beliefs enables you to distance yourself from your habitual ways of thinking and thus encourages the objective habits of mind your instructors want to foster. Your exploration can also help you discover ways to ground your argument in assumptions, values, and beliefs you share with your readers. (You may wish to review Todd Carpenter's essays, which appear on pages 191–97 to see how he achieves this goal.)

Sometimes your exploration may enable you to realize that you face special challenges when it comes to writing an effective academic argument on a particular subject. For example, freewriting about your feelings about gun control may help you realize that your convictions about this issue are so deeply rooted in your beliefs, values, and assumptions that you will have to work hard to maintain academic standards of objectivity in an argument about this subject. Understanding this about yourself beforehand can save you a great deal of time and frustration.

3. Engage in an Internal Dialogue with a "Devil's Advocate" to Help You Critically Examine Your Values, Assumptions, and Beliefs.

Becoming aware of your values, assumptions, and beliefs can help you better understand why you have adopted a particular stance toward an issue or a problem. You may nevertheless find it difficult to step outside your habitual ways of thinking to consider whether others might reasonably hold differing views—and yet much academic writing demands just this ability. Many writers find it helpful to engage in an internal dialogue with one or more "devil's advocates," persons whose views differ considerably from their own. If you were writing an essay arguing that the federal government needs to increase funding for college student loans, you might engage in a mental or written dialogue with a hard-headed pragmatic congressperson or corporate executive whose concerns about the national deficit might cause resistance to such an argument. Their challenges might help you recognize that assumptions you have made about the need for all students to have access to a college education are not universally shared, that other assumptions—such as the need to balance the federal budget—might reasonably take precedence. Your dialogue has helped you learn that you must not only make your own assumptions explicit but provide good reasons why your assumptions are valid and consider competing assumptions as well. Your dialogue might even help you realize that you need to limit or modify your goals for this essay.

4. Engage in Real Dialogues with Your Classmates about Your Subjects.

You're probably already aware from informal discussions that even friends and family members can disagree about complex or controversial subjects. When you discuss current events with your friends or family, for example, they may naturally formulate questions that require you to reconsider not only your stance toward an issue or problem but also the assumptions, values, and beliefs that undergird this position. You can draw on this natural activity of mutual inquiry to help you explore your values, assumptions, and beliefs. This may take the form of informal dinner talk with friends. But your instructor may also ask you to work more formally in groups. If you engage in formal group discussions with classmates, be sure to follow these steps.

- Decide how much time each student will have to discuss his or her work in progress. Appoint a timekeeper to enforce these limits.
- The writer should begin by describing the controlling purpose or thesis of the essay and then briefly list the assumptions, values, and beliefs that led to taking this position. The writer should then invite group members to ask questions designed to provide perspectives on these assumptions, values, and beliefs and to explain different views that others might reasonably hold.
- Group members should let the writer facilitate the resulting discussion. The writer should feel free to ask group members to clarify or elaborate on suggestions. Group members should

remember that their goal is not to attack or criticize the writer's assumptions, values, and beliefs but rather to help the writer gain additional perspectives on them.

When you argue, you must consider not only your own assumptions, values, and beliefs but also those of your readers. The student writing about the Forest Service plan would present a very different argument to the local branch of the Sierra Club than to representatives of the Forest Service. In arguing to the Sierra Club, the student, almost assured of agreement, might focus primarily on how the group might best oppose the plan and why members should devote their time and energy to this rather than other projects. The argument to the Forest Service would be quite different. Recognizing that members of the Forest Service would know the plan very well, would have spent a great deal of time working on it, and would obviously be strongly committed to it, the student might decide to focus on a limited number of points, especially those that the Forest Service might be most able and willing to modify. The student might also assume a less aggressive or strident tone so as not to alienate the audience.

In academic argument, of course, your reader is generally your instructor. In this rhetorical situation, the most useful approach is not to focus on your instructor's individual biases or interests or to try to "psych out" his or her views on your topic. Rather, you should consider the values and beliefs your instructor holds as a member of the academic community. In writing for an economics or a political science instructor, the student arguing against the Forest Service plan should provide logical, accurate, and appropriate evidence for assertions. He or she should avoid strong emotional appeals and harsh expressions of outrage or bitterness, focusing instead on developing a succinct, clearly organized, carefully reasoned essay.

Application

Think of an issue that concerns you. Perhaps you are involved with or have been following a campus controversy. You may oppose a decision made recently by your city council or some other elected body. Or you may be committed (or opposed) to broad national movements such as the efforts to provide public child-care facilities, house the homeless, or improve public transportation.

After reflecting on this issue, use the guidelines presented earlier in this section to analyze your values, assumptions, and beliefs. Then respond to the following questions.

1. Given your assumptions, values, and beliefs, what challenges would writing an academic essay on this subject pose for you?
2. To what extent did your analysis help you understand that others might reasonably hold different views on this subject? Make a list of the opposing arguments that others might make in response to your subject; then briefly describe the assumptions, values, and beliefs that might lead readers to make these counterarguments. How might you respond to these arguments?
3. Now write the major assertions or arguments you would use to support your controlling idea or thesis. Below each assertion, list the assumptions, values, or beliefs your readers must share with you to accept that assertion.
4. How have the guidelines and this application helped you understand how to write an effective academic argument? If you were to write an academic argument on this issue, how would you now organize and develop your ideas? What strategies would you now use to respond to the assumptions, values, and beliefs of your readers?

USING EVIDENCE APPROPRIATE TO YOUR ARGUMENT

Whenever you argue, you are engaged in the process of giving good reasons why your reader should accept your conclusions or judgment. Arguments are not all alike, however. A student reviewing a play or a movie faces different challenges from one advocating laws requiring mandatory use of seat belts in cars. These two tasks require not only different analytic skills but also different kinds of evidence.

Arguments can be characterized in a number of ways. All of these systems are somewhat artificial, for the categories describe "pure," unmixed arguments, whereas in actuality many arguments are hybrids. Still, considering your potential argumentative task can help you determine how best to limit your thesis, select appropriate and persuasive evidence or support, and organize your ideas. In *Elements of Argument,* Annette T. Rottenberg categorizes arguments according to the nature of the thesis or claim. All arguments, she notes, involve *claims of fact, claims of value,* or *claims of policy.* Some essays focus on only one of these claims. More often, however, writers draw on all three approaches to support and develop their ideas.

Claims of fact

These claims state that something is or will be true.

- Eastern European weight lifters consistently outperform their western counterparts.
- ABC University fails to provide adequate funds for the library.
- Orientation programs for first-year students help them adjust to college life.
- When used properly, organic fertilizers and pesticides can be just as effective as their chemical counterparts and much less harmful and expensive.

When arguing about a claim of fact, you often support your thesis by using examples, statistics, and statements by authorities on the subject. Even though you use data to support your claim, however, you must still define and interpret this information. You should recognize that reasonable people can disagree about just what the facts are. For instance, scientists sometimes disagree about the results of rigorously controlled studies. In academic argument, the distinction between a fact and an inference (a conclusion or an interpretation of a fact) is often subject to debate. Consequently, you should not assume that the facts are obvious. Many facts are open to multiple interpretations; such interpretations play a crucial role in academic argument.

Claims of value

Claims of value assert a judgment.

- Euthanasia is a humane alternative to the pain suffered by patients with terminal illnesses.
- None of the *Star Trek* movies has matched the original television series for wit and originality.
- Maslow's psychological theories describe the nature of human motivation better than do those of Freud or Pavlov.
- The news media's obsession with the private lives of politicians is harmful to the practice of democracy.

Claims of value attempt to prove that something is right or wrong, just or unjust, effective or ineffective, well crafted or poorly constructed. If you go to a movie with a friend and then argue about how well the actors performed, you are arguing about a claim of value.

Your experience arguing about movies may help you understand an essential requirement for a claim of value: acceptable criteria for judgment. You could hardly defend the merits of a movie because you liked the color of the heroine's dress or because you think that gangster movies set in Chicago are always good. Even if you've never studied films or read movie reviews, you know that if you want your opinion to be taken seriously by others, you need to base your arguments on such commonly accepted criteria as the quality of the acting, the script, and the direction; the significance of the theme; or the movie's ability to draw you into the action. When writing an academic essay about a claim of value, you need to be especially concerned with identifying criteria or standards for your analysis. Otherwise, you may be charged with relying on mere opinion rather than informed judgment or with focusing on trivial issues.

Claims of policy

Claims of policy assert that something should or should not exist or occur.

- Student fees should not be used to support this college's athletic program.
- The federal government should direct more funds to public transportation and less to constructing new highways.
- American executives should adopt some aspects of the Japanese style of management.
- Students should boycott the *Playboy* photographer who will visit campus this term to recruit models.

When you assert a claim of policy, you are implicitly arguing that some current problem must be remedied. There would be no reason to provide better child care, for example, if current facilities were adequate. Essays making claims of policy often begin with necessary background information. Next the proposed policy must be carefully explained and supported. The support for a claim of policy often comes from statistics and similar forms of evidence. A student advocating increased support of child-care programs might cite the number of children needing child care as well as the number of placements available or include the comments of a noted child psychologist on the need for high-quality care.

When you argue about a claim of policy, beliefs and values often play a crucial role in your argument. They do so because they strongly influence how you (and your readers) interpret data. Two individuals reviewing statistics about the number of children needing child care might draw very different conclusions. "This is evidence," the first might think, "of the need for our state to provide public child-care facilities." The second might conclude, "This is evidence of the breakdown of the traditional American family. We need to convince mothers that staying home and caring for children is the most important job possible."

As a student writing academic arguments, you need to recognize how personal values and beliefs may influence your advocacy of a policy. You must also recognize that readers will, in turn, be influenced by their values and beliefs. Ignoring their concerns or attempting to force your own preferences on them weakens your argument and creates a negative image of you as the writer.

Application

Think again about the issue you wrote about in response to the application on page 277. Formulate a tentative or working thesis statement that reflects your current position on this issue. Identify whether this thesis statement asserts a claim of fact, of value, or of policy, and then list the major evidence you would use to support this thesis. Finally, write a brief statement explaining why this evidence is appropriate, given your thesis statement and the kind of claim it makes.

ACKNOWLEDGING POSSIBLE COUNTERARGUMENTS

Academic argument is modeled on inquiry rather than debate. Your task in an academic argument is not to persuade your instructor to agree with you but to demonstrate that you can reason, and write, in a logical, coherent manner. This approach requires that you consider both sides of an issue. Discussing and responding to counterarguments in the body of your essay is one of the most effective ways to demonstrate that you have analyzed an issue from a number of perspectives—that you have seriously looked at all sides of the issue and drawn reasonable conclusions.

Earlier sections of this chapter provided a number of ways you can discover counterarguments to your own position. For instance, you can have an internal dialogue with one or more "devil's advocates," or you can discuss your subject with a group of classmates. You might even decide to interview someone who holds a position different from your own. Being aware of your own values and beliefs can also help you identify possible counterarguments. The student arguing against the Forest Service plan might consider the views of someone with different values, perhaps someone who believed in the importance of economic development, such as a worker for a lumber company. Finally, reading and research can expose you to the ideas and arguments of others.

How you use the counterarguments that you identify will depend on your subject and your rhetorical situation. In some instances, these counterarguments can play an important structural role in your essay. After introducing your essay and indicating your thesis, for example, you might present the major counterarguments to your position, refuting each in turn. You might also group these counterarguments, responding to them at an appropriate point in your essay.

Group Activity

The following activity will help you recognize possible counterarguments to the thesis you have been writing about in the applications on pages 277 and 281. To prepare for this group activity, be sure that you have a clear, easy-to-read statement of your tentative or working thesis and of the major evidence you would use to support this thesis in an academic essay. Now spend five to ten minutes brainstorming a list of possible counterarguments to your working thesis.

Bring these written materials to your group's meeting. Determine how much time the group can spend per person if each student is to get help with his or her writing. Appoint a timekeeper to be sure that the group stays on time. Then follow this procedure.

1. Have the writer read his or her working thesis, evidence, and possible counterarguments.
2. Have members of the group suggest additional counterarguments that the writer has not considered. Avoid getting bogged down in specific arguments; instead, focus on generating as many additional counterarguments as possible.

Continue following this procedure until each student's work has been discussed.

When you enter a college or university, you join an academic community, one with unique values, beliefs, and methods of inquiry. Yet few members of that community will discuss these directly with you.

Instead, your history instructor explores the impact of printing on the Renaissance imagination, and your political science instructor focuses on recent events in the Middle East. Your instructors leave it to you to understand the academic rhetorical situation and to master the skills necessary to succeed in their courses. You don't have to face this challenge alone, however. Your composition instructor and your classmates, acting as both coaches and supporters, can help you understand and develop the critical thinking, reading, and writing skills necessary for success in college. What's at stake in your composition course, then, is not just earning a passing grade or fulfilling a requirement but becoming a fully participating and successful member of the academic community.

Activities for Thought, Discussion, and Writing

1. Chapter 9 presented a number of readings on education in America, including George Leonard's "End of School" (pages 226–31) and a diverse selection at the end of the chapter (pages 239–48). Now that you have read this chapter's discussion of academic argument, return to these earlier readings and evaluate their strengths and weaknesses as arguments. (Even though several of the readings are not traditional arguments, they nevertheless implicitly take a position about education and hence can be analyzed as arguments.)
2. Read a daily newspaper for a week. (You may want to read one of the well-respected national newspapers, such as the *Christian Science Monitor* or the *Wall Street Journal.*) Paying particular attention to the editorials, see if you can find examples of arguments making claims of fact, value, and policy. Analyze the effectiveness of these arguments. Be prepared to bring examples of each kind of argument to class for discussion.

   Also try to find at least two or three examples of mixed arguments—arguments that focus on more than a single claim. How do these arguments differ from those that focus on a single claim?
3. This chapter has presented activities designed to improve your understanding of academic argument. The application on page 277, for instance, asked you to identify the values, assumptions, and beliefs that have led you to hold strong views on an issue. The application on page 281 asked you to formulate a tentative or working thesis and to list the major evidence you would use to support it. Finally, the group activity on page 282 encouraged you to acknowledge possible counterarguments to your thesis.

Drawing on these activities, write an essay directed to an academic reader on the topic you have explored. If you need to revise your tentative or working thesis, feel free to do so.

EPILOGUE

GOING ON: WRITERS—AND WRITING—"IN PROGRESS"

What does it mean to be a writer? Now that you have read *Work in Progress* and have written a number of essays, you know that writers are not geniuses endowed with special powers but rather people who use the resources of language to communicate with others. As a student, you primarily write essays, reports, examinations, and other academic forms of writing, though you may relax by writing poems or letters to friends or by keeping a journal. But what will you write once you graduate?

To better understand the kinds of writing students do once they leave college, I recently wrote to students from previous composition classes, asking them to describe the role that writing plays in their current lives. Here are some of their responses:

> I'm always writing. In my daily life, I write out of necessity: "to do" lists rank high. My ability to persuade with writing brought me to my present job, and I write for my work frequently. But I write for personal reasons too--lyrics mostly. (The form fits the time I have.) And as I've gotten more involved with community activities I've written grants for nonprofit agencies and notes for presentations. I'm a member of the board of directors for a child-care center; my writing skills have proved invaluable in this position. I want to give back to my community, and my writing allows me to do this.
>
> MARY McCOY
Sales/Consignment Coordinator,
Nonprofit Resale Shop
Eugene, Oregon

> I'm an avid letter writer, and--especially when I'm traveling--a journal keeper. Since I am a high school teacher, I also depend on writing to communicate to students about their work, to share informally with

colleagues, and to create formal documents, such as grant proposals.

HOLLY HARDIN
High School Teacher
Hood River, Oregon

I don't do much work-related writing, but I do write in relation to my hobby. I wrote for a club newsletter for several years and still contribute to other related publications. Writing is a skill that I value, even though my current job doesn't require me to write a lot. It gives me confidence to know that if I need to put something in writing, I can do it competently.

DINA ELDRIDGE
Restaurant Manager
Newport, Oregon

Currently I draft responses to charges my company receives from the Oregon Bureau of Labor and Industries. My writing must be clear, concise, and persuasive. I don't do as much writing in my personal life as I'd like to: my goal is to write more letters!

KIM SMITH
Employee Relations Manager
Portland, Oregon

As a newspaper editor who also writes a lot of stories for the paper, I place a premium on well-organized, well-done material. It's not reasonable to ask readers to stick with the stories I write and edit if they're not organized and well written. Lately I've also been doing a different kind of writing, writing just for myself. About four years ago I started keeping a journal, and now nearly every night I write in it--about whatever I want and without any pressure to meet anyone's expectations. I just write, and that's fun.

STEVE LUNDEBERG
Sports Editor
Albany Democrat-Herald
Albany, Oregon

Writing is an essential component in my profession, law enforcement. Anything I write can, and often does, appear in court. I spend enormous amounts of time writing. I write court documents, memos, letters to professionals, and teaching materials. I also write short stories, essays, and journals. Writing used to be a task, but now it is a pleasure, an integral part of my life.

JACKIE TURLE
Police Officer
Eugene, Oregon

As you can see, writing plays an important role in these individuals' lives. Most write a good deal in their work lives, but they also write for personal and for civic reasons—to express their creativity, to record the events of their daily lives, and to participate in social and community affairs. If queried five years from now, these individuals might be engaged in different writing activities. But they will undoubtedly still be writing.

How did Jackie Turle, Steve Lundeberg, Mary McCoy, and the other individuals whose statements you have just read develop the skills necessary to meet the challenges they currently face as writers? All began by taking a composition course like the one you are taking now. Doing so enabled them to develop a strong foundation they could build on as they moved through their undergraduate years and into the workplace. Central to this foundation are four key insights about writing:

1. Writing is a process, not a mysterious or magical activity. You cannot entirely control the writing process, but through practice, introspection, and collaboration with others you can learn to respond more effectively and more efficiently to the demands of writing.
2. Rather than relying on rules or formulas for writing, you can make appropriate decisions as a writer by analyzing your rhetorical situation. Doing so encourages you to ask commonsense questions about your own role and purposes as a writer, the needs and expectations of your readers, and the textual conventions appropriate for your writing.
3. Reading and writing are mutually reinforcing processes. Through reading you can increase your sensitivity to the forms and situations of writing.
4. Writing is naturally a collaborative, rather than a solitary or lonely, activity. People who take their writing seriously interact regularly with others who share their interest.

Writers who wish to continue to grow and develop understand that just as writing is always work in progress, so too are writers always "in progress." All writers find that writing is sometimes a chore. But those who take their writing seriously find ways, as Jackie Turle indicated, to make writing "a pleasure, an integral part" of life.

Now that you are nearing the end of your composition class, what can you do in the future to continue your development as a writer? Here are some suggestions from former students like those you heard from earlier:

> Do lots of writing. Learn how to accept feedback and criticism. Don't be afraid or unwilling to rewrite. Reading--especially careful reading where you pay attention to style as well as content--can help you develop your writing skills. Believe me, it's worth it. It is only by the process of communication that we, as humans, make ourselves known to others. The more effectively you communicate, the greater chance you have of standing out, of being noticed.
>
> DAVID FOWLER
> Senior Technical Writer
> Hillsboro, Oregon

> Writing is nothing to be afraid of. Anyone with a pen and paper can do it. The next time you think you can't deal successfully with the process of writing, just go to the library. There are a lot of amazingly good books in there--and as many really lousy ones. They were all written by people like you.
>
> DENISE KAUFMAN
> Musician and Landscape Gardener
> Corvallis, Oregon

> Take more writing classes and classes where language in general is important. My journalism classes gave me a wonderful grounding in mechanics. Short-story writing helped me see how important each word can be to the meaning of a sentence. If instructors in other classes allow you to rewrite, do it. And take the time to form writing groups with students from your classes--it really makes a difference.
>
> LAURA STEINERT
> Graduate Student
> Corvallis, Oregon

> Try everything thrown at you. Give it all an honest effort. Find a place and time where you can write well and schedule it in.
>
> GREG O'SHEA
> Teacher's Aide
> Laguna Beach, California

Read. Read for pleasure; read to learn what other writers do. It will help your writing. Also, look for opportunities to write with others; I've really come to enjoy collaboration--melding ideas and styles. And I always learn something new about writing when I work with someone else.

BRIAN JOHNSON
Counselor
Hood River, Oregon

Try keeping a journal. Don't be uptight about it or you'll never continue; just write when you want to. It keeps the juices flowing, and it makes great reading later. And whenever you can, get responses to your writing. There's something wonderful about seeing someone reading and responding to your work. When I see a glint of understanding or the beginning of a smile on a reader's face, I know my work's been worthwhile.

JUDY STOCKTON
Teacher and Small Business Owner
Tangent, Oregon

The suggestions you have just read all encourage you—as your composition class and this textbook have encouraged you—to take yourself seriously as a writer. As the former students who responded to my questionnaire told me over and over again, when they were undergraduate students they did not necessarily imagine that they would be doing the kind of work—and writing—that they now do. But because they took their own writing seriously, they were able to meet both professional challenges and their own personal goals. You don't need to be an expert to understand writing and to write well. As former student David Fowler says: "The successful writer is the writer who can remain flexible, who can question and adapt, who can be inventive while remembering basic principles of effective writing." Like David Fowler, Kim Smith, Denise Kaufman, Greg O'Shea, Judy Stockton, and the others whose words you have read, you can make writing an important—and successful—part of your personal and professional life.

Acknowledgments

American College of Surgeons advertisement. Copyright 1994, American College of Surgeons. All rights reserved.

"Beauty Shop"/What's on your Powerbook advertisement. © Apple Computer, Inc. 1993. Used with permission.

From *The Little Rhetoric and Handbook*, 2/e by Edward Corbett. Copyright © 1982, 1977 by Scott, Foresman and Company. Reprinted by permission of HarperCollins Publishers. Adapted from "Discovery through Questioning: A Plan for Teaching Rhetorical Invention," by Richard Larson in *College English*, November 1968. Copyright 1968 by the National Council of Teachers of English. Reprinted with permission of the publisher and the author.

From *Writing with Power: Techniques for Mastering the Writing Process* by Peter Elbow. Copyright © 1981 by Oxford University Press. Reprinted by permission.

Peter Elbow and Pat Belanoff from *A Community of Writers*. Copyright © 1989 by McGraw-Hill, Inc. Reprinted by permission.

Carole Feldman, "Challenges Outside Classroom Threaten U.S. Teens, Study Says." Copyright 1993 by the Associated Press. Reprinted by permission.

John H. Flavell, Eleanor R. Flavell, Frances L. Green, "Development of the Appearance-Reality Distinction," *Cognitive Psychology* 15 (83), 95–120. With permission.

John H. Flavell, "Really and Truly," reprinted with permission from *Psychology Today*. Copyright © 1986 (Sussex Publishers, Inc.).

John H. Flavell, "The Development of Children's Knowledge about the Appearance-Reality Distinction." Copyright © 1986 by the American Psychological Association. Reprinted by permission of the American Psychological Association and John H. Flavell.

"To Mr. Winslow" by Ian Frazier. Reprinted by permission; © 1993 Ian Frazier. Originally in *The New Yorker*. All rights reserved.

"The New Traditionalist" advertisement by *Good Housekeeping*. Reprinted by permission. Copyright 1989 The Hearst Corporation. All rights reserved.

"Any Questions Class?" cartoon by Matt Groening. From *School Is Hell* © 1987 by Matt Groening. All rights reserved. Reprinted by permission of Pantheon Books, a division of Random House, Inc., New York. All rights reserved.

From "A Portrait of Lorenzo de' Medici" by Francesco Guicciardini. From *The Portable Renaissance Reader*, ed., intro. by James Bruce Ross and Mary Martin McLaughlin. Copyright © 1953, renewed © 1981 by Viking Penguin, Inc. Used by permission of Viking Penguin, a division of Penguin Books USA, Inc.

Harper's Index. Copyright © 1993 by *Harper's Magazine*. All rights reserved. Reprinted from the November issue by special permission.

Burton Hatlen, "Writing Is a Craft That Can Be Learned, Not an Effortless Outpouring by Geniuses," © 1988, *The Chronicle of Higher Education*. Reprinted with permission.

"Para Teresa" by Inés Hernández-Ávila from *Con Rayón, Corazón: Poetry*. Copyright © 1987 by Inés Hernández-Ávila.

Brian Jarvis, "Against the Great Divide," from *Newsweek*, May 3, 1993. © 1993, Newsweek, Inc. All rights reserved. Reprinted by permission.

Jamaica Kincaid, "Girl," from *At the Bottom of the River* by Jamaica Kincaid. Reprinted by permission of Farrar, Straus & Giroux, Inc.

Robin Lakoff, from *Language and Woman's Place*. Copyright © 1975 by Robin Lakoff. Reprinted by permission of HarperCollins Publishers.

George Leonard, "The End of School," originally published in the May, 1992 issue of *The Atlantic Monthly*. Copyright George Leonard.

Cullen Murphy, "Going to the Cats," © 1987, Cullen Murphy, as first published in *The Atlantic Monthly*, August 1987.

Jane Bryant Quinn, "How to Read an Annual Report." Reprinted by permission of International Paper Company.

"It's Time to Grade Parents," by the editorial staff of *The Sunday Oregonian*. Copyright © 1993, Oregonian Publishing Co.

UNICEF letter. Reprinted by permission of U.S. Committee for UNICEF.

"John's Losing His Hair" advertisement for Rogaine. Courtesy of The Upjohn Company.

Nicholas Von Hoffman, "Gun Crazy." Copyright © 1993 by Nicholas Von Hoffman. Reprinted by arrangement with Virginia Barbar Literary Agency, Inc.

Index

Instructor's Manual to Accompany

Instructor's Manual

to Accompany

Lisa Ede's

WORK IN PROGRESS

Third Edition

Instructor's Manual

to Accompany

Lisa Ede's

WORK IN PROGRESS

Third Edition

Prepared by

Lisa Ede

and

Suzanne Clark

St. Martin's Press New York

Manufactured in the United States of America.
9 8 7 6 5
f e d c b a

For information, write:
St. Martin's Press, Inc.
175 Fifth Avenue, NY 10010

ISBN: 0-312-10108-2

CONTENTS

Instructor's Manual

to Accompany

Lisa Ede's

WORK IN PROGRESS

Third Edition

1. A FEW WORDS ABOUT WORK IN PROGRESS

Work in Progress addresses students as a writers, in a rhetorical situation. Instead of assuming that as students they must learn to write by following directions from teacher and text, this approach locates them in the sphere of writing. They are apprentice writers, to be sure, but nonetheless fellow writers, ready to learn the secrets of the craft: its messiness, chaos, uncertainty, ambiguity, as well as its shaping, transforming power.

Of course, as teachers of writing, we have always tried to get our students to become writers, to take themselves seriously, and to become active problem-solvers as they write. In that sense, this text has very familiar, recognizable goals. What may seem new and perhaps unfamiliar is the way in which Work in Progress asks students to undertake their composition studies in the role of writers. The goal of becoming a better writer is punctuated by completed papers, but it is inherently work in progress. Such a goal is dynamic, not final.

From the beginning, Work in Progress asks students to investigate, describe, and question the concrete circumstances of their writing. They are encouraged to see themselves as part of a community of writers--to read each other's work, to exchange tips and ideas, to discover for themselves how they read, and how their understanding of this process and of textual conventions can influence their own writing. They are encouraged to become aware of and respond to their rhetorical situations, including in particular their situation as students writing in an academic environment. They learn to see their writing as work in progress and to take charge of their own writing processes, including evaluating and revising.

Work in Progress is not a panacea, but it can have important consequences for you and for your students. The worried freshmen who think they must learn how to write once and for all in a single term will be relieved to discover that their task has a more human scale (though it sometimes takes weeks in class before this realization finally strikes). And your familiar frustration with not being able to cure all your students' writing ills also can be relieved as students move from viewing themselves as patients suffering from linguistic dis-ease to regarding themselves as healthy (if beginning) writers, capable of learning to make their own diagnoses and to manage their own plans.

Work in Progress invites students into the collaborative circle of writers that we, as experts, know--where writing is always risky, uncertain, and sometimes painful but also a rewarding and eminently social activity. This text teaches principles of writing not as certainties but as strategies, ways of going on despite encountering the inevitable problems. It will help you change the nature of your authority from isolated expert to advanced fellow participant. It will help you establish your class as a community of writers. We believe that writing is a powerful component in the work of both individuals and groups. So this text demonstrates not only how to write, but how writing can be an instrument of learning.

We proceed, however, with a certain humility. Since teaching, like writing, is work in progress, and the classroom a unique rhetorical situation, the possibilities for using this text are multiple and complex. This instructor's manual aims to give you as much help as we can about workable plans for teaching and as much information as we can about useful ideas and about our experiences teaching this text. As fellow teachers, we offer strategies, not certainties; we offer this instructor's manual as an act of collaboration.

2. HOW TO USE THIS INSTRUCTOR'S MANUAL

This instructor's manual is designed to complement and support Work in Progress. In writing this manual, we were particularly aware of the needs of beginning teachers of writing--teachers who bring many strengths to the classroom, but who lack extensive pedagogical experience and who may be just becoming acquainted with research in composition studies. We hope in this manual to provide concrete suggestions that will enable beginning teachers to teach confidently and effectively--to embark successfully on the work in progress that teaching always comprises. We also hope, however, to provide helpful, stimulating resources and suggestions for experienced teachers of writing.

This instructor's manual is divided into the following four sections:

--Section 1 provides an overview of and rationale for Work in Progress; it also discusses alternative ways of using this text and presents suggested course plans for quarter and semester-long classes.

--Section 2 presents practical strategies for teaching, including using collaborative learning, handling the paper load, and responding to students' writing. It contains suggestions for teaching writing assignments, including free writing, brainstorming, interviewing, the writer's notebook, and essays. Although your program doubtless includes some form of teaching evaluations, this section suggests some ways to include ongoing assessment as part of the collaborative processes of the course. It concludes with a brief bibliography designed to acquaint those unfamiliar with research in composition with some important resources for instructors.

--Section 3, the longest section of this manual, provides chapter-by-chapter suggestions for teaching the concepts and activities presented in each chapter of Work in Progress. Beginning instructors, in particular, should find this section helpful in preparing for class discussions and activities and in responding to students' writing.

--Section 4 includes sample assignments and student papers from instructors who have taught Work in Progress. These materials are included here so that you may reproduce them for use as class handouts.

We have made certain changes in the Instructor's Manual for this third edition of Work in Progress:

--We have added material on collaborative practices and a section on evaluating collaborative teaching.

--We have added theoretical works as further reading on important concepts.

--We have taken advantage of the responses from students and instructors who used the first and second editions of Work in Progress.

We wrote this instructor's manual to be used by beginning and experienced teachers of writing. If you have suggestions about how this manual could be improved, please write to us in care of St. Martin's Press, College Division, 175 Fifth Avenue, New York, NY 10010.

3. OVERVIEW AND COURSE PLANS

Rationale for the Basic Features of *Work in Progress*

Unlike longer, and often more prescriptive, texts, Work In Progress provides a conceptual framework that can stimulate effective classroom instruction, yet it also offers instructors considerable autonomy and flexibility. This approach reflects the authors' belief that composition texts should support and enrich, but not dominate, the life of the classroom.

Work in Progress richly reflects and enacts recent research in composition and rhetoric, yet it is also a practical, commonsensical textbook. It attempts to convey complex theoretical ideas in a manner that is neither intimidating nor irrelevant to students. Its most distinctive features include the following:

--full discussion of the concept of the rhetorical situation, including strategies that students can use to determine the most appropriate way of approaching any writing task
--explicit support for and reinforcement of collaborative learning and writing activities
--increased attention to the process of reading, and to reading and writing as dynamic, interdependent activities
--a strong emphasis on the importance of social context and of textual conventions of writing
--full discussion of the demands of academic writing
--a variety of student and professional examples, including numerous comments by students about their writing practices
--activities interspersed throughout the text, as well as at the end of each chapter, which encourage students to apply the concepts and strategies discussed in the text

How *Work In Progress* Is Organized

Work in Progress is divided into three major parts. Part One, "Writing, an Introduction," has the following chapters:

--Chapter 1: Writers Writing
--Chapter 2: Understanding the Writing Process
--Chapter 3: Understanding the Rhetorical Situation
--Chapter 4: Writers Reading

These four chapters establish the conceptual and pedagogical framework for the text. Together, they enable students to develop a sophisticated, yet commonsensical, understanding of writing as a means of communication, of the writing process, and of the rhetorical situation. In Chapter 4, they learn the significance of textual conventions. The discussion and activities in these chapters also encourage students to begin to think of themselves as writers and participants in a community of writers. Activities new in this edition prompt them to evaluate their understanding of the text, and to write an essay together, as a group collaboration.

Part Two of *Work in Progress*, "Practical Strategies for Writing," includes the following four chapters:

--Chapter 5: Strategies for Successful Invention
--Chapter 6: Strategies for Successful Planning and Drafting
--Chapter 7: Strategies for Successful Revision: Managing the Revision Process
--Chapter 8: Strategies for Successful Revision: Revising for Structure and Style

As the title of Part Two suggests, these four chapters introduce students to a variety of practical strategies they can use as they plan, draft, and revise. Here, the text emphasizes not a single prescribed series of steps or strategies that students must follow but a repertory of strategies they can draw upon working alone and with others, depending on their purpose and situation. This edition contains quite a bit that is new. Chapter 5 has extended the approach to invention with added material on research. An extensive section on planning and drafting collaboratively in Chapter 6 and a section on revising collaboratively in Chapter 7 will help you assign cowritten essays, if you wish.

Part Three of *Work in Progress*, "Connections: Writing, Reading, and Reasoning," consists of the following three chapters:

--Chapter 9: Understanding the Reading Process
--Chapter 10: Understanding Academic Audiences and Assignments
--Chapter 11: Understanding Academic Analysis and Argument

This final part of Work in Progress initiates students into the reading and writing that they will do as members of the academic community. Students learn approaches to analyzing texts that will help them read more critically and write more effectively. The text offers suggestions for analyzing disciplinary conventions and for understanding what is expected in assignments. In these and other ways, Work in Progress shows students ways to approach writing academic analyses and arguments. This edition features a new section of readings in Chapter 9 on the theme of education.

Finally, each chapter in Work in Progress includes activities designed to help students understand and apply the ideas presented in the text. Three kinds of activities--explorations, applications, and group activities--are interspersed throughout each chapter. Activities designated as explorations are designed primarily to stimulate students' understanding of and response to the text. Many explorations ask students to reflect upon previous writing experiences or to brainstorm, freewrite, or talk with others in response to discussions in the text. Activities designated as applications ask students to apply concepts or strategies presented in the text. Those designated as group activities involve students in carefully designed collaborative learning and writing experiences. In general, assignments lead students to reflect on writing and the rhetorical situation of learning to write as both the subject of a critical inquiry as well as the process they are undergoing.

This edition includes increased references to the use of computers and other technologies in connection with writing. It also offers readings and assignments that should allow you to take cultural differences into account and to discuss them as part of the rhetorical situation which students must address.

How To Take Advantage of the Flexibility of *Work in Progress*

Work in Progress is an innovative textbook, but it is also a practical textbook, one that can be used effectively by teachers employing diverse approaches to the teaching of writing. Part of this flexibility can be attributed to the text's brevity. Instructors using this text can be assured that they will have time for a variety of classroom activities--from peer response groups to the analysis of readings or discussions of writing in the disciplines. Students who have used Work in Progress have consistently praised the text as both easy and interesting to read. Consequently, instructors are not required to spend large amounts of class time explaining the basic concepts in the text. Instead they can engage the class in discussions of substantial rhetorical issues or of the numerous and diverse examples of student and professional writing. Furthermore, the text's many activities--more than any one instructor could assign--can stimulate numerous discussions and interactions. Our point here is that instructors truly are free to determine the degree to which they want to tie classroom discussions or activities directly to the text.

How can instructors who favor different approaches use Work in Progress? Those who wish to engage students with collaborative learning activities, for example, will find substantial support for these approaches in this text, based on the idea of writing as an interactive or dialogic process. Part One of Work in Progress, "Writing: An Introduction," devotes considerable attention to the writing process, a discussion that is reinforced in Part Two, "Practical Strategies for Writing." Furthermore, the explorations, applications, and group activities interspersed throughout the chapters all reinforce a process-centered, collaborative emphasis. You may wish not only to use collaboration as a learning strategy, but also to have students write some assignments in collaboration. New to this edition is a full discussion of collaborative writing, which should prove useful to teachers who wish to engage their students in a full range of collaborative activities.

Instructors who favor using the modes of discourse, writing across the curriculum, or thematic approaches to the teaching of writing can also use Work in Progress effectively. (Of course, these approaches are often used in conjunction with collaborative, process-oriented teaching practices.) Like many traditional rhetorics, Work in Progress suggests topics in the text but does not require their assignment. Thus instructors wishing to base class discussions and topic assignments on the modes of discourse, disciplinary conventions, or specific themes or subjects can easily do so.

Although Work in Progress contains a number of essays by students and professionals and thus can be used as the only text for a course, it can be combined with other texts as well. Like most rhetorics, Work in Progress can be supplemented by a handbook that can serve as a reference on grammar and usage for students. More important, perhaps, Part Three on reading and academic writing more directly supports and reinforces the use of a reader than do many traditional rhetorics, which may contain brief examples of professional or academic writing but lack explicit comment on the reading process or the nature of academic writing. Work in Progress can thus be assigned very effectively with a traditional reader, a collection of readings exploring a particular theme or subject, a reader focusing on writing across the curriculum, or even a novel or nonfiction work, such as Richard Rodriguez's Hunger of Memory or Mike Rose's Lives on the Boundary.

Finally, we would like to note that Work in Progress has most often been used in first-year writing courses, but has also been used successfully with intermediate and advanced composition students, including a number of future writing instructors in courses on teaching writing. Students in these classes reported that the text enabled them consciously to recognize and discuss understandings that had largely been implicit, if present at all. In anonymous evaluations of the text, students consistently recommended that Work in Progress be used in future intermediate and advanced composition classes.

Because we believe that Work in Progress can be used successfully with quite diverse approaches to the teaching of writing, as well as with different levels of students, we would appreciate hearing from instructors who have used Work in Progress in their composition classes, and we would particularly appreciate receiving copies of syllabi, assignments, or other handouts that indicate how practicing teachers have integrated Work in Progress into their classroom practices.

Course Plans

In the following syllabi, we present possible ways of organizing your quarter or semester course using Work in Progress with or without an accompanying reader. Although these plans follow the sequence of the chapters in the textbook, you should feel free to vary the order of the chapters in ways that best suit your classroom. Following these syllabi are suggestions about variations in chapter order to accommodate the situation in your course.

Suggestions for Using Work in Progress without a Reader

--Plan to take advantage of class time to develop collaborative learning activities. In addition to the group activities described in the text, you can regularly have group members brainstorm in response to assignments, analyze readings, and respond to works in progress.

--Work in Progress stimulates reflection on the processes of learning and writing--of education--which you may wish explicitly to make the subject of your course. The reading portfolio on education which is new to this edition can help such an approach. If your students are making new transitions into academic life, they may especially appreciate the opportunity to reflect critically on the institution and their experiences as writers within it.

--Use the writing assignments suggested in Work in Progress, or design your own series of assignments based on the modes of discourse. If you ask your students to keep a Writer's Notebook and write responses to all the prompts as they work through the reading, they will amass an impressive amount of material appropriate for reflection. Professor Bob Inkster at St. Cloud University has students write about their reading, about learning in other classes, about observations from field trips--all as a basis for drafts and finished papers.

--You may wish to develop assignments based on strands of or linked to a specific theme or issue. This is the approach used by instructors in the Writing Program at Florida State University. For example, led by Professor Wendy Bishop, instructors developed several different approaches to Work in Progress, working collaboratively on different strands to differentiate their teaching. Kathy Burton used a packet of media readings from magazines and newspapers for a "public media" approach. Kim Haimes-Korn and Gay Lynn Crossley suggested "authority" as a topic, using a packet of various academic pieces together with student papers to help students explore finding their own voice in an academic setting, and Ron Wiginton used a "personal discovery" approach. Cindy Wheatley-Lovoy had students explore the characteristic style of three disciplines for a research-oriented approach featuring their investigation of "Writing across the Disciplines."

--Many instructors wish to photocopy packets of materials for use in their classes. Sample essays written by previous students in response to assignments can be particularly helpful. See Section 3 of this manual for sample assignments and student essays available for your use.

Quarter Syllabus for Work in Progress

Major assignments: five essays, developed from invention through rough and final drafts

Week 1
Work in Progress Preface, Prologue, and Chapter 1
Assign essay 1

Week 2
Work in Progress Chapter 2
Rough draft of essay 1 due; in-class peer response

Week 3
Work in Progress Chapter 3
Final draft of essay 1 due
Assign essay 2

Week 4
Work in Progress Chapter 4
Rough draft of essay 2 due: in-class peer response

Week 5
Work in Progress Chapter 5
Final draft of essay 2 due
Assign essay 3
Turn in all work to date in a folder
Midterm course evaluation

Week 6
Work in Progress Chapters 6 and 7
Class meetings canceled: conferences (may be with individuals or with groups)

Week 7
Work in Progress Chapter 8
Rough draft of essay 3 due: in-class peer response

Week 8
Work in Progress Chapter 9

Final draft of essay 3 due
Assign essay 4

Week 9
Work in Progress Chapters 10 and 11
Rough draft of essay 4 due: in-class peer response

Week 10
Work in Progress Epilogue
Final draft of essay 4 due in folder with all written work from the quarter

Finals Week
Essay 5 written in class as final examination

Semester Syllabus for *Work in Progress*

Major Assignments: Eight essays, developed from invention through rough and final drafts

Week 1
Work in Progress Preface, Prologue, and Chapter 1
Assign essay 1

Week 2
Work in Progress Chapter 2
Rough draft of essay 1 due: in-class peer response

Week 3
Work in Progress Chapter 3
Final draft of essay 1 due
Assign essay 2

Week 4
Work in Progress Chapter 4
Rough draft of essay 2 due: in-class peer response

Week 5
Review of and practice with concepts in Part One of *Work in Progress*
Final draft of essay 2 due
Assign essay 3
Turn in all work to date in a folder
Course evaluation

Week 6
Class meetings canceled: conferences (may be with individuals or with groups)

Week 7
Work in Progress Chapter 5
Rough draft of essay 3 due: in-class peer response

Week 8
Work in Progress Chapter 6
Final draft of essay 3 due
Assign essay 4

Week 9
Work in Progress Chapter 7
Rough draft of essay 4 due: in-class peer response

Week 10
Work in Progress Chapter 8
Final draft of essay 4 due
Assign essay 5

Week 11
Work in Progress Chapter 9
Rough draft of essay 5 due: in-class peer response
Turn in all work to date in a folder

Week 12
Work in Progress Chapter 10
Final draft of essay 5 due
Assign essay 6

Week 13
Work in Progress Chapter 11
Rough draft of essay 6 due: in-class peer response
Assign essay 7

Week 14
Work in Progress Epilogue
Review and Practice
Final draft of essay 6 due
Rough draft of essay 7 due: in-class peer response

Week 15
Completion of activities, reflections on writing and group procedures
Final draft of essay 7 due in folder with all written work from the semester

Finals Week
Essay 8 written in class as final examination

Suggestions for Using Work in Progress with a Reader

--In selecting a reader, you might choose any of a number of excellent texts available, use a collection that you gather yourself, or you might consider other kinds of reading appropriate to a composition class, ranging from anthologies of materials for writing across the curriculum to collections of short stories and interviews with writers. If you are interested in emphasizing the reading-writing connection, you might want to use a collection of essays gathered around a single theme. Whatever your choice, Work in Progress allows you great flexibility and freedom in developing your course.

--You might make essay assignments from the suggestions in Work in Progress or from assignments accompanying the reader. You might also wish to develop your own essay assignments to suit your situation. Many of the activities and essays in the text can readily be adapted for use with readings. Section 5 of this manual also supplies sample assignments accompanied by student essays.

--When you construct your course schedule, you might want to alternate days when students respond to reading with days when they write and work in groups. This pattern is especially useful during the beginning weeks of the class when students are reflecting about their own histories as writers and the kinds of writing processes they might use.

--Consider regularly using writing as a way to help students respond to their reading and learn the material it covers. For example, have students write opening and closing summaries of class discussions, responses to discussions, and questions or issues they wish to raise.

Quarter Syllabus for a Class Using _Work in Progress_ with a Reader

Major Assignments: eight reading assignments; five essays, developed from invention through rough and final drafts

Week 1
Work in Progress Preface, Prologue, and Chapter 1
Read and discuss assignment A from reader
Assign activities from _Work in Progress_

Week 2
Work in Progress Chapter 2
Read and discuss assignment B from reader
Assign essay 1

Week 3
Work in Progress Chapter 3
Read and discuss assignment C from reader
Rough draft of essay 1 due

Week 4
Work in Progress Chapter 4
Read and discuss assignment D from reader
Final draft of essay 1 due
Assign essay 2

Week 5
Work in Progress Chapter 5
Read and discuss assignment E from reader
Rough draft of essay 2 due
Midterm evaluation of the course

Week 6
Work in Progress Chapters 6 and 7
Class meetings canceled; conferences (may be with individuals or with groups)
Final draft of essay 2 due
Assign essay 3

Week 7
Work in Progress Chapter 8
Read and discuss assignment F from reader
Rough draft of essay 3 due

Week 8
Work in Progress Chapter 9
Read and discuss assignment G from reader
Final draft of essay 3 due
Assign essay 4

Week 9
Work in Progress Chapters 10 and 11
Read and discuss assignment H from reader
Rough draft of essay 4 due

Week 10
Work in Progress Epilogue
Completion of activities, reflections on writing and group processes
Final draft of essay 4 due in a folder with all written work from the quarter

Finals Week
Essay 5 written in class as final examination

Semester Syllabus for a Class Using _Work in Progress_ with a Reader

Major Assignments: thirteen reading assignments; seven essays, developed from invention through rough and final drafts

Week 1
Work in Progress Preface, Prologue, and Chapter 1
Read and discuss assignment A from reader
Assign activities from _Work in Progress_

Week 2
Work in Progress Chapter 2
Read and discuss assignment B from reader
Assign essay 1

Week 3
Work in Progress Chapter 3
Read and discuss assignment C from reader
Rough draft of essay 1 due

Week 4
Work in Progress Chapter 4
Read and discuss assignment D from reader
Final draft of essay 1 due
Assign essay 2

Week 5
Review and practice concepts from Part One of _Work in Progress_
Read and discuss assignment E from reader
Rough draft of essay 2 due
Midterm course evaluation

Week 6
Class meeting canceled: conferences (may be with individuals or with groups)

Week 7
Work in Progress Chapter 5
Read and discuss assignment F from reader
Final draft of essay 2 due
Assign essay 3

Week 8
Work in Progress Chapter 6
Read and discuss assignment G from reader
Rough draft of essay 3 due

Week 9
Work in Progress Chapter 7
Read and discuss assignment H from reader
Final draft of essay 3 due
Assign essay 4

Week 10
Work in Progress Chapter 8
Read and discuss assignment I from reader
Rough draft of essay 4 due

Week 11
Work in Progress Chapter 9
Read and discuss assignment J from reader

Final draft of essay 4 due
Assign essay 5

Week 12
Work in Progress Chapter 10
Read and discuss assignment K from reader
Rough draft of essay 5 due

Week 13
Work in Progress Chapter 11
Read and discuss assignment L from reader

Final draft of essay 5 due
Assign essay 6

Week 14
Review *Work in Progress* Chapters 9, 10, and 11
Read and discuss assignment M from reader
Rough draft of essay 6 due

Week 15
Work in Progress Epilogue
Completion of activities
Reflections on writing and group processes
Final draft of essay 6 due in folder with all written work from the semester
Prepare for essay 7

Finals Week
Essay 7 final draft written in class as final examination

Suggestions for Assigning Chapters out of Order

Work in Progress has eleven chapters, arranged in three sections, which you can use in various orders to suit the aims of your course. When you follow the order given in the book, the first part orients students to writing, to their own composing processes, to the rhetorical situation, and to reading as a writer. The second part, Chapters 5 through 8, introduces students to strategies for writing, moving from invention and planning through drafting to revision. In the last part, students integrate reading with writing and look specifically at academic writing. Many instructors will find that proceeding through the text as organized supplies the logical order that they wish for the course. However, *Work in Progress* has worked very well for instructors using all kinds of orders. Other ways to arrange the order of presentation include the following three examples.

Beginning a class with Part Two makes sense if you want your students to start thinking about and experimenting with writing strategies immediately, reserving reflection on concepts such as the rhetorical situation and the writing process until later in the term. An assignment sequence with this emphasis would look like this:

--Chapter 5: Strategies for Successful Invention
--Chapter 6: Strategies for Successful Planning and Drafting
--Chapter 7: Strategies for Successful Revision: Managing the Revision Process
--Chapter 8: Strategies for Successful Revision: Revising for Structure and Style
--Chapter 1: Writers Writing
--Chapter 2: Understanding the Writing Process
--Chapter 3: Understanding the Rhetorical Situation
--Chapter 4: Writers Reading

--Chapter 9: Understanding the Reading Process
--Chapter 10: Understanding Academic Audiences and Assignments
--Chapter 11: Understanding Academic Analysis and Argument

If you choose to emphasize the reading-writing connection, particularly if you wish students to think in terms of academic writing in their first assignments, begin the class with Chapters 3 and 4 so that students understand the concept of the rhetorical situation, then go to Chapters 9 through 11.

--Chapter 3: Understanding the Rhetorical Situation
--Chapter 4: Writers Reading
--Chapter 9: Understanding the Reading Process
--Chapter 10: Understanding Academic Audiences and Assignments
--Chapter 11: Understanding Academic Analysis and Argument

Finally, should you have a two-term composition sequence, consider using Work in Progress as one of your textbooks for both terms. A logical arrangement would be to choose for the first term a reader that emphasizes either personal writing or writing that reflects the students' situation and community. One of the multicultural readers now available would be very suitable. Accompany reading assignments with Parts One and Two of Work in Progress. In the second term, choose a reader organized around issues or a theme, or select a collection of academic essays and arguments. Begin by having students review Part Two on writing strategies and them move to Part Three.

Term One
--Chapter 1: Writers Writing
--Chapter 2: Understanding the Writing Process
--Chapter 3: Understanding the Rhetorical Situation
--Chapter 4: Writers Reading
--Chapter 5: Strategies for Successful Invention
--Chapter 6: Strategies for Successful Planning and Drafting
--Chapter 7: Strategies for Successful Revision: Managing the Revision Process
--Chapter 8: Strategies for Successful Revision: Revising for Structure and Style

Term Two
--Review Work in Progress Chapters 1-8 and ask students to use the chapters on strategies (Chapters 5-8) as a reference for this term.
--Chapter 9: Understanding the Reading Process
--Chapter 10: Understanding Academic Audiences and Assignments
--Chapter 11: Understanding Academic Analysis and Argument

4. TEACHING PRACTICES

This section of the instructor's manual discusses a number of effective teaching practices, focusing on the following:
--Using collaborative practices
--Handling the paper load
--Responding to student writing
--Using writing assignments
--Evaluating teaching
--A brief bibliography: further reading in composition studies

Using Collaborative Practices

Writing classes increasingly make use of collaborative practices, some as supplements to a traditional, instructor-centered classroom and others as the informing principle of the course. What choices might you make? Instructors plan their writing classes with very different goals in mind, which increasingly may include writing collaborative assignments, so from start to finish, the project is done by a group or a team. Students enter college writing classes with widely differing kinds of previous experience with collaboration. In this section of the Instructor's Manual, we will make suggestions that should help you discover the collaborative practices that are most appropriate to your situation.

What is collaboration? In one sense, writers cannot avoid collaboration, because they must incorporate other points of view into their discourse in order to be rhetorically effective; writing is dialogic. If you think of knowledge as socially constructed, then everything we know is the effect of collaboration. Collaboration can enhance this process and take advantage of the learning fostered by explicitly taking other views into account. Conflict as well as cooperation is at the heart of effective collaboration. Class discussions that articulate multiple points of view and the possibilities of differences as well as agreements provide one important benefit of collaboration.

The collaborative practices described in Work in Progress help students first of all to work together on the goal of learning to write. When students collaborate their primary job is to produce knowledge about their writing, not to build friendships or even to share knowledge about other areas, although those may be important benefits. In addition, this text supports specifically collaborative writing assignments, which may include having groups write entire essays together. Collaboration works best if you can shift student attention so that they see their first task as the work-in-progress of learning to write rather than the short-term goals of producing papers with good grades. You may need to make this explicit on your syllabus and in your grading procedures.

To insure effective collaborative learning experiences, instructors must pay as much attention to group dynamics as to content. Although the role of the instructor moves out of the spotlight, your collaborative roles as structurer, responder, consultant, and facilitator demand great skills and remain chiefly responsible for the success or failure of the class. Collaborative classes do not teach themselves. In the final part of this section, we provide some explicit ways of evaluating your teaching success in such a classroom.

Following are some additional suggestions for using collaborative learning groups in classes.

1. Recognize that collaborative learning challenges both you and your students to learn new roles. Instructors need to learn to trust the collaborative learning process. They have to be able to exchange the certainty of a well-prepared, well-delivered lecture for the uncertainty of peer interactions. They have to be able to put aside the hierarchies of expertise in order to make time for apprentice writers to talk about their craft. Instructors also need to recognize that their general pedagogical assumptions and practices will influence students' perceptions of collaborative learning. Those who tend to be authoritarian in most of their dealings with students, for instance, or who obviously value the instructor's wisdom over students' inexperienced opinions may find it difficult to convince students that they genuinely want them to collaborate with one another. Additionally, the writing program needs to support collaboration. It is important for evaluations of instructors to acknowledge the importance of collaboration and to look specifically for good collaborative practices.

Students will enter college writing classes in the context of an academic community that tends to favor competition, not cooperation, so students may be suspicious of group activities. Some may have no experience with collaborative groups. Many will be used to focusing on short-term goals and assignments, so that they prefer tasks oriented toward solving specific problems rather than geared toward the long-term goal of progress in writing. Work in Progress mediates this problem by integrating group activities with the topics of each chapter so that students can see how their work is related to the concepts they are learning.

2. Acknowledge the importance of resistance. Collaborative practices need to make a place for students' resistance, which may very well mark a point of great interest. Ask your students to write about resistance to discover the forms it takes in your class. Resistance to collaboration may reflect ongoing problems in relations among students that they are reluctant to address. Group activities in Work in Progress carefully define tasks so students can choose the amount of personal exposure they want to risk. Since the institution constructs the instructor as an authority, who insists on certain points of view, procedures, due dates, or standards, you may find resistance to all of these appearing as resistance to you. You will make resistance more productive if you ensure that students understand you want diverse responses and expect the assertion of differences.

3. Remember that collaborative learning can involve more than the use of peer response groups. Many instructors use peer response groups in their writing classes. Such groups enable students to read and respond to work in progress, and we strongly recommend their use. Collaborative learning groups can function in other ways, however. Group activities suggested in Work in Progress utilize a number of approaches. Students brainstorm together, compare responses to check lists and guidelines, analyze responses to readings, and write and revise together. Collaborative learning activities need not be time-consuming. An instructor might want to have students spend ten minutes in groups discussing a question generated by a reading, for instance, before leading a full class discussion on the same issue.

4. Develop ways to foster students' collaborative learning skills. Instructors can improve students' ability to work collaboratively in the following ways:

--using collaborative practices from the very first day of the term
--demonstrating a collaborative approach through participation and example
--observing and interacting with groups as they work together
--demonstrating through grades and other means that collaborative learning counts in your class
--taking class time to discuss effective group dynamics and to respond to students' anxiety about group work
--encouraging students to monitor their group's effectiveness through self-evaluations and peer evaluations
--engaging students in role-playing activities

Instructors might allocate time during the first two or three classes to help students learn to work collaboratively with each other. Students need to develop a willingness to explore a topic without anxiety about being wrong, and to negotiate the making of meaning. Beginning groups will benefit from heterogeneity and from assignments that encourage diverse responses, since the greatest threat to effective collaboration is a premature shutting down of differing perspectives.

It is especially important to start with what students know. On the very first day students can freewrite their responses to a question like "How can writing help you succeed in college?" and collect their responses in small groups. Such a question could be simply boring and predictable if there were a right answer, but encouraging students to come up with unpredictable answers will set another, more productive kind of standard for group activities. Next the groups could try to write a collaborative answer to the question "Why write?," taking the various responses into account, and report to the class as a whole. Such a sequence establishes from the first that group work is work, not a break, but also that it requires heterogeneity to be productive.

The prologue of Work in Progress exemplifies the productive differences in experiences and abilities that a writing class may bring together. If students go on to do the activities in Chapter 1, they may compare responses to the question about college writing with their answers to the first question about their own previous experiences with writing. Work in Progress begins with commonplace understandings about writing. "Guidelines for Group Activities" in Chapter 1 provide specific suggestions to help students orient themselves.

Talking about writing, and writing about talking, students begin to weave a network of connections between speech and the written language--connections that for many students have been hard to make or non-existent (writing, to many students, is always someone else's language, probably the teacher's, or maybe Shakespeare's or Melville's or even Alice Walker's). Talking makes the community of student writers literate about their shared experiences.

Talking also leads students to collaborate with one another, to be excited about each others' work, and to see writing as a social act rather than a solitary one. The scene of writing enlarges from the isolated garret to include parts of the world--class, library, fields, stores, family, work.

After talking, the activities should return to writing, and the text has a number of suggestions about essays students might write as the result of their inquiries. These essay assignments ask students to synthesize what they have learned through writing exercises, exploration, reflection, and discussion. Students put into writing what they have learned about writing.

5. Structure groups and collaborative activities carefully. How should groups be chosen? There are some advantages to allowing students to form their own groups, but in general you should structure groups yourself, especially at the beginning of the class. In so doing, remember that groups work most effectively when members bring a variety of strengths and experiences to group activities. Alternatively, you could form groups for most activities randomly--counting off students in groups of three or four, for instance--but allow students to choose long-term peer response groups of five.

How are collaborative assignments different from others? When you assign groups to collaborate on substantial projects (activities that involve more, for instance, than responding to a reading or a series of questions and then reporting back to the class), you should structure your assignments with particular care. Effective collaborative learning assignments share the following characteristics:

a. They require collaboration for the project to be completed successfully. Otherwise, they may seem like a waste of time to some students.

b. They are explained in writing so students don't have to begin by arguing about the assignment.

c. They suggest how the project or activity is to be complete, and they suggest how the group should approach each stage of the assignment. They may also suggest possible roles for group members (recorder, timekeeper, reporter, and so on).

d. They build opportunities for self-evaluation and peer evaluation into the assignment.

e. They encourage group members to negotiate issues of authority and responsibility; they also encourage creative conflict while protecting minority views.

How can collaboration be graded? Simple check-off systems can provide the basis for a grade on collaborative work, using records submitted by groups at the end of each class. For important, lengthy collaborative learning projects, students can receive a group grade. You can incorporate feedback generated by trouble-shooting and self-analysis in the determination of this grade. Students can submit individual portfolios reflecting their participation in a group project to help demonstrate excellence in leadership and good citizenship. Finally, students can submit peer evaluations in the form of letters assessing the contributions of other group members.

6. Take advantage of the differences among students that collaboration can help to address. Working together requires careful leadership by the teacher to successfully organize group work, to initiate dialogue and provide

a model of interaction, to keep the class as a learning community focused upon its specific goals of studying writing, and finally, to establish the basis for a sense of community and for good citizenship within that community.

What worries some instructors are the problems students might encounter working together. Sometimes students have simply not had enough experience with collaborative learning, and so the course will be useful for them in this respect. But what about the moments when students encounter conflict? You as the instructor can help here not by lecturing, but by providing a model of non-divisive responsiveness. What you show them is how to engage in a dialectical exchange, which takes the other person's point of view into account without abandoning one's own. One of the reasons a teacher-centered classroom limits the possibilities for learning is precisely that it avoids or even represses conflict. Such a discussion is made much easier by the fact that everyone has a stake in the dialogue--everyone has writing that is under discussion.

To insure that everyone has a stake in group process, as well as to make sure students do their work, you may want to make it a prerequisite of participating in collaborative groups that each member has brought the needed assignment. Those who have not done the writing can work alone or in a separate group.

7. Assign multivocal as well as univocal collaborative essays. Rather than working in the group to produce a seamless document projecting agreement, your groups might try a collage or collection of their various texts, perhaps simply juxtaposed or else assembled with connecting explanations and transitions. Highlighting rather than smoothing over the differences in voices, styles, and perspectives has been an increasingly popular practice among feminists and others who want to keep cultural characteristics distinct, a way to honor differences as well as to suggest the collective mode of some groups' decision-making. Sometimes texts are even written in different languages. Of course, it would be an illusion to suggest that such documents reflect a total lack of hierarchy or selection, since someone must make choices at some point. Nonetheless they allow groups another option besides imposing a consensual style or argument on members who see the consensus as a distortion.

This discussion of collaborative writing and learning is necessarily brief. For further information see the following:

Clark, Suzanne, and Lisa Ede. "Collaboration and Resistance." The Right to Literacy. Ed. Andrea A. Lunsford, Helene Moglen, and James Slevin. New York: Modern Language Association, 1990: 276-285.

"Collaborative Writing." Special issue of Technical Communication: The Journal of the Society for Technical Communication. 38.4 (1991).

"Collaborative Writing in Business Communication." Special Issue of The Bulletin of the Association for Business Communication. 53.2 (1990).

Ede, Lisa and Andrea Lunsford. Singular Texts/Plural Authors: Perspectives on Collaborative Writing. Carbondale and Edwardsville, Ill.: Southern Illinois University Press, 1990.

Forman, Janis, Ed. New Visions of Collaborative Writing. Portsmouth, N.H.: Boynton/Cook, Heinemann, 1992.

Gere, Ann Ruggles. Writing Groups: History, Theory, and Implications. Carbondale, Ill.: Southern Illinois University Press, 1987.

Lay, Mary M., and William M. Karis, eds. Collaborative Writing in Industry: Investigations in Theory and Practice. New York: Baywood, 1990.

LeFevre, Karen Burke. Invention as a Social Act. Carbondale and Edwardsville, Ill.: Southern Illinois University Press for the Conference on College Composition and Communication, 1987.

Spears, Karen. Sharing Writing: Peer Response Groups in English Classes. Portsmouth, N.H.: Boynton/Cook, Heinemann, 1988.

Handling the Paper Load

To make your responses to student writing more effective, communicate them before the final draft of an essay appears for grading. Students need readers in order to revise and to change; comments on a final draft are apt to seem irrelevant or nothing more than justifications for the grade--not an easy kind of response for an instructor to make. Instructors should also seek out alternative ways to increase the amount of and kind of responses students receive before their final drafts. Instructors can talk with students about their writing in brief conferences and longer, more extensive sessions. Some instructors like to tape-record comments for students as they read. Brief, focussed reading of certain sections can be more helpful than global corrections. Students can hand in drafts with those sections they are particularly worried about marked for comment, or with questions attached. In computer labs, instructors can answer questions as they arise in the process of revision.

The fact is that students need to write much, much more than writing instructors can reasonably hope to evaluate, and instructors who try to micromanage their students' writing are probably wasting their time and being overdirective. Students do need wide-ranging responses to their writing; they can find other readers through the use of peer response groups and through sharing their work with friends, family, roommates and others. Instructors can greatly increase the focus and effectiveness of their evaluations by pressing students to draw upon other resources for help, such as writing centers, and by expecting students to do their own correcting of mechanical problems. If students must read papers aloud--even tape them--they will rapidly improve their ability to correct many of their own problems of voice, syntax, style, diction, and even punctuation.

In response to the awareness that instructors of writing should focus on the writing process as well as on the written product, many instructors have reduced the number of essays they require students to complete in a single term. This reduction insures that students will have time for planning activities, peer responses, and revisions. By limiting the number of assignments, instructors have reduced one difficulty traditionally associated with the teaching of writing: instead of grading eight or ten essays by each student in a single term, many instructors now grade four or five. Although this aspect of the paper load is reduced, other problems quickly appear. How can instructors keep track of and give credit for the prewriting, drafting, and revising they require or encourage students to complete?

We suggest that instructors cope with the paper load created by multiple drafts by detailing in the clearest, most straightforward terms what they expect of students. A handout that specifies what students are to turn in for writing assignments will help both you and your students organize their work more efficiently. The following handout suggests the information you should provide to students:

A NOTE TO STUDENTS ABOUT WRITING ASSIGNMENTS

Because I want to provide numerous opportunities for you to revise your writing, I have limited your assignments to five essays--roughly one essay every other week. Thus you will have time to engage in numerous planning activities, participate in peer response groups, and revise your writing. All of these activities are important to your improvement as a writer. Consequently, when you turn in the draft of an essay, I want to examine not just your final typed draft but all that preceded it. I can only study the process you used to write an essay if you organize your work carefully. (Doing so will also help you keep track of work in progress.)

Whenever you hand in an assignment, please be sure to include ALL of the following items, arranged in the order listed below. Please paper clip related items, such as invention and other planning materials. Turn in all material for an essay in a file folder or pocket folder.

1. invention and other planning materials--all the notes, diagrams, random jottings, lists, or other things that you wrote down to stimulate or collect your thinking before and during drafting

2. rough drafts--all working drafts, numbered in order of completion (and also with pages numbered in each draft and in decipherable, if not legible, handwriting and form)

3. peer response form--indicating the name of the student who responded to your work

4. your revision--typed, please, in a final draft with each page numbered

5. statement from you (handwritten is fine) that answers the following questions:

a. How did you write this essay?
b. What aspect or aspects of this paper are you most satisfied with, and why?
c. What aspect or aspects of this paper are you least satisfied with, and why?
d. What did you learn about yourself as a writer by working on this essay?

Responding to Student Writing

The dialogue you establish with students through your responses to their writing plays a crucial role in determining your effectiveness as an instructor--and their likely success as a student. Much has been written about instructors' comments on students' writing, so we will limit our discussion to several important principles.

1. Make your comments to students count. Remember that your job is not to comment on every strength or weakness in a student's essay but to provide advice that students can use as they write and revise. Better to concentrate on a few salient points than to overwhelm them with a multitude of suggestions and corrections.

2. Make comments that reflect your reading process. Indicate when you're intrigued, confused, or puzzled. Ask questions. Respond to the content of the essay. Let students know that a person (not a grading machine) is reading their work.

3. Be sure to find ways to tell students what they are doing well. Write summarizing statements that say what worked, what was persuasive, what was accomplished.

4. Comment on the rhetorical situation of the essay. Frequently an early draft of an essay will suffer from an incomplete or poorly developed sense of situation. Your comments about the situation that the paper implies can help the student think more clearly about this aspect of writing.

5. When you make suggestions for revision, focus on strategies rather than on specific content. For example, if a draft is rambling or incoherent, you might ask the student to write a descriptive outline or to summarize the essay and then to reflect on the degree to which it fulfills his or her controlling purpose.

6. Help your students understand your comments by giving a public reading of one or more student papers, commenting as you go. By showing students how you read their writing, you can demythologize the process and help students better interpret your comments as well.

7. Publishing students' writing provides a wider audience for them. You can easily produce a class publication. If you have no resources whatsoever, ask students to bring 25 copies of their best essay to class during the last week or so of the term. Perhaps you will want to provide copies of a title page. Often a student will contribute art work or lettering talent or a computer graphic for the cover. Desktop publishing expands the possibilities enormously. If you are assembling the volume yourselves, you can collate the copies by putting one page per desk in a circle around the

room and letting students collect their own "books." Bring a stapler. Or, you can have the whole thing copied and bound at a local copy center for a charge of about $5 or so a copy, if students want to pay the price.

The result is a collection of essays with histories the students may know very well, remembering the rough drafts and the struggles of composition from their groups. It is also a collection that provides a sort of reference, a cross-section of what one class of students produced--and that helps all of them to orient themselves in the academic world. Finally--not the least of its assets--publication gives students a reason to take the last step of editing seriously, as more than the personal crotchet of their group members or their instructors. Some instructors have classes buy packets of selected examples of student writing drawn from past terms. Finally, some programs, such as the Composition Program at the University of Arizona, publish books of essays selected from student submissions together with comments and questions.

Using Writing Assignments

1. Freewriting: When you have students do freewriting assignments, be sure to keep them "free." The basic idea is that writers will not be held accountable for the kinds of problems or errors that would ordinarily discount the value of their efforts in the economy of the classroom. Freewriting has "use" value rather than "exchange" value: it doesn't "count" in the same way that final drafts count.

It sometimes helps to define freewriting by the amount of time spent producing it. Ask students to write for five, ten, or fifteen minutes. You will often find that in the first four or five minutes they write down everything that they are used to thinking or saying to themselves, and the next few sentences come more slowly, from less automatic responses. You might want to structure your freewriting assignments accordingly, asking them to spend at least seven to ten minutes on topics that they probably have rehearsed quite a bit already.

2. Brainstorming: Brainstorming is a form of listing that may be done by a group or by an individual. Given a topic or problem, they are to write down every idea that comes to mind, as quickly as possible. The only rules are: (1) don't stop to elaborate and (2) don't censor the list.

We like to tell our classes that it's not a real brainstorming session unless they produce at least some ideas that are exotic, crazy, terrible, ridiculous, or reprehensible. The idea is to produce excess. When we do a brainstorming session in class, we ask students to go back and circle the items that are incredibly awful. If they have none, they need some.

Like freewriting, brainstorming works especially well as a mode of invention when it is detached from the critical judgments that will prune and restrain things later on for the final draft. Brainstorming encourages creativity--the production of a number of ideas.

3. Interviewing: A number of the exercises in this book ask students to interview others--peers, family, tutors, older students, instructors--for various kinds of information about writing. These interviews serve collectively to help students construct a realistic idea of the rhetorical context within which they write. The interviews also help students to step out of their isolated writing habits, and to think about asking others for information and help as a natural part of the writing process.

Most classes will benefit from guidance on the process of interviewing. Even if they have done "interviews" before, often they are still doing rather perfunctory research. In order to give them some direction and some sense of the possibilities of an interviewing assignment, instructors may have students role-play the interview first. For example, ask one student to play the role of an instructor in his field, and another in the same field to interview him. On the board or an overhead projector, list additional ideas for questions submitted by other class members. Ask all to take notes during the interview and check them against one another for the accuracy of their understanding. Instructors who invite speakers or panels into their classes can take advantage of the occasion to compare students' notes the next day. The hidden problem of interviewing will immediately become evident--that students very often hear what they expect to hear rather than what is said, just as they also misinterpret what they read when they do research. Finding this out during the kind of informal interviewing suggested in this text will provide a low-anxiety entry into working on the problem.

In sum, students can improve their interviewing by setting up questions in advance to serve as guidelines, keeping careful notes about what was said, double checking difficult or startling answers, and using quotes accurately.

4. The Writer's Notebook: The writer's notebook functions like a journal, a place where students are encouraged to write freely, explore ideas, to reflect, or to record messages to themselves. Is there a difference between a notebook and a journal? Perhaps not, in fact. However, writer's journals often contain extended pieces of writing and reflect the writer's desire to describe what she or he experiences, while a writer's notebook might contain all sorts of things, including quotations, plans and schedules, clusters, or random thoughts, and might be more oriented to instrumental purposes.

Perhaps an argument for calling this assignment a "notebook" rather than a "journal" might be that the "journal" has become associated with more personal, expressive writing. But you may wish just such expressive writing, and you should follow your own preferences in both title and suggestions for contents. The fundamental idea is to have students experiment and explore, using writing to learn and reflect--producing much more material than they eventually use in class essays.

If you wish to require students to keep the notebook, you may ask them to pass it in at the end of the term. It makes a logical part of a portfolio, if you are using that system. You don't, however, want to have students putting off a last-minute ordeal of filling a notebook, as our experience with assigning journals has sometimes proven. And giving credit for the notebook may be less important than giving notebook work attention as part of the class--not necessarily by responding in writing. (You probably don't have time.) Opportunities to use notebook material and to reflect on and discuss selected entries throughout the course of the term will help integrate using the notebook into the rest of students' writing. Or ask to see notebooks every other week or so, together with a comment from the student reflecting on the experience of keeping the notebook and notes about possible uses for the material. You can simply keep a check list recording the fact that you have seen the notebook.

You will find that skimming notebook or journal entries frequently can be a valuable way of getting feedback about the progress of the class. If students are prewarned that you will be reading them, they can avoid unintended embarrassment, or you can simply ask for the student's comments alone, without the bulk of the notebook (or the possible invasion of privacy).

The one thing you should not do with a notebook is give it a grade or any other form of critical evaluation. It needs to be exploratory.

See pp. 45-46, Chapter 2 for an extended description of the writer's notebook and a list of possible uses.

5. Essays: Most writing classes base final grades on essays that have been developed into final drafts and handed in perhaps every other week (four or five per quarter, six or eight per semester). A length of two to four pages works well. If you wish to assign longer papers, you'll probably reduce the number accordingly. But you do not need to ask students to write only finished essays. You may want your students to try out many of the essay ideas prompted by assignments in the text and to choose just a few of the most promising to work into final draft form. Many instructors have students submit a portfolio of drafts and a certain number of essays chosen for revision as the basis for evaluation at the end of the term.

When you decide on the essays you would like students to write, whether you use suggestions from the text or other assignments, you can develop a more elaborate explanation of the essay assignment to help your students, together, perhaps, with samples of student work to serve as models. Sample essay assignments and student essays are collected at the end of this section.

6. Research: Writing classes often must teach students how to think about research without specifically teaching the research methods of particular disciplines. This is not as impossible as it seems. Rhetorical inquiry provides a basis for all research, and you can help students take the first steps toward a responsible approach to the research projects they will be assigned in later classes. No matter what kind of research students might encounter, they must analyze the rhetorical situation (What is the exigency that prompts writing? Who is the audience?) and the conventions that are necessary or appropriate. They must develop some form of argument. *Work in Progress* can help with this process through its emphasis on analyzing the rhetorical situation, its careful articulation of bridges between oral discussion and written projects, its attention to the place of conventions, and its opportunities for considering the differences and possible relationships between personal, informal writing and impersonal, formal writing.

For work on the rhetorical situation, see Chapter 3; for research and invention, see Chapter 5 (which has a section on the library and on interviewing, questionnaires, and observation); for critical reading, see Chapter 9; for academic assignments and audiences, see Chapter 10; and for academic analysis and argument, see Chapter 11.

Evaluation of Your Teaching

Teaching, like writing, takes place within a rhetorical situation. You will surely wish to assess in an ongoing way how your class is going and make adjustments to improve instruction during the term. The frequent sampling of students' experiences, ideas, drafts, and reflections which *Work in Progress* suggests will serve as an important means of keeping in touch with your class, so that these informal moments of evaluation can take place powerfully with no special structure beyond the dialogic form of instruction. Informal write-to-learn activities can also provide useful feedback. You might end a class period, for instance, by asking students to: 1) write one thing they've learned as a result of class discussion or activities; 2) write one question they have or a difficulty they're experiencing. Such comments can give you a good sense of the "pulse" of your class.

Still, you will probably wish to provide for some more formalized kinds of evaluation. Your students may have plenty of opportunities to give you feedback about how they are doing; yet, they may not take full advantage of the possibility. There may be misunderstandings about your aims and procedures that you need to address straightforwardly; students may believe you expect them to be good students in terms defined by teacher-centered and/or lecture-dominated classrooms, for example. They may also expect you to be a good teacher according to such norms. Thus you may wish to take time periodically to explicitly evaluate the progress of the class. You can do this yourself, by asking students for anonymous comments or soliciting comments and suggestions in an ongoing way--perhaps with a suggestion box, or an E-mail location.

You can also benefit from bringing others into your classroom to observe and comment. If your institution provides the opportunity, try midterm evaluation visits from an instructional center or from colleagues, whose interviews with your students can reveal trends you had not noticed and whose observations of the class can give you the benefit of a disengaged opinion. Obviously, the benefits of such visits depend on the collegiality and shared understanding in your program. They should be "formative" rather than "summative" evaluations--that is, directed toward improving instruction rather than making judgments about your teaching ability. Such evaluations should begin with a conference before the visit when you discuss your goals and your concerns and a postvisit conference when you can hear the views of the evaluator and explore any changes you want to make.

When the class has finished, your teaching will be evaluated in a more conclusive way. Perhaps students will be asked to fill out an evaluation form and/or write brief comments. Many institutions, which are beginning to pay more careful attention to teaching, are asking for teaching portfolios. Your own notes and reflections about the class, together with the syllabus, sample papers, hand-outs, and even letters from students are items that may eventually contribute to a portfolio representing your teaching of that class in a final evaluation.

The following are qualities often included in institutional evaluations. Although teaching evaluations may seem to assume a teacher-centered classroom, their most important components are also important functions for the teacher of a classroom using response groups and collaborative activities. Think about ways to determine how well your class is doing--and how well your students understand your approach.

1. Did the teacher make this class interesting? A more helpful term instead of "interest" might be "commitment" or "engagement." Work in Progress tries to show your students how to build their own sense of commitment to writing assignments rather than depending on teachers or on the contents of assignments. The frequent responses to their concerns and to their work that are a part of a collaborative classroom do, however, make a major component in generating interest. You can improve students' engagement in your writing class through the quality of their interactions with you and with other students. And you can teach them how to permanently improve the quality of their interactions in other classes and with other instructors as well.

2. Is the teacher well organized? When you teach a writing course, all the recommendations made for organizing collaborative writing groups are appropriate. That is, it's very important to make goals clear, timelines definite, agreements explicit--and it's also very important to attend to group process, making sure everyone understands, has a chance to contribute, feels disagreement has a place, and knows what responsibilities they have. Unlike lecture-centered classrooms, whose success may seem to depend on the teacher's preparation alone, writing classrooms depend on the students' participation as well for their success. In particular, this may mean thoughtful attention to the organization of response groups and collaborative assignments. It also means organizing ways to keep track of the many kinds of writing and reading you ask them to do, whether graded or not.

3. Did the teacher give clear assignments? Were the expectations clear? Our experience suggests that students greatly appreciate explicit guidelines. The many "Guidelines" available in Work in Progress should help them know what to do, step by step as they work through the process of writing. They will also appreciate explicit assignments from you (see the last section of this instructor's manual for samples), and help with understanding the grading system you will use. Students generally find essay writing and essay exams less "clear" than "objective" measures. If you find this to be true for your students, you might want to talk with them about ways of evaluating the complexities of writing and collaborative work.

4. Have you learned significantly from this course? For a writing class, this question should not be translated as "Have you learned to write yet?" As we who are professionals in the field know very well, writing is not a content that can be mastered once and for all. Your class ought to help students plan and critically assess their own writing projects, within a rhetorical situation that is appropriate. This sense of critical authority, this increasing self-confidence in learning more about how to write--and not learning to write in any final way--may be their most significant achievement in your class.

Further Reading in Composition Studies

The following bibliography does not attempt to list all the works that might be included in a basic bibliography of works on composition. Rather, we have included here those works that, by their broad scope or bibliographic emphasis, provide useful introductions to the field of composition studies. Should you wish to know more about the theoretical and research basis of *Work in Progress*, you may find useful the following essays on the teaching of writing by Lisa Ede: "Teaching Writing" in Lindemann and Tate's *Introduction to Composition Studies*, cited below, and "Methods, Methodologies, and the Politics of Knowledge" in Kirsch and Sullivan's *Methods and Methodologies in Composition*, also cited below.

Bartholomae, David and Anthony Petrosky, eds. *Ways of Reading: An Anthology for Writers*. 2nd ed. New York: St. Martin's Press, 1990.

Brandt, Deborah. *Literacy as Involvement: The Acts of Writers, Readers, and Texts*. Carbondale, Ill.: Southern Illinois University Press, 1990.

Bullock, Richard and John Trimbur. *The Politics of Writing Instruction, Postsecondary*. Portsmouth, N.H.: Boyton/Cook, 1991.

Elbow, Peter. *Writing with Power; Techniques for Mastering the Writing Process*. New York: Oxford University Press, 1981.

Enos, Theresa. *A Sourcebook for Basic Writing Teachers*. New York: Random House, 1987.

Flower, Linda. *Problem-solving Strategies for Writing*. 2nd Edition. San Diego: Harcourt Brace Janovich, 1985.

Harkin, Patricia and John Schilb. *Contending with Words: Composition and Rhetoric in a Postmodern Age*. New York: Modern Language Association, 1991.

Kirsch, Geza, and Patricia Sullivan. *Methods and Methodologies in Composition Studies*. Carbondale, Ill.: Southern Illinois University Press, forthcoming.

Lindemann, Erika; and Gary Tate. *An Introduction to Composition Studies*. New York: Oxford University Press, 1991.

Lunsford, Andrea and Robert Connors. *The St. Martin's Handbook*. New York: St. Martin's Press, 1989.

McClelland, Ben W., and Timothy R. Donovan. *Perspectives on Research and Scholarship in Composition*. New York: Modern Language Association, 1985.

Rottenberg, Annette T. *Elements of Argument: A Text and Reader*. 2nd Edition. New York: St. Martin's Press, 1988.

Tate, Gary. *Teaching Composition: 12 Bibliographic Essays*. Rev. ed. Fort Worth: Texas Christian, 1987.

5. SUGGESTIONS FOR TEACHING FROM WORK IN PROGRESS

PROLOGUE: Entering the Conversation

As they begin to read this book, your students will encounter a sketch representing the author's students in a dialogue with her about writing. Students beginning a writing program often believe that the study of composition is precisely not a conversation, but rather something closer to learning a foreign language. Some fear that working with readers other than their teacher would be some form of cheating. Kenneth Burke's notion of rhetoric as an ongoing conversation provides a much more enabling analogy. The idea of writing as a "conversation" emphasizes the collaborative and suggests that we draw upon our wider linguistic experiences to write. This book invites students to take such an approach from the beginning.

The prologue shows how important writing students can be to one another and how much they can learn by talking to one another. At the same time, the prologue also emphasizes the diversity of students who might be in a writing program. Writers not only come from diverse cultures and personal situations, which may impact their writing, but they also have very different preferred methods for working. However, they most particularly have in common the fact that they all engage in talk about writing.

The writing course might also begin with a kind of prologue. In addition to talking about the syllabus and about assignments on the first day, students can usefully write a brief paragraph to prompt their memory and then talk (perhaps in small groups) about previous writing experiences. Talking and writing will both be important means--and useful tools--of learning in this course and others. We've found that it's a good idea to ask students to do a little of everything you want them to do during that term on the first day.

CHAPTER 1: Writers Writing

In this chapter: Guidelines for Group Activities

This chapter orients your students to their rhetorical situation in a writing class. It begins with a list of ways that people might use writing when writing isn't assigned for a class: as a journal, as notes, as a proposal, for a bulletin board, to prepare a plan, to write a family history, and even to help the process of writing academic essays. Thus it stresses a commonsense approach to writing, giving students credit for what they already know--their "rhetorical sensitivity"--and forecasting the factors and choices that may enter into learning to improve their writing. In particular, this chapter counters some of the expectations about a writing class that many students bring with them. It stresses the interactive nature of writing, its complexity, and the need for students to use their judgment in making decisions; rules and formulas are useful as guidelines, not as absolutes. The chapter speaks of writing as a process and focuses attention on that process as it is situated in culture and in a specific context. Finally, Chapter 1 introduces students to the idea that writing is not necessarily a solitary agony, but rather something that benefits from collaboration with others. The classroom can function as a writing community rather than an aggregate of isolated individuals.

This chapter can support several emphases. You might want to stress the conceptual, discussing the idea of rhetoric and the nature of writing, and the problem of describing effective writing with rules. You might want to stress the practical, setting your class up right away as a workshop and engaging students in the process of writing, reading, and exchanging responses. If you are using additional reading material, you can use the commonsensical approach of this chapter to encourage your students to start right in on content-centered writing, making writing decisions, rather than waiting to be told exactly what to do.

Concepts

1. Writing as Work in Progress: Chapter 1 asks students to begin thinking of writing not as a singular act, started and finished in one (perhaps painful, last-minute) sitting, but as a complex process of choices involving rhetorical sensitivity. As they begin to analyze their writing, they will find a number of ways to work on improvements rather than imagining that they must work on everything at once.

2. Rhetoric: Students often have no idea what "rhetoric" means. They may have heard the expression "that's just rhetoric" used to complain about a political speech or an advertisement, and so they may think of writing as "rhetorical" when it wrongly values form over content.

Ironically, student papers also frequently suffer from being too "rhetorical" in this sense, because they worry more about the effect (getting a good grade) than about their ideas. But you might want to point out to your students that rhetoric does not, inherently, necessitate this kind of imbalance. Rhetoric takes into account the interaction of reader, writer, text, and context. It overlaps with the study of communication, language, and discourse. In the medieval system of learning, the basic subjects in the lower division of the liberal arts, or the "trivium," included logic, grammar, and rhetoric. Rhetoric was distinguished from the other two by its situational, practical nature.

Clearly, part of what rhetoric has to offer is a way to study the expressions and representations of culture. Thus you will find that this text's rhetorical approach allows you to easily integrate other cultural texts into your writing program. You will also find that the rhetorical approach helps students see the continuity between their own writing and the writing produced around them. Rhetorical study can apply equally to the freewriting produced by a freshman and the article she reads in Harper's, to the student's review and the textbook for his psychology class.

You can begin right away to encourage your students to adopt a rhetorical way of thinking about all the texts they encounter. One way to do that is by asking students to consider how the various elements of rhetoric interact whenever they are looking at a piece of writing--whether written by one of them or by a professional writer. Who is the writer? What is the writer's persona? Who is the reader? What is the context? How does the text reflect these considerations?

3. Rhetorical Sensitivity: Students already have a commonsense knowledge about writing which they can both draw on and improve. They acquire this rhetorical sensitivity just as they acquire language, through experience. Of course, students in your classes vary widely in the amount of previous experience with written texts, which they bring to this writing course, and you will want to take their very different degrees of rhetorical sensitivity into account. What kinds of things have they read and written before? What experience have they had with the academic writing they will be doing in the future? Are many of your students better attuned to oral presentations than to written texts and thus more sophisticated about what "sounds right" than about how to arrange an essay? Do you have students who feel so uncertain about every detail of written language that they must approach it as a "foreign" kind of discourse? Students who are, in fact, nonnative speakers?

You can help students translate some parts of their "rhetorical sensitivity" into their written work by asking them to explicitly identify what they know--not necessarily in particularly sophisticated vocabularies. When they explain what works, to you or to other students, they are making their knowledge conscious and accessible.

Most students, for example, know quite a bit, perhaps even from watching television, about how a story should be structured, and they can apply that knowledge to narrative passages in each other's compositions. Most understand, tacitly, how devices that frame and structure a text help orient the reader--they can point out that they don't understand what an essay is about and that the writer needs to beef up the opening without needing much formal instruction on the topic of introductions.

On the other hand, students who have never read a persuasive essay or a critical review cannot understand what it should be like from a series of rules. If they have no prior experience with the kinds of texts you want them to write, students need plenty of examples and models to follow.

4. Rules and Formulas: Chapter 1 asks students to exercise judgment about what does and does not work in their particular rhetorical situation. It points out that general rules, such as "never use I," ought to be questioned and don't universally apply.

When they reconsider rules they perhaps once accepted, your students may feel liberated from arbitrary constraints, from the sense of being bound by rules that did not always seem reasonable. But you may find that students do not altogether welcome the end of dictatorship. Many continue to long for a tidy recipe which would enable them to cook up passable writing every time.

Most of us, in fact, would welcome some relief from the messy chaos and anxiety of writing, especially when that writing is being evaluated. So it is tempting to restore the formulaic--easier, even, to grade papers if there are some rules that either have or have not been violated. But research suggests that the formula is a temptation we ought to resist.

The problem is not that rules inevitably hamper creativity. After all, many sonnets illustrate how forms can stimulate creative solutions to their constraints. What damages the ability of students to learn how to write is an attitude of rigidity about the process that keeps them from thinking things through or having the confidence to change plans. Research on writing blocks (notably by Mike Rose) suggests that students who suffer from such blocks have a tendency to think about writing inflexibly, to follow rules or formulas as if they were absolute, and to stop writing rather than to try another approach that might better suit their subject or their audience or their aim. The point, then, is to help students to proceed flexibly, regarding rules as conventions or strategies rather than as directives. Asking students to examine rules critically and to use them as strategies rather than as scientific law should help students gain confidence, even when they run into problems with an assignment.

With all of this said, we will of course go on supplying our students with handy hints, rules of thumb, guidelines, heuristics, and even useful recipes--all wonderful tools if used rhetorically rather than absolutely, as probabilities rather than mathematical certitudes. And for rhetorical reasons as well, we recognize the importance of adhering to the conventions of standard written English.

To help focus students' anxiety about breaking rules, try this exercise. Ask them to write a paragraph that violates as many rules as possible. Run a contest for the worst paragraph in the class, if you like. You might then go on to point out that breaking grammatical rules is not the only way to write a perfectly terrible paragraph, as the Bulwer-Lytton Fiction Contest illustrates. By exaggerating the most banal clichés of the genre, such as variations on "it was a dark and stormy night," the winners of this contest are those who produce the worst samples of gothic and romantic fiction. In writing, the most conventional can also be not the best but the worst.

5. Writing as a Process: The idea of the writing process is introduced here briefly and will be expanded in later chapters. By analogy with a number of other activities; which you may wish to explore with your students, writing involves a performance of complex skills adapted to varying situations, requiring a great deal of practice and benefitting by setting goals and assessing progress. Here you might want to go on to specify the implications of this view of writing as a process for the way you are organizing your class.

6. The Writing Community: If writing is not a series of algorithms to be memorized but rather a social process much like a conversation in its general structure, then the collaborative model can help reformulate expectations about the way a classroom should work. Keep in mind critiques of the ways collaboration might stifle student resistance or opposition as you set up your class, so you will encourage debate and acknowledge tendencies to impose a normalizing consensus. There are a number of ways to organize a class as a writing community, with greater or lesser emphasis on using class time for learning groups. All have in common the attitude that students should be encouraged to exchange ideas at every stage of the writing process, and that writing at its best takes advantage of all social resources, rather than happening in isolation. Instead of concluding that only the writing class can be a "writing community," ideally students will use this approach to extend their roles in the academic community as they continue their education.

This chapter offers Guidelines for group activities. The Teaching Practices section of this instructor's manual offers additional suggestions for collaborative structures. There are many different forms of collaboration in contemporary writing practices. This book contains material on developing a rhetorical sensitivity to the collaborative nature of all writing and on using collaborative groups to help students learn to write as well as teaching students to work together on specific projects. For more information about the history of collaboration, current types of collaboration in business and industry as well as academic contexts, and a discussion of theory of collaborative writing, see Lisa Ede and Andrea Lunsford, *Singular Texts/Plural Authors: Perspectives on Collaborative Writing* (Carbondale and Edwardsville Ill.: Southern Illinois University Press, 1990).

Activities

(p. 10) Exploration: This exploration asks students to list the kinds of writing they do. You might want to start this exercise on the very first day of class because it immediately moves students into one step of the writing process, affords an opportunity for students to share writing experiences, and establishes the fact that students *are already writers*. If you want to help class members to know one another and begin to establish the class as a community, put the responses up on the board or on an overhead transparency. The result will be an informal survey of the kinds of writing the students have done and their reasons for writing. You will establish the first evidence that you take them seriously as writers simply by the act of listening to their responses, some of which will probably be "I never write unless I have to," and other expressions of duress. Press them to define for themselves what they consider to be productive and satisfying writing experiences. This exercise concludes by asking them to write one or two paragraphs that make these differentiations. This activity is important in two ways. First, by doing this students take their own experience seriously and they take an analytical perspective toward those experiences. Second, it involves students in a workable model of a writing process--first listing, then drafting paragraphs.

(p. 12) Exploration: This exploration is to help students think methodically about writing. It asks students to examine the elements of a successful experience with writing. Without previously discussing what criteria should define successful writing, you can use this exploration to find out how they define "successful." They will often be surprised by the variety of criteria other students bring to bear, if you give them a chance to talk about their responses with each other. (You may be surprised as well.) But more important, this exercise gives students the beginnings of a method for managing their own writing, discovering what works or does not work in their own practice. The discussion of what "successful" might mean will continue throughout the course, as more complex aspects of the rhetorical situation come into view. With luck, you can complicate the supposition that success means a good grade, as well as showing the various judgments that come into play in assigning grades.

(p. 16) Exploration: This exploration asks students to demonstrate their understanding of "rhetoric" and "rhetorical sensitivity." In discussing this assignment, you may fruitfully spend some class time exploring some different situations the students might describe: the text suggests a job interview, a wedding, a sports event. What about situations that emphasize the difference between public and private discourses--for example, a family holiday, an appearance on television, a conversation between friends, the same story told to a newspaper reporter? Thinking about the doubleness of rhetorical conventions, ask students to decide how free and how limited their situation might be, from conventions of such things as dress to conventional expectations about how much you should know. When would they feel they needed to learn more about the conventions? Do they prefer writing tasks with specified conventions, or writing that is very open-ended?

(p. 17) Application: This application asks students to list rules that they have never understood or fully accepted and then to write a brief explanation about their reasons for questioning one of them. Tell them to look at a handbook or at a book about style such as Strunk and White's Elements of Style, if they are unsure about what kind of rules might be at issue. After this exercise, you may wish to have them look at documents from the history of rules and usage, from the rules for rhetorical exercises that Shakespeare might have been taught, and/or the rules imposed on American students in nineteenth-century, one-room schoolhouses. The McGuffey's Reader reminds us, for example, that teachers once paid a good deal of attention to oral reading, and (in spite of admonitions to trust nature) they imposed rules for correct pronunciation which aimed to remedy the faults illustrated in a number of charts such as the following:

RULE II: Avoid the *omission* of unaccented vowels

INCORRECT	CORRECT	INCORRECT	CORRECT
sep'rate	sep-a-rate	mem'ry	mem-o-ry
'pear	ap-pear	'pin-ion	o-pin-ion
'special	es-pe-cial	par-tic'lar	par-tic-u-lar

Can your students give any reasons why such rules would be valuable? Why they might not be?

(p. 17) Group Activity: This activity asks students to discuss in groups the rules they are questioning and to select one for further deliberation. The exercise suggests that you use groups to frame arguments against--and in favor of--a selected rule. Thus the students are asked to think rhetorically rather than grammatically, using judgment rather than correctness as a standard.

These discussions may usefully forecast topics that will be taken up later on in the course. As an example, a group may question whether paragraphs need topic sentences, by analogy with the rule about essays needing a thesis. There will perhaps be some contention in the class about certain rules: many students, for example, feel strongly about academic rules against sentence fragments, which they encounter frequently in everyday prose. Many students have computer programs that check their papers not only for spelling, but also for grammatical correctness. As an additional exercise, have them run two or three samples of prose through their computer's grammar check--something of their own, but also some samples from textbooks or readers. Discuss whether they agree with the computer program's recommendations, and what cannot be included in its checker. For example, how useful are comments about sentence length?

The exercise concludes with a class discussion about conclusions. Students understandably want most of all to know about your list of necessary rules and how their developing common sense will connect to their grades. You might want to deal with this hidden agenda by pointing out that rules and grades don't have much to do with each other, since the point is that good writing requires the exercise of judgment and choice. However, you also can point out that certain errors of spelling and usage are not acceptable.

(p. 19) Exploration: Freewriting is a technique that can help students suspend attention to context, audience, and conventions momentarily in order to focus on developing ideas. It does not necessarily reject all concern with these aspects of the rhetorical situation, but rather emphasizes one use of writing: writing is a powerful tool in the production of thought. It's best if you have students do their first freewriting in class so they understand how to put everything aside and simply keep writing. Ten minutes is a workable length of time. If you occasionally take class time for freewriting and then reflecting or responding to the writing, you encourage attention to the process and underline its importance. If you write along with the class, so much the better.

Students' opening responses to this Exploration can serve as a montage to jump start your next class meeting. Here are some samples from our students:

When I write I feel like I'm in jail . . .
Writing means trouble . . .
Writing is like going into a long, dark tunnel . . .

(p. 23) Application: If you make it a class assignment to go interview a writing assistant at the writing center, you might forewarn the center about the date you choose. Freshmen in particular are often surprisingly shy about seeking out help, so it makes sense to encourage them to become familiar with what is available, especially if they have no other introduction to the services. Assigning an interview has the advantage of removing any imagined stigma from students' going to the writing center.

(p. 26) Group Activity: Even if you do not wish to establish on-going groups in your class, you might want to help students form collaborative support groups to meet outside of class. Usually at least some students in a class will be interested in such a voluntary group. Once they get together and organize, they might meet once or twice a week to read and respond to each other's work, exchange ideas and discoveries, and make suggestions to each other. Support groups outside class, in other words, can serve the same kinds of functions that in-class groups serve. However, they do not really substitute for in-class groups, because, without your help and modeling, they sometimes have difficulty focusing, and, without a required schedule, most students have trouble finding meeting time.

Activities for Thought, Discussion, and Writing

You may wish to assign these activities as entries into a writer's notebook. Additionally, numbers 2 and 3 under this heading are good starting points for an essay assignment.

Number 1: This activity asks students to write down concrete goals for themselves as writers. This paragraph can help to give you a better sense of how well students' expectations for the class articulate with your sense of what they can expect to accomplish. However, when you look at the goals your students write down, you may find that some students still have very little ownership of their writing and very little understanding of what a writing goal might be. Their goals may be vague rephrasings of something a former teacher told them they should do or a stab at psyching out what you want them to have as goals, rather than anything they have a deep commitment to accomplish. One of the real achievements of the term's work on writing may finally show in the extent to which students are able to formulate concrete, realistic, attainable goals for their writing.

Number 2: This freewriting asks the writer to explore feelings and values associated with writing. You may be surprised, as we have been, by responses that articulate the separation students perceive between school writing and private writing. Many students talk about good and bad school writing experiences solely in terms of the grades they received. Part of what they will learn from you is how to talk about successful writing.

Number 3: This activity suggests an interview of other students and some form of report on the results, either to the student's writing group or in the form of an essay.

A number of the exercises in this book ask students to interview others--peers, family, tutors, more advanced students--for various kinds of information about writing. These interviews serve collectively to help students construct a realistic idea of the rhetorical context within which they write. The interviews also help students to step out of their isolated writing habits and to think about asking others for information and help as a natural part of the writing process. Work in Progress offers several opportunities in later chapters to use interviewing as a means of researching writing. This exercise offers informal practice for an activity you may wish to teach more formally later on. See page 127 for "Interviewing Guidelines" and the Teaching Practices section of the instructor's manual for more on interviews.

Interviewing other students will not necessarily inspire your students with positive reports about the worth of writing. Some of the technical majors at our university, for example, told Composition 121 students they didn't see much reason for anything but preparation for technical writing! Some of our freshmen students were upper-division, having put off their freshman writing to their junior or senior year. This encounter with the realities of the rhetorical situation allowed, at least, for some exchange about what a beginning writing class should teach. We can, after all, argue that there are defensible reasons for teaching a humanities version of the essay, especially if we question the characterization of writing as merely a basic (remedial?) skill, and we see rhetoric as a humanity.

Number 4: This exercise asks students to freewrite about their experiences working with group activities. Like writing, groups draw upon rhetorical knowledge and context in order to function, and students will benefit by making assumptions and conventions explicit. Like the other exercises here, this can give you valuable information about your class. If you sense that students feel considerable awkwardness about working together, you may wish to work with them specifically on ways to improve the usefulness of group work.

CHAPTER 2: Understanding the Writing Process

In this chapter: *Guidelines for Analyzing Your Composing Process*
Guidelines for Keeping a Writer's Notebook
Guidelines for Managing Your Time
Guidelines for Writing with a Word Processor
Guidelines for Collaborative Writing

This chapter introduces your students to the writing process. Its purpose is to demystify the rituals of writing and the sense of isolation so that students will learn to regard their own writing practices as open to interaction, analysis, and change. In particular, the chapter emphasizes ways that expert as well as beginning writers may work to improve on raw inspiration. Students will learn some of the different forms planning, drafting, and revising may take in the experience of various kinds of writers. Work in Progress encourages students to think about how they can develop these composing processes in their own way through learning and practice. By opening up various possibilities to students, the text shows them how to develop more flexibility and more conscious decision making about writing habits that may have seemed ineluctable as fate. Many students will find themselves changing their writing processes when their situation changes. Under the pressure of deadlines, for example, they may sometimes abbreviate planning or revising. The composing strategies they study in this text and in your classroom will help them make choices wisely about how they approach planning, drafting, and revising in changing circumstances. Finally, this chapter introduces a discussion of informal and formal collaborative writing.

Concepts:

1. Magical thinking and the students' history as a writer: Many students believe writing requires a natural talent or inspiration, and so hard work does not make much difference in how well one can write. Such a belief greatly influences their writing habits, discouraging many students from making the effort to change the way they write. Furthermore, writing is so complex and multiple, it probably most resembles learning a second language--it only seems natural once you've acquired considerable fluency, which is never acquired overnight in one extraordinary outburst of passionate scribbling. This process of naturalization, however, helps convince many students that such magic exists.

You may want to take time to talk with your students about the way they think about writing. A useful technique is to ask them to brainstorm associations with the word writer. Typical responses include: genius, glasses, dead, brilliant, reclusive, creative, eccentric. Or ask them to do a freewrite beginning with the words "A writer is someone who . . ." Many students think writers are in touch with some kind of magic--and out of touch with their everyday experience. Teachers find it productive to discuss some of their own writing processes with students, even if the students do not regard academic lives as particularly "everyday."

When you discuss revision and procrastination, you will find students especially full of mystical superstitions. Many of our students have stories about an essay they wrote at the last minute and received an A, while another essay was revised and revised but only received a C. As such folklore illustrates, students often seem to want to believe that the result of their writing is beyond their control. Of course, frequently those last minute A papers worked well because the students tried nothing new and just repeated what they'd already mastered, and the much-revised papers may have represented some genuine learning, not fully assimilated or polished enough for an A. The shortest distance between an assignment and a finished paper is not the best direction to take for learning to write: industrial efficiency provides a poor model, even though students may later want to write with such efficiency. You can use portfolio evaluation, organize your assignment grading to shield students from too-early grading of newly learned approaches, or let later drafts and papers compensate for early poorer grades.

This text is structured to interrupt the automatic and unconscious writing habits of your students. In this chapter they will be asked to reflect on their experiences as a writer and their representations of the craft. You may want to structure your classroom and requirements further to resist the habits of magical thinking.

2. Composing strategies: Chapter 2 asks students to identify the composing strategies that work best for them and to recognize differences among individuals in what works. The distinction between a strategy and a rule is exactly that criterion; if one strategy doesn't work, another one is called for. Students who think in terms of strategies rather than rules, Mike Rose's research suggests, are less apt to suffer from writing blocks. Students who think of writing as something they can pragmatically and systematically learn to do will be in a better position to put the strategies that work into practice. At the same time, the exercises in this chapter will help to encourage your students to examine the ways writing is bound up with their own history and sense of identity. Thus strategic rhetorical choices are deeply involved as well with the development of an ethos, a sense of writing authority, and the ethical choices writers must make. If a rule seems merely technical or a matter of skills, rhetorical strategies are much more.

3. The writing process: planning, drafting, revising: Your students may be surprised to find significant variations in the way different people manage the writing process. Most of our students find it liberating to realize that individual writing processes might be different. They welcome the idea that heavy planners and heavy revisers and sequential composers might all have acceptable approaches even though they are apparently at odds. The situation often determines the best process, so no writer should depend upon a single way of writing.

Since many of your students have probably not had much chance to experiment, they can try a new model if the one they use doesn't work very well, or deliberately exaggerate the opposite of their usual manner in order to develop flexibility.

Many students have never become aware of the writing process because they dislike revising so very much. They find heavy revising unimaginable--they are so used to squeezing out work one stingy word at a time to fulfill an assigned length that they just can't imagine ever revising anything voluntarily. To counteract this, try asking students to overwrite a draft--to bring in twice the number of pages that the finished essay will have--so they can discover the advantages and disadvantages of heavy revision. For example, since those pages are written with the expectation of heavy revision, students often find them quite a bit easier to write than usual. You can also combine freewriting with heavy revising to good effect. For further information see Muriel Harris, "Composing Behaviors of One- and Multi-draft Writers" (College English 51.2 [February 1984]: 174-191).

4. Procrastination: You might find it useful and enlightening to take your students' intense desire to procrastinate seriously rather than letting it seem (unconsciously) a kind of moral issue. Does it ever really work better to procrastinate? Our students have evolved some rambunctious theories--just waiting to be confirmed by research--to argue that it does. Meanwhile, most of us continue to draw distinctions between healthy amounts of planning and putting the draft off until the last minute out of less desirable (if understandable) motives. Some students who procrastinate are avoiding something that causes them anxiety. We tell them we understand. Writers almost universally agree that sitting down to write is very hard, even painful, certainly something that one would be willing to clean the house and weed the yard to avoid. You can lower the anxiety barrier, though, by encouraging students to write uncritically at first. John McPhee says he hates to write because he knows the first draft will inevitably be bad, less than what he wants. He hates having to produce bad writing to get to the good

stuff. So do our students, especially since they feel far less confident about ever managing to revise the bad into the good.

A less acceptable motive for procrastination is simply that most college students don't make their writing class the first priority of their studies. You might want to discuss this frankly, letting students talk about their frustrations with requirements while pointing out that the writing course realistically requires rather large amounts of time. In our experience, most students really do want to become better writers, but they let themselves slip into a kind of resistance to the prescribed. When you are pragmatic rather than prescriptive, you make it harder for them to slide into such thinking.

Finally, some students procrastinate because they are rotten with perfection, and putting things off until the last minute allows them to make choices that are pragmatic rather than ideal. Using the class as an audience can help to limit and particularize the abstract sense of a transcendental audience that often accompanies perfectionism.

5. Monitoring and the composing inventory: Monitoring is that cognitive function that supervises and directs the composing process, keeping watch and making strategic suggestions according to what's happening. The word comes from the Latin monere, "to warn," and the whole function may seem overly critical to some of your students. What you say and do as an instructor when you coach them can help model the monitoring that your students internalize. You may also want to explicitly encourage students to change their ways of thinking about what they are doing when they write, putting aside, while they write a first draft, the critical perfectionist editor within in favor of a more flexible, practicing explorer.

6. The writer's notebook: See the Teaching Practices section of the instructor's manual for a more detailed discussion of planning assignments to use a writer's notebook or journal in your class.

7. Effective time management: Don't be afraid to talk with your students about your own writing habits and rituals and what works for you.

The testimony of many professional writers suggests that a regular turn at the writing desk is essential, whether one feels productive or not. Surprisingly, some of the students who have the most trouble with blocks and procrastination are people who don't allow themselves to stop writing once they have started. With this kind of "must work until death" attitude, small wonder that they put off writing. Sometimes it helps to suggest that such students keep both ends of a schedule--sticking to their planned quitting time even though they can imagine writing much, much more. One student found that it seemed revolutionary to go to bed at a reasonable hour the night before the paper was due, letting himself say that what he had completed was, if not perfect, nonetheless good enough. He had spent all the time he reasonably had available to work on the paper. Still, the next day when he turned his paper in, he was still not quite sure he had done the right thing. (What if he could have moved the paper from a B to an A sometime between 2:00 and 4:00 A.M.?)

Encourage students to get in the habit of talking to others who somehow manage to get writing done, and done adequately, so they stay in touch with the realities of changing writing situations.

8. Writing with a word processor: This section of the text will be helpful to students throughout the term. You may find, as we have, that many students take up the computer during the term as they find out its usefulness for revising, and they can then keep referring back to these suggestions.

9. Collaborative writing: Writing with groups of people is an increasingly common practice. Whatever else happens, it requires an explicit, commonly understood set of plans and schedules for writing. Thus experience with a collaborative writing project will help your students to articulate the writing process and discover how others write. Collaboration requires students to address differences and perhaps discover what's at stake in their own perspectives. If you mark the significance of such exchanges, students will increase their understanding of the interaction between author and audience in the rhetorical situation. The chapter provides guidelines for collaborative groups, emphasizing the importance of working to make them

successful and acknowledging conflict rather than imposing consensus. John Trimbur has advocated what he calls the "rhetoric of dissensus" as a dialogic way of thinking about such collaborative work. ("Consensus and Difference in Collaborative Learning," College English 51 [1989]: 602-16). That is, in order to avoid silencing group members who might not share the dominant opinion in the group, students need to be taught not to rush to consensus, but rather to solicit the various perspectives within the group, most particularly if they disagree.

Activities

The first three activities in this chapter are coordinated to lead students from their responses to reading to a collaborative task growing out of their own writing. It is a model as well, then, of ways you can integrate informal, personal writing with reading, collaboration, and discussion.

(p. 35) Exploration: This exercise asks students to read essays by a student, Mary Kacmarcik, and a professional writer, Burten Hatlen, and then to respond to a list of questions about their own writing by freewriting or making a list. The questions may help them to be more specific and detailed about their reflections on writing and their history as a writer. Point out that even personal recollections can usefully be enlarged by a list of pertinent issues.

(p. 36) Application: This exercise asks students to use information generated by their lists in order to write a letter about themselves as a writer. The format encourages them to write informally and probably more personally than an essay, and you can make use of these letters in several ways which are discussed below. The next exercise brings them into a group activity. Later you may ask students to write an essay on their history as a writer, using Kacmarcik and Hatlen as models, or to write an essay comparing their own experience with writing to that of others.

(p. 36) Group Activity: This important activity uses student letters about writing experiences as the basis for group discussion. You keep their exchange focused by asking them to report to the whole class after a certain amount of time. This discussion can be an important source of information for you as well as for your students about the general profile of the class. You might give groups twenty to twenty-five minutes to answer the questions, and then take another ten minutes to hear reports of the results. Notice that students are asked to work toward a sense of group cohesiveness first, by identifying commonalities, then asked to note differences, and finally asked to report common goals. Differences will often reflect context and situation. Many students have histories as writers that are really histories of the teachers they had--good and bad--and chronologies of grading dramas. Do you want to make time to discuss the experience of evaluation here--of being graded, and more generally, of having writing evaluated by others? Such concerns seem a digression, yet the thought of the eventual audience obviously reaches into the apparently isolated writing process from the first.

How are your groups doing at this point? Do they feel reasonably comfortable with each other and with the idea of group tasks? If some are working with a great deal of awkwardness and inhibition, you might want to give some attention to group processes. See Teaching Practices for some more general suggestions.

The process of comparing personal responses and then making generalizations about agreements helps build the capacity to collaborate and also moves students from the kind of personal expression they may find familiar to the process of drawing inferences and making generalizations. Later, when they understand more about describing and evaluating composing processes as well, you might ask students to write an essay that analyzes the characteristic approaches to writing they observed in these letters and reports.

(p. 43) Application: "Guidelines for Analyzing Your Composing Process" asks students to identify and describe their own characteristic style of composing. The exercise is important, leading them through guidelines they can use to thoroughly examine various aspects of their own composing practices and attitudes. This puts your students in the position of taking an analytic attitude, as if they were doing research about their own writing. Students usually very much enjoy figuring out their composing style. Interestingly enough, a real willingness to change often seems to come out of this analysis--many students start to experiment with writing processes and timing as they see composing increasingly as a matter of making choices that they can control. The guidelines asks your students to decide for themselves which writing practices work well, and also to decide on ways to do better. It makes a good entry for the writer's notebook, which they will think about more specifically later in this chapter.

(p. 44) Group Activity: Students are to discuss responses to the "Guidelines for Analyzing Your Composing Process" and draw wider conclusions about the writing process. You might have to limit time for talking about individual responses to the questions in order to get groups to move firmly toward making some statements about writing. Then, although it takes an extra ten to fifteen minutes, if you have time it's worth having groups report back the results of their thinking. If you record these on the board, on butcher paper, or an overhead, you move the class from thinking mostly about their own work to making generalizations about the nature of the writing process which they can pursue as well.

(p. 46) Application: This assignment asks your students to reflect on the writer's notebook and to look at it as a tool in furthering writing projects. If you are assigning such a notebook, you might also explicitly assign periodic reviews for reflecting and planning. If you ask students to hand in notebooks from time to time, you can ask students to hand in these comments as well. See Teaching Practices for further details. Even if you are not assigning a writer's notebook which you will check, this application invites your students to try it for themselves, an option you can reinforce simply by periodically calling attention to it.

(p. 47) Group Activity: This exercise asks groups to generate suggestions for effective time management. After about ten to fifteen minutes, ask groups to report back to the whole class with their advice. This is an opportunity for you to get a sense of your class; some may need explicit advice about academic study skills, while others may have a long history of experience organizing their studies and managing their time.

Here is an additional activity you may wish to assign:

> For your next writing assignment, establish a rough schedule detailing how you will manage your time planning, writing, and revising as you work on the assignment. Your schedule doesn't need to be elaborate, but do write it down. As you work on the assignment, note the changes you make (if any) in your schedule. After completing the assignment, take a few moments to reflect on this experience. Did you find it helpful to establish a schedule for your work? Would you follow this process in the future? If so, would you plan to balance your time any differently?

Here is another activity to engage students in making schedules and planning ahead:

> Your instructor has probably either given you a written syllabus for your writing course or described the main assignments and indicated approximately when they will be due. Take half an hour to read and think about these writing assignments. If you are keeping a writer's notebook, copy these assignments into your notebook; otherwise, set up a separate manila folder or large envelope for each assignment. When ideas related to these assignments occur to you, write them in your notebook or add them to the appropriate folder or envelope. Simply copying your assignment and establishing a place to keep notes about them will start you thinking about possible topics and approaches. Now look at the due dates for each assignment. Compare these to the dates

when you must turn in major projects or take tests in other classes. Try to formulate a general plan for accomplishing the work you need to do this term. You may want to use a calendar (or weekly charts with a section for each day) in order to note due dates and eventually to outline a work sequence. Finally, read and think about your first writing assignment. After realistically considering your academic schedule, family and social obligations, and the demands of the assignment, rough out a schedule that will provide reasonable time for planning, drafting, and revising. Your instructor may also ask you to write an essay describing the major academic challenges you face this term and explaining how you plan to meet them.

You might also ask students to try a writing schedule for an assignment they will have in another class. Often these aren't due until the last part of the term, so many students are shocked at the very thought of planning so far ahead. Make a note to return to this assignment, perhaps even as part of a final analysis or final examination, asking students once again to think about the effects of planning and make changes, if appropriate. Meanwhile, in order for them to practice, have them concentrate on the first assignment due in your class.

<u>Activities for Thought, Discussion, and Writing</u>:

Number 1: This assignment encourages students to learn more about their own composing process, and to do so by conducting a mini-case study of themselves as they work on a writing project. Keeping a detailed process log is essential to the success of this assignment, for the process log enables students to get beyond vague generalities about their writing--generalities such as "coming up with ideas is hard" or "revising makes me nervous"--to more specific understandings of the strategies they employ (and the habits they draw on) when they write. Students are often surprised by what they discover when they analyze their process logs. Students sometimes overestimate how long they typically work on their writing, for instance. Recording when they start and end each work session helps them become more aware of the amount of time it can take to make significant progress in writing.

Depending on the nature and goals of your course, you can use this assignment in various ways. You may have students keep process logs and write an informal analysis of what they have learned by studying their own writing as a prelude to a class discussion of this activity. Or you may make the case study one of your course's major writing assignments.

Number 2: This assignment asks your students to write an essay about procrastinating. It's a subject that releases a great deal of pent-up energy. It's also a topic that allows most students to draw on extensive personal experience. So students generally find it easy to write a first-draft essay about procrastination. I like to encourage students to take the fun seriously; that is, to imagine some attitude toward procrastination besides automatic responses of guilt and pleasure, to rethink and revise themr first impressions. Procrastination is an especially important problem for your class because it forecloses the possibility of learning to revise. In other words, it may be a way of not learning much of what there is to be taught in a writing class.

Number 3: This assignment suggests that students read interviews and essays by professional writers about their work. One possible mode of organization for the class would use such a collection as a reader throughout the term (see Teaching Practices for detailed suggestions and plans). Or you might want to make some of these essays and interviews available to accompany this chapter. There are also a number of films and videotapes of interviews with writers.

Ask students to respond in writing to what they read. In particular, ask them to point out whatever might have been unexpected. Do they find it surprising that best-selling author Anne Tyler speaks of herself as only a housewife who is "still just writing"? Do they agree with Alice Walker that a writer can't afford to risk having more than one child? Ask students to think about how the context affects the writer, and how they themselves are affected and influenced <u>as</u> <u>writers</u> by the place they live, by their daily lives, by the people they know, by their favorite routines, by the weather, and by the past.

Number 4: This assignment puts students to work on a systematic ongoing project of self-examination and self-consciousness about their writing habits. You can assign this meta-analysis together with another writing assignment, and you can go on to use a version of such analysis for each assignment the student turns in for evaluation.

CHAPTER 3: Understanding the Rhetorical Situation

In this chapter: Guidelines for Analyzing Your Rhetorical Situation

This chapter defines the concept of "rhetorical situation," showing how to analyze it and how a more acute sense of the relations among the elements of rhetoric and the world will enable your students to write more effectively. Your students have perhaps already learned to think about their readers when they write. They need to understand that the "reader" is both more and less specific and concrete than they think. To help them develop confidence in making judgments, you might stress that, just as the rules for writing are not absolute, no magic or mathematical formulas exist for figuring out what the rhetorical situation is or how to address readers. A writing project involves making choices; taking the various factors into account helps point toward a solution, but it also helps to point out complexity that might come into play.

Greater complexity helps improve writing, but students sometimes resist acknowledging it; they want to intuit the rhetorical situation or reduce it to easily controlled dimensions so they can solve the writing problem expeditiously. Some say they feel blocked when there's too much to take into account. We are sympathetic: don't all writers have moments of wishing the rhetorical situation were more clearly defined for us, more limited, even more formal? And of course most of us as teachers are used to hearing students say plaintively "I don't know what you want," even when we think we've made an assignment crystal clear. To help students gain better control over defining their writing tasks, Work in Progress provides general "Guidelines for Analyzing Your Rhetorical Situation" in this chapter. For a list of workable criteria for academic writing, see the discussion in Chapter 10 of standards for academic writing.

Analyzing the rhetorical situation may seem fascinating if it is genuinely practical or demanding and difficult if it is just an abstract exercise. In talking about the rhetorical situation, it helps to keep students thinking concretely about their actual situation as writers. You might want to insert some speculation, for example, about how the weather is shaping their prose, using regional writers for comparison with themselves. You might ask how their peer group or other groups they feel a part of affect their writing. Furthermore, the classroom itself is always part of the rhetorical situation for students. For instance, students' essays are almost always, in some respect, an argument for a positive evaluation. (Don't you sometimes feel that argument as a sub-text when you grade, as a demand for reasons if you don't give an A or B, or an appeal for pity?) Keep on discussing your class as a rhetorical situation, using it as a ongoing, complex, and rich concrete example.

Concepts:

1. Rhetorical situation: Chapter 3 defines the concept of rhetorical situation in terms of the writer, the reader, and the text. If your course structure permits it, you may want to discuss the rhetorical situation more broadly as well. Critical theory has led many in English departments to conclude with Terry Eagleton that the discipline might best be described as rhetorical studies. Furthermore, more recent work in sociology, anthropology, psychology, political science, and philosophy has also demonstrated a turn to rhetoric, a sense that culture might be defined in terms of rhetorical situations. Inquiry like that of Clifford Geertz shows how rhetorical analysis could involve everything we know--all our knowledge of culture, the way it works, its codes and conventions, our grammatical competence, our vocabulary, and all our knowledge about the world, what it is and what it ought to be. The problem, then, is to separate out what is relevant and needed for a given writing project without being too reductive or egocentric.

This chapter asks students to think about writing projects in several different situations. In order to provide an artificially limited rhetorical situation for students to focus on, ask students to write brief assignments from roles. You might use these exercises as in-class writing, perhaps for groups to do together. Give them suggestions, the more extreme and melodramatic the better, such as: write a letter to the bank about an error, first as a well-known millionaire, then as a single mother of four who keeps barely afloat by working two jobs. Have them choose an unfamiliar role. Ask the women to write as men and the men as women. Exaggerate the theatricality and inevitable role-playing in the classroom to help students see the significance of the rhetorical situation.

You can help your students develop their rhetorical sensitivity, their tacit, commonsense knowledge about rhetorical situations by encouraging them to ask again and again about different kinds of texts: What makes this writing work? What makes it effective--from the perspective of writer, reader, text? This chapter connects analyzing the rhetorical situation specifically with planning to write, establishing intentions and goals. The "Guidelines for Analyzing Your Rhetorical Situation" (pp. 59-61) will help students turn analysis into strategy.

For further discussion of the rhetorical situation, you might want to consult the following works, listed in chronological order:

Bitzer, Lloyd F. "The Rhetorical Situation." Philosophy and Rhetoric 1 (January 1968): 1-14.

Vatz, Richard E. "The Myth of the Rhetorical Situation." Philosophy and Rhetoric 6 (Summer 1973): 154-161.

Consigny, Scott. "Rhetoric and Its Situations." Philosophy and Rhetoric 7 (Summer, 1974): 175-186.

Jamieson, Kathleen M. Hall. "Generic Constraints and the Rhetorical Situation." Philosophy and Rhetoric 7 (Summer, 1974): 162-170.

Brinton, Alan. "Situation in the Theory of Rhetoric." Philosophy and Rhetoric 14 (Fall 1981): 234-248.

Biesecker, Barbara A. "Rethinking the Rhetorical Situation from within the Thematic of Difference." Philosophy and Rhetoric 22 (1989): 110-130.

2. The Writer: This chapter portrays the writer as a persona that we choose when we write, an appropriate image. In other words, the writer is rhetorical, produced by the text, and writers need to change the persona representing themselves to suit different rhetorical situations. Students identify so closely with the "I" of their writing that they believe they always write simply as themselves. They may not notice how naturally they can change registers when they move from informal to formal situations, for example. Try explaining this with an analogy: you change persona in response to a situation, just as you change clothes, wearing jeans for one occasion; formal dress for another. You can probably help most students improve their control of the rhetorical situation by asking them to think about just how the writer needs to "sound" or "look" to be convincing. Students who have already internalized a good repertoire of successful approaches to writing will be able to write unself-consciously, to simply feel "sincere" and also write well, but other students will be liberated if you encourage them to write parodies or play roles.

This analogy to theatricality has, of course, some limitations: good writers seldom adopt more than a few roles or "personae." Instead, they develop authority, a "voice," made up of knowledge, experience, character, commitment, and a deep understanding of appropriate conventions. Student writers suffer because they haven't done this yet. Their recurring attention to the problem of "who is the writer here" will help them acquire strategies and devices that work for them.

3. Readers: Unlike an audience physically present at an oral presentation or performance, the rhetorical reader in a writing situation does not necessarily correspond to a single person or group of people. Instead, the reader holds a role or position in the discourse which the writer and the situation both help to define. For example, think about the readers of the letters and advertisements appearing at the end of Chapter 3. The writers of

these examples didn't know more about the individual reader than information about the context could provide. In fact, these writers had an obligation not just to appeal to the reader, but to create the reader as a participant. In a sense, then, the reader is anyone who might respond to the text's address. The writer develops a relationship with the reader, cuing the reader about the role to take.

For these reasons, students need to imagine their readers clearly and sympathetically, neither viewing them as the blank unknown, nor limiting them to knowable persons such as instructors they might be able to "psych out" or the other members of their writing groups. Don't let your students get trapped by their tendency to think of readers too literally, as if they had to have a precise psychological profile of an individual or demographic read-out of a crowd before they could think about the reader. The reader exists as a relationship and a role in the rhetorical situation. For further reading about the concept of reader and audience, see:

Ede, Lisa. "Audience: An Introduction to Research." College Composition and Communication 35 (1984): 140-54.

Ede, Lisa, and Andrea Lunsford. "Audience Addressed/Audience Invoked: The Role of Audience in Composition Theory and Pedagogy." College Composition and Communication 35 (May 1984): 155-70.

4. Text: You might want to point out to your students that the word "text" in this book refers to all examples of writing, and not just to a book required for a class. When students analyze a text, they need to consider the conventions of form, style, and logic that govern its presentation. Although rhetoric evolved from the study of speeches and students can benefit from analyzing the rhetorical situations of oral presentations on television and in classrooms, a written text differs from spoken language in ways that sometimes create difficulties for students. Texts operate according to conventions and codes of written language which students frequently don't know or haven't yet mastered. Some students may not have read enough to develop a firm common sense about academic writing. They will benefit by consistently thinking about the conventions of form and evidence that might apply in a given situation and by learning to seek out models to help them acquire these conventions. You might explore rhetorical conventions that they do know well--such as, the "Top Ten List" David Letterman uses--so they can see what kinds of tacit understandings might be included and also to understand that they can, with practice, become adept at more academic forms of writing.

5. Aristotle's Appeals: In this chapter, the traditional Aristotelian categories for persuasive appeals are introduced: logos, pathos, and ethos. Your students may not be used to thinking about writing as an act of persuasion (or, indeed, as practical in any respect whatsoever), even though it's easy enough to point out the persuasive component of all writing. The examples of persuasive writing, which accompany this chapter, will help them see the three appeals at work. Even images, such as those in advertisements, work not as objective evidence but as means of persuasion, in ways your students can probably specify.

Later, when students look at academic writing, you can point out how more subtle forms of the same appeals work to make a text authoritative and convincing. Scholarly work in fields like Women's Studies often points out the persuasive aspect of even the most objective-seeming writing. See, for example, Evelyn Fox Keller's Gender and Science.

The appeal to logos is based on evidence and reasoning. So it is the most powerful appeal in most academic writing. Remind your students to consider the appeal to reason even in papers they do not regard as objective or papers about issues or personal experiences. For example, their analyses of their own writing histories or processes go beyond an appeal to pathos or ethos, even though those are the primary appeals. You, as a person interested in composition research, may find yourself as the reader drawn in by the logos, by evidence and analysis of certain writing processes, and not just by your interest in your students' feelings and characters.

The appeal to _pathos_ is based on emotion or on values, beliefs, and desires. When students think about how to effectively address readers, they need to think about the readers' values and attitudes as well as more obvious kinds of feelings. What assumptions are the readers likely to accept? Aristotle lists certain commonplaces human beings are likely to share or apply commonsensically to large groups of people. For example, the old are likely to respond to appeals for greater security, while the young respond to appeals for change. Through class discussions, you can elicit your student's contemporary understanding of what might seem commonsense knowledge.

Many students have studied persuasion as part of units on propaganda and logical fallacies. Sometimes they have translated the idea of logical fallacy into a rule banning everything that is not _logos_. They may think you want them to write dry-as-dust informational prose, appealing to evidence alone. You can point out that sometimes a heavy emphasis on _logos_ is inappropriate. Further, writers who rigorously segregate _pathos_ from _logos_ are apt to produce unmitigated sentiment or unmitigated fact. If students are encouraged to consider all three appeals carefully, they will find it easier to plan balanced papers that are well adapted to their purposes.

The third appeal, to _ethos_, turns to the good character of the writer, to the audience's willingness to believe what the writer says. The persona adopted by the writer helps convey the appeal to _ethos_. Because students are particularly vulnerable and are writing from a position of little authority, they often struggle with angst about being convincing. This is not a problem that finding a personal voice can fully solve, and it is not easily resolved by imitating the _ethos_ of another either (including the teacher). Since _ethos_ is deeply involved with the interaction of individual, ethics, and rhetorical situation, it is an especially difficult but fruitful starting point for discussion.

Activities

(p. 59) _Application_: This application asks students to apply their understanding of the elements of rhetoric to three letter-writing situations. Most students will find that they already have, and will enjoy making explicit, a considerable amount of tacit knowledge about rhetorical situations. Some students have difficulty doing this analysis, or seem very impatient with reflection. And that difficulty may not always be a symptom of ineptitude. (At least one good student wished we would just get to the point and tell him the right way to do the letters.) These are students who need to understand that rhetorical reasoning doesn't involve a single right solution, but requires them to make decisions based on ways of thinking about rhetorical situations.

It may help in such cases to give students sample materials by someone else to read and analyze first, to see the kinds of choices other writers have made. If they are working in groups, and exchanging the answers to this question, members of the group will be helped by hearing the variety of acceptable ways that others might handle the rhetorical situation.

If you have a whole class with very little self-confidence and/or experience writing, spend a little time reading and talking about familiar examples as a class before you ask them to analyze rhetorical situations on their own. Then supply as much practice as possible, such as the activities at the end of the chapter.

(p. 66) _Exploration_: This activity asks students to decide whether Lynn Hansen's essay, "Burgdorf Hot Springs," achieves the goals she has set for herself. This work allows them to rehearse the kind of careful analysis they should apply to each other's papers when they function as readers.

(p. 68) _Exploration_: This activity asks students to write a paragraph or two about how a different readership, such as that provided by the _New York Times_, might have changed the essay above. To help them define readership, you might bring in several week's worth of the _New York Times_ Sunday edition and go through it with them, looking for evidence of interests and expectations. You might repeat this with other publications, and later, with other essays.

(p. 69) Application: This activity asks students to read introductions from two articles about stress. They will talk about the differences between one article that tells a story and invites the reader's identification with a personal experience of stress and the other article that summarizes information and invites the reader to think analytically about the relationship of stress to certain kinds of work. You might ask your students to look in particular at the pattern of common assumptions in the two introductions--what the writer assumes that the reader will already know or agree with or want to know. What do they assume about ordinary readers? Ask them as well to think about the stylistic cues: sentence length, complexity of syntax, diction. If you have time, you might also ask students if they think the way a text addresses them could change their minds. Can they see how the role of the reader might act as a means of persuasion or how the writer, by invoking the role of the reader, might direct the reader's response?

(p. 75) Exploration: This activity asks students to apply their understanding of appeals (ethos, pathos, and logos) to a student essay. Like the earlier analysis of a student essay, this practice will help students not only with their own writing, but also in giving helpful responses to each other's papers.

Activities for Thought, Discussion, and Writing:

Number 1: This analysis of a UNICEF letter requesting charitable contributions asks your students to think about the assumptions the writer made about the rhetorical situation and how they influenced the plan for writing. In order to keep this from being a discussion that is misleadingly abstract or formal, you might want to begin a discussion (or ask students to begin writing) by addressing the content of the letter from the reader's point of view. Ask students just to respond, describing their feelings as they read. Ask them next to describe their reactions to the request for a contribution. Were they persuaded? Why or why not? Does this reaction have anything to do with beliefs, values, or ideology? How about gender? Once students have thoroughly described their reactions, ask them to analyze the kinds of assumptions the writer made about what might appeal to them. Are they the readers of this letter?

Number 2: This activity asks students to find some examples of writing that fails to address them as readers. They are to explain the reasons in a paragraph or two. This explanation will begin to define explicitly what assumptions students bring to their reading. You might ask them to formulate commonalities in small groups and discuss expectations that function as group norms for the whole class. Remind them that this kind of information is important to a wide variety of writers, from academics to marketing specialists. Then remind them that their expectations as readers can themselves be shaped by a persuasive text.

Number 3: This exercise asks students to analyze the appeals to ethos, pathos, and logos in advertisements. Most students are used to analyzing advertisements critically. You can extend their practice doing rhetorical analysis by asking students to think about how words might replace the appeals represented by visual images in the advertisements. Following discussion, some students may wish to write about the questions raised by the appeals of advertising.

Suggestions for Further Activities

1. Ask students to write an analysis of their rhetorical situation for an essay or writing project upon which they are currently working. Ask students to do this for the next assignment in your class, one of the essays suggested in the text or another project that you have assigned. If your next

assignment <u>is</u> to do a rhetorical analysis of some kind (for instance, of the material at the end of Chapter 3), your students will encounter the metalinguistic nature of this kind of analysis; it can always comment on itself. Or you may wish to assign a persuasive essay like the examples used in the chapter. Frequently the "reader" in this analysis will be other class members and yourself--an interesting reason for general discussion.

Here are some brief suggestions for essay assignments:

a. Write a description of a place you particularly enjoy for readers of a travel magazine or for a brochure designed to inform tourists about your area. Choose a specific magazine and analyze its likely readers, or interview a local travel agent or member of the Chamber of Commerce about the likely readers of a travel brochure.
b. Write a persuasive essay about an issue of importance to you, asking your readers to take some specific step as a consequence of your argument. Choose an issue and an audience that you know personally very well.
c. Write a response to an article or essay or advertisement. Begin by describing your experience as a reader. Then analyze its rhetorical situation and its appeal to the reader.
d. Write an essay examining the context of your writing, placing yourself in your region of the country or as a member of a group or a historical period.

<u>Group Activity</u>: Exchange the above analyses and discuss responses. This activity offers students a chance to check their understanding of the rhetorical situation against the way a partner perceives it and to make suggestions to each other. If this is a good time for a group analysis of the way students see the rhetorical situation of your composition classroom, use one pair as a "model" exchange for class discussion after everyone has had a chance to talk. Whole group discussion makes less sense here if the assignment is not the same for everyone.

2. Ask students to draw up a plan for writing an essay (like Monica Molin's on page 72) based on Aristotle's three appeals. This activity asks them to translate analysis into a plan for action, making decisions about their writing on the basis of thinking through how they will appeal to their readers.

This is a particularly important principle to rehearse, a process that you will want students to use every time they write. You might want to point this out and return to it from time to time during the term, asking again for explicit or written statements reflecting the results of students' rhetorical analysis. You might also point out that what seems like a somewhat artificial exercise right now will eventually, with practice, begin to seem like a natural part of planning to write, becoming part of their rhetorical common sense. You can do this with individuals or have the students plan collaboratively, in small groups.

3. Ask students to compare and contrast the rhetorical situations of two letters, one that was easy to write and one that was difficult. Then have them reflect about what makes writing easier, and consider the ways that factors outside themselves might influence the difficulty of a writing task. It encourages them to consider their context as part of the job. This is particularly helpful if you have students who are having difficulty understanding the concept of the <u>rhetorical situation</u>.

CHAPTER 4: Writers Reading

This chapter shows how the perspective of a reader can enable students to understand different kinds of writing. It introduces students to the role played by textual convention in changing rhetorical situations. It emphasizes the interconnectedness of literacy, showing how both reading and writing are acts of composing and how writing depends upon knowledge gained from reading. It demonstrates how students may become more conscious about making connections between their reading and their writing, showing them how to read like a writer, rhetorically. This is a powerful means of access to understanding the various disciplinary conventions. The assumption that students can learn something about the available forms of writing by reading selections of rhetorical material is not new; it has, in fact, underwritten the long tradition of using rhetorical readers in composition classes. However, Work in Progress emphasizes the rhetorical situation of texts, directing students to pay attention to forms in specific contexts rather than forms artificially cut off from their connections to discursive communities and their intellectual and cultural history. This chapter pragmatically addresses the rhetorical situations of academic discourse and encourages students to become more critically aware of their variety.

Concepts

1. Academic discourse: Most rhetoric and composition theorists agree that the academic reading and writing tasks students will encounter through classes belong to a rather specialized discourse. Part of what we are teaching is how to succeed in this academic discourse community, which may be very alien indeed to some students, and questionable to others. Work in Progress does not ask your students to master a specific form of writing; rather, it encourages them to develop a readerly, rhetorical approach to writing which will enable them to assess any discourse's possibilities and limits. You may wish to help them analyze, for example, the rather strict set of methods represented in scientific writing. Students get into trouble writing when they approach the process as if a single format and style were appropriate for any course. A piece of writing that makes the conventions strange or obvious can help: the chapter includes a twelfth-century letter to home from two brothers who are students. You may also wish to help them look for the cultural and social implications of discourses. Your students should learn not only to emulate but also to critique certain examples of academic writing. This chapter includes an exercise about textbooks. For an essay discussing the broader issues of academic discourse, see Peter Elbow, "Reflections on Academic Discourse: How It Relates to Freshmen and Colleagues" (College English 53.2 [February 1991]).

2. Textual conventions: This chapter will direct students to pay attention to the functions of conventions ranging from the very general to the very specific: persona, genre, style, organization, and diction, among others. Rather than looking at these conventions formally, out of context, this chapter shows students how to analyze the ways the rhetorical situation might condition the choice of form, and the ways that conventions shape reading. Introductions to three different reports of the same research by psychologist John Flavell show how textual conventions shape the reader's experience and how some conventions--understood in the context of a professional journal--can even limit the ability of the uninitiated to understand at all. These textual conventions, bound to the rhetorical situation, are part of what students will learn about their disciplines. Students will improve their reading if they understand that they need to look for such conventions, and they will improve their writing if they understand that textual conventions can give them accepted ways of organizing material. This understanding, in other words, will help demystify the reading as well as the writing process and alert students to recognize the role that textual conventions play in our construction and interpretation of texts. As they

begin to look for such conventions, reading like a writer, they become a "noticing" reader, newly aware of what works and how it works.

Activities

(p. 87) Exploration: This exercise uses the twelfth-century letter to home. First, students should find textual features--the anachronistic ones will be easy to cite, if not to describe. For example, the letter begins with a salutation in third person ("their . . . parents; their sons"). "Filial obedience" might be a phrase that would not spring readily to the lips of contemporary writers, however wonderful their relationships to parents. Whether you have students write two or three sentences about this in class or out, have them read several aloud or even take the time to have them work for ten minutes in a group to see how much they can discover, how the letter compares to one they might write, and even speculate about what the differences mean. (Why might twelfth-century students want to call themselves "obedient"? Why do students seem, across the centuries, always to need money?)

(p. 89) Exploration: This exercise asks your students to write paragraphs about the introductions to three articles by John Flavell. These lists should reveal some of students' tacit assumptions about the meanings of forms, connecting conventions of writing with readers' resultant assumptions about an article's intention or purpose. Your students will probably vary widely in their ability to decode the formats of these introductions. Some will simply get stuck at saying the first one's easier than the others. To help improve the ability to analyze and decode conventions, discuss the results of the brainstorming together with the comparison of these introductions before students do the next exercise.

(p. 98) Application: The questions in this exercise will lead students to further examine the differences and similarities among John Flavell's three introductions.

1. This question asks students to look at the way examples are used in each text. The examples are so various that some students may not know what kinds of things to count as an "example." Does the citing of other studies work as examples? In the third excerpt, examples include: "the sun looks like it moves around the earth but it really does not" and "it appeared that S-R theory could explain language development," because the authors want to argue the significance of the research for the general philosophical issue of appearance and reality in scientific knowledge. How do students think about the function of such examples? The three excerpts use very different examples, some from other sources than the research, because each makes a different argument, with a point which is defined by a very different community of interests, not only increasingly specialized, but increasingly theoretical. Students may be surprised to find there are three arguments here, given that all report Dr. Flavell's research. Ask students to look at the widening circles of "significance" that each address, to try to list the claims, and then to indicate the function of examples as evidence and as illustration for the various claims.

2. This question asks students to examine the writer/reader relationship and how it is cued. Ask them to imagine who they would need to be, what they need to know, and what interests they should have as the reader of each excerpt. You can be playful about reconstructing this imaginary reader, to try to discover how discursive cues operate; whether the cues appeal to psychological position, or knowledge, or economic status, or . . . ? If you were advertising in the classified section of a paper, what requirements would you want to list? Why? Is the reader cued by these excerpts best defined by job description? Degrees earned? Personal habits? Appearance?

3. This question asks students to compare the two abstracts. The American Psychologist abstract summarizes an article which reviews the findings of a half-dozen years of research, while the Cognitive Psychology

abstract summarizes the results of three specific studies which the article reports. Ask your students to see if they can see differences beyond the greater specificity of the second, differences reflecting empirical research methods and intentions.

4. This question asks students to look at style in the three excerpts. They may talk about the difficulty of syntax and vocabulary and the effect the style has on accessibility. Ask them if the style has anything to do with logos, with what knowledge it is possible to convey.

5. This question asks students to consider the reader once again, this time thinking about what prior knowledge Dr. Flavell assumes in particular instances. For example, the Cognitive Psychology article assumes knowledge about developmental psychology, and in particular about the work of Piaget. Point out that one of the problems for the general reader might be that these assumptions are not spelled out--someone who hasn't studied any psychology at all might not know what field of knowledge "developmental problem" refers to. Knowing what has been studied and what there is to know may be as important as the possession of facts.

6. This question asks students to think about the author's persona and the appeal to ethos. As they describe the image of the author and the way it is developed in each article, students are considering factors that contribute to academic credibility or authority. Ask them whether they themselves could adopt a similar persona. What techniques would work for them? Which could they not use? Why?

(p. 99) Exploration: This freewriting assignment invites students to characterize academic writing as they have experienced it so far. In particular, they should think about their own successes and failures and the differences among academic disciplines. Often students attribute these varying experiences to individual differences: their own talents or lacks and the personal decisions of instructors. They received an A or a C but they do not know why, they may report. Look together at the "Characteristics of an Effective Academic Essay" on p. 88 and think about what kinds of writing might not meet these criteria and still be successful. Ask them how their work does and does not succeed, according to this list and according to the evaluations they have received. If they have done very little writing, ask them to answer in terms of the differences in reading.

(p. 100) Application: This interview assignment asks students to write about their specific understanding of the writing demands in another course after asking questions of a teacher. Since this proactive approach to learning will be very helpful as they go on with their academic career, and it establishes contacts that will help beginning students to engage more fully with college experiences right now, it is probably worth the time to make sure students can effectively do this interview. If they are one of five hundred in a writing-intensive chemistry course, they may need to interview a T.A. rather than the professor. If all the students in writing courses carry out such interviews in the same week, they will flood teachers of entry-level courses. Some teachers will have circulated a description of their writing requirements. You might look at a few examples in class before students begin the interviews and ask them to examine their teacher's handouts closely so they can ask more focused questions. (See Teaching Practices for a discussion of interviewing.) Since this exercise explores the realities of the academic writing and reading situation, you can usefully move to discussions that compare and contrast the ways you are handling material in this class to the various practices in other classes on campus. The opportunity to be pragmatic and descriptive will probably interest your students very much and be useful to them as well.

Alternatively, you may wish to arrange for a panel of speakers from various disciplines to address composition students. Although students miss the opportunity to carry out an interview, this may solve logistical problems. Or arrange for the panel first, and then send students out on their interviews.

You may wish to use students' interview summaries and two paragraphs of reflection about academic writing as the first draft of an essay assignment. The following Group Activity will help them develop their ideas.

5. (p. 101) Group Activity: Students go on to collaborate by answering questions about their interview and comparing and contrasting the responses various group members found. This activity requires several rounds of discussion and writing. The process really needs to include time for them to write down statements and examples. You will probably need to allow at least half an hour for individual groups and another fifteen minutes for their reports and class discussion.

Activities for Thought, Discussion, and Writing

Number 1: This activity provides an occasion for students to use writing to evaluate what they have learned and the textbook's approach (so far), and to formulate questions. You may wish to add evaluation of other elements of the class, such as work load, pace, and group work, together with other readings and materials you have used.

Number 2: This activity takes yet another step toward establishing connections between reading and writing, asking students to apply the "Guidelines for Analyzing Your Rhetorical Situation" to a selection they choose for its success. They are to imagine themselves as the writer. Here they are making explicit the conventions that characterize their preferred reading. Your remarks about their selection process will make a great deal of difference: they may choose pieces that they actually prefer, or they may choose pieces that represent what they imagine as excellence, perhaps far from their private choices of reading. What do you want them to analyze? Here is an opportunity to discuss the differences between the reading they are encountering in their classes and reading directed to another kind of audience.

Number 3: This exercise asks students to analyze two textbooks they are using for classes. You may want to work through this process either as a specific writing assignment or as a group activity. You may also wish to encourage students in the habit of such analysis. Have them record their observations in their writer's notebook and invite them to do the same for other reading assignments they encounter in college. Give them an opportunity from time to time to orient their remarks in small groups and in class discussions in the context of reading they have done. Ask them frequently what makes the works they read effective--or not.

Number 4: This assignment of a collaborative essay asks students to work in a group to summarize and reflect about what they've learned from the interviews of teachers. They might begin with the answers they wrote earlier to questions on pages 100-1. If you need to make sure everyone has heard a few very good interviews, have the whole class take notes on those before they begin to work in the smaller groups. Some group members will probably want to go back and ask the teachers further questions once they begin to make comparisons. You can help them resist oversimplifying or generalizing by asking them to compare and contrast: provide evidence that "academic writing" is not one single form of discourse as well as show similarities.

Suggestions for Further Activities

Have students bring in examples of articles appearing in publications that appeal to a specialized audience. Work in pairs or in small groups to brainstorm lists that record the unfamiliar reader's first impressions. Discuss the approaches and the conventions of format and style that are at work. You are aiming to develop an awareness about the regularities of discourses and their relationships to readers. Your class may lead you to spend more time comparing a vernacular they prefer to unfamiliar academic argument or to concentrate on differences among academic discourses. Their heightened awareness of discursive conventions will help them orient their writing appropriately to the rhetorical situation.

You may also wish to use this discussion of conventions and academic discourse to consider multicultural texts and to compare cultural assumptions about form and style.

CHAPTER 5: Strategies for Successful Invention

In this chapter: *Guidelines for Group Brainstorming*
Guidelines for Group Troubleshooting
Guidelines for Conducting Library Research
Guidelines for Field Research and Interviewing
Guidelines for Designing and Using Questionnaires

Together with Chapters 6, 7, and 8, this chapter suggests specific strategies your students can use to improve their composing processes. The chapters focus on one aspect at a time: inventing, planning and drafting, global revising, and local revising. Exercises ask students to try out the various strategies and to evaluate the results. Experienced writers are pragmatists--flexible and collaborative. These chapters emphasize the practical--what works to get the writing job done. You will find suggestions drawn from modern research on writing and from the older traditions of rhetoric as well. These four chapters may also function like a handbook, furnishing ideas your students will return to again and again and supplying specific guidelines that you may use as references throughout the term.

Work in Progress urges students to take a writerly, pragmatic approach to these chapters, actively sorting through suggestions to determine those to add to their own best writing practices and those that might work in a given situation. Some students in the past may have been required to use certain procedures, such as outlining or clustering. These techniques themselves are just fine, unless students treat them as algorithms rather than heuristics; as if they had to replace the power of judgment with mechanically applied procedures. You can help mitigate the sense of alienation or the tendency of students to shortcut engagement with the processes of writing. Keep specifically and concretely referring to the rhetorical situation of each writing project. And, on the other hand, give students time to experiment with the strategies in a playful or exploratory way. They ought to try most of the approaches sooner or later--and now is the time for them to try something unfamiliar.

Chapter 5 presents a number of strategies for invention. If you have students go through this chapter with a particular assignment in mind, you may want to have them be selective about the methods of invention they try. Ask them to come back to this chapter several times during the term with other assignments in mind or have students experiment with all the techniques, returning to use the most appropriate ones more extensively.

Concepts

1. Strategies for invention: This chapter presents invention as both a matter of individual effort and a matter of communal processes, giving students ways to tap into what they already know and suggesting ways to use dialogue and collaboration to add other resources. As you work through the strategies presented in the text, you may find it especially helpful to frame the tasks in these two ways, as both an individual and a social effort.

When students come from widely differing discursive communities, and/or have little experience negotiating among social differences in conventions, they often have difficulty with the process of invention. Past experience does not provide them "naturally" with successful ideas. Or, to put it another way, extending the discourses they know, or learning another discourse, becomes part of the task of invention.

Students who are overly formulaic about invention may be freed to see new connections by informal processes like clustering. On the other hand, students who do not have much experience with academic discourse--at times the majority of our classes--may not think of using even very common patterns like cause-effect, or comparison-contrast. They may be especially helped by the traditional topics, since they do not know the kinds of questions which might conventionally be asked, or answered, in an argument.

2. Informal methods: These strategies may seem to work best for certain kinds of writing--for example, the informal, experience-based, or personal essay. However, they provide ways to get started on all kinds of writing, to get going even if the writer is not "in the mood," as the selection from a student's journal suggests. Informal methods include freewriting, looping, brainstorming, and clustering. See the Teaching Practices section for comments on freewriting and brainstorming. Looping, the alternation of freewriting and analysis, helps students learn to read their work productively and develop a sense of purpose. You can also "loop" with a group--have students freewrite for five or ten minutes and then write brief responses to each other's work. This kind of exercise creates a certain intensity and focus that may be especially helpful to get students started on a project. Clustering has a similar ability to generate commitment; many students use visual mapping of some kind as their preferred method of getting underway, substituting the cluster for an outline, and developing more and more elaborate graphics and figures as they plan.

3. Formal methods: These strategies help guide students beyond informal methods, showing them some directions for systematic investigation. The text discusses journalist's questions, tagmemics, and the topical questions adapted from Aristotle. Many students like the systematic and comprehensive quality of the topics and find that having the list at hand can prompt an angle of thought that might have been otherwise ignored. Your students can enlarge their habits of invention as they become familiar with these conventions of analysis and argument, especially if they have tended to think of subjects only in terms of narratives or descriptions. A few enthusiasts may go overboard, perhaps putting their subjects diligently through all (or a number of) the topical paces with the hope of making a paper that is truly encyclopedic. In addition, students sometimes make the mistake of confusing invention and arrangement. Answering the questions doesn't solve the problem of order, as you might want to point out, though the topics do suggest some possibilities for later arrangement.

4. Inventing collaboratively: Collaborative invention means much more than working on a collaborative project. All writers, in a larger sense, necessarily work collaboratively since they draw on the language, research, and ideas of others. The strategies for "inventing collaboratively" in this chapter emphasize the social components of invention and show students how to look outside themselves for ideas. These collaborative strategies may also provide bridges from one form of discourse to another and thus help students who might flounder in isolation. Protect students against the coercive potential of group consensus-making by encouraging diversity and divergent reasoning. This chapter includes specific "Guidelines for Group Brainstorming" and "Guidelines for Group Troubleshooting."

If your students have not had much experience working in groups, you may want to pay special attention to troubleshooting. Hold a group trouble-shooting session, and then have students freewrite for ten minutes about the experience. The freewriting evaluation is an important part of the introduction to trouble-shooting which you will want to follow up on. Have groups list strengths and weaknesses and make some decisions about how to improve on problem areas. You may want to discuss common findings with the class as a whole. Work as a consultant with groups that seem to need further help--most frequently because members are reluctant to give firm advice or suggestions about problems. But note that the trouble-shooting format helps a great deal with this, because the writers ask specifically for the assistance they want.

5. Research: This chapter emphasizes the variability of the research process, making a number of suggestions to enhance the discovery and elaboration of ideas. "Guidelines for Library Research" reflect the principle that research is a type of invention, collaborative invention perhaps, not a matter of locating authorities to quote. The students must still behave as writers, actively determining their purpose and carrying out research

accordingly. Ask students to think about their knowledge of the library and freewrite for ten minutes about what they know. This can provide you with valuable information about your students' problems with the library. Either collect the freewrites or take oral reports. Your students' responses will give you some advance warning about problems with upcoming work on academic writing and reading. You may want to find out if your library has brochures, tours, or special introductory programs for students. They may need specific information about access to electronic databases and Internet resources. Additionally, you might want to discuss research sources other than books, some of which may not be in the library, such as research on film or using videotapes.

Evaluating resources for research is especially difficult for students and critical for success. The "Guidelines for Library Research" offer a series of specific questions to help students think about the library sources they have found. If you are working through a research topic with your class or intend to do so later in the term, you will want to have them bring sources to class so you can address these questions with as much detailed attention as you might give a written draft.

Interviews, questionnaires, observations, and other sources of information in "field research" can be important sources of information as well. While disciplines that use these methods extensively (such as sociology, political science, or anthropology) have very thoroughly considered protocols for them, students can also use them less formally (and of course, as social scientists wuld warn, with no right to claim scientific validity). The text provides a set of "Guidelines for Interviewing" and "Guidelines for Designing and Using Questionnaires," as well as some suggestions for using close observation as a research tool. Ethnographic observation in particular has become a widely employed research method. Students gain considerable critical understanding of cultures through such observation. As anthropologists have been careful to warn us, however, the study of other people's behavior and values always needs to take account of the beholder's perspective as well, to make explicit the inevitable ethnocentrism and bias and correct it to the maximum extent possible.

Activities

(p. 111) Application: This exercise asks students to use the process of looping on the topic of "family," or another topic they choose. It will help your students both to generate material and to focus on what is significant about it. Looping is a powerful method; many of your students will find strong subjects for writing. Some will be enchanted when they discover their unknown resourcefulness. If you have assigned the essay on family as a possible writing project, your only problem may be getting students to set aside their looping to try other forms of invention in the chapter before they complete their essays. Or you may want to arrange your schedule differently, letting students work through one project and then come back to forms of invention appropriate to another.

(p. 113) Application: This exercise shows students how to use brainstorming to develop ideas around a topic. Students commonly use brainstorming and listing as a kind of opening shotgun approach and then have trouble elaborating and developing their subject. Here they are integrating brainstorming with other modes of invention.

(p. 115) Application: This exercise adds clustering to the methods of informal invention. If you have students who have not tried clustering before, you may be amazed at how liberating it seems for many of them. Students who respond well to visual representations may also want to try out more elaborate graphic schemes or maps for arranging their ideas.

(p. 115) Group Activity: Here is a chance for students to evaluate together the informal modes of invention they have been exploring. The questions ask them to think about how different composing and learning styles as well as differences in situation might influence the effectiveness of these approaches. Since students are often used to thinking of themselves as individuals, most may feel very comfortable with the informal methods. It's reassuring to discover ways they can tap their own authority. After they have worked through the formal methods, you might ask them again to assess their effectiveness and to make comparisons with the group.

(p. 118) Application: This exercise uses journalists' questions and tagmemics. Topics that are issue-oriented work best in trying out the strategies. If your students are working on the "family" essay, they may move into more general questions about families or perspectives on family issues, from changes in the nuclear family to the advent of "new" families with same-sex partners and so forth. Many students find it rather difficult to negotiate the difference between private and public domains of discourse in a single essay, though the possibility of doing so is an interesting one. Feminist research suggests that private and public forms of writing may be associated with gender for some students. If you see a gendered preference in your class, you might want to discuss the issue.

(p. 120) Application: This exercise continues the work on strategies of invention for the subject your students have chosen. Notice that the topics work as methods of discovery and will also work to suggest ways of arranging and developing the subject so that invention overlaps with drafting.

Activities for Thought, Discussion, and Writing

Number 1: This activity puts the practice work on invention to use on an essay exploring family. Topics that draw on students' personal experiences help them make bridges from the familiar writing to the academic. But there is a danger: such topics also tap a formidable store of stereotypes, clichés, and automatic responses. Informal methods of invention help bypass this ready banality, partly by generating so much material that students can get beyond it and also by allowing contradictions and complexities to be described before they are hidden by premature explanations. Going on to formal methods of invention will press students to engage the topic of family critically and place it in a larger cultural and historical context.

Number 2: This essay evaluating a group brainstorming or troubleshooting session has the merit of being grounded in empirical observation. Because it connects to improving a real-world activity, with consequences, it short-circuits the often hidden rhetorical situation of the classroom. If you decide to give your whole class the assignment, perhaps you will want to have groups exchange task and observer roles. Members can also collaborate on notes, brainstorm results, and discuss recommendations as a group.

Number 3: This assignment asks students to experiment with and evaluate a strategy not used before. It encourages students to use the strategies from this chapter again and again during the term and with various writing assignments. You might explicitly assign a new strategy of invention whenever the group seems to be lapsing into hasty invention or individual students need extra work.

CHAPTER 6: Strategies for Successful Planning and Drafting

In this chapter: *Guidelines for Planning Your Essay*
Guidelines for Evaluating Your Controlling Purpose
Guidelines for Drafting
Guidelines for Organizing and Developing Your Ideas
Guidelines for Collaborative Planning and Drafting

Chapter 6 discusses planning and drafting. It goes on from the work of Chapter 5, connecting planning and invention, emphasizing the different ways to plan, and grounding the concept of the controlling purpose in the rhetorical situation. Then the chapter suggests procedures for successful drafting. It discusses the shift from thinking about a writing subject to thinking about presenting ideas for readers. The chapter also includes a section on collaborative planning and drafting with specific suggestions for carrying out a writing project with others.

Concepts

1. Controlling Purpose: Students often have trouble with finding a purpose because they try to invent one arbitrarily, in isolation. If writing is social and not the act of a solitary individual writing alone, then the goals of the writer develop out of the discursive community, not from acts of individual will alone. The sense of a purpose arises out of the individual writer plus the rhetorical situation--out of the potential readers, their concerns, the conventions of their discourse, and the additions the writer wants to make to the communal conversation. However, choosing an appropriate, interesting purpose doesn't always appear as a conscious, carefully articulated process, but rather, like other functions of language, as something that is tacitly understood. So planning must involve both conscious work and a kind of unconscious intuition or playfulness. This chapter suggests ways to evoke and determine a sense of purpose.

In this chapter, the controlling purpose is defined as "a capsulized or condensed summary of your rhetorical situation." When you ask students to think about their goals for a particular assignment, ask them to define their purpose in just this way--analyzing the rhetorical situation, describing it succinctly, and stating what they want to accomplish. This chapter provides Guidelines that may serve as a useful check list for future projects. Recognize that a good deal of preliminary invention and even drafting may take place before the writer has a good sense of the controlling purpose. You don't necessarily want to insist that students submit a firm statement about controlling purpose before they begin drafting, for example, though making that effort and calling it tentative might help them. Defining the task at any stage brings into view the specific work that remains to be done.

2. Planning: A draft written without any plan whatsoever may waste a good deal of a student's time--and yours, because it is hard to comment helpfully on a loose collection of materials. Define planning in an open-ended way, as part of an exploration or inquiry into a question at issue so students can find a starting point that doesn't foreclose their options. Problems with invention, controlling purpose, and planning tend to be related so you can often help students work on all of them at once by referring them back to work from Chapters 3 and 5 on the rhetorical situation and on invention.

Sometimes students have trouble with planning because they are exploring their topics--asking questions--and they imagine that they need to have reached conclusions or taken a stand before they can proceed. You may want to remind these students that a plan can also consist of a series of questions, issues, or problems to be raised for the writer as well as the reader. Many kinds of writing projects do not require the kind of conclusiveness that students are apt to associate with authority. Rhetorical planning is a form of inquiry so that thinking about how to write is intimately connected with thinking about what to write. Remind students that planning may seem like cycles of work and play.

Many students do very well using looping, freewriting, or discovery drafts, written without a plan to discover what the topic has to offer. Such processes combine invention and drafting. But how can you usefully comment on such work? You can mark passages you find especially effective or interesting and point out connections as you notice them. If the whole draft seems fairly coherent, you can summarize what it seems to be about. Have students mark passages they find promising for your comments, or have them ask questions based on such a draft.

3. Drafting: The "Guidelines for Drafting" make specific recommendations to help students. You might want to talk about your own practices here--emphasizing differing practices for different kinds of writing. You might also want to address the tremendous gap students often experience between the ideal and the real situation of their writing. You may have many students who continue to procrastinate--often because they simply don't have much time and their writing is not a high priority, or not high enough. You can respond to this problem through group activities and your own coaching. Frequent attention to the work in progress keeps students from putting writing aside until the last minute. This scheduling of frequent attention is one of the advantages a writing class can offer. Talk about the impact of problems they are having. Is it hard to get time at a computer? The Guidelines include some suggestions for taking advantage of computer capabilities. Are they making good use of available resources? Are they giving themselves enough time per session to get going? Many students have unrealistic ideas about the time they need to write, and they simply are not scheduling enough lengthy sessions until the very last moment. At this point you may also see the cycles of writing and reflection paying off as students begin to have a sense of ownership about their writing, a sense that they understand how their own writing processes work rather than feeling dependant on their teachers.

This chapter includes some suggestions for overcoming resistance to drafting. These include using rituals, just getting started without trying for perfection, talking to others, and freewriting about the resistance itself. You might want to set aside some time in class for students to freewrite about their resistance, allowing volunteers to read their results to the class. Or discuss resistance, acknowledging that most writers experience it sooner or later. Other comments on resistance appear in the Teaching Practices section.

4. Organizing and developing: Some students think of drafting as nothing but a problem of organizing and developing their ideas, with little discovery involved. The more conventional and well-rehearsed the topic, the more this is apt to be true. Drafting, in other words, may include varying amounts of invention and arrangement. This chapter provides separate guidelines for the intermediate processes of organization, focussing on building strong connections between questions of content and questions of form, between the writer's ideas and the reader's expectations. It is here that students should concentrate on making their ideas explicit by unpacking code words, working on a thesis statement, and using conventional formats to signal organization. Here instructors may usefully remind students of organizational formulas: problem-solving, cause-effect, definition, comparison-contrast.

5. Planning and drafting collaboratively: Working collaboratively gives students less flexibility in exchange for the added power of group work. A set of guidelines provides some very specific questions for groups to use in order to open up discussion, emphasizes the importance of articulating and communicating shared understandings, advocates taking advantage of electronic technologies, and warns against a cut-and-paste method. Collaborative writing works best, in other words, when the writers work on group processes as they go, and it is likely to run into trouble if writers simply split up the duties and go their separate ways. As you assign collaborative projects, build in

time and place for these group exchanges and check to make sure that students are genuinely collaborating on their effort.

Activities

(p. 133) Exploration: This freewriting exercise in effect asks students to explore their biases about planning before they begin to read. Discussing the variety of responses in the class might be helpful as well, particularly when you feel your class is especially worried or resistant to opening up their usual procedures.

(p. 136) Application: This activity asks students to use the Guidelines to evaluate their controlling purpose; you will want students to use these questions again and again as they develop a controlling purpose for subsequent essays. You may want to refer to the list of questions in comments you make on drafts, when it seems that students need more work on their controlling purpose. Students frequently, for example, choose a topic and describe it, as if their purpose were purely aesthetic or formal. Or they take on too large a task, so that the essay they write can't possibly succeed.

(p. 141) Exploration: This exercise asks students to evaluate their methods of making plans and to think of ways to improve these methods. Since some students seem especially resistant to internalizing planning, these questions may help them to start thinking purposefully about their usual strategies. Putting the practice into words makes it available for monitoring and change.

(p. 141) Group Activity: Following up on the individual reflections about plans, this group activity summarizes planning practices and some conclusions about them. In the class discussion that follows, explore the variety of planning methods without prejudice, but also press students to make decisions about alternate methods with which they will experiment. Since planning and drafting so often feel like a regimen being prescribed for students, their vows to do better can easily have no more long-term effect than vows to go on a diet. The only thing they really need to pledge is sufficient time and attention to practice so that they have a chance to internalize new approaches.

(p. 147) Exploration: Like the above exercise, this exploration of drafting habits will help students internalize explicit strategies.

(p. 147) Group Activity: Like the group activity on planning, this exercise will help students to see the variety of drafting approaches available to them and, at the same time, press them to try new strategies that might improve their work.

Activities for Thought, Discussion, and Writing

Number 1: Writing an essay about writer's block offers students a chance to have some fun, perhaps to make impassioned descriptions about the past dire straits they've been in because of writing blocks or the extreme measures taken for a cure. It encourages students to become analytical about resistance as well. This is an assignment that lends itself to collaboration too; a group could tackle it together, if you want them to do some collaborative writing. They could describe some of the experiences they've had with the problem and then conclude with some group recommendations for solutions to writing block.

Number 2: This activity asks students to keep a record as they write. Comparing proposed and actual planning and drafting activities helps students to take a more extensive look into their actual writing processes. You might ask them to compare the results with the earlier descriptions of themselves that they have written.

Number 3: This assignment asks students to interview a nutritionist, lawyer, engineer, teacher, salesman, baseball player, or doughnut shop manager--whoever seems to be working in a field they might want to enter or even in a field they are simply curious about. (See Teaching Practices for notes on interviewing.) Students are to ask how their subjects plan writing, how they draft, whether they work collaboratively or alone, and what technological aids they use. Some students will interview spouses, relatives, and friends because they feel reluctant to approach strangers in their jobs. Unfortunately they miss a wonderful opportunity to initiate conversation in the workplace and ask questions that will reveal much about the nature of the job. You may find the results interesting enough to warrant class discussion. Then students write an essay about their findings.

Suggestions for Further Activities

The extensive planning needed for collaborative writing to work well is not easy to fit into a class schedule. You can, of course, ask students to do this work on their own time. But in order to launch a successful first experience with collaborative writing, set aside a period of time in each class for a week. During this time you can sit in on groups briefly to make suggestions about their process. More importantly, students see both how much time collaborative sessions might need, and (with luck) they see how much more fruitful collaboration is with some investment in communication.

As a variation on Activity Number 2, have students work in pairs to observe each other's composing process. This requires the composer to talk about what she or he is doing with planning and drafting while the other student observes and records. When both have done their work, they may compare notes about what they saw.

CHAPTER 7: Strategies for Successful Revision: Managing the Revision Process

In this chapter: *Guidelines for Responses from Friends and Family*
Guidelines for Responses from Your Writing Group
Guidelines for Using Your Instructor's Responses
Guidelines for Revising Objectively
Guidelines for Collaborative Revision

Chapter 7 addresses the larger questions of revision, asking students to think about revision as a time when they can look at their work as a reader, seeing it differently--perhaps more objectively--and bringing it to completion. The chapter provides suggestions for using feedback from various sources: friends and family, classroom groups, peer tutors, instructors. You will find a sample student paper included here as well, in rough and final draft.

By now your students have probably accumulated a great deal of material to work on and perhaps much longer rough drafts than they are used to revising. If so, you'll find this accumulation very helpful. Students are often stingy revisers because they so fear cutting out one single hard-earned word. Many of your students have probably been amazed and gratified by the sheer number of pages of writing they can produce when they do freewriting and loops or apply Aristotle's topics. For the first time, they have too much, their drafts approach or exceed the page limits, and they must make choices about what to include.

The experience of <u>cutting things out</u> is so novel and so wonderful for some students that for the first assignment that focuses on revising, we frequently encourage them to overwrite their drafts; that is, to make the rough draft perhaps twice as long as the final paper might be. Many students can hardly believe that they would actually write more than needed for a composition assignment or that it would feel so easy to do. Students who have suddenly discovered that they can invent more words fairly easily are ready to enter into a new economy of revision, based not on scarcity but on abundance. Writing too much is also especially helpful if you have some students who still can't seem to take the risk of making genuine changes in their papers.

Nevertheless, revising sometimes poses some difficult issues. For example, if students come to class with the kind of draft that we associate with automatic writing--something facile and acceptable that they've learned to produce without much risk--they may find it very hard to open the draft to inspection. Some work sounds good and says little. Revising may just make that more obvious. Or, on the other hand, if students bring work that has come out of freewriting, has a number of rough edges, but also has a lot of character, they sometimes seem prone to revise it into more stereotypical, less exciting forms. There's as much art to revising as to inventing and perhaps as little guarantee that the result will be wonderful. But you can increase your students' chances of success by multiplying their options. If a student has several possible essays to develop into a final draft, for example, he or she can choose the one that seems most promising for revision. If students know a number of people from whom to seek responses and a number of ways to try revising, they are not so apt to feel at a dead end. If they see revising as part of a process that they understand and can freely tap, they may extend their writing resourcefulness in ways that will make revising the most rewarding part of a project. And finally, as they learn to use a growing sense of audience, they will be able to revise more firmly within a well-conceived rhetorical situation.

The section on revising collaboratively in this chapter will help your groups work on their project together. Group members function not only as writers, but also as a sample audience and as a peer response group. From the variety of responses, students can become more knowledgeable about evaluating for revision.

Concepts

1. Revision: This chapter emphasizes the larger dimensions of revision, giving examples of genuinely new visions or approaches to rough drafts that allow students to write a more successful version of their papers. This kind of global revision requires that the writers allow their dialogue with others to influence the way they read their own papers--that they take readers seriously. The chapter points out how this differs from editing, with its concern for correctness. To show them the difference, ask your students to read each others' drafts through quickly to determine the gist of what is said, so they could repeat it without the help of written pages in front of them. The problems they encounter getting at a gist, and the differences of opinion about what it is and whether it suits the author's intention, are matters for global revision. Then, if you want them to experience proofreading, have them read the last paragraph of the paper, word by word, backwards from the end, checking for errors in spelling. Contrasting these two activities clarifies the point: revision is concerned with the production of meaning.

2. Revising collaboratively: This chapter makes many suggestions about getting responses to a rough draft. You might want to ask the whole class to try some of them: for example, listening to a paper read aloud by someone else or asking every student to meet with a writing assistant at the writing center. Students can make use of responses from other students, from family and friends, from writing assistants, and from the teacher. The chapter has Guidelines for using each of these various kinds of responses.

The chapter also makes important, specific suggestions for using response groups as an integral part of revising. Many writing-across-the-curriculum programs have found that such response groups are helpful to students writing papers in content area classes; if your institution has such a program you might want to tell your students something about it. Teaching your students how to use a response group will help them greatly in the future; our students testify to this. Responses from peer groups and from the instructor are, of course, examples of variations in interpretation which students have already had to take into account. Frequently, however, students tend to regard variations as some kind of error, either in the reader or in the writer, rather than as the inevitable differences that need to be negotiated to improve communication. Talking about reading each other's papers as a process will help them to see the dialogic nature of their understanding. This chapter gives some specific suggestions for the kinds of responses a group might use from Peter Elbow and Pat Belanoff's Sharing and Responding. Peter Elbow does a good job of insisting on the contradictory-seeming nature of these response-group exchanges. He says that as a reader, you are always 100 percent right about your response, but the writer is always 100 percent right about her intention as well. And it's a good idea to get both out in the open before the process of negotiation starts. See the Teaching Practices section of this instructor's manual for further comments about collaborative learning.

Finally, the section on revising collaboratively gives specific instructions for groups who are working on a writing project together. As the group moves into the final stages of a project, the need to coordinate carefully becomes even more pressing. When you teach students how to write together, you shift their attention from making isolated judgments to negotiating consensus about procedures and goals. As a number of commentators have pointed out (including the authors), the movement toward consensus which is required for a collaborative project, offers a microcosm of the powerful forces that converge to influence students during their education. So, too, it offers an occasion when you can use your leverage as a teacher to support a fuller participation and attention to diversity of voices than a less self-conscious group might allow, maximizing "productive conflict." You can call attention, for example, to the possibility noted by feminist theorists that gender differences mean female students are less likely to assert their perspective. You can ask groups to compensate but also to recognize the increased productivity that full participation of all group members will allow. Furthermore, you might point out that moments of difficulty and resistance or loss of focus in groups mark problems not only with the functioning of the group but also with what is written.

3. Samples of student revisions: Rosie Rogel's essay, "Memories," provides an example of how descriptive outlining helps her revise a paper on the topic of "family." Kira Wennstrom's paper on a personal experience shows the responses of her writing group in the margins. You may wish to add samples from your own collection to show on an overhead transparency or make them available in a class file on reserve.

Activities

(p. 160) Exploration: This assignment asks your students to reflect on their experiences with revision, distinguishing it carefully from proofreading. Encourage them to share stories of disaster, triumph, and mistaken opinion, and try to get some sense of how much revision your class has done in the past, either by asking them to turn in written responses or by holding a class discussion. You may have a number of students who "just can't revise." Don't be surprised if you have several students report that they ruin everything they revise: it's a common, self-serving superstition; in some cases it may even be true. The trick for you is to establish an atmosphere where taking a risk looks worthwhile and trying something new that doesn't work will not ruin the writer's G.P.A. Trying new writing approaches may very well cause a momentary regression in the writer's mastery.

(p. 165) Group Activity: This exercise asks students to think about how they perceive peer responses and to conceptualize what kinds of responses they prefer. Since this isn't necessarily something easily put into words, the collaborative part of the exercise helps students adapt or add to what they might have simply borrowed from the chapter. More importantly, it helps the group function more effectively. Often students say they want "tough," "critical" responses and don't get enough of them. As group members come to trust each other more, they are more willing to risk a critique that entails substantial revisions.

(p. 173) Application: This exercise asks your students to work out a descriptive outline first for their own paper and then for another student's essay. Exchanging descriptive outlines allows them to compare their own readings of their essay to another's. This is also an important exercise for students to learn objectivity and forms of response, using Rosie Rogel's essay and descriptive outline as a model.

Activities for Thought, Discussion, and Writing

Number 1: This assignment asks students to reflect on their revising practice in a way that may help promote their objectivity about their writing. At the same time you can also encourage them to have fun with their descriptions, to include all the relevant data (such as time taken out to watch a movie on television), and to try to find good metaphors for the process such as building a wall out of a pile of bricks or encountering foggy weather on page three. Analogies from Activity Number 2 below might be useful. Students' observations about group collaboration might easily be incorporated as well. If you have them write essays, they may be like Horatio Alger stories or like the confessions of revising sinners, perhaps with some repentance at the end. Most often, they will be structured as expositions of problem-solving. Some students might want to write arguments advocating a better way of revising. Have collaborative writing groups keep a log of their meetings and records of their procedures--agreements, revising sessions, information networks, ground rules--as well as their decisions about writing goals and responsibilities. Asking questions about the effectiveness of the process is an ongoing necessity for such groups.

Number 2: This exercise asks students to use analogy as a way of describing and understanding the complicated processes of revision. Take the opportunity to point out how analogies structure a whole attitude into the comparison as well. If revising is like cleaning house, it's primarily a job of cutting and clearing out. What gets omitted is dirt and junk and disruption, with a premium on orderliness and clarity. If revising is like adjusting binoculars, it's primarily a matter of bringing the parts into focus so they all work together to form a single picture, just as the controlling idea establishes a single, clear image. If revising is like a forest fire, a lot of valuable timber might get burned in the ruthless process of making room for new growth. Use these examples to help your students get started thinking of their own.

Number 3: This assignment, like Activity Number 1 above, asks students to reflect on revising with some depth and thoroughness in a way that will improve their objectivity about the process. By interviewing other students about their revision strategies and by drawing comparisons, students may see how they can make some useful choices about their methods, and they may also develop some further understanding about the relationship between revising strategies and the kinds of writing that seem to result. If this is a class assignment, or option, it makes some sense to have all the students doing this interviewing work together in groups of three. Perhaps this is a good opportunity for them to talk with people not in their usual response group. The resulting essays could be developed individually, or the group could collaborate on a single essay that summarized the experiences of the group.

CHAPTER 8: Strategies for Successful Revision: Revising for Structure and Style

In this chapter: *Guidelines for Evaluating Your Focus, Content, and Organization*
Guidelines for Revising for Coherence
Guidelines for Revising Your Style

This chapter continues the discussion of revision, moving on to consider matters of structure and style. The big issues--attention to focus, content, and organization--come first, complete with a checklist of questions to help guide analysis. Then the next step is to think about coherence. Finally, the chapter gives detailed advice about working on style.

Concepts

1. Focus: The controlling purpose gives focus, but this is not simply a matter of the writer's solitary will. It grows out of the rhetorical situation, and the writer's clarity about what's at stake. A lack of focus shows up as a mismatch between the essay intended by the writer and the essay read by the reader. Focus, therefore, depends heavily on the relationship between the writer's goals and the writer's understanding of the rhetorical situation, the conventions and expectations at work.

2. Content: Content develops and elaborates the controlling purpose of the writer. Most students have heard a good deal about the need for more specifics and greater detail in their work, but to know what kind of elaboration is needed they need to have a strong sense of purpose and a sense of what reader's questions they might be responding to.

3. Organization: Students revise organization by moving from the preliminary drafts on their subject to forms that will accommodate their readers. Writing has a beginning, a middle, and an end in the reader's mind, if not in the writer's text. So the writer needs to ask whether these elements all work suitably, and whether more detailed organizational schemes are required. Some types of writing, for example, have highly conventionalized formats for their organization. While the introduction and conclusion are important, your students also need to consider as organizational questions now (with the reader in view) some of the material they first thought of in the process of invention: how much evidence, definition, elaboration, or reasoning is needed; how much do they need to acknowledge other perspectives or other arguments; how much background or context must be included; and how much is too much.

4. Coherence: Many students are surprised to learn that there are specific techniques that can improve coherence quickly in their work. The sense of coherence arises from the reader's ability to follow the connections between sentences and between paragraphs in a piece of writing. Transitions, pronouns, and the repetition of key words and sentence structures help produce coherence. These are cuing devices that your students can quite consciously add to their work without changing it much, sometimes with a great increase in clarity.

5. Style: Style reflects all the choices of the writers such as syntax, order, and diction. But there are some basic guidelines that may help students develop a more effective style. This chapter analyzes some examples and explains some of the elements of good style, about how to work on sentence structure and variety, how to use concrete language, and how to reduce wordiness. An analysis of just how good style is effective may go further than such rules to illustrate the principle. Using the paragraph from The River Why, for example, ask students to decide which of a collection of dramatic sentences might contribute the most to the whole. There are several good candidates in the paragraph; we might start out the discussion by admitting that we couldn't have decided on just one choice. Surely the second sentence, which uses "because of fishing" as its anaphoric refrain, needs to

be one of the chosen. But then comes context matter for some good discussion. You might ask if students thought any of the sentences did not really contribute much. Why does the writer need both sentences three and four; the first is a general observation, and the second an analogy that repeats concretely the comparison with other prodigies? (Why do writers ever need to include both abstract and concrete versions of the same idea?) This is an analysis you could usefully do with the whole class in order to model the lines of discussion possible.

6. Voice: Although we use the term voice to talk about the sense of personal presence created by the writer, it's misleading and perhaps a bit mystifying to talk as if a writer had only a single way of sounding that was essentially and authentically the writer's own. A few students regard stylistic flexibility as hypocritical or unfaithful to their true selves, but nevertheless students need to develop several modes of personal and impersonal address for varying writing occasions. There are, assuredly, political and cultural implications in the voice a writer adopts. Furthermore, most of us can't just switch easily from one voice to another. Nevertheless, some students will face continuing problems with their writing because they cannot reconcile their sense of personal voice with the kind of objectivity demanded in academic writing. Aristotle's broader notion of the writer's ethos is a helpful corrective. You might want to offer some ways out of the impasse.

Here's a suggestion for students who are having trouble imagining themselves taking on a persona that seems alien. This resistance could, for example, take the form of students wishing to write only confessionally, rather than adopting an objective voice of authority; or wishing to write only as if they were being interviewed on television after winning a football game, rather than in the academically authoritative voice of an egghead professor. Have such students write a parody of the voice they find most objectionable or most difficult to imitate. Making fun of the voice removes the objections. When they don't have to be successful in the pretense, students can gain some experience practicing the persona. And of course some academic writing lends itself rather easily to parody. A certain theatricality is helpful to the first efforts at taking on new roles.

Activities

(p. 194) Application: This exercise asks students to read Todd Carpenter's paper on a national bottle law in the same way that they are reading each other's essays, both noting changes and making suggestions. Take this opportunity to double-check their perceptions by discussing the results with the whole class. Students should emerge with a better ability to gauge how much room there is for differences in reading and recommending and how much agreement there is on basic responses to revision. You might pay special attention to students who feel lost here. A few may continue to have severe problems with revising because they are so very unused to reading critically.

(p. 197) Application: This exercise asks students to write an analysis of their own draft, using the questions on focus, content, and organization appearing earlier in the chapter. The sample analysis written by Todd Carpenter provides a model. This prepares students to list specific goals for revising their essay.

(p. 201) Application: In order to define voice, this exercise asks students to find two passages from their current reading, one of them with a personal voice and the other with a public voice. The questions that follow are designed to help students make connections between their response to persona or voice and the rhetorical strategies that produce the effect of voice. The example in the text of a personal "voice" is from a Ken Kesey essay on the rodeo. The example of a public voice is from an article written by journalism students for Rolling Stone, called "Don't Call Me Slacker." Even though they might feel generationally closer to the latter topic, they should easily be able to see how much less visible the writers themselves are As they discuss these passages, ask them also to think about the different effects of authority and believability in these "voices," and how they are related to a rhetorical situation.

Activities for Thought, Discussion, and Writing

Number 1: This exercise asks students to put into practice on their own draft suggestions for improving coherence. After they have tried out the suggestions, you can ask students to discuss the results. You may want to make such intensive checks a regular part of the classroom routine for a while, at least until you think students are beginning to resolve their questions about coherence.

Number 2: Like the preceding exercise, this one asks students to apply the chapter's Guidelines, this time for revising style.

Number 3: A list of questions direct students' reading of Ian Frazier's essay, "To Mr. Winslow," asking them to focus on style and structure. Their first description of the style may take the form of vague impressions. Ask them to locate a word or sentence in the essay itself that seems to represent its style. Ask them to talk about persona in terms not only of character but also as tone. When they locate examples of effective prose style, they will surely fix on the use of concrete words and, perhaps, sentence variety. Ask them if the sentences that are not concrete seem excessive, or what function they perform. What is the purpose of the following sentences:

> "These words echoed in the media as reporters quoted and misquoted them."
>
> "Finally, I found a wooden stake broken off about half an inch above the ground: the base of the memorial cross, probably--the only sign of the unmeasured sorrows that converge here."

As they compare the passages they think characteristic of the writer's persona, ask students to work on attending to the interaction of textual form and the production of meaning. You will need to discuss the results in groups or as a whole class. The exercise would work well for group collaboration. You can then take group reports to the class as a whole. Since there will be a number of students who feel less than authoritative about their reading analysis, you will need to have some form of closure for them--not necessarily total agreement, but an opportunity for them to get the idea of how others are talking about style.

To get the discussion started, ask what the major connections are. What major elements are repeated? You might mention the idea of over-determination; many elements of a good essay function in several different ways at once. And important ideas get repeated several different ways.

Number 4: This exercise asks students to bring an example of a well-written essay to class, together with reasons why they think it demonstrates the principles of style. Ask them to find connections between the advice in Work in Progress and their preferred reading material. While the examples students bring to class may not always seem as wonderful as they hope, it is very enlightening to find out what students think of as good style. What will you do if they bring a number of examples from popular magazines and edifying books? It's probably worthwhile to look at the selections with some objectivity, reflecting on the rhetorical situation. Be sure to include a discussion of the context of these passages. How do certain publications circumscribe the available personas? Are there conventions of voice at work? How about the persona of Ian Frazier and New Yorker magazine style? Discuss the interaction of genre, audience, publication, and style.

CHAPTER 9: Understanding the Reading Process

In this chapter: *Guidelines for Effective Reading*
Guidelines for Previewing a Text
Guidelines for Annotating a Text
Guidelines for Summarizing a Text
Guidelines for Analyzing the Argument of a Text
Guidelines for Keeping a Reading Journal

Chapter 9 returns to the complexities of reading, the other term for that deceptively simple pair, reading and writing. Here Work in Progress goes on from the process analysis of reading, which is first addressed in Chapter 4. Chapter 9 pays special attention to the kind of critical reading skills students will need in college, and the rhetorical analysis that will help them to make connections between their reading and their writing. You will find a number of specific suggestions and examples to help students read a text more effectively. In particular, there are questions for analyzing the reading process, "Guidelines for Effective Reading," that consider texts within a rhetorical situation and help for previewing, annotating, outlining, summarizing, and analyzing. Short texts provide material to understand critical reading, including Jamaica Kincaid, "Girl" and an excerpt from Robin Lakoff, Language and Woman's Place. Then a group of texts about education enable students to carry out a more sustained rhetorical inquiry, so they can think about each reading in the context of larger arguments and in the discursive context of other kinds of texts that deal with the same topic.

Concepts

1. Reading: Like writing, reading is a complex process, far from a basic skill, and, like writing, it occurs within a rhetorical situation. Furthermore, although it is frequently assumed that reading is a fairly passive activity--again, all readers have to do is decode a text--reading turns out, like writing, to involve actively all the student's linguistic and cultural problem-solving strategies. As the far-ranging research on literacy suggests, both reading and writing are deeply implicated in culture and in the interpretations that culture directs. Most students recognize that literary texts require interpretation--a practice that requires a lengthy apprenticeship. But they generally have not extended the practice of critical reading to other kinds of texts. Once given the tools for analyzing their reading, students can consciously improve their critical thinking and their selection of materials, rather than relying solely on instructors for direction. For further reading, see David Bartholomae and Anthony Petrosky, eds. Ways of Reading: An Anthology for Writers. (2nd ed. New York: St. Martin's Press, 1990).

2. Writing and reading texts: Writing results in a visible product; it is a physical activity. Students can easily see that they contribute to writing; they are producers; they do actively write, even though they may not think of themselves as writers. Because of this, it is easier to make students critically aware of their writing processes than of their reading processes. The careful attention to their writing process in this class, however, has made students conscious of their own ability to manage, direct, and control complex processes in ways that will help them a great deal as they turn to thinking about reading and integrating their reading with their writing. What they have found out about the writing process will help the class overcome taking the reading process for granted too. See Robert Tierney and P. David Pierson, "Toward A Composing Process Model of Reading." Perspectives on Literacy. (Ed. Eugene R. Kintgen, Barry M. Kroll, and Mike Rose. Carbondale, Ill: Southern Illinois University Press, 1988, pp. 261-272).

3. Critical reading and the dialogue: You may find yourself in all classes repeating over and over the idea that critical does not mean "finding something wrong." When we assign a critical review essay, inevitably four or

five papers will go through obviously <u>pro forma</u> rehearsals of faults to prove they have fulfilled the requirement. This is true not just of freshmen, but also of seniors, which suggests a widespread discursive habit at work here, not just a misunderstanding about the meaning of the term.

Connecting critical reading with the idea of the dialogue may prove especially helpful to your students' understanding. Students think of the written text as the author's monologue, which they may either accept or reject. Thinking of their interaction with the text as a form of dialogue helps to encourage active understanding, analyzing, and evaluating instead. Classroom dialogue rather than the monologic lecture helps model critical thinking for them as well.

Elizabeth Flynn, in <u>Gender and Reading</u> (Baltimore: Johns Hopkins University Press, 1986), has outlined a way of thinking about this dialogue that may help students distinguish critical reading from habits of mind that block adequate response. She places readers on a continuum between the extremes of "submissive" and "dominant" responses. Extremely submissive readers lose themselves in the text, and their responses tend simply to amplify the way the text organized material, echoing even its very phrases and vocabulary. Students reading too submissively will frequently repeat phrases such as "then it says" or summarize plots rather than address ideas. Extremely dominant readers don't get beyond their own expectations, finding only what they already expected to learn or rejecting the text out of hand. Phrases such as "I could not relate to this article" obviously signal a failure of dialogue. They also signal a certain unwillingness or inability to analyze what might be causing the gap between reader and writer. Another mark of a dominant reading might be an aberrant interpretation that fails to take into account the apparent intentions of the writer. Between these two extremes comes dialogue, negotiating the differences between the reader's knowledge and expectations and the writer's work.

4. <u>Previewing</u>: The questions for previewing ask students to notice the publishing history of the text, the author, the title, the format and organization, and to survey the text quickly to predict what it will include and what response the reader might have to it. Notice that some clues about the usefulness of a text can be uncovered just from entries in the library catalogue. Previewing extends all the way from a decision about whether to read the book at all to organizing the reading work around appropriate questions. Students often imagine they must read everything and understand everything in a text if they are to use it at all, a dangerous assumption when it prevents them from taking on reading that is difficult. Previewing ought to function as an active assessment of the material to be read.

5. <u>Annotating</u>: Suggestions for more active ways of interacting with the text than simply underlining include the following:

1. asking questions
2. noting terms and vocabulary and identifying key words
3. noting main ideas, passages, and points brought up in class
4. responding not only to ideas, but also to style
5. using a reading journal for notes and comments

These are ideas worth assigning; a number of students won't already have such habits in their repertoire of responses. You might also suggest that students try freewriting in response to reading, using "writing-to-learn" as a tool for critical reading. Occasional pauses in class for this kind of written response will give students an idea of how it might be used on their own.

Visual maps, from outlining to clustering, may also help students annotate and respond to a reading. Note that the logic of outlining is easier to learn when students use it to see the structure of reading than when they use it to make preliminary writing plans.

However, since outlines of reading materials are frequently used for research papers, they are also frequently the source of problems with documentation and plagiarism. Point out to students that they are obligated to give credit to the source for _ideas_ they rephrase in notes as well as to sources of quotations.

Some students may benefit from other methods of visualizing the structure of readings. Just as many students find mapping or clustering a more accessible tool for organizing their own writing, they may also find a visual diagram easier than an outline for getting at the main points of written material. For another use of visual representation, see the example of clustering in Chapter 4.

6. _Summarizing_: Many students have difficulty writing a good summary. Since a summary involves finding the main ideas, it involves all the other aspects of critical reading as well. Ask students to write a number of brief summaries of things they have read, such as they might for general notes.

You can also help students work on determining the main idea. Have students do antisummaries, or "vagaries," collecting divergent and supplementary sentences that they would _not_ include in a summary. The object is to avoid clear references to a main idea. Challenge students to come up with the most incoherent or unexpected collage possible from the most rational and coherent discourse, perhaps from technical writing or from philosophy (historical writing is fun, but perhaps too easy). Strengthen the convergent thinking muscles by exercising the opposite as well. This exercise also shows students how well-knit texts work through redundancy and reference to lock all elements together.

7. _Analyzing the argument_: Students often are asked to analyze and evaluate material that to them, does not appear to be an argument in the conventional sense because it is presented as a reasoned analysis. The questions in this chapter help make the significant structure visible for students, beginning with the major claim or thesis (whether explicit or implicit) and the appeals that the writer uses to argue in favor of the thesis--to argue _logos, ethos, and pathos_.

When students are asked to read and report or to do research, instructors expect them to get at the significance of what they have read. Yet most students have a hard time understanding how to do that. They do not know how to analyze arguments to discover what is at stake. Frequently they do not know enough about the field to be able to recognize what's at stake. And they very often do not read material as if it were an argument at all. Accustomed to reading in order to recall information, students are used to neglecting the significance of what they read, and furthermore the context of academic work often requires them to read in this passive way. Students assume that their professor knows what's significant and what is not and that by the time they reach graduate school, they may find out too. Unfortunately, it's hard for students to write unless they can find some way to figure out the important arguments before they graduate. They have to know enough--or read enough to learn--to get the point of the essay or article or book or story that they are reading. Only then can they write about it.

Students can learn how to be critically self-conscious about their reading. They need to know if they have gotten the point and why or why not. When they reflect about their reading processes, they come to know their own knowledge and experience and their limits. They learn to consider whether they know enough about psychology or computers to read the samples in the text. Some find it an enormous relief to realize that their reading skill is not a matter of raw talent and ability, but rather something that is guaranteed to get better as they go on in their education. The reason why it's sometimes hard to find the significance of a work doesn't need to be a mystery or a crime.

8. _Reading responses_: This chapter suggests that students use freewriting responses to their reading as an aid to understanding, and points out the way that writing can help make reading a more active process.

9. _Portfolio on education_: This chapter includes a number of readings on education. George Leonard's "The End of School" provides a point of reference. Leonard's argument that the key to school reform lies in taking the viewpoint of the learner opens up an invitation for the learners in your class to connect the question of learning to write with the larger issues of

education. His utopian speculations about a "Metaschool" of the future define education in the broader context of the culture and evolving technologies. A newspaper editorial argues that "It's Time to Grade Parents"; an Associated Press story reports on the Education Department's statistical study of American youth; a New Yorker essay, "Gun Crazy," comments on the death of a teacher; an editorial by a sixteen-year-old in Newsweek argues that schools should teach black and white students to get along; a poem "Para Teresa" by Inez Hernandez reflects on the different ways two Chicana friends see school; and Matt Groening gives us the "School Is Hell" perspective (which also informs The Simpsons). How does culture interact with the goals of education? These readings point to the rhetorical situations of students in a program of writing instruction.

Activities

(p. 218) Exploration: This exercise has students freewrite in response to the items in a "Harper's Index." When they reflect on the experience, perhaps they will see the reader's share in the making of meaning, as they detect patterns and themes and think about the habits and assumptions they bring to a text and how facts generate interpretation.

(p. 218) Application: Here the chapter provides two readings with extensive follow-up questions to guide student responses. After they have answered the questions, they should reread the selections in order to note the process of revising in reading. Have students write out their answers to the questions in order to prepare for the group activity that follows. The first text, "Girl," by Jamaica Kincaid, is a very short story, while the second is an excerpt from Robin Lakoff's Language and Woman's Place. The first question asks students about their expectations. They can discuss their differing responses to the literature and to the more scholarly prose. The second question asks them to reflect about how their own assumptions and values might have influenced their reading of two texts about women in society. Ask them to notice how the very prediction of a kind of bias in the text corresponds to a bias in their responses, whether favorable or resistant. The third question asks them to look more closely at the very process of reading to see if they detected shifts in their constructions as they read. The fourth question asks students to look at the roles of author and reader and to compare these in the two texts. The fifth asks what three or four factors most influenced the difficulty of reading. And the sixth asks what kind of person might find the texts easy and pleasurable. Or if they seemed easy and enjoyable reading, what are the reasons? After these questions, students are asked to reread and to list several ways the second reading was different. These questions focus on the process rather than on the content of the material. They ask students to think about how expectations, their knowledge of terms, values, and previous knowledge might influence reading. Be sure to tell students that the point is to monitor their experience, not to find a correct answer.

(p. 222) Group Activity: Comparing responses to reading helps students see how individual reading processes differ and yet how certain commonalities arise as well. Students should begin to get a sense of how they read in comparison to their peers and perhaps even learn new ways to improve their critical reading.

If you have a number of students who focus only on interest or on liking or not liking the material, try returning to the rhetorical appeals presented in Chapter 3. Help them become sensitive to appeals that address their powers of critical reasoning, logos, as well as ethos and pathos.

(p. 226) Application: This application asks students to preview the article,"The End of School." It's important to have students write their answers down so you can compare the initial impressions gained by "skimming." Students who are prone to wildly divergent first impressions of their reading need to know what others see; students who worry about their mildly divergent first impressions need reassurance about the usual range of readings. Press students to make guesses about what they think the point and possible significance of the article will be.

(p. 232) Application: This exercise asks students to annotate "The End of School" just as they would any reading in preparation to write an essay. Many students annotate only by highlighting; discuss the advantages and disadvantages of this practice. What might be the consequences (good and bad) for being able to respond verbally or for locating the main ideas?

(p. 233) Application: This exercise asks students to write a brief summary of "The End of School." Advise students before they begin that summaries often start most effectively with a sentence naming the piece and stating its thesis or main idea. Summaries also follow the order of ideas, not necessarily the order of presentation in the original. Since the problems students have with summaries carry over into their research papers, try to go through the process thoroughly. Many students have severe problems distinguishing the most important ideas from the illustrations, examples, and evidence that they can safely omit. Discuss what is left out of the summaries as well as what is included. Do you want to discuss the problem of citations at this point? Our students admit learning to summarize for "reports" from elementary school on by changing a few phrases in the original and leaving other phrases out. So it probably won't suffice to say "put it in your own words."

(p. 234) Application: This exercise asks students to use the questions in the text to develop a critical reading of the argument in "The End of School," considering claims, the author's interests, evidence, key terms, emotional appeals, and their response as reader, conditioned by their own values and beliefs.

(p. 234) Group Activity: Students need their written preview, annotations, summary, and analysis of argument from the previous activities. This group activity offers the chance for them to compare and contrast responses to "The End of School." Then they are to offer conclusions about critical reading which, if all goes well, will reflect both their recognition of the diversity of responses but also the idea that there is considerable agreement about the main features of the reading. The most important conclusion they need to draw from this is that their reading is much richer, more complex, and more responsive after they use these critical reading strategies.

Activities for Thought, Discussion, and Writing

Number 1: This exercise asks students to analyze two textbooks they are using for classes. You may want to do this as a specific writing assignment or as a group activity. You may also wish to encourage students in the habit of such analysis. Have them record their observations in their writer's notebooks, and invite them to do the same for other reading assignments. Give them an opportunity from time to time in small groups and in class discussions to focus on the context of their reading. Ask them frequently what makes the works they read effective or ineffective.

Number 2: This exercise asks students to do a critical reading of the materials on education included in the chapter. Then it provides a series of questions for them to answer as they reflect on their reading.

"It's Time to Grade Parents" appeared as an editorial just as students were heading back to school. How does this influence the rhetorical situation? Does it seem optimistic about the year ahead? What's at stake in this editorial? What, in other words, do they mean by "today's education debate"? In assessing the responsibility for successful education, what part should "the niftiest curriculum or the shiniest school facilities and . . . stratospheric school spending" play? If the rhetorical situation includes a crisis in school taxes and reluctant taxpayers, does that change your students' interpretation of the piece?

"Challenges outside Classroom Threaten U.S. Teens, Study Says" is an Associated Press report of the Education Department's statistical study of

American youth. Like the "Harper's Index," it shows how suggestive facts can be, but it also offers several layers of interpretation. First, there is what Richard Riley says, which is that American youth are holding their own. And then there are the facts that the reporter finds most significant, the "story" of "challenges": "violence, AIDS, drugs . . ." There is an intriguing quote from the school principal, Princess Whitfield, about school as a haven from outside pressures. If your students were to write a piece about the state of American education, what would their controlling idea be?

A New Yorker story, "Gun Crazy," comments on the death of a teacher. This is not the same death that Ian Frazier wrote about in the essay in Chapter 8, and its tone is quite different. Students can usefully compare the two. In particular, they could reflect about which seems more effective, the uses of style, what kind of argument each seems to be mounting, and to what end.

An editorial by a sixteen-year-old in Newsweek, "Against the Great Divide," describes an almost complete separation between black and white students in the same school. Students may find their readings of this influenced by a number of important arguments about racial separatism currently going on, including those that advocate separatism to increase success for African-American students, or at least for the boys. (Just as some feminists believe that same-sex schools are better for girls). But this article assumes that such a divide is not good. The rhetorical situation of this article is rather unusual for Newsweek. Should readers consider the age of the writer? The location of the school (St. Louis)? Why did his experience at summer camp in Michigan differ so much from his experience at school? And how does that example change the argument?

"Para Teresa" is a poem by Inéz Hernandéz. It powerfully addresses the accusation of betrayal of one's people that threatens students who do well in learning-school culture. It also is written on what Gloria Anzaldua has called "la frontera," the borderlands of languages where English and Spanish intermingle. The poem complicates the ideal of integration in the previous essay. What impact does the form of poetry have here?

Matt Groening's cartoon creations include not only School Is Hell but also Bart Simpson, that well-known underachiever. What is the view of education presented here? Are students sympathetic to the desire for satisfactory answers? Do they agree that the answer is usually "no"? Compare irony here to its use in "Gun Crazy." Does it depend on very different views of school discipline?

The questions to guide student responses ask them to make comparisons among these texts. They are to keep careful track of their expectations and impressions, first from skimming and then from a more analytic reading. In particular they are to think about the relationship of author and readers for each, their relationship to one another, and then to develop through answering the questions some responses to the ideas about education that emerge from their encounter.

Number 3: Next, students are asked to return to George Leonard's essay on "The End of School." Ask them to explicitly identify juxtapositions of texts that alter their reading. Perhaps "Life in Hell" looks a bit like an illustration for Leonard's portrayal of middle school and high school. But how would Fernandez' falling out with her friend be addressed within the Leonard model? And so forth.

Number 4: Finally, the chapter closes with an essay assignment. Students can either write about their own views about education, or respond to one of the readings. In either case, ask them to consider when they have finished how many ways their writing was impacted by the extensive reading. Were they to go on with a more ambitious project, they could combine both, or work collaboratively to write a group essay on education that incorporated ideas from the reading.

Suggestions for Further Activities

Ask students to interview an expert or a more advanced student in their area about their reading. If you are teaching lower division students, you might ask them to consult with upper-division students in their major; if undergraduates, ask them to interview graduate students or other knowledgeable sources. What do they typically read in classes in their field? How much reading is generally assigned? How difficult do they find this reading? Do their instructors discuss these readings extensively in class, or do they assume that students have assigned materials and discuss other subjects? What role do the readings typically play in these courses as a whole? What advice would these upper-class students give to a new student, like yourself, about the best way to approach the required reading in this field? (See Teaching Practices for a discussion of interviewing.) Ask students to report the results in class. This exercise offers the opportunity for students to research and describe the contribution of reading to their rhetorical situation in college, so it is well worth going on to assign an essay that summarizes their results.

Like most inquiry that aims to investigate genuinely interesting questions, your students' work will encounter real-life difficulties. When they report their findings to each other, in groups and to the class as a whole, they may have wildly varying information. And, unless you suggest that they exercise considerable care, some of their interviews may not be very reliable, either because the answers are superficial rather than considered, or because the interviewees don't know everything they should about the reading they are expected to do. For example, juniors and seniors do not always know systematic ways to review the literature for a research project or what "the literature" might include in their discipline, even though they may be trying to do research projects. Since this exercise explores the realities of the academic writing and reading situation, you can usefully move to discussions that compare and contrast the ways you are handling reading material in this class to the various practices in other classes on campus. The opportunity to be pragmatic and descriptive will probably interest your students very much, and be useful to them as well.

CHAPTER 10: Understanding Academic Audiences and Assignments

In this chapter: *Guidelines for Identifying the Assumptions behind the Assignment*
Guidelines for Generating Interest in and Commitment to an Assignment
Guidelines for Getting Started on an Assignment

This chapter and the next turn to the rhetorical situation of academic writing, drawing on the idea of textual conventions and the experience with analyzing their reading which students encountered in Chapters 4 and 9. In particular, this chapter discusses the expectations students need to consider when their audience is academic, pointing out that academic discourse depends on reason, analysis, and argument, that it deals with complexities and so resists oversimplification.

Your students will find here a list of possible responses to their recurrent question: "What does the instructor want?" And they will find specific suggestions about academic writing assignments and how to develop plans to complete them successfully.

As they work through this chapter, students will find it helpful to have a current writing project in mind so they can put the suggestions into practice.

Concepts

1. The academic audience: What do members of an academic community look for, as readers of their students' writing? Not, perhaps, what some of your students may expect--that is, not just evidence that students have done the assignment, or even just evidence that they learned what they were told. Students may improve their ability to assess academic writing situations if they see their instructors as people thinking about a certain body of knowledge rather than as just evaluators of student papers. That means that individual instructors evaluate papers within a set of disciplinary standards, and students will have to learn something about the discipline, not just about general writing, in order to succeed. Fortunately, the work on rhetorical situation that students have done will help them analyze academic assignments and understand what further inquiry is needed to get the job done.

Through a position of mutual inquiry and shared rationality, rather than the adversarial relationship of student to grader, students may be able to give instructors what they really do want: evidence of thought. On page 251, the text lists characteristics for effective writing. A sample essay written by Tessa McGlasson for a history examination appears on pages 254-57.

2. Analyzing academic writing assignments: Although assignments range from the very broad and general to the very limited and specific, key words, such as define or evaluate, point to appropriate strategies. You might ask students to note that these key words suggest varying levels of complexity--an evaluation or a defense may include definition, analysis, and summary, for example. Students frequently mistake the intent of an assignment, responding with a simpler mode than the assignment requires or oversimplifying complexity. For example, in critical reviews students may simply write summaries instead of including evaluation. Or they may include nothing but evaluative conclusions with no summaries of the contents or definitions of criteria.

3. Identifying the assumptions inherent in the assignment: Identifying assumptions requires students to ask: What is the rhetorical situation of this class? Students often rely heavily on carefully specified objectives, believing that they can understand only limited and explicit course objectives. When extensive objectives are listed, however, students may read them mechanically, as simply a list of disconnected objects with coercive intention. And worse, they may fail to think any further about what purposes the class may have.

Since students need to learn what kinds of connections might be made in a given discipline and how assumptions might be examined critically, they should be encouraged to formulate and reformulate for themselves what they see as the directions and purposes of their classes. Then the questions on page 260 will help to focus students' own inquiry, perhaps helping them to make suggestions as if they were the professor, or to guide group work. Chapter 11 will provide further help with appropriate methods for analysis.

4. Building commitment: Commitment to an assignment is not quite the same as interest, even though both are ways of describing what motivates writers. Most students will readily admit that finding a way to make a writing assignment interesting is a big part of their struggle. Working on strategies of invention in your class has probably already showed them ways to get started--whatever the academic writing project--without inspiration, or even prior interest. A lack of engagement in writing assignments leads students to do them in a perfunctory or superficial way, skipping the process of thought that their professor expected--sometimes because the student does not understand the steps of inquiry that support the final piece of writing. In many disciplines this might include research through reading, but sciences and even social sciences might expect a careful description of experimental methodology as well. Students who work through assignments carefully are in a position to ask questions about methods and expectations they do not understand.

An especially good way to get involved in an academic topic--to enter into the conversation already going on in that field--is through reading. This may be seen as prewriting, or even prereading, a preliminary step that may not involve taking any notes at all, but rather making annotations and jotting down questions and remarks in the writer's notebook. Without your encouragement, many students regard this kind of reading as a waste of time because it does not seem to lead efficiently to the final product. Consequently, they fail to give themselves sufficient time for reading and thinking about the topic.

In addition to the suggestions of strategies that insert students into the discourse, this chapter includes a set of guidelines for countering resistance to required assignments.

5. Preparing to do an assignment: Although this section lists questions helpful for managing writing assignments, some knowledge about writing has to be acquired by practice. This knowledge will become part of students' rhetorical common sense once they master this kind of planning, but just thinking about it or nodding agreement won't do. They might just as well nod agreement to the way irregular French verbs are conjugated.

Activities

(p. 251) Exploration: If students have been exploring their writing situation frequently during the term, so that most of the stereotypical responses have already been exhausted, this opportunity to freewrite about the academic situation may produce insights and unforeseen questions.

Some students will probably raise questions about the seemingly arbitrary differences in expectations among classes and their regular mystification about what expectations are. If they do, it's a good lead right into the next section on criteria for effective academic writing.

(p. 257) Group Activity: Using Tessa McGlasson's essay, admittedly an especially good one, students should be able to find examples that meet the criteria for effective academic writing. Presenting the results in class will allow you to talk about their interpretations of criteria, some of which may startle you. For instance, many students think that a significant topic needs to be a hot issue of some kind, typically as defined by the evening television news.

(p. 263) Exploration: Notice the two important steps of this exercise in freewriting about a difficult or frustrating academic writing experience. If your students are likely to express fervent antipathies to some academic writing experiences, or to present a formidable inability to deal with a lack of commitment, you might want to provide in-class time for writing about this. You can then explicitly divide this freewriting into two parts, asking students first to focus thoroughly on the way the problem felt and then asking them to turn to the way they now imagine themselves handling it. In any event, it's important not to leave them with the conviction of frustration and ineptitude.

Activities for Thought, Discussion, and Writing

Number 1: Interviewing instructors can be important not only for giving students a chance to find out about matters they usually think of as top secret or a forbidden mystery, but also for prompting them to speak rationally about their classes and their major fields with members of the faculty. This ability to get precise understandings about assignments is crucial. Previous practice with interviews ought to give them some confidence in carrying this out. They need to be particularly careful to check their understanding of what is said and to report it accurately. What methods and conventions are assumed in the assignment that the student must have understood to write it?

You may wish to have a panel of instructors come to your class, either to supplement individual interviews or to provide an alternative way to interview faculty. Some situations make the logistics of individual interviews difficult. Your colleagues will not increase their friendliness toward writing classes if nine hundred freshmen seek interviews frantically during the same week.

The information students bring back may well be very useful to other students who do not usually have the chance to ask faculty such questions. You can ask your students if they would like to spend class time hearing the results.

Occasionally students are intimidated or have difficulty understanding their instructors, and their reports seem vague and misleading. Faculty members may not always be accessible. Faculty members do not always know just how many of their assumptions about disciplinary writing need to be made explicit for beginners. In any event, you will be able to tell quite a bit about how well students understand their academic situation from their ability to carry out this assignment. Chapter 11 will offer further help with disciplinary differences.

The text gives an essay as the final step of the exercise. You might want to gauge the accuracy and depth of the interviews before you assign an essay summarizing and commenting on the results. If the interviews reveal difficulties, you might find that students will benefit from writing an essay about why they still do not understand the goals of undergraduate education or of a particular class, or why they feel anxious and frustrated about the analytic and argumentative skills required. Most classes, after all, are mixed experiences, and students may not understand the goals of a great professor for years.

Number 2: This activity asks your students to put the suggestions from the chapter into practice. Students should follow the steps of analyzing their assignment, recognizing its assumptions, developing commitment, and creating a plan for writing. Then they should evaluate this planning process.

Do as you did with writing processes: keep both the positive and the negative aspects of students' discoveries out in the open as matter for discussion. Students who labor through this planning in a perfunctory or distanced way may have trouble imagining themselves ever doing it again. Their genuine distance from understanding the assumptions of the disciplines they are studying is not remedied quickly. Can students write and plan in the absence of understanding? Your job is to persuade them that they can at least make a beginning and that such a beginning is itself the work of understanding. Maybe it will help your students to know how much we all labor in the dark when we write, making assumptions and guesses without the kind of certainty that would be reassuring.

Number 3: This essay asks students to assess their present situation in college. It's a version of an assignment that has long been traditional for composition classes: several generations of college students have entered their freshman year and written about what college is like for them. But your students are now equipped to write about expectations and experiences much more analytically and critically. You might want to have them freewrite a few times in an intensely descriptive mode, or have them narrate the events of an hour as they imagined it, and an hour as it really is, so they have some body to their speculation.

CHAPTER 11: Understanding Academic Analysis and Argument

In this chapter: Guidelines for Developing an Appropriate Method for Your Analysis
Guidelines for Analyzing Your Values, Assumptions, and Beliefs

This chapter, continuing the examination of academic writing begun in Chapter 10, guides students through the process of using analysis to write an academic argument, situating themselves in subjects from biology to art history to economics to business. It discusses choosing a topic and thinking about a purpose in the light of the topic's broader significance. It directs students to consider what frameworks or methods are usual and appropriate for the discipline they are writing in. It points out the chief characteristics of academic discourse: reasoned argument proceeding from a thesis and making assumptions and beliefs explicit. It reviews three kinds of argumentative claims and the kinds of evidence that they require. Finally, it explains why academic arguments must take counterarguments into account and how students can include the other side in their writing.

As students begin to think about how arguments take shape differently in different disciplines, they will be able to draw on what they learned in Chapter 10 by studying the assumptions behind writing assignments. Nevertheless, there are real and difficult challenges involved for students who must figure out, often for themselves, what approaches are preferred for each subject matter.

Concepts

1. Analysis and argument: In academic discourse or inquiry, analysis and argument are intimately related. Even in disciplines such as literary criticism, which students sometimes imagine as a matter of personal taste, unsupported appeals to emotions or beliefs (or both) are unacceptable; they look too much like raw ideology and offend the rationality of the profession. Reasoning is the process that needs to appear in academic writing. When your students understand that they need to include analysis to develop their immediate responses, they won't feel so frustrated about the problem of evidence. Often our students have felt utterly blocked by needing to "support" a response such as "this poem seems sort of depressed." Because they want to imitate a scientific model, they go looking for "facts" to buttress a conclusion, instead of articulating their processes of analytic thinking.

You may also find that your students have trouble seeing how analysis and argument connect. A journal article on acid rain, defining and explaining cause and effects, might seem to them to be purely factual with no argument. Academic argument is addressed to a critical reader, and our students, used to the arbitrary certainties of the print media, are not habitually critical readers, even after they've thought about the reading process. If students think of the academic audience as composed of critical readers, that may help them see how to use analysis to argue for a point or to make claims.

At this point someone in the class might feel free enough to say: "Wait a minute! That's where we started in this class! Imagining everyone in college with a red pencil! Now you want us to go back to the anxieties of knowing we're writing for a 'critical reader' after our brief days of happiness and freedom in our composition class?" And maybe somebody else in the class would answer something like this: "Well, we started out thinking 'critical' meant looking for something wrong, marking out those run-on-sentences you liked so much, or telling us our ideas stink. Besides, we all had a tendency to take it personally." An exchange like this is an opportunity to point out that argument, analysis, and critical thinking go on all the time in class. Like rhetorical common sense, reasoning is something your students have been doing all along without knowing it.

2. Significance: Knowing what is significant and interesting in a field is part of what it means to be an expert. Nevertheless, students who write well have both the ability to focus on a manageable purpose and a sense of the wider implications, of how their topic fits into larger issues which they will not address directly. For instance, an essay on the plausibility of the fool in *King Lear* bears on the general discussion of the fool the assignment evoked and also on the question of effective characterization in drama. It's a mistake for a student writer to think he or she must draw conclusions about either of these larger issues as part of the specific purpose. Note that significance often seems to arise at the intersection of two topics under discussion in a field, as a function of their relationship. Point out to students that one way to discover a worthwhile approach is to relate two well-discussed themes.

3. Methods for analysis: Students have the tough but inevitable task of figuring out the preferred methods of analysis for the disciplines they study. This chapter recommends that they first use the instructor as a model, analyzing his or her methods, noticing the evidence and the kinds of questions asked. Then students might apply some of the approaches for critical reading, looking at written models.

Instructors do model the kinds of thinking they want to endorse, and students who actively work to understand and imitate those methods learn how the discipline works. In this way, successful students do "psych out" the instructors as models of inquiry; passive students run into problems because they expect to be told what the instructor wants.

4. What's at stake in an argument: Frequently students have a hard time understanding what the thesis of an essay ought to be because they do not think in terms of argument, taking a position on a topic. They need to address an audience, not just a topic. But the academic audience is unfamiliar. And peer response groups don't automatically provide a good sense of an audience that is committed to the ideas of a certain discipline. Ask group members to participate in determining what's at stake by imagining what convictions might be unsettled or overthrown if the writer proves a certain point.

5. The role of values, assumptions, and beliefs: Even academic writing depends on a number of assumptions that remain unexamined. You might want to talk about these with your students, looking at some academic writing to decide what assumptions are made, what remains unexamined, and why. Show students how disciplines as interpretive communities have patterns of shared assumptions. A challenge to these assumptions is generally a major enterprise, a disciplinary revolution and not just a brief examination of assumptions. For example, a basic assumption in writing about literature has been the idea that literary texts are different from other kinds of writing--and better. Feminism, cultural studies, and poststructuralism have all challenged this assumption, generating considerable theoretical controversy. Scientific discourse also undergoes changes. Thomas Kuhn has written in *The Structure of Scientific Revolution* about how scientific assumptions (or knowledge) come to be challenged and overthrown.

Students often raise very interesting questions about disciplines because they naively do not know what is taken for granted. However, the truth is that students will seldom succeed in revolutionizing a discipline; their argument will fail instead to seem effective. Students need to be aware of these regular patterns of disciplinary assumptions or bases in order to write successfully. Even the challenges that appear as legitimate operate within discursive limits or as arguments about limits.

Students also need to think about what their own arguments depend on and how they might be challenged. What do your students write about as if everyone agreed, or shared the experience, when they know that isn't the case? Peer groups can help with this, pointing out assumptions that *someone* might challenge without the onus of a personal confrontation. Cultural diversity in your class helps insure that provincialism will be challenged. You can help by making it clear that such questioning is valuable.

As students work through the "Guidelines for Analyzing Your Values, Assumptions, and Beliefs," they may realize how much the goal of academic objectivity depends upon a relationship of dialogue with other writers and other texts. If academic inquiry progresses through argument, then writing that appears outside argument will also appear outside the interest of academic readers. Without defending some of the cultural limits of academic discourse that may be indefensible, you can show students various ways to deal with such limits other than assaulting a brick wall or giving up.

6. Appropriate evidence: What seems appropriate evidence for an argument depends in part on the kinds of claims being made. Annette T. Rottenberg's categories, presented in the text, include claims of fact, claims of value, and claims of policy. As your students think more carefully about the kinds of arguments they might be writing, they will learn to sort through evidence in terms of its relationship to their point.

When writing arguments, students often fail to connect evidence to purpose. They may assume that facts speak for themselves, and their only obligation is to accumulate a great stack of them. Student writers need to think about the principle of selection, and about how they and others might interpret those facts. Often they need to make their interpretive assumptions explicit. You can usefully comment on this when you read drafts.

Students also often fail to show the relationships among judgments, criteria, and examples. For instance, in evaluations or critical reviews, students may say a play was "well done," but they don't explain their standards for good plays or cite particular instances. Students may not know how to negotiate the difference between widely accepted standards and personal preferences, especially because entertainment values have encouraged them to think that raw response is enough. You might ask your class whether they think the Nielson rating is good evidence for a claim of value--for saying whether a television program is good or not.

Finally, students have problems with advocacy, perhaps in part because they think "everyone has the right to their own opinion," and also because they are influenced by the spectacle of public debate. As a result, they are apt to separate problem-solving from a reasoned consideration of values, issues from argument. A student may, for example, examine a hot topic such as child abuse or drugs or teen pregnancy by collecting arguments as if they were facts, submitting a collage of problems and solutions rather than thinking through the various positions and their relative merit.

When students submit position papers, taking a stand against abortion or in favor of the rain forest as their thesis, they may mistake passionate opinions and emotional revelations for an invitation to discuss issues. You may want to address directly the forms of public debate your students are used to hearing and reading and ask them to look at them critically. What kinds of models have influenced students' ideas of good arguments? Can they bring some examples to class? Should they be relying on these models?

7. Counterarguments: Students need to understand the importance of considering counterarguments in academic writing. Thinking of counterarguments will help students recognize and answer possible challenges to their assumptions. Considering counterarguments also will shift their reasoning from diatribe to dialogue. Their thinking begins to be more complex. The counterarguments can serve as an important way of organizing an essay. And members of peer groups can learn to represent possible counterarguments, stimulating a more active consideration of writers' positions.

You can encourage students to assume critical roles even when they have limited knowledge or don't feel critical. Use group work to dramatize the practice. The more theatrical and arbitrary you make this role-playing, the easier it will be for students to learn to play the devil's advocate, raising counterarguments for themselves. If you exaggerate the parodic aspect of this role-taking, you will avoid finding yourself in the old rhetorical dead end of seeming to advocate cynicism. You can have them argue one side and then the other without asking them to take up an ethos which could cynically argue both sides. Or take a few topics for general discussion and pass out pieces of paper assigning positions ("You are a logger in favor of cutting old-growth timber." "You are an environmentalist, against cutting old-growth timber.") Ask students to write out slips of papers representing various positions on their topics to perform this exercise in their groups. Point out how learning to reason from the standpoint of the other is also an exercise in empathy and a recognition of our real inner ambivalence. It is important to be able to take a position and also to suspend the argument in its favor long enough to hear other perspectives.

Activities

(p. 269) Exploration: This freewriting exercise asks students to explore their concept of argument and their attitudes toward being involved in arguments. Most students see argument, like critical, as negative. This is not a small problem. It's not just a matter of redefining terms. Their resistance to seeming critical and argumentative may very well keep some students from writing effectively. If you can get them to articulate their discomforts, they may be able to take positions more assertively--and more thoughtfully. They may begin to make distinctions between arguments that appeal to reason and arguments that make them uncomfortable by appealing to emotions. Class discussion will also reveal interesting differences among people about what kinds of arguments seem acceptable. See if your class feels these differences are based on gender, ethnicity, race, religion, politics, region, family conventions, or other factors. Does your class agree on what is the touchiest subject, the argument everyone would like to avoid?

(p. 272) Application: This activity asks students to answer three questions about the analysis of rhetorical situation, rough draft, and final draft of the essay "Why Isn't There a National Bottle Law?" which appeared in Chapter 8. First, they are to find the thesis statement ("The United States government should require every state to have a bottle law or constitute a national bottle law.") This enables the writer, Todd Carpenter, to argue for more than a change of attitude (the rough draft just said "What a shame.") Readers now find themselves asked to think about taking action--making a law. So the addition of a thesis shifts the way all the paper's reasons and evidence will be read. Ask your students to point to specific consequences in the paper. Are there sentences whose meaning or impact seem to change when viewed from the perspective of the added thesis?

Next, students analyze and list changes in the revised draft that make it a more effective academic argument. The second draft is more academic in a number of ways, from style to the specificity of evidence. Some students may nevertheless prefer the more relaxed tone of the first draft; if so, you can speculate about style and rhetorical situation. When they turn to the third question, students can imagine changes appropriate to the rhetorical situation implied by an ecological group rather than an academic setting. Would such a group prefer a more relaxed tone? Wouldn't they want great precision about evidence? Would Todd need to add material about the impact of discarded bottles on all environmental efforts? Or comparisons with other environmental projects?

(p. 277) Application: This exercise asks students to analyze their own values, assumptions, and beliefs about a possible writing topic. They are to list opposing arguments as part of their analysis. This not only helps them to imagine counter-arguments they might address, it also will reveal much about their own commitments. Those in danger of being overinvolved in an issue are encouraged to think about their unexamined assumptions and whether or not they want to examine them. Those who habitually choose topics because they seem obvious or workable begin instead with a sense of commitment to an issue. Ask your students to repeat this freewriting and analysis for each essay topic they consider.

(p. 281) Application: This exercise asks each student to develop a workable plan--thesis, claim, and appropriate evidence--for writing an argument. Since all the elements must mesh, you might encourage students to weigh their options carefully, perhaps rewriting the thesis after thinking about evidence and claims or listing questions about claims and evidence for group discussion.

When students find, as many will, that all three claims can work for their issues, have them arrange the claims in hierarchical order so they can see how to organize their evidence. Does the writer on teen pregnancy think that the most important claim is one of fact, for instance, arguing that teen pregnancy is a problem connected with poverty, disproportionately affecting girls from low-income families? Or the most important a claim of value, for instance, arguing that teen pregnancy creates problems for mother and child that include poverty? Or is the most important a claim of policy, for instance, that the government ought to fund programs to prevent teen pregnancy because it increases poverty and all its accompanying problems? Should the writer, in other words, emphasize facts about the nature of teen pregnancy, examples of the problems faced by poor teen mothers or a explanation of social programs to help teen mothers?

Often the emotions associated with a much-discussed public issue make the issue seem self-evident, so, for example, it seems obvious that teen pregnancy is bad. Refusing to take the self-evident for granted can sometimes give a student a lead for their thesis. For example, the writer could observe that teen pregnancy seems a persistant problem in the face of mass education about sex and birth control, asking if there are other reasons why teens keep getting pregnant.

(p. 282) Group Activity: This exercise asks your students to think of as many counterarguments to a thesis as possible, without pausing at this point to develop any of them. You may need to practice this assignment several times when you first assign it so that everyone gets a feeling for what counterstatements might be like. You might also bring a couple of statements to class on each of the next two or three days and challenge students to produce counterstatements, writing them down as a list or brainstorming aloud.

Activities for Thought, Discussion, and Writing

Number 1: This activity pulls together the material from this chapter about arguments and the material on analysis of reading from Chapter 9. Carefully using the analytic tools they have been developing, your students may be able to examine these arguments--especially the nontraditional forms--from a more critical perspective than their immersion in the norms of reading the media can allow. Listing and discussing both strengths and weaknesses, the students should understand that the point is not simply to accept such readings *or* simply to dismiss them as propaganda, but to see them as more complex efforts to persuade.

Number 2: Analyzing newspaper editorials for a week provides practice in thinking about claims of fact, value, and policy. The object is not to find airtight distinctions among arguments because most editorials will, in fact, mix their claims. Furthermore, your students, like all audiences, will read for the appeals that seem persuasive to them, and tend to give priority to them. Students will probably disagree about what the major claims of many editorials might be so the exercise provides practice in identifying claims of different kinds.

When they bring the editorials to class, their discussion may reveal that different individuals or groups see the same editorial differently. There is a reader's share even in the structure of claims and evidence. You might ask students what this discovery suggests for their own arguments. Ask them to consider how editorials work effectively--how claims prove anything--in spite of their various readers. Resist letting the discussion resort to "everyone to his or her own opinion," since that does not solve the puzzle of effective argument.

Number 3: This essay assignment pulls together the separate steps in preparing an argument that students have worked on throughout the chapter.

Encourage students to refine their ideas as they develop their essays. If they have, indeed, worked their topic through the various exercises, they have probably found themselves with considerable material. Nevertheless, the task will not necessarily be easy; the complexity now revealed will, in fact, make it a less familiar essay assignment. Most students have developed shortcuts that allowed them to write, but also reduced their effectiveness in the long run. You may, in other words, find yourself at this point needing to reassure your students that the more sophisticated essay they are about to write will serve them better in their academic careers--and that such writing also takes practice to master.

EPILOGUE

What have your students learned as they finish your course? Not everything they need to know, they should understand, in order to write well. Instead, they have learned how to enter into a process of writing. Paradoxically, precisely by working with groups and doing collaborative writing, they have become more independent. They can use the rhetorical methods they have practiced in your class to continue to learn. They have had some experience with making group work productive and with interviewing others to improve their writing.

One of the institutional situations all writing classes face is the demand that instructors teach students how to write once and for all. As students learn to actively work with other instructors in various disciplines to improve their writing, they may preserve and even improve on the gains they have made in your course. They know how to use writing to help them understand their reading and their coursework as well as how to write better on examinations and assignments. You have put it in their power to go on--and now it is up to them to do so. Your students have a realistic, pragmatic assessment of their own writing on which to build.

6. SAMPLE ASSIGNMENTS AND STUDENT ESSAYS

In the following pages we have collected sample assignments and student essays for your use, written for courses using Work in Progress as their text.

Assignment for a Critical Review of an Essay

Writing a critical review is a basic step for most kinds of research. It involves not only reading for what the author intended to say but also reading "critically." Accordingly, your task for this essay will be twofold: you need to communicate the content of the original essay, and you also need to evaluate the essay.

Choose any one of the essays in our collection of readings as your subject, whether we have read it in class or not.

You may wish to start by writing a first-impression response, recording your reading experience before you go on with any analysis. After first reading the essay, freewrite whatever comes to mind--whatever strikes you, confuses you, or reminds you of something. Write down phrases that leap out without yet thinking about why. In this first response, your own initial prejudices and opinions may very well emerge, too. Again, don't try to sort all this out yet. If you write this kind of first-impressions response, you'll use it as a discovery draft, a way to think. In fact, you may use almost none of the text from a first response in a later critical essay. What the response does is to help you see what you thought.

Next go to work on trying to understand what the writer intends to say. What is the writer's rhetorical situation--why is he or she writing? Are you the audience? Can you summarize the main points of the essay? How are the writer's most important themes developed? Are there certain phrases which seem to make the point especially well--phrases you might want to quote? In this work for understanding, you try to set your own feelings and opinions aside, even though your point of view will necessarily color what you see.

Finally, look at the essay "critically." Of course, that does not necessarily mean that you will say something negative; it means that you will interpret, analyze, and evaluate. Look at the essay from another point of view--move away from your posture of unquestioning attention. Ask questions. Does the writer miss something that ought to have been taken into account? Does the writer "cheat" by making assumptions that ought to have been questioned? Why is the essay effective? How do style and arrangement contribute to its effectiveness? What are the implications of the writer's points? If an essay seems memorable, it is frequently because we can see many other examples supporting its claims or observations. What makes the essay interesting? Does it tell you something new? Does it say something you always thought but never could quite express? Do you agree or disagree-or both?

You may organize your review in two parts, with the summary coming first and the critical evaluation second. Or you may organize it around three to five main ideas, or sections, with each paragraph including both your summary and your critical commentary.

Use a bibliographical entry to head your review instead of a title. If you quote an entire sentence or passage, note the page number in parentheses at the end. Quotes longer than four lines must be indented five spaces. The finished length should be two to four pages, typed.

Sample Critical Review of an Essay (Wrigley, Robert. "The Swing, the Snow, the Skull of a Hare." Northwest Variety. Ed. Lex Runciman. 1987.)

In the essay, "The Swing, the Snow, the Skull of a Hare," Wrigley states, "I think that we are all regional writers, that we all carry with us the landscape we have come to call home" (Wrigley 140). The belief that a writer is or is not regional leaves much to be debated. A recent article in Oregon Focus magazine, titled "We Are the World," by Doug Marx does just that. Marx argues, "All this literary talk about regionalism is, if not pure bunk, at least artificial in the given text" (Marx 9). In contrast, Wrigley has strong feelings that there is something about the climate or the soil that inspires people to write.

Wrigley admits without shame that he was drawn to the Northwest and to Idaho by geography. His writing reflects the mountains and canyons, the wild, far-falling rivers, and the exhilaration he feels around them. Wrigley writes: "I was struck as I am again and again by the beauty of this irregular landscape, this dramatic unlevelness. It appeals to me, I think, for the same reasons swinging did when I was a child. It is up and down, it is rhythm on a dazzling vast scale" (Wrigley 140). He relates his love for the landscape to his enjoyable memory of swinging. Can this same simile be made in the far-flat Midwest? One of the distinctions of a well-written essay is that it introduces the reader to an idea that he or she would never have thought of otherwise. Could someone who has lived all of life in the Midwest make such an analogy? People who live in different regions may not think to associate the same things because they don't see the same scenery.

Wrigley, his wife, and his son borrowed a friend's cabin in the mountains near where they live and spent most of their Thanksgiving holiday there one year. He picturesquely describes how one morning he slipped into his skis for a trip through the woods and up onto a flat-topped knoll. Here is a sample of his vivid description: "From on top you can see across Hells Canyon, with the Seven Devils Mountains on one side and the Oregon Wallows on the other. The sky was clear; it would be a gorgeous and frigid dawn" (Wrigley 142). Wrigley is again describing a region of great inspiration to him. There is something about snow-covered mountains that amazes people and causes them to wonder. There is a feeling of a stimulation when people can stand at the top of a mountain and sense that they can see forever. Wrigley ponders the same excitability: "I thought to myself how in the seventy or eighty square miles of this little mountain range there were likely no more than six or seven people, and all of us had gotten here on skis or snowmobiles; there were no plowed roads here this time of year. It was that feeling, that exquisite melancholy, that silent, still exhilaration that the earth, and art, can bring on" (Wrigley 142).

As Wrigley proceeded on, he saw the tracks of a snowshoe hare. At the moments he saw the tracks, they reminded him of the summer before when he and his son went camping and found intact the skull of a hare. They took it home and boiled it in bleach. It is now on his son's dresser and is one of his most prized possessions. This experience inspired him to write the poem, "The Skull of a Snowshoe Hare." One of the lines in the poem has great significance because it relates nature to human understanding in a very subtle way: "If we relish the artifacts of death, it's for a sign that life goes on without us" (Wrigley 143). Thoughts like these can be understood by people, despite the region they live in, but it is the region that has created the images to bring on the thought. Wrigley explains, "It is a quieter poem than usual. Blame that on the tenderness of the subject, the landscape softened under snow" (Wrigley 143).

Marx states: "Are Homer, Shakespeare, Tolstoy, Balzac and Dickens in any sense 'regional'? Probably--but the fact of our being able to locate their stories within this or that geographical boundary has little bearing on our appreciation of them" (Marx 10). Marx says that these authors are in a "sense" regional. Maybe their type of writing wasn't meant to be regional but was, in a sense, because it was unavoidable. Nevertheless, some writing displays more regionalism than others. Marx may be missing what Wrigley describes as "that feeling, that exquisite melancholy, that silent, still exhilaration that the earth, and art can bring on" (Wrigley 142). The sensations described by Wrigley are ones that a reader can experience while reading his essay. Vividly describing the land can be almost as effective as actually seeing it, and more so if it is seen differently. Regionalism is very apparent in "The Swing, the Snow, the Skull of a Hare," as Wrigley gracefully meant it to be.

Assignment for a Critical Review of Reading from an Academic Area

Your chief task in this essay will be to read an essay or article critically and then write an analysis of it, arguing for your understanding of its purpose.

For your reading, choose an essay from a field in which you may find yourself doing further academic work. Your selection process will be an important aspect of this assignment because you will need to consider the rhetorical situation of the essay you choose very carefully. The best selections will be sound arguments written in conventions that are accessible to you. Look carefully at the three articles written by Flavell in *Work in Progress*. If you were to begin with the version appearing in *Cognitive Psychology*, do you know enough about the disciplines to read it critically? How about the version from *American Psychologist* which is written for a wider audience, even though still professional? Finally, turn to the essay appearing in *Psychology Today*, written for the general public. Here your question changes--you no longer wonder if you know enough to read and write a review. Instead, you must ask if the essay contains enough academic "meat" for you to work on. In this case, the essay is an easier-to-read explanation of substantial, important research: it would be a good choice. Watch out for popular essays which are written by journalists, not experts, and may simply summarize a whole issue, or essays which are loose and speculative. As you can see, your ability to judge the integrity of material you might use for research is an important part of this assignment.

You will want to review the *Work in Progress* chapters on reading and on academic writing very carefully. Follow suggestions for a careful reading of your article, paying particular attention to the section of Chapter 8 on analyzing the argument and answering the questions there. Then turn to Chapter 10 and follow the suggestions for writing analysis and argument. Write a rough draft of your review from these reading and writing notes.

As you see your ideas about your review essay take shape, you will need to be ready to step back and consider its "frame" or context. You need to provide some sense of how this article or essay fits into the ongoing work of improving our knowledge. Be as concrete as you can. Your writer has some obligations to do this for you, but you also need to demonstrate your awareness of the rhetorical context in which this essay is appearing.

While your review will include evaluation, you do not need to say whether you liked or did not like the essay. The aim here is to enter into a dialogue of ideas, and your disagreements should take that form.

You may use quotations. Do not, however, let a quotation make your argument--lead into it with your point or a paraphrase. Head your review with a bibliographical entry giving the author, title, source, and date of your essay. Include a copy of the essay you are reviewing with your paper.

Sample Critical Review (Johnston, Jim. "Advertising." Communication Arts, May/June 1987.)

After millions of dollars of research and audience testing, it appears that a trend among many major companies and their advertising agencies is to create commercials that rely on vivid, visual imagery, stunning music and cinematography. Yet, are these commercials serving their purpose, persuasive communications? In a short editorial essay in the May/June 1987 issue of Communication Arts magazine, Jim Johnston adamantly argues that many flashy, expensive commercials are fundamentally lacking central ideas.

Although he admits many advertising agencies are producing high-priced commercials that are entertaining and enjoyable, they are not presenting rational reasons for persuading their viewers to buy. Johnston presents his readers with the newest advertising campaign for Chevrolet. It's made up of what many commercials have borrowed from past hits from the Beatles, MTV, and Miami Vice: "Music without meaningful words. Flash without substance. Visual pyrotechnic without any real idea." He isn't saying that these devices weren't successful for the Beatles, MTV, and Miami Vice, but their use isn't intended to serve the same purpose. Advertising, in the true historical sense of the word, is to employ communication to persuade the masses or a target audience, not entertain you. "The Heartbeat of America is today's Chevrolet" is certainly impressed on our minds, but this isn't enough, even with its spectacular visual clips, to give a person a reason to buy a Chevy.

To defend his stance, Johnston says that audio/visual excitement and a strong central idea can coexist in a thirty-second spot, and he gives specific ad campaigns that successfully integrate both. Hal Riney's Bartles & James campaign is one of those which Johnston says is splendidly entertaining and also has an astonishing clever idea. Riney's commercials aren't successful because a meaningless phrase like "The Night Belongs to Michelob" is flashed across a screen dozens of times, but because they present a simple persuasive message that even a sourpuss would chuckle at.

Johnston brilliantly makes a powerful statement about the current advertising world. He makes a point that is so eye-opening that many of his readers may very well reconsider the direction of the next commercial that they produce. This short essay could easily have been a powerful speech at the next Addy Awards, as he makes comments and observations that he might have expressed to any advertising colleague.

In a sense, Johnston is creating his own ad. And he is doing a very good job at that. He uses valid arguments and examples to create a persuasive ad for ideas to his target audience, the advertising community. He doesn't rely on dazzling clips from commercial spots to make his point but promotes it with witty, ironic undertones that are just as successfully entertaining. And no dummy could miss his central idea. He appears to have covered all the bases in his ploy to persuade us. Or has he?

Are these companies really washing millions of dollars down the drain in their idea-less, flashy hype? I doubt it. Johnston appears to overlook, maybe intentionally, that these companies initially incorporate thorough research and audience testing before ever deciding which method of persuasion to employ. Instead of giving us cold, hard facts about why we should buy their product, a large majority of television commercials purposefully appeal to our emotions. Are these trends toward focusing on emotional appeal in commercials implicitly telling us something? Have these corporations concluded that the general American public is comprised of mindless imbeciles who can't intelligently absorb rational reason but most rely on their emotions to guide their purchasing habits? It appears so. Johnston naively assumes in his assertions that there are rational reasons for buying anything. I have trouble finding rational reasons for buying a $50,000 Mercedes Benz over a $10,000 Ford Taurus when both have essentially identical functions. Are there really valid enough reasons for buying a Michelob beer over a Budweiser? I'm sure it must be because "The Night Belongs to Michelob."

Assignment for an Argument

As Corbett notes in his Little Rhetoric and Handbook, "Argument is that form of discourse in which the write attempts to persuade an audience to adopt a certain position or to behave in a certain way." Argumentative writing, Corbett adds, "tries to achieve one or more of the following objectives":

--to reinforce the reader's present position
--to persuade readers to modify their present position
--to persuade readers to reject their present position and to adopt another one
--to persuade readers to act in a certain way
--to dissuade readers from acting in a certain way (120)

This assignment asks you to create a rhetorical situation that involves argumentation, as defined above. To do so, you need to focus not only on a topic for this assignment--the importance of bicycle safety, the need to protect the remaining virgin forest in the coastal range, reasons why students should shop at the 1st Alternative Coop instead of supermarkets, and the need for students to become computer literate--but also on a particular rhetorical situation.

Suppose, for instance, that you decide you're interested in promoting bicycle safety. The following are just a few of the rhetorical situations you could create involving this general topic:

--You could write a letter to the head of traffic safety urging him to enforce bicycle regulations on campus more strictly.

--You could write a letter to the head of traffic safety urging him to revise the current bicycle regulations in some way.

--You could write a letter to the local newspaper urging bicycles riders in your town to follow bicycle rules more closely. (This letter would be quite different from the previous one. Can you see why?)

--You could write a letter to the student newspaper urging drivers and pedestrians to be more courteous to and observant of bicycles riders.

--You could write a letter to the local newspaper urging drivers and pedestrians to be more courteous to and observant of bicycle riders. (Again, this letter would differ greatly from the preceding one.)

--You could role-play as a member of the campus cycling club. (Does one exist?) As such, you could propose that the club sponsor events designed to encourage bicycle safety.

Although all these essays or letters would involve the same general subject, bicycle safety, they would vary in important ways because of the different rhetorical situations to which they respond.

Hints:

--Be sure to choose a topic you know a lot about. Avoid such "large" issues as abortion, religion in the schools, handgun control, and so on unless you are particularly well informed (and concerned) about them.

--Be sure your topic is not too broad. Remember, you're going to have to persuade your audience, which means that you're going to have to marshal a lot of supporting evidence. If you try to deal with a topic that's too broad, you won't be able to be specific enough about any single aspect to be persuasive.

--Be sure to choose an audience with which you are to some degree familiar. You may choose to write to a specific person (your parents, your dorm counselor), a group (student government, the campus Environmental Task Force) or a larger audience (the readers of the student or the local newspaper). In each case, your knowledge of and projections about your audience will play a critical role in the development of your argument.

--Early on in your planning you should develop a pro and con list of arguments related to your topic. This will help you think more concretely about your topic; it will also help you anticipate objections from your audience.

--Consider your purpose in writing--your persuasive intent--carefully. It might be more realistic, for instance, to attempt to argue that the library should establish a committee to consider the feasibility of longer hours than to argue that the library should offer longer hours. The latter commits you to proving that the library can do so--that is has the money, the staff, and so forth.

Sample Argument

Student's Statement of Intentions

My persona is myself--a college student who has worked through school as a waitress. I hope I've taken on a light tone, yet made a serious point.

After much soul-searching, I've decided that I'll put this in the Oregonian in the point-of-view section. Anyone reading the paper who has eaten at a restaurant will see the headline and possibly consider reading this. As this isn't a hard-news story, only the person who enjoys reading features in a newspaper will read this. I don't think one has to be a raging intellectual to enjoy the article; in fact, it's rather simply written. A person who enjoys lighter reading will perhaps enjoy reading this. The major constraint is that, as with most everything in life, the person who most needs to read this probably won't, i.e., the "insensitive customer."

I want to say that being a waitress is sometimes a difficult job, and customers should be sensitive to this fact, and tip accordingly (when the service merits it).

WAITRESSES ARE PEOPLE TOO

The next time you eat at any kind of food-service establishment, please take time to notice the person who serves you your meal. I could have asked you to notice the food-service employee who serves you your meal, but I said "person" for a specific reason. Why? Because a food-service employee is a person too, an individual with feelings, dignity, and, quite possibly, tired feet.

How do I know? I speak from experience, especially in the tired-feet realm: I'm a waitress. Now waitressing isn't going to be my lifetime career, heaven forbid. I'm working part-time to put myself through college. But that isn't necessarily the case with all my colleagues. Some are single mothers who didn't have a chance for further education. Some are working because their husbands are disabled or unemployed. There are those who have taken the job just to help their families make ends meet. But whatever the reason, all of us have the task of ensuring that you have a satisfactory and enjoyable meal in a pleasant and relaxing atmosphere.

And that ain't always easy to do.

Not to the untrained eye, waitressing might look like a fairly uncomplicated chore. Take order, pour coffee, bring food, and presto! Job done. A co-worker's husband recently echoed the "waitressing-is-easy" belief when he said to me, "It must be a relief to get there and lose yourself in some mindless work."

What his wife sees in him, I'll never know.

This "mindless work" includes keeping a constant eye on your section of tables so nobody creeps in unnoticed, taking orders while trying to remember who had what special with which salad dressing, trying to place the correct dinner in front of each member of a table of twenty without making a mistake--not to mention the six tables of customers who all sat down at the same time and who want their service all at the same time.

Now I can understand why we might end up mindless, but start out that way? I hardly think so. And those problems I mentioned are the tip of the iceberg. (And no, I'm not talking lettuce!) I didn't say a word about grouchy cooks, surly customers, screaming children, slippery floors, broken dishes, lazy co-workers, or those jolly folks who order three-course meals five minutes before closing time.

Now before I proceed much further let me note that, yes, I realize I haven't mentioned waiters. That's because, as a rule, the majority of men employed as waiters are working exclusively in more expensive restaurants. Let's be realistic: the day-to-day drudgery of the food-service profession is 99.9 percent borne by women. The fancy restaurant conjures up the image of a refined and intimate atmosphere where tips, those marvelously tangible tokes of appreciation for a job well done, are much more generously given. After all, who is going to leave fifty cents for a $50.00 meal? So the waiters have it pretty good. Besides, when was the last time anyone made a waiter dress in a polyester miniskirt uniform and wear heels?

But work in the everyday coffee shop or family restaurant differs drastically. There, the level of respect for waitresses and the difficulty of their job takes a nosedive. That's where the image of the nonentity--the unintelligent, gum-snapping bimbo--comes to mind. The waitress Vera, a character on the popular television show Alice, is giddy, scatterbrained, and not too bright: a typical (?) waitress. Vera seldom has any tables to wait on, but maybe that's how she keeps her job. In a real restaurant, she'd last a week, tops.

So what should customers expect of the average waitress? I'll tell you what I expect: a pleasant demeanor, a full coffee cup, prompt service, and a willingness to help if any problem comes up during the meal such as cold food, spilt milk, or an order change. I don't think that's unreasonable. But when customers expect the waitress to discipline their children, laugh at jokes that were new when Lincoln was president, or endure grouchiness that only the family dog is supposed to put up with, the line is drawn. I suppose what I'm trying to do is encourage you to treat your waitress like the person she actually is. No, I'm not suggesting that you invite her to sit down for a steak with you and your family; you don't even have to exchange names and birthdates. But do recognize that she too appreciates a please and a thank you just as much as the next human being. Emily Post aside, however, politeness isn't everything. If you don't leave your waitress a tip, no matter how nice you are, your name is mud. Seriously, if you "stiff" your waitress, don't expect marching bands, red carpet, and a key to the city when you eat at that restaurant again. Your reputation as a good customer will have been tarnished with the label of "cheapskate."

Now I'm not saying a tip is appropriate in every circumstance. I can still remember the tight-lipped waitress who earlier this month "waited" on my table in name only. I practically had to tackle her to get some more coffee, and then she looked like she would rather have poured it on me than serve it. I wanted to apologize for even coming into the restaurant. I still don't know what her problem was, but I didn't leave her a tip. She didn't deserve it in the least. However, for every unfriendly incompetent, there are five gracious professionals. These are the ones who merit the appreciation shown only by a generous tip.

Unfortunately, it's difficult to put those negative experiences with waitresses out of your mind. But remember, a pleasant restaurant meal is a two-way street. Human nature being what it is, a waitress will respond to customers the way she is treated. As a waitress, I have vivid memories of some customers I would just as soon forget. For example, there was the man who berated me just for asking if he wanted cheese on his hamburger. "If I'd wanted cheese," he snapped, "I would've asked for it!" Then to his friend at the table he said, "Why do they always ask that stupid question?" At times like that, the phrase "grin and bear it" takes a personal meaning. But for every rude and arrogant customer, there are five courteous and gracious customers who show their appreciation by leaving generous tips while treating me like a human being.

The keys to a positive restaurant experience for both parties, then, are mutual respect and understanding of each other's needs. (My, this sounds like marriage!) As a waitress, I need to be both cordial and sensitive to customer necessities. As a customer, you need to give me credit for being an individual with thoughts, feelings, and a tough job on her hands. You may be surprised how the quality of your service will improve if the waitress knows you're going to treat her well. A waitress can bloom under the application of your courteous appreciation. Go ahead and try it next time you're in a restaurant--make someone's day!

<u>Assignment for a Review</u>

Reviews may inform, evaluate, persuade, and entertain. (Many reviews represent a subtle and complex mix of these purposes.) There is no standard or "formula" review: the exact shape of a review depends upon a number of related factors such as audience, purpose, and means of publication.

Some reviews are largely informative. This would be appropriate, for instance, if you decided to write a review for the student newspaper comparing the three best-selling touring bikes in a certain price range to help students decide which is the best buy. Even here, however, there is an implicit argumentative edge to your review: if you're in the market for a touring bike, you should consider brand X; it's the best buy.

Some reviews are largely evaluative. After a brief rundown of the movie's plot and basic cinematic techniques, some critics focus almost entirely on evaluating a movie's script, acting, photography--its overall success. These reviews also have an implicit or explicit argumentative edge: you should (or shouldn't) see this movie.

Some reviews, though partly informative or evaluative in intent, also aim to entertain. When a writer reviews the ten best Sunday brunches in Oregon, as David Sarasohn recently did in <u>Oregon</u> magazine, the best approach may be to treat the subject wittily and lightheartedly--to engage the reader as much with style and wit as with information or critical acumen. Even here, though, the writer's argumentative function as a reviewer holds true: though his style is casual and witty, David Sarasohn is still telling readers--arguing--which restaurants have the kind of brunch worth spending hard-earned money on.

When you start to think about your review, don't just consider various subjects. Consider the rhetorical situation as a whole. You can review almost anything--movies; restaurants; places to ski, hike, fish, run, swim, play tennis, study, be alone, meet interesting people, or drink good coffee; all sorts of equipment such as stereos, bikes, calculators, food processors, fabrics, or tennis rackets. This list is endless. But when you decide what to review, you've just begun to define your topic. Who is your audience? How knowledgeable are readers about your subject? (You would write a very different review of this years' best running shoes if you were writing for the student newspaper versus <u>Runner's World</u>.) Are your readers already interested in your subject? (If you're writing about the best places to backpack in the Central Cascades for readers of the <u>Sierra Club Newsletter</u>, you can assume fairly strong interest. If you're writing about the same topic for readers of your local newspaper, you probably can't.) You also need to consider the image of yourself that you want to project in your writing, your persona. You may choose to adopt a serious, distanced persona. You may choose to be witty, sarcastic, casual, or whatever.

As the writer, it's your responsibility--and your freedom--to shape your review so that it best reflects your intentions, the needs and interests of your readers, your (hypothetical) means of publication, and your subject. Have fun!

<u>Note</u>: Be sure to remember the recommended length of 2 to 4 typed pages; choose a rhetorical situation that realistically calls for an essay of roughly that length.

Sample Review

Student's Statement of Intentions

I am writing a review of the movie The Deerhunter. I'm not addressing my review to a specific audience; instead, I'm assuming an audience of intelligent readers, people who are already interested in and knowledgeable about films in general and Cimino's work in particular. I want to appear casual and yet knowledgeable.

THE DEERHUNTER

Focusing on a small Pennsylvania steel-mill town and the effects of the Vietnam conflict on some of the young men and women who live there, Michael Cimino's The Deerhunter gives us a rich, tightly woven story. One of several made in the last few years that explores facets of the American involvement in Vietnam, this film presents the viewpoint of those small-town men who went off to fight in foreign jungles believing that America was still The Beautiful. Despite the horrors of a war that held no meaning for them, despite the painful losses that they suffered, the characters in this film still cling to that ideal.

I first viewed Deerhunter right after its release, and its initial impact overwhelmed me. Cimino has masterfully created layer upon layer of cinematic reality. The first hour of the movie is a carefully crafted exposition of the town of Clairton, Pa, with all its grit and charm, and of the relationships between the major characters, forming a solid base for the more swiftly moving Vietnam footage and denouncement. This film is too lengthy, according to some, but I cannot think of a single shot that is not a necessary part of the whole; like an Altman film, it relies on the totality, gathering its effectiveness and strength from the sum of these parts.

Upon subsequent viewing, I have found that the film's impact is lessened by my knowledge of the plot. I think that this problem is accentuated by the intensity of the film's impact during my first viewing since after a year I still recalled much of it shot for shot. Even so, I continue to marvel at the texture and fullness that it has.

The violence that is a part of this story--a horrifying version of Russian roulette in which the Viet Cong pit one prisoner against another--is bloody and necessary to our understanding of the deep psychological anguish that the men undergo. It makes us realize that a superhuman control is needed by Michael (Robert DeNiro) to save his buddies, Nick (Christopher Walken) and Steven (John Savage), from the mental and physical damage imposed by this terrifying game and from the war itself.

In many respects this is a buddy film. Three young men who grew up together, who work together and play together, end up going off to war together. Boisterous, daring types at home, they are confronted with a war that pounds at their minds, rips at their bodies, sends them back to the familiarity of their town as strangers. Through all of this, the unity of friends is what makes survival possible. I generally dislike buddy films because they tend to make women appear as peripheral adjuncts to men and portray men as one-sided good old boys, but The Deerhunter manages to escape these pitfalls. The script itself can take much of the credit for this success since it allows the men to relate to each other in a caring, loving manner. The excellent acting by the cast members is also responsible for the wholeness of the characters they play. DeNiro injects the part of Michael with all of the strength and control that it requires, with Walken and Savage superbly completing the triad of close friends. The women have smaller parts, but they have just as much reality for us. Meryl Streep (as Linda) is especially fine in giving life to a character that might otherwise have been overlooked.

One of the only real problems with Deerhunter is that once in a while the cuts (exterior to interior, scene to scene) are confusing. In some instances this can be seen as effective--in the sequences of a disintegrating

Saigon, for example--but in most cases it is merely disconcerting and annoying. Also bothersome is the insistence of the screenplay on some rather unbelievable coincidences such as the scene in which the hometown buddies are reunited in the middle of a field near a Vietnamese village. Sure it could happen, but. . . .

Ah, but there are other coincidences, other miracles here. Is this actually a reality that we are presented with? More like a dream, it seems to me: a dream where you spend your paycheck over pool and beers at the local tavern, a dream where you are lifted from your home and a new bridge only to find yourself in a strange jungle with a gun, a dream--no, a nightmare--where you lose your closest friend, track him down beyond all possibility, and find him again, tell him that you love him, only to have his life blood slip through your fingers. It is the American Dream, a little the worse for wear.

Assignment for an Analysis of a Writing Sample

In your earlier essays, you've been focusing on writing in response to a particular rhetorical situation--one of your own making. In this essay, you are, in effect, to turn the process around: you are to study one or more samples of a particular genre of writing and analyze, among other things, the rhetorical situation to which it implicitly responds. This analysis is designed, of course, to help you become more sensitive to the constraints and options that all writers face.

Choose a specific kind of writing--generally, though not necessarily, one with which you are either already somewhat familiar or interested in learning about. Such kinds of writing might include the following:

--certain genres or subgenres of fiction (hard-boiled detective fiction, Harlequin romances, science fiction stories)

--a magazine devoted to a particular subject or aimed at a limited audience (*Runner's World*, *Field and Stream*, *Oregon Magazine*, and so on)

--a general news magazine (*Newsweek*, *Time*, and so on)

--professional writing in your field (one or more issues of a professional journal, a series of reports or memos)

--a particular kind of writing published in newspapers or magazines (editorials, news stories, advice columns, and so on)

--the writing of a specific columnist or writer (Ann Landers, George Will, Pauline Kael, and so on)

After you have decided on the kind of writing you want to analyze, choose a reasonable sample. Using the guidelines in Chapter 8, analyze your sample. (As always, you'll want to read the sample student essay very carefully as well.) The final step, of course, is to write your analysis. For this assignment, the general outline for your rhetorical situation is, quite simply, that you are writing an essay for this class with me, your instructor, as the intended reader. The general constraints of academic writing (that I am looking for a clearly organized, well-developed essay) would obviously obtain in this situation.

Sample Analysis of a Writing Sample

Student's Statement of Intentions

I have chosen to analyze Nancy Drew teenage detective stories because of my own familiarity with them as I grew up. I was always intrigued by the exciting, true-to-life episodes and characters from the mystery stories. My friends and I would make up our own mystery adventures, based on Nancy Drew stories, complete with hidden clues. Each of us would choose a character to portray, and I usually ended up being Nancy.

I am writing this as myself to an audience interested in the contents of teen mystery stories. This is a straight analysis format that could possibly be used as a guideline for writing such stories.

This Nancy Drew analysis could be part of a book that contains similar analyses of other teen detective stories (such as the Dana girls, the Hardy boys, Trixie Belden, and so on).

Parents could use this book as a guide to what their children could read. Educator might also benefit from such a book.

NANCY DREW: A MYSTERY TO SOLVE

> As the structure--the old, creaky hanging bridge--swung around, Nancy clutched the railing for support, but it too was unsound. The decayed wood gave way, and the girl plunged violently forward to meet the turbulent waters of the swollen stream.

Eight- to fourteen-year-old girls are usually so engrossed in the Nancy Drew mystery story they are reading that they won't put the book down until they finish. As soon as they experience one exciting adventure with Nancy Drew and her friends, girls are eager to puzzle their way through another mystery. Carolyn Keene, the author of these teen detective novelettes, urges her readers through the series with a promotional line woven into the last few paragraphs of each book.

> Again Bess smiled in admiration of her chum's cleverness. No matter how many mysteries Nancy solved, the Marvin girl never ceased to be amazed at each new one. She was to stand aghast at the solution of the next problem, The Clue of the Tapping Heels.

Young girls easily get caught up in the exciting, fast-paced Nancy Drew episodes. They can begin to frame the story through the setting, and they can anticipate a clue about the forthcoming mystery by the end of the first chapter. From there on, the plot of the mystery rapidly unfolds and sustains a quick pace throughout successive chapters.

Chapters vary from as little as four pages to a maximum of twelve pages in length. From one chapter to the next, transitional paragraphs leave the reader hanging for a split second--just long enough to prick the reader's curiosity--then quickly pick up the idea begun in the chapter before. For instance, the following paragraph shows how a new chapter carries through the action from a previous chapter, in this example the bridge collapse in the quotation opening this paper.

> The current was swift, and before Nancy could battle her way to the shore she found herself carried far below the point where the haunted bridge had stood. Bedraggled, and with her clothes muddy and torn, she pulled herself out on the slippery bank and sat there for a moment in the rain, trying to regain her breath.

The paragraphs, each composed of no more than five sentences, flow naturally because the sentence structures vary and are just complicated enough to interest adolescent readers. Variation in sentence length prevents reading from becoming too tedious.

The vivid, descriptive language--the extensive use of action verbs, adjectives, and adverbs--of the omniscient narrator and the characters replaces illustrations; there are rarely more than three sketches in a Nancy Drew book. This induces the young reader to participate actively with her imagination and encourages her to envision the scenery and the action taking place.

The constant dialogue among Nancy Drew and the other supporting characters also draws young girls into the action and gives them a sense of being a part of the conversation, elevating the story to a personal level. It is at the personal level where girls wish to identify with the intelligent, eighteen-year-old amateur detective. Nancy Drew portrays a role model that younger girls look up to. She possesses many well-balanced characteristics, both physically and mentally. Being athletic and physically attractive does not detract from Nancy's feminine and well-mannered behavior. And despite her independence and ability to make her own decisions wisely, she readily accepts advice and guidance from her brilliant criminal-lawyer father, who taught her to think quickly and rationally. People's needs and feelings are important to the young sleuth's way of thinking; she demonstrates this by her friendly understanding and thoughtful attitude toward them.

Nancy's peaceful home environment contributes to her own well-being. A nice, comfortable, two-story house in a pleasant suburban neighborhood is her residence. Here she lives with her father, Carson Drew, and their housekeeper, Hannah Gruen, who frees Nancy from tedious domestic chores and occasionally gives her motherly advice. When the young detective is not busy solving a case (usually at the beginning of the story), she can be found at home adding to or improving her physical and mental skills. The varied interests of Nancy's reading audience are catered to by her wide range of abilities: drawing, skiing, riding, golfing, ad infinitum.

But to prevent young girls from envying Nancy's character, the author has taken care not to overdo Nancy's perfection and her comfortable station in life. Carolyn Keene has included a tragedy in the heroine's life--the death of her mother when she was only a four-year-old girl. Because of this tragic element, readers can empathize with Nancy. Her motherless life also explains her need to be independent and her ability to be compassionate with other characters who have their own woes.

The writer introduces the characters early in the reading so the reader can establish their relationship to the entire action of the mystery. Nancy's immediate family, her closest girl friends Bess and George, and her boyfriend Ned Nickerson, constitute the supporting characters that round out Nancy's role and add fullness to the amateur detective stories. Bess is extremely timid and unsure of herself, whereas her cousin George, as her name implies, is tomboyish and impulsive. Ned always helps out when a young strong college man is needed for protection.

The importance of these primary characters could not be measured without the secondary characters: the protagonists and the antagonists. Without these actors there would be no mysteries for Nancy Drew to solve, no villains to outsmart, and no victims to rescue from disastrous circumstances.

As Nancy first probes her adversaries and then actively tests her cunning wits against them in each of her adventures, she exposes to her young readers the diverse personalities, values, and standards inherent in different people from all walks of life. In this capacity, Nancy Drew mystery stories not only provide exciting reading, but each story teaches its adolescent readers a valuable moral, ethical, or social lesson.

When each of Nancy's exciting cases is nearly solved, there is a heightened sense of drama when one more action comes into play, keeping the attention of young readers at the very end.

Each Nancy Drew mystery book puts Nancy and her readers in a different situation in a variety of settings across the country or around the world. A boy or girl can pick up and read just one book out of the whole numbered series without being confused about the identity of the Nancy Drew characters, or he or she can read the entire series without getting bored by repetitious plots.

Young readers enjoy sharing new secrets with Nancy Drew; it satisfies them to know that they were with her through every twist and turn, using valuable clues in unlocking mysteries and bring villains to justice. The value of rational decision making, good attitudes, and manners is one thing that young readers can learn as they develop a familiarity with Nancy Drew. Nancy Drew is like an old friend whose exciting life readers can take part in.

Assignment for an Interview

The minimum requirement of this assignment is that you interview one or more persons and use the results of the interview (whether recorded in notes or on tape) as the data for an essay. As the following examples should indicate, the form and purpose of your essay may vary with the reason why you choose to interview someone. Possible reasons include:

--to inform, to entertain, to illuminate. We're all naturally curious about people. What was it like to live through the Great Depression? How do the women who work as maids in the dorms feel about their jobs--and about students? What is the typical campus day of a disabled student like? Assuming that you choose appropriate readers, you can almost guarantee that you'll have an interested audience.

--to make or support an argument. Sometimes we interview people to prove a point, to search for answers that only someone in the know can provide. Such interviews can result in essays that explicitly attempt to persuade. Other interviews (for instance, an interview with a poor migrant worker) can also function as implicit arguments.

As always, in considering how best to respond to this assignment, be sure to consider the rhetorical situation in general, not just the person or people you'll interview. Going into each interview, you should have an idea not only of why you want to interview this person, but also of the general focus of the resulting essay. Who will read this? Why should they be interested? Where will the essay be published? What constraints will the means of publication provide?

In class, we'll talk about some of the formal considerations this essay raises. (What format should you follow? Should you include or delete your questions? What role should you as interviewer play?) We'll also discuss some questions of process. (Should you use a tape recorder or just take notes?) And we'll consider the ethics of interviewing. For now, though, there are a few closing suggestions.

--Don't assume that you need to find an unusual, exciting, or bizarre person to interview. Some of the best interviews simply reveal the richness inherent in even the most ordinary of people.

--Be sure to review the use of quotation marks.

--Save the notes or tape of your interview. Sometimes looking at notes or listening to the original interview can help solve problems that arise.

Sample Oral History

Student's Statement of Intentions

I am writing about my father's experience as a boy growing up on a farm in Nebraska. I want to try to recapture the event that he told about as best as I can, and I have tried to preserve the character of my father's speech when doing so.

The purpose of my paper is to record a piece of my family history in writing, to identify with a different way of life, and to learn more about my father.

My audience is myself and my brothers and sisters. I also plan to save this essay and let my children read it to give them a little knowledge about their family history. It may help them to know their grandfather better and may also enable them to get a feel for what their great-grandfather was like.

My paper may also be of interest to my cousins. Our families are scattered around the United States and have very little contact with each other. This paper is one piece of the history that unifies our family, so it would probably be interesting to them.

I don't have a means of publication in mind. This paper could, however, be an excerpt from a book on our family history.

I was a little apprehensive about interviewing my father at first. I was afraid that the artificial circumstances surrounding the interview would distort the character of his casual speech and inhibit his natural storytelling ability. It was difficult to decide exactly how to approach him about the interview, and finally I just sat down on the couch while he was reading the newspaper and began to ask him questions. He had to think awhile at first, but soon his past began streaming back through his mind, and his stories unravelled faster than I could record them.

He began by telling about the chores on the farm in Nebraska. "There was always something to be done, and we were just expected to do it--not for money or allowance or anything. I had to gather eggs and cobs. We used cobs in the stove for cookin' and heatin'. I'd have to go pick 'em up out of the hog yard after the hogs ate 'em clean. That was a messy job; boy, I hated it!

"My brothers had to milk the cows and water the livestock. All of us helped in separatin' the milk. We had a hand-turned separator that separated the cream from the milk.

'We had to shock the wheat; we'd put together seven or eight [shocks] in bundles to dry out. We'd let it sit and dry, then we'd come along with a hayrack pulled by horses or a tractor, pick up the bundles with pitchforks, and put 'em on the hayrack. Then we'd take 'em to the thrashin' machine to get grain. All the neighbors worked together for thrashin', we'd move from farm to farm and help each other out. Usually only one family had a thrashin' machine, and everybody had to pay a charge to the owner to use it.

"We always had large dinners with lots of potatoes and gravy and platters piled with meat. Then after dinner--lunch was called dinner--we had lunch at about four o'clock in the afternoon. We'd have sandwiches, and we might have had a beer after shovelin' grain. I got to drink the bottom of the bottle.

"In the wintertime we didn't do too much except go to school. We went to school in a one-room country schoolhouse with all eight grades in the same room. We had to walk a half mile through the pasture in knee-deep snow.

"Of course, we still had to feed the animals in the winter. We fed the cows in the lots since we couldn't turn 'em out to pasture 'cause the grass was all dried off. Sometimes we turned 'em out into the cornfield and let 'em eat what was left. And we still had to milk 'em morning and night; 'course we all had our share of that. Everybody had more or less . . . oh, I don't know . . . things just had to be done.

"Then every Monday was wash day. We had a gasoline-powered washing machine. I used to fall asleep listening to it on the sofa. That was when I was just a little bitty fart and Mamma was still alive."

Dad stopped talking every once in a while, as if he had to probe his mind to remember some of the details. When there was a lag in the conversation, I would prompt him with another question. I was curious about how the death of his mother changed life on the farm, so I asked him about it.

"I was pretty young when Mom died; I didn't really understand everything that was going on," he started. Mom died in 1942; I must've been about six years old. We had an aunt that stayed with us awhile--Claire Rooke was her name--but most of the time we had housekeepers. But us five boys were more than they could stand so most of 'em didn't last very long. Hazel Sickman was the longest one we had. She'd stick her head out the front door and holler whenever she wanted something. If she wanted eggs, she hollered, 'Eggs!' If she wanted cobs, she hollered, 'Cobs!' I can hear her yet. I mostly had to go get 'em for her because everyone else was busy with chores.

"We had one housekeeper with a son and daughter. Alice Ann was the daughter's name, and Freddie was the son. Alice Ann was spoiled, and she used to pick on her little brother. She was kind of fat, and she used to take his candy away from him. That's why Bob wired up the toilet; he didn't like the way Alice Ann used to pick on her little brother."

There was a sudden change in topic as Dad began to explain the reference to the toilet seat. "Bob charged up the outhouse seat with a magneto from the tractor and some wire," he said with a chuckle. "Then, when someone would sit down, he'd turn it on and shock 'em. Alice Ann wouldn't go out there after awhile, and she had to have a pot in the house. She kept saying that spiders were out there biting her. Anyway, one time Bob made the mistake of doing it while Dad was in there. I don't remember exactly whether Bob ran or what, but Dad came out with one suspender unhooked and hoppin' mad, and that was the end of the magneto and the toilet seat!"

By now my dad was really enjoying himself. He told numerous stories of mischievous antics performed by him and his brothers. I listened in amazement to some of these almost unbelievable tales and thought to myself how similar the experiences were to something that you might see on The Little Rascals television show.

"When the Kempsters [city slickers from Portland] used to drive back to Nebraska to visit," Dad recalled, "we used to play pranks on them. One time we put Loretta on the Shetland pony, Jerry went into the barn and shook the oats bucket, while we fixed the barn door so that the bottom was opened but the top was closed. The horse went running into the barn [for his food] under the top part of the door, and Loretta got knocked off." Dad thought back on this event and began to laugh out loud.

I asked my father how often he and his brothers were punished for their shenanigans. My dad answered, "There wasn't much Dad didn't know about. He used to use a razor strap to paddle our behinds."

Dad began another story. "I remember a time when brother Jerry and I pulled the car with a tractor to get it started. Dad had tried to start it but couldn't so he walked to the highway and hitched into town. We got it started and were racing around our driveway. (It was shaped like a semicircle and went up in front of our house and around.) We thought we were doin' Dad a favor by getting his car started--'course, we were having a little fun doin' it. Well the neighbors told Dad, and we both got the razor strap for that one!

"And then there was the time that my older brother John and I were riding our bicycles up to the main highway. He decided he was going to smoke a cigar. He'd take two or three puffs and stick it in the handle bar. Dad saw him smokin' it, and when John got back that night Dad said, 'I understand you like cigars.' John didn't know what to say. Then Dad made him sit down and smoke one cigar after another until he turned green.

From these and other episodes, I was beginning to picture my grandfather as a mean, unreasonable, and quick-tempered man, and I voiced this image to my father. He was quick to deny its validity, saying that his father wasn't all bad. Dad said that Grandpa was strict and strong willed, but that he was only doing what he thought was best for his boys. He also said that Grandpa was reluctant to accept new ways and illustrated this with the following story.

"One time Jim put a radio on a tractor," Dad said. "Dad didn't like it and told him to take it off. Well, one day Dad took the tractor out, and you could hear the radio playin' a half mile away. Then he told Jim he might as well leave it since he already had it on there."

I was interested in knowing how the economic conditions in the late thirties and early forties had affected my father's upbringing. I asked him whether his family had felt any of the effects of the Great Depression.

"The WPA built our outhouse for us," he began. "That was one of Franklin D. Roosevelt's job creators for gettin' through the depression.

"We didn't have to buy much because we raised mostly everything we needed. We had a garden and raised our own meat. We stored our salt pork in a barrel in the basement. There was no refrigeration, only an icebox.

"We never had a lot of stuff. For Christmas we usually only got one present. My clothes were hand-me-downs and so was my first bicycle. We had to go barefoot a lot--cut my foot one time and nearly bled to death. They had to pack it in flour to stop the bleeding. Well, anyway, I never felt deprived or anything; we just didn't expect much.

"The oldest boys went to boarding school in Missouri for a couple of years. Dad found it hard to get everyone to school in town during the winter, so he thought he'd send 'em to a Catholic boarding school to give 'em a good education. That's how he died--he was going down after 'em and got in an accident."

I had known that my grandfather had died in an automobile accident but had never known the circumstances. I waited for more.

"Nobody knows all the details, really," Dad continued. "He was driving in the rain and hit a drain in the highway. The tire blew out, and the car flipped end for end. He lived twenty-one days in the hospital before he died.

"After Dad died, I went to live with Aunt Monica on her farm in Giltner. We moved that summer to Hastings and lived in a basement apartment for a year or two. Then she bought a house, and we moved again.

"Aunt Monica was pretty strict. We had to be in the house by nine o'clock on week nights. She had a son by the name of John. I suppose there was some friction between us (John and I)--competition or whatever you want to call it."

It seemed Dad was implying that relations between Aunt Monica, John, and himself were a bit strained, but he volunteered little information on this subject when I asked about it. Maybe he didn't want me to get a bad impression of one of my favorite aunts. Whatever the reason, Dad changed the subject.

"I went to high school at St. Cecilia's. The nuns were pretty strict. I got my hand slapped with an eighteen-inch ruler for not filling a pew in church. There were only seven people in it, and there were supposed to be eight. My palm got slapped ten times, and I had to go to the principal's office. Another time I got whacked for polishing an apple on my pantleg in class. I thought I was paying attention, but the teacher didn't, so she whapped me.

"When graduation night came," Dad seemed to sigh with relief, "We had planned a big party. My brother Jerry had come back from Portland, but I didn't know it. Well, one of the other fellas, Don Webber, was supposed to tell me to go straight home after the graduation. He didn't, so I went to the party and got a 'little' inebriated. I had to climb in the window to get in that night, and Aunt Monica met me on the stairs and kicked me back out. I was told to leave--lock, stock, and barrel. I ended up sleeping in the porch swing that night.

"The next day, I got on my motor scooter and rode out to Aunt Irene's farm, and she was pretty understanding. She took me in for a while, but since Jerry was going back to Portland, I went and got my stuff and came out here with him. I was seventeen when I came out to Oregon."

Dad stopped here, and it seemed as though he was signaling the end of the interview. I guess he felt that this was where his growing up ended and a new phase of life began. I sat for a while, letting everything he had told me sift back through my mind, and tried to remember his expressions and tones in detail. I felt that I knew my father better now that I ever had before.